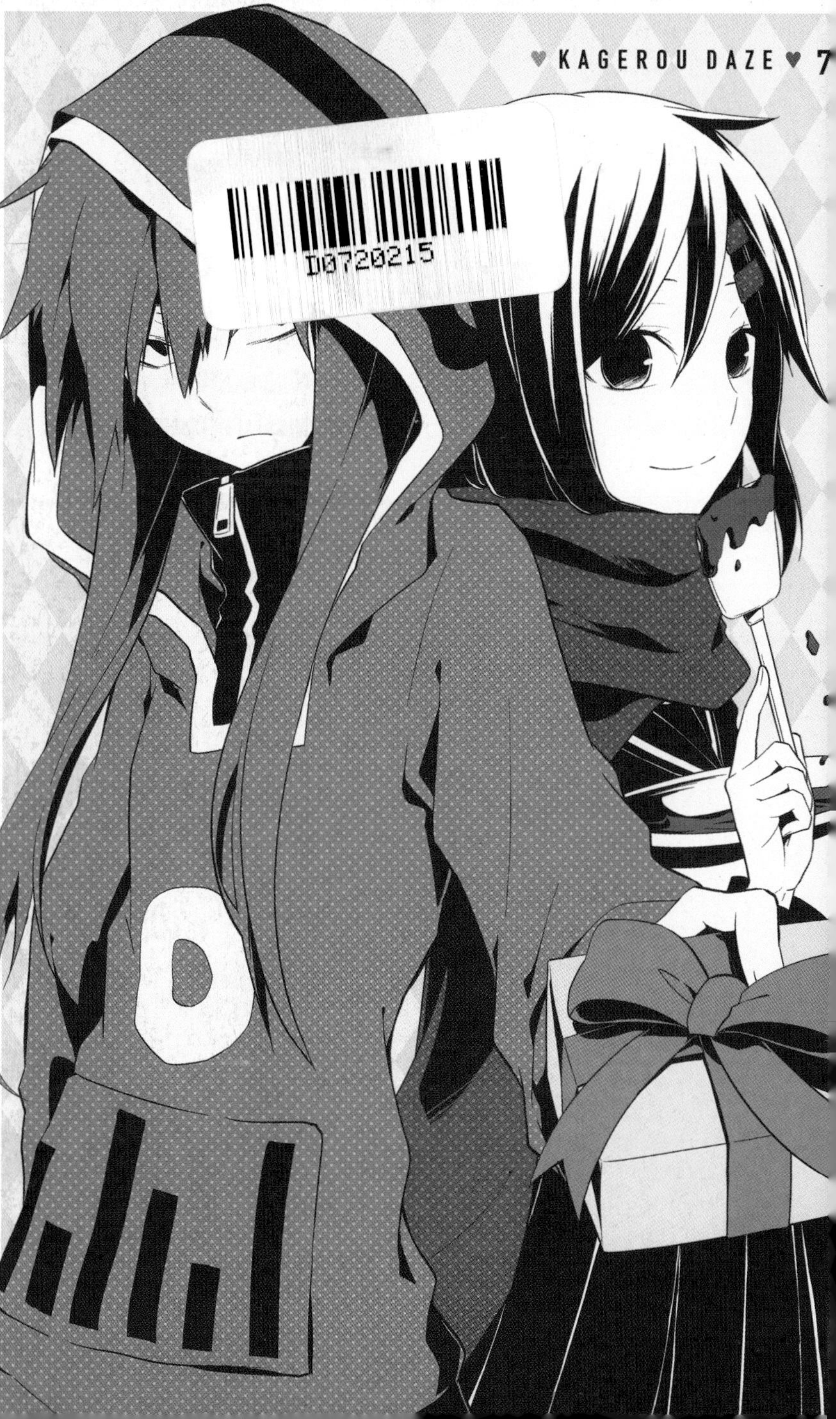
♥ KAGEROU DAZE ♥ 7

KAGEROU DAZE 7

CONTENTS

31 >> SHINIGAMI RECORD I

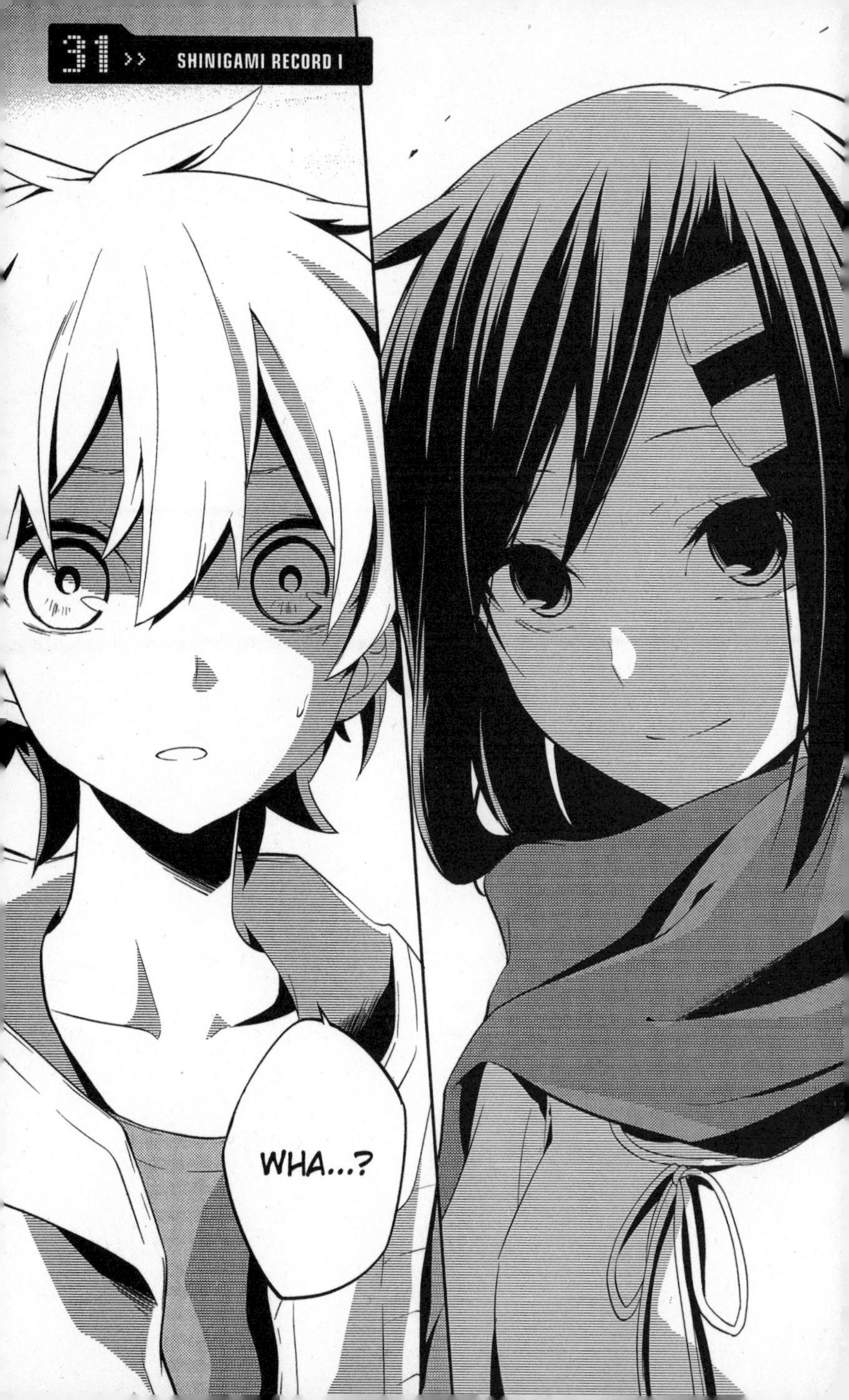
WHA...?

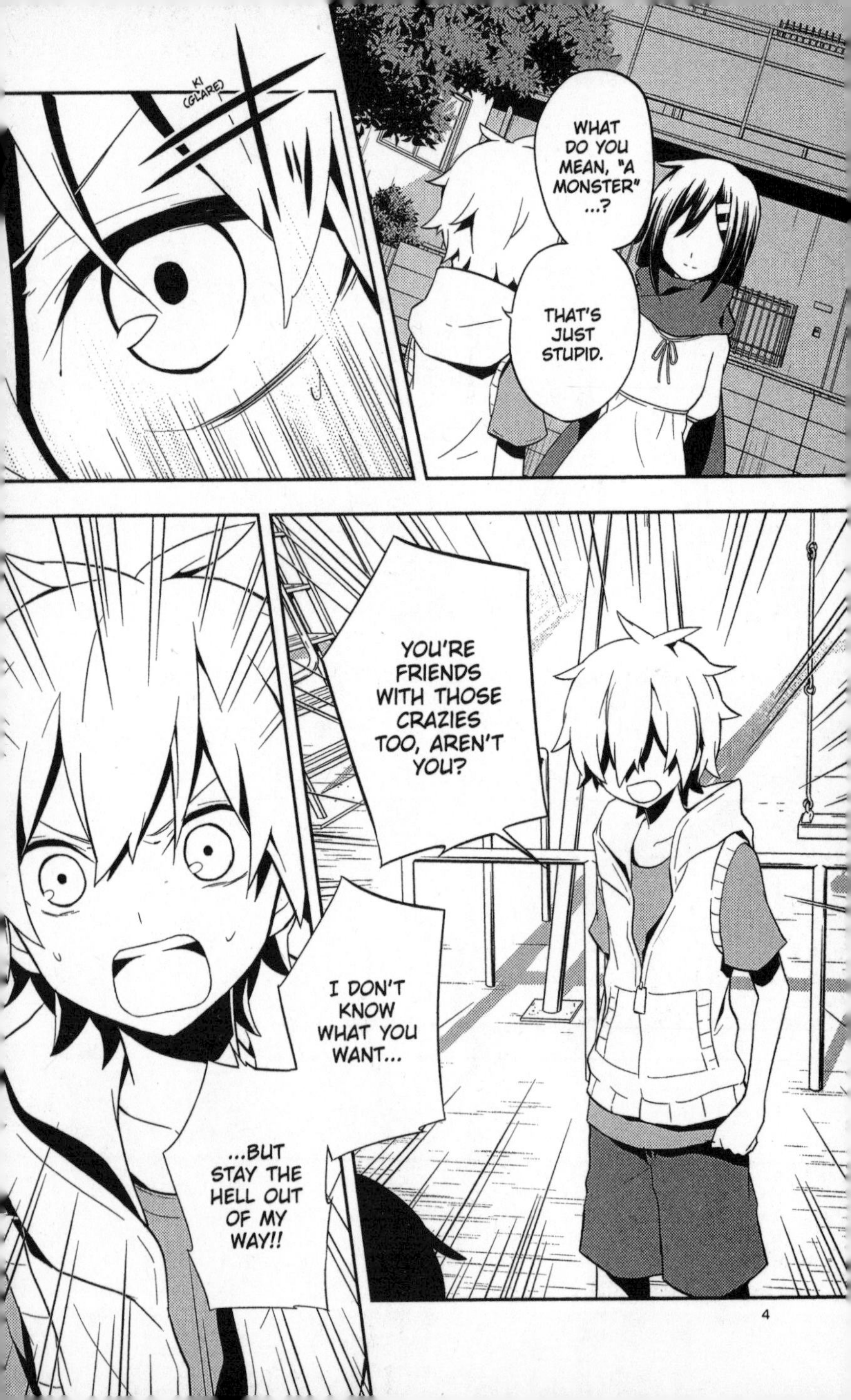
WHAT DO YOU MEAN, "A MONSTER"...?
THAT'S JUST STUPID.
KI (GLARE)
YOU'RE FRIENDS WITH THOSE CRAZIES TOO, AREN'T YOU?
I DON'T KNOW WHAT YOU WANT...
...BUT STAY THE HELL OUT OF MY WAY!!

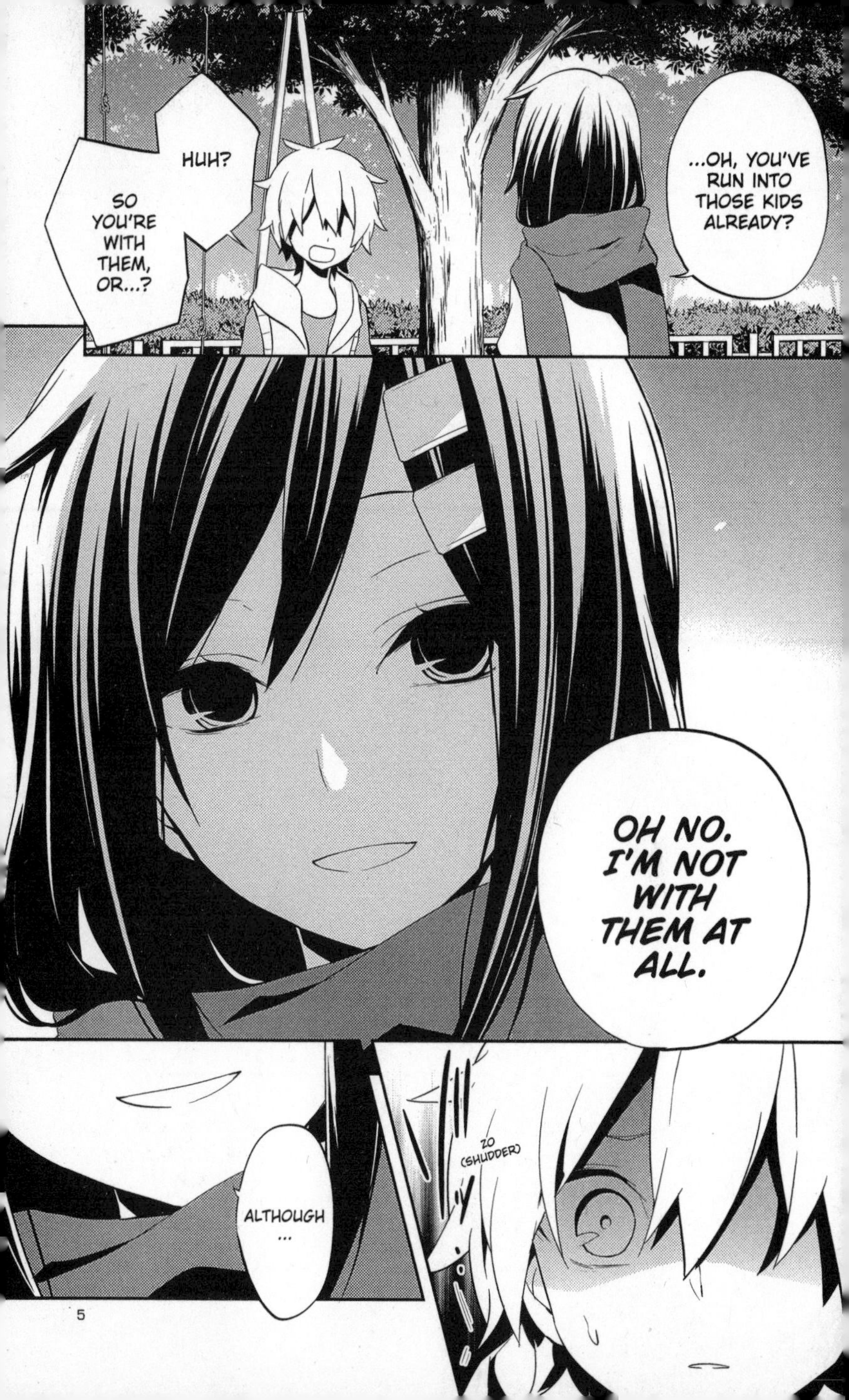
...OH, YOU'VE RUN INTO THOSE KIDS ALREADY?
HUH?
SO YOU'RE WITH THEM, OR...?
OH NO. I'M NOT WITH THEM AT ALL.
ZO (SHUDDER)
ALTHOUGH ...

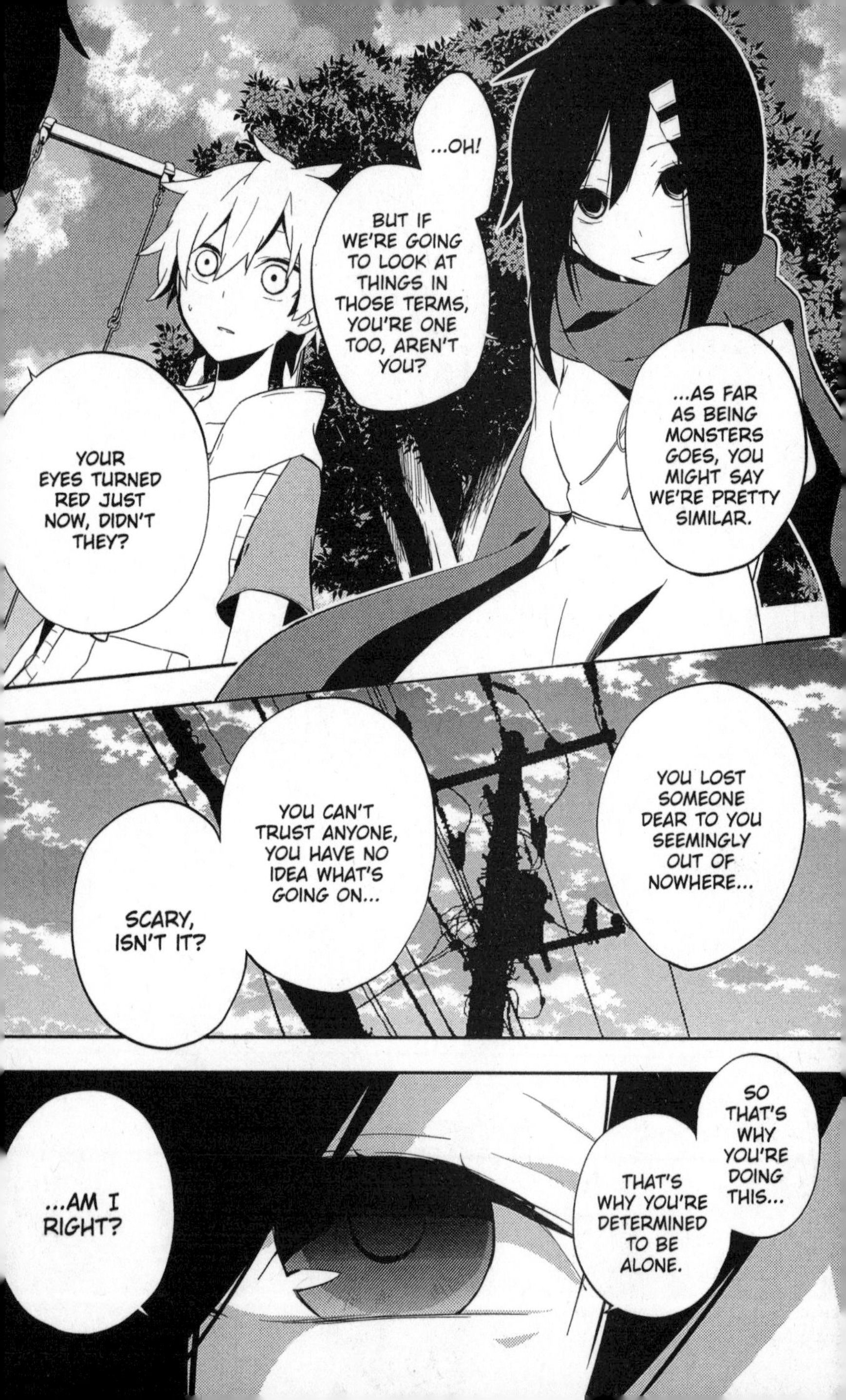

...OH!
BUT IF WE'RE GOING TO LOOK AT THINGS IN THOSE TERMS, YOU'RE ONE TOO, AREN'T YOU?
...AS FAR AS BEING MONSTERS GOES, YOU MIGHT SAY WE'RE PRETTY SIMILAR.
YOUR EYES TURNED RED JUST NOW, DIDN'T THEY?
YOU LOST SOMEONE DEAR TO YOU SEEMINGLY OUT OF NOWHERE...
YOU CAN'T TRUST ANYONE, YOU HAVE NO IDEA WHAT'S GOING ON...
SCARY, ISN'T IT?
SO THAT'S WHY YOU'RE DOING THIS...
THAT'S WHY YOU'RE DETERMINED TO BE ALONE.
...AM I RIGHT?

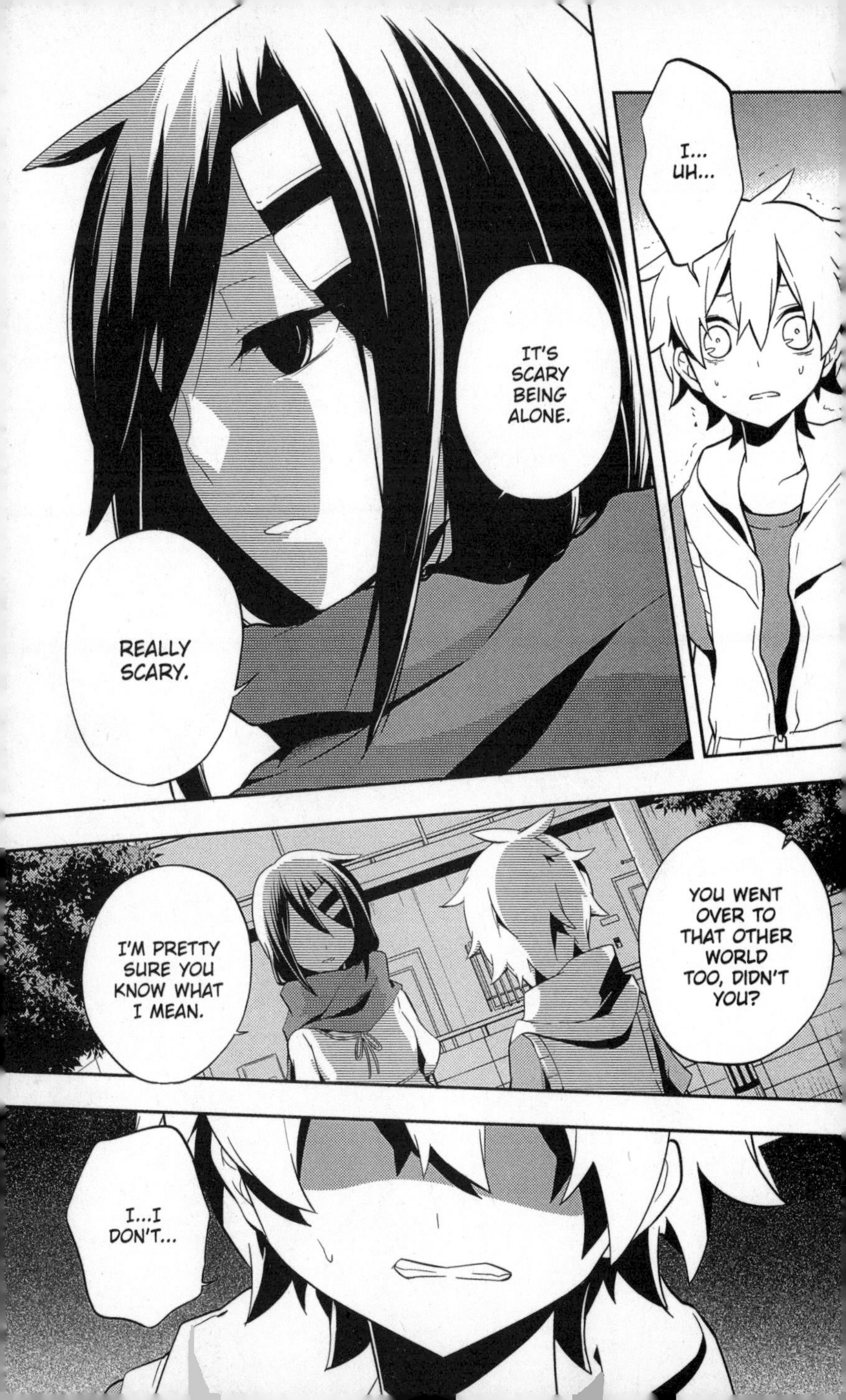
I... UH...
IT'S SCARY BEING ALONE.
REALLY SCARY.
YOU WENT OVER TO THAT OTHER WORLD TOO, DIDN'T YOU?
I'M PRETTY SURE YOU KNOW WHAT I MEAN.
I...I DON'T...

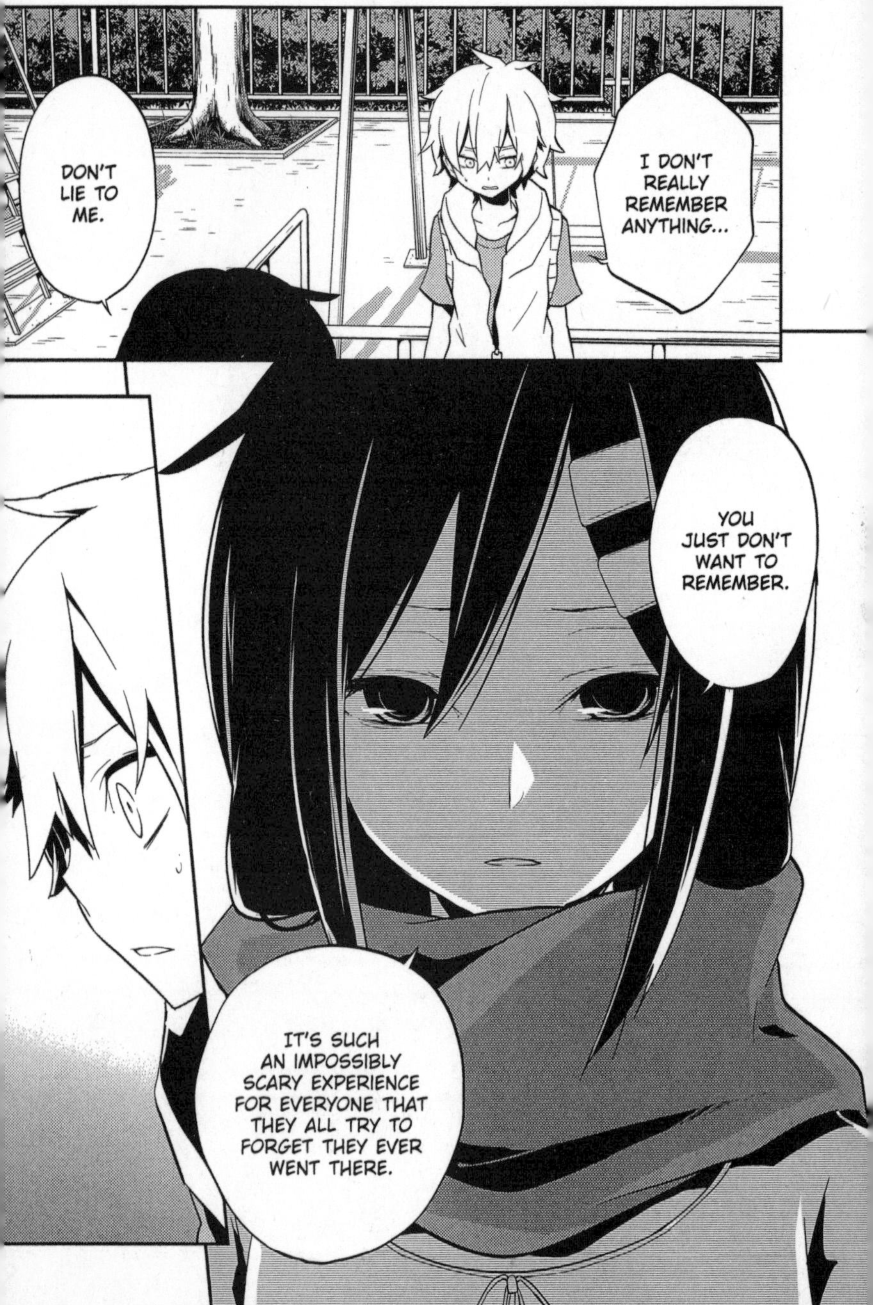
I DON'T REALLY REMEMBER ANYTHING...
DON'T LIE TO ME.
YOU JUST DON'T WANT TO REMEMBER.
IT'S SUCH AN IMPOSSIBLY SCARY EXPERIENCE FOR EVERYONE THAT THEY ALL TRY TO FORGET THEY EVER WENT THERE.

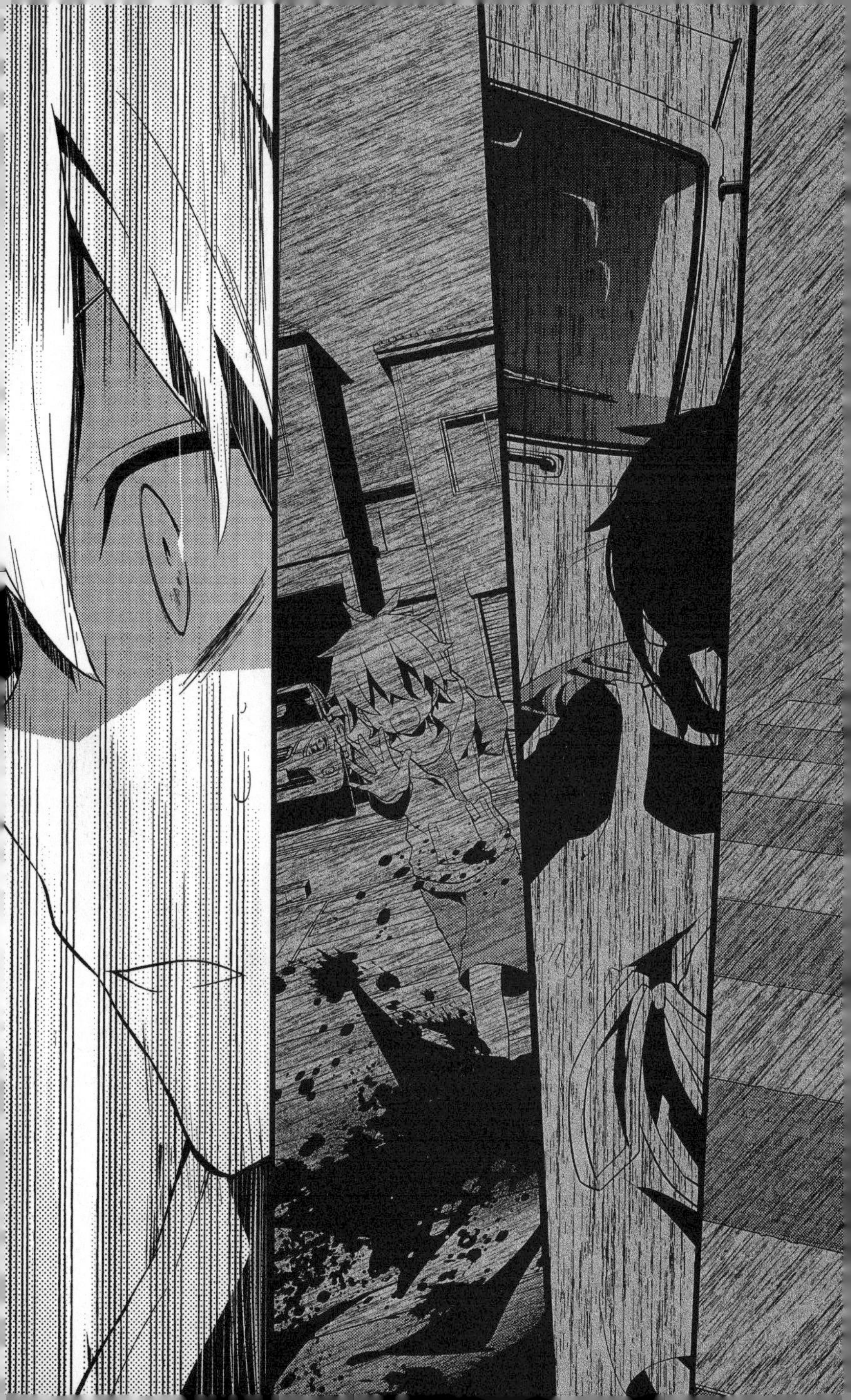

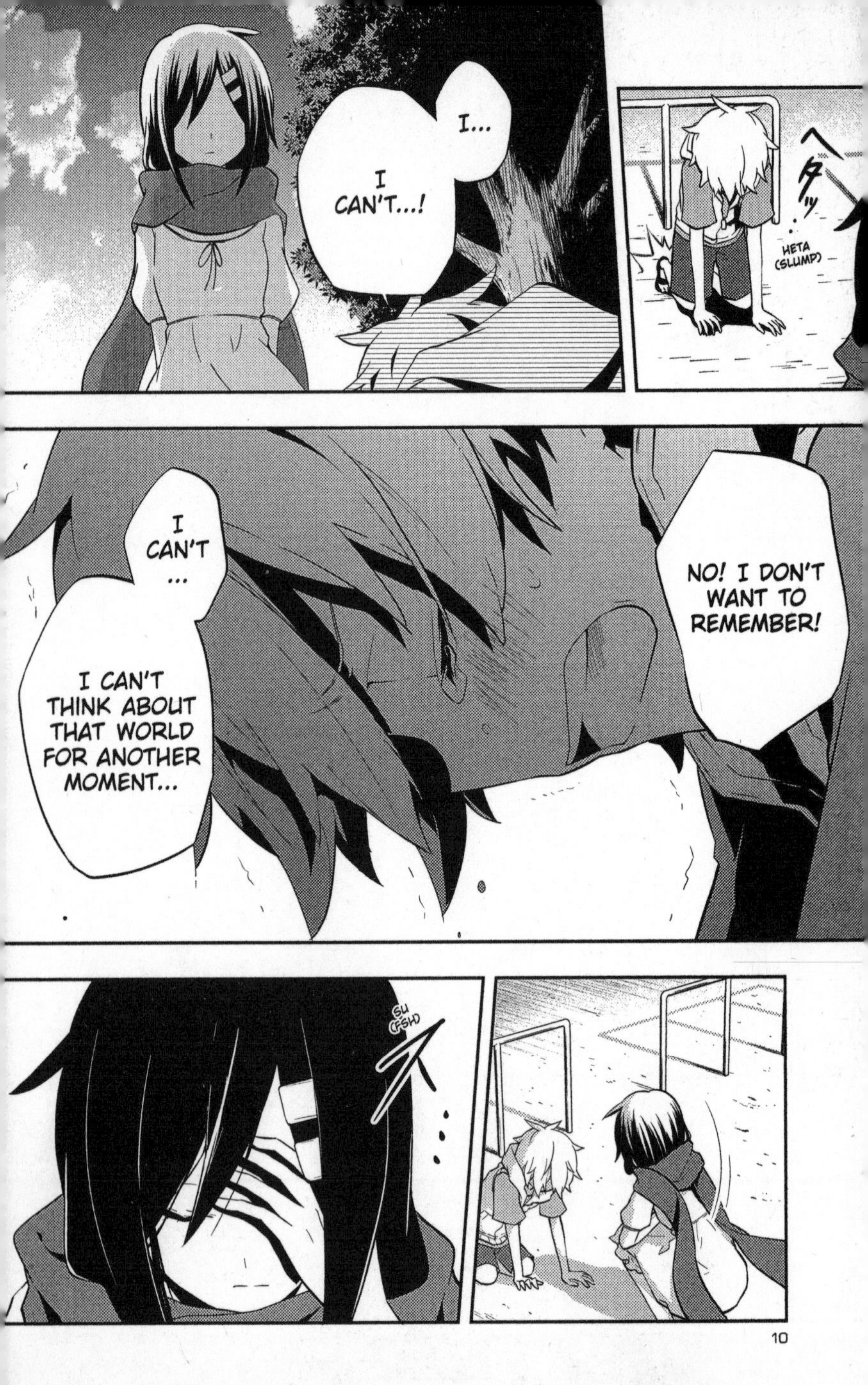
ヘタッ
HETA (SLUMP)
I...
I CAN'T...!
NO! I DON'T WANT TO REMEMBER!
I CAN'T ...
I CAN'T THINK ABOUT THAT WORLD FOR ANOTHER MOMENT...
SU (FSH)

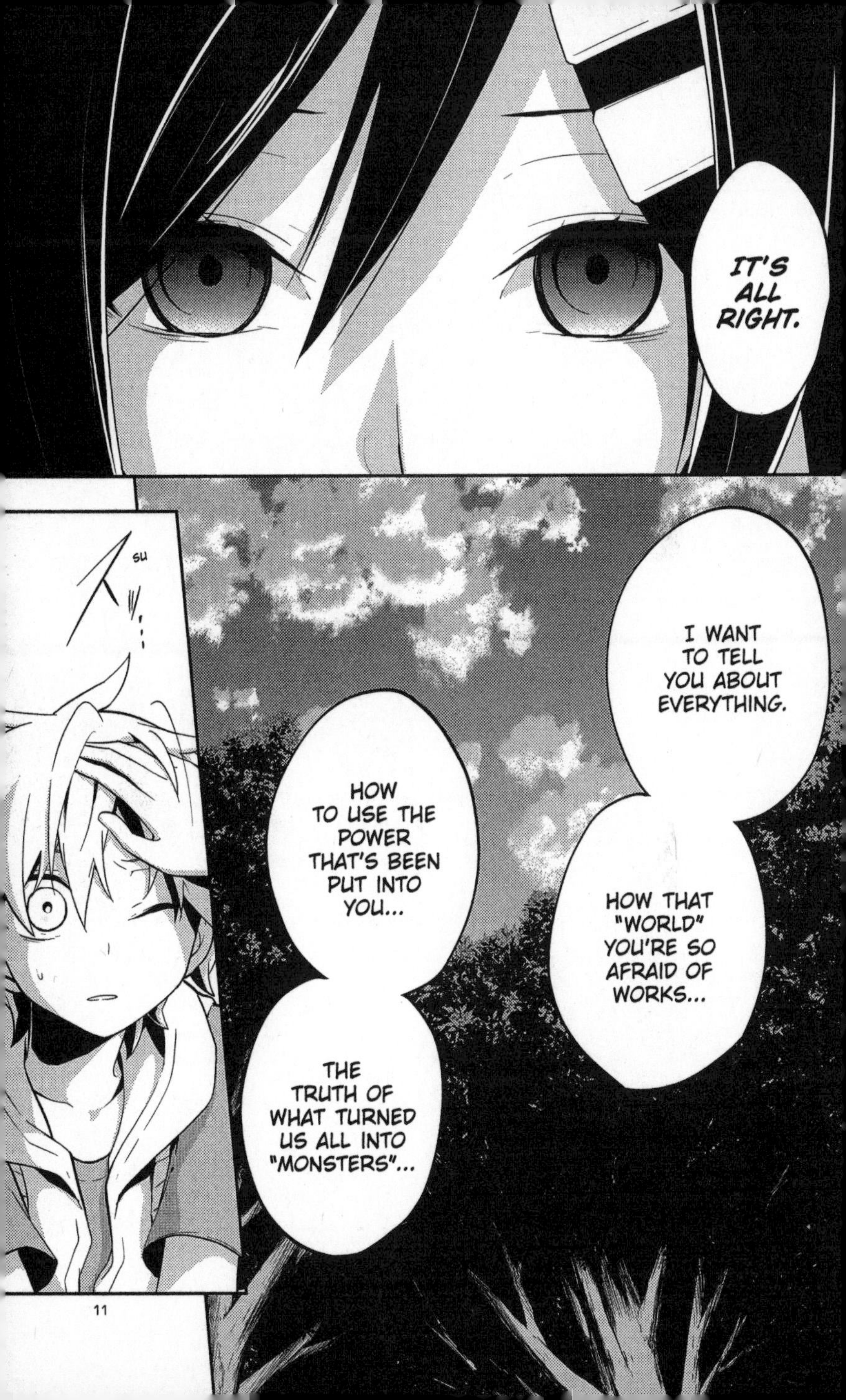
IT'S ALL RIGHT.
I WANT TO TELL YOU ABOUT EVERYTHING.
HOW THAT "WORLD" YOU'RE SO AFRAID OF WORKS...
HOW TO USE THE POWER THAT'S BEEN PUT INTO YOU...
THE TRUTH OF WHAT TURNED US ALL INTO "MONSTERS"...
SU

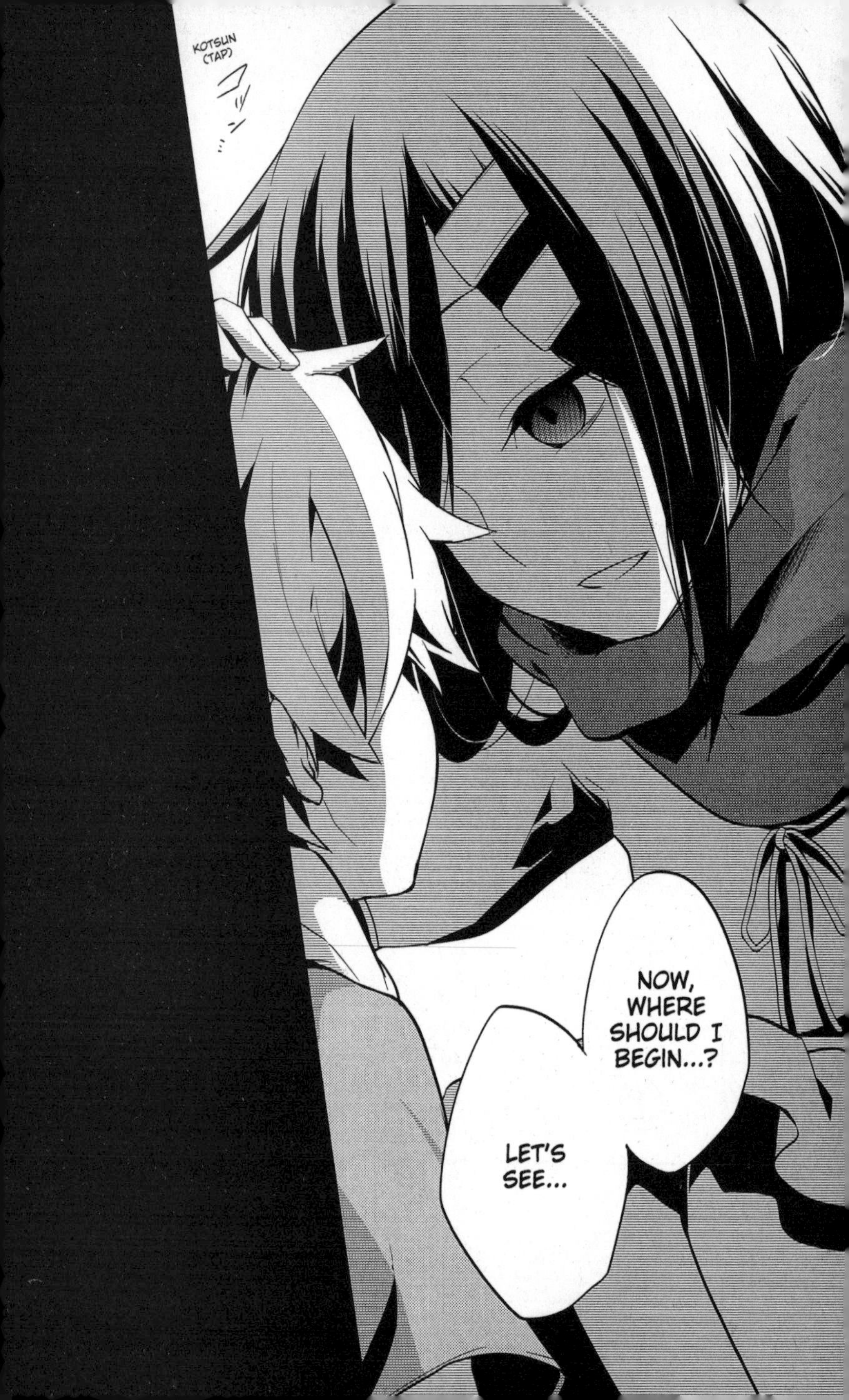
KOTSUN (TAP)
NOW, WHERE SHOULD I BEGIN...?
LET'S SEE...

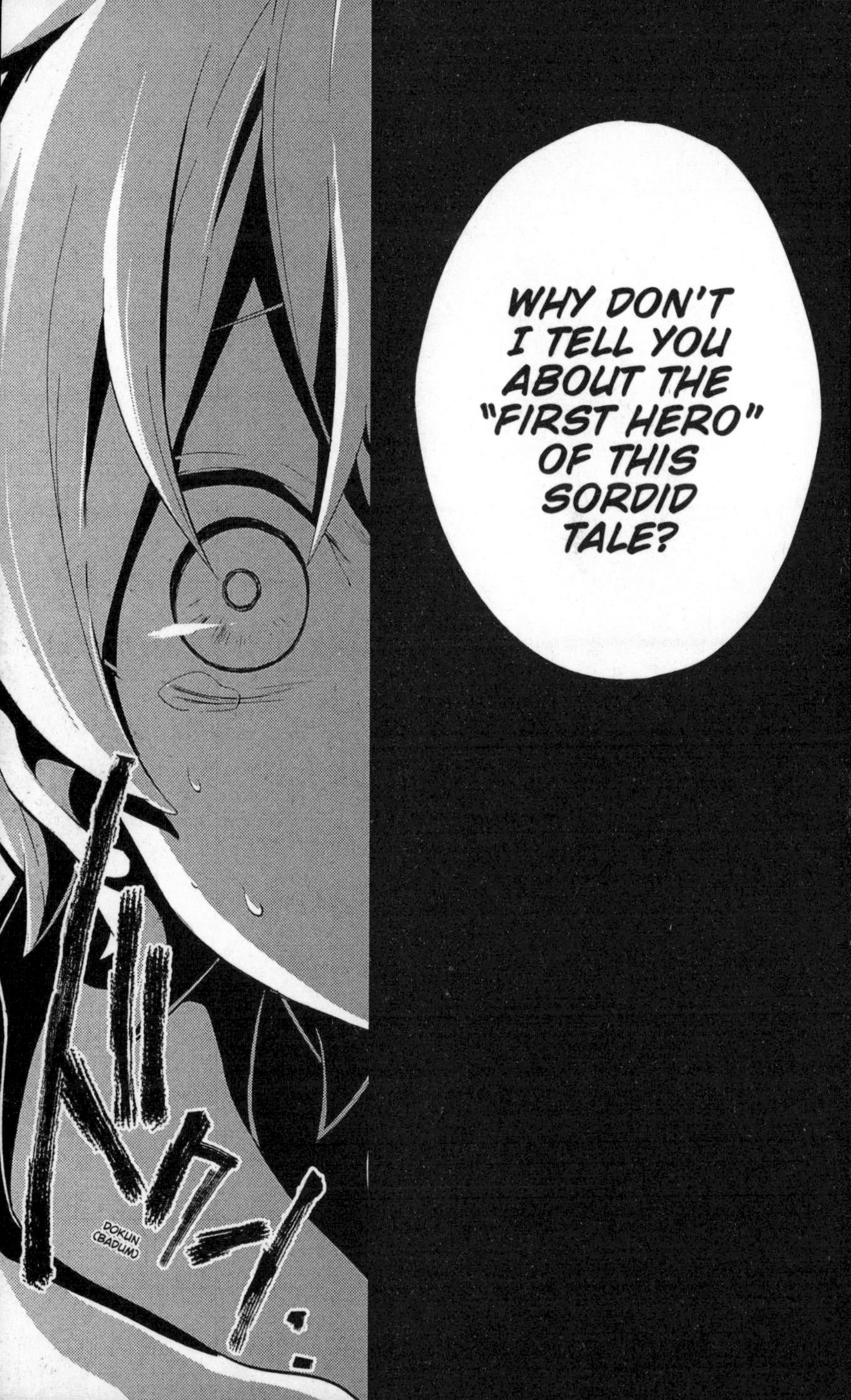
WHY DON'T I TELL YOU ABOUT THE "FIRST HERO" OF THIS SORDID TALE?
DOKUN (BADUM)

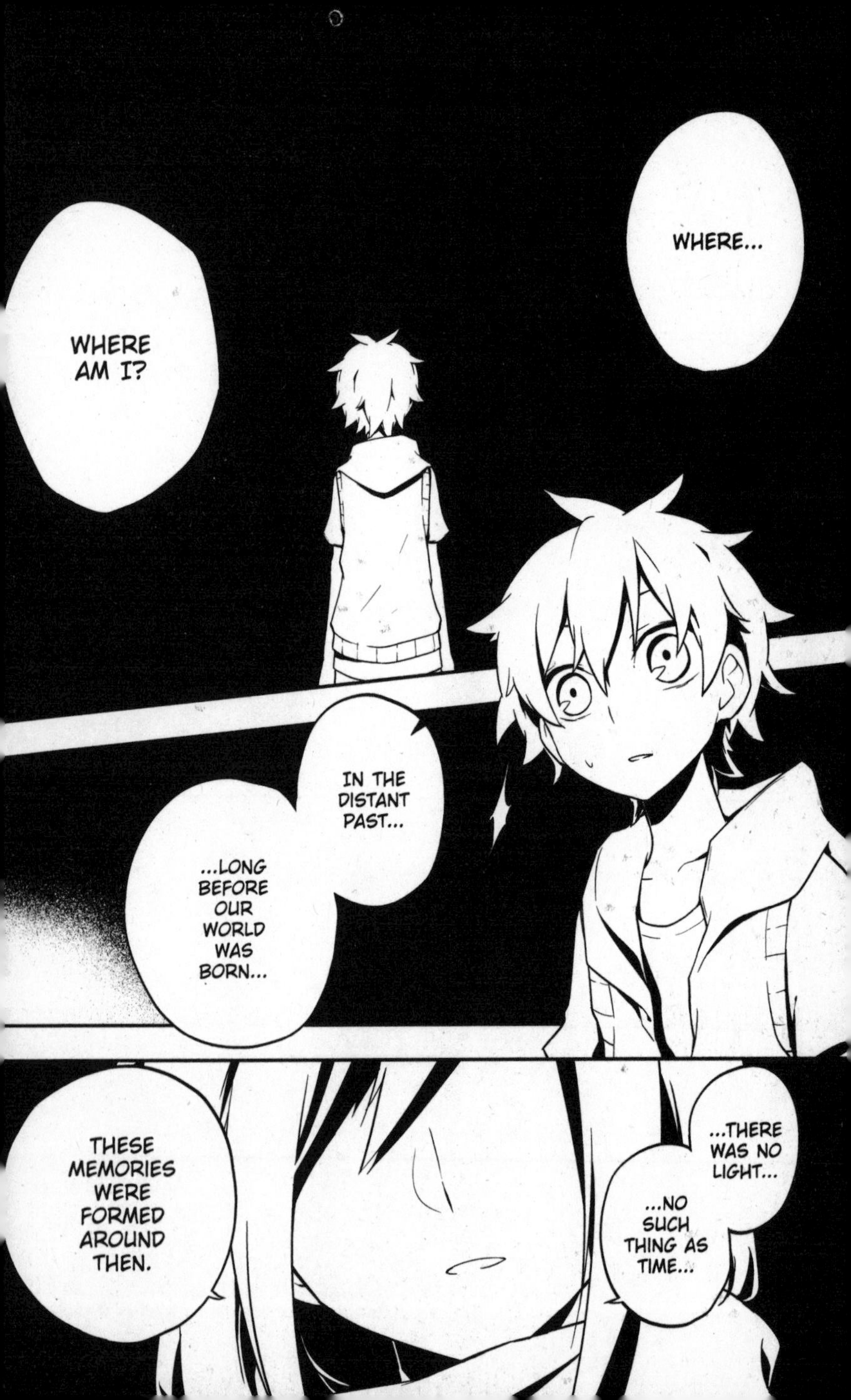
WHERE...
WHERE AM I?
IN THE DISTANT PAST...
...LONG BEFORE OUR WORLD WAS BORN...
...THERE WAS NO LIGHT...
...NO SUCH THING AS TIME...
THESE MEMORIES WERE FORMED AROUND THEN.

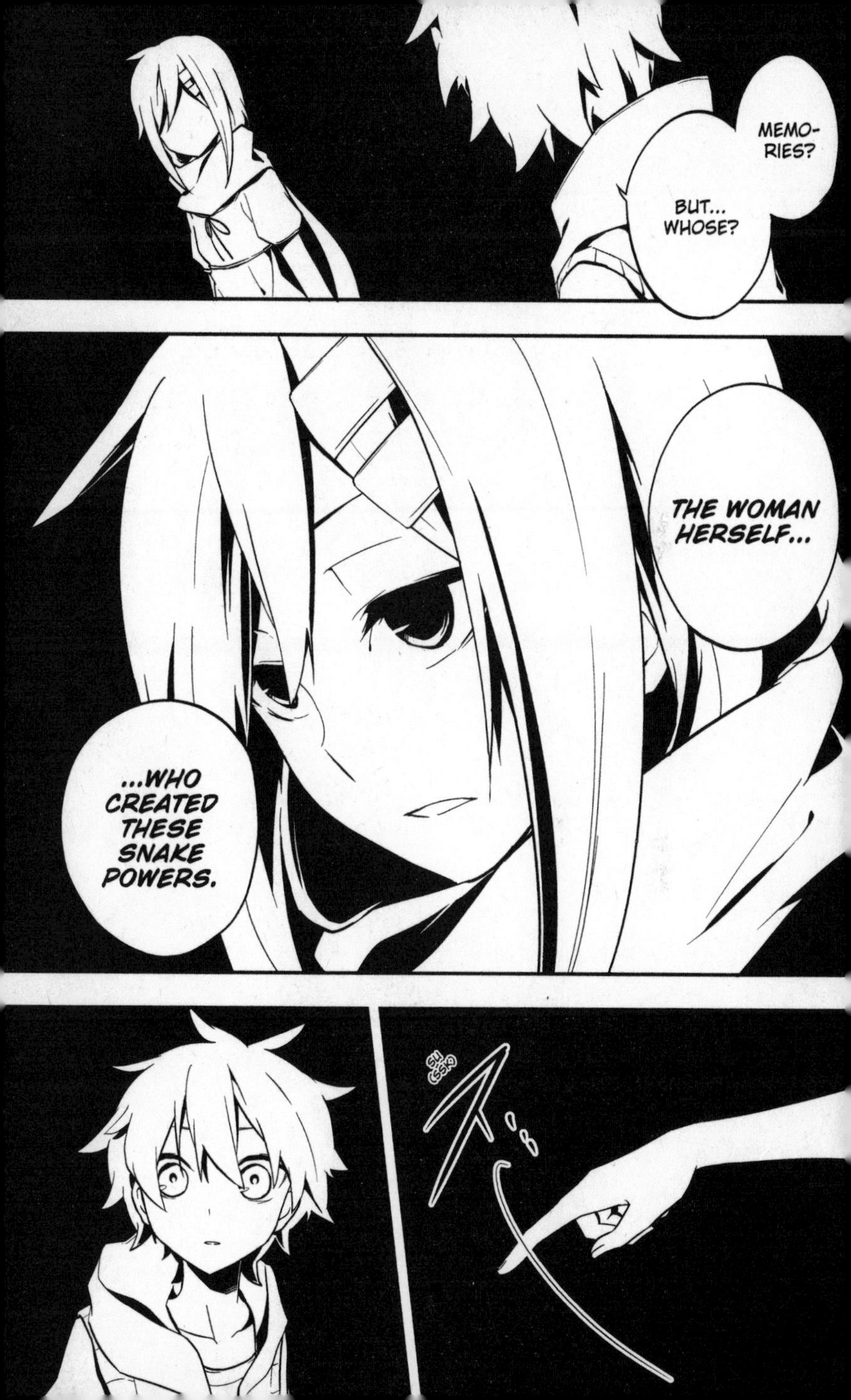
MEMO-RIES?
BUT... WHOSE?
THE WOMAN HERSELF...
...WHO CREATED THESE SNAKE POWERS.
SU (SSK)

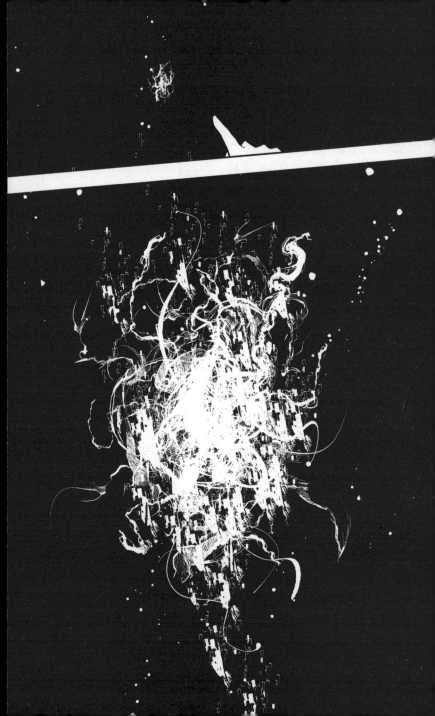

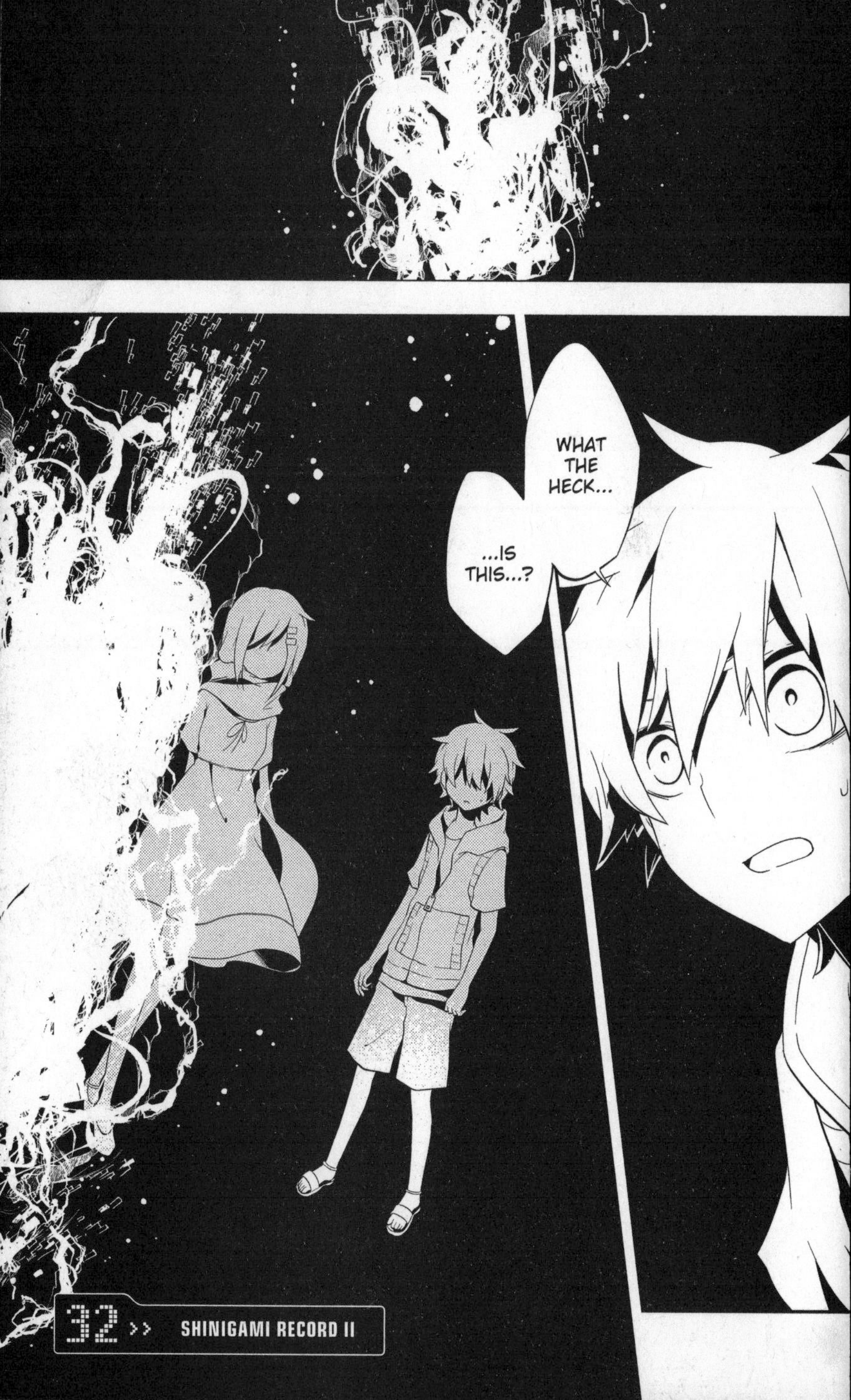
WHAT THE HECK...
...IS THIS...?

32 >> SHINIGAMI RECORD II

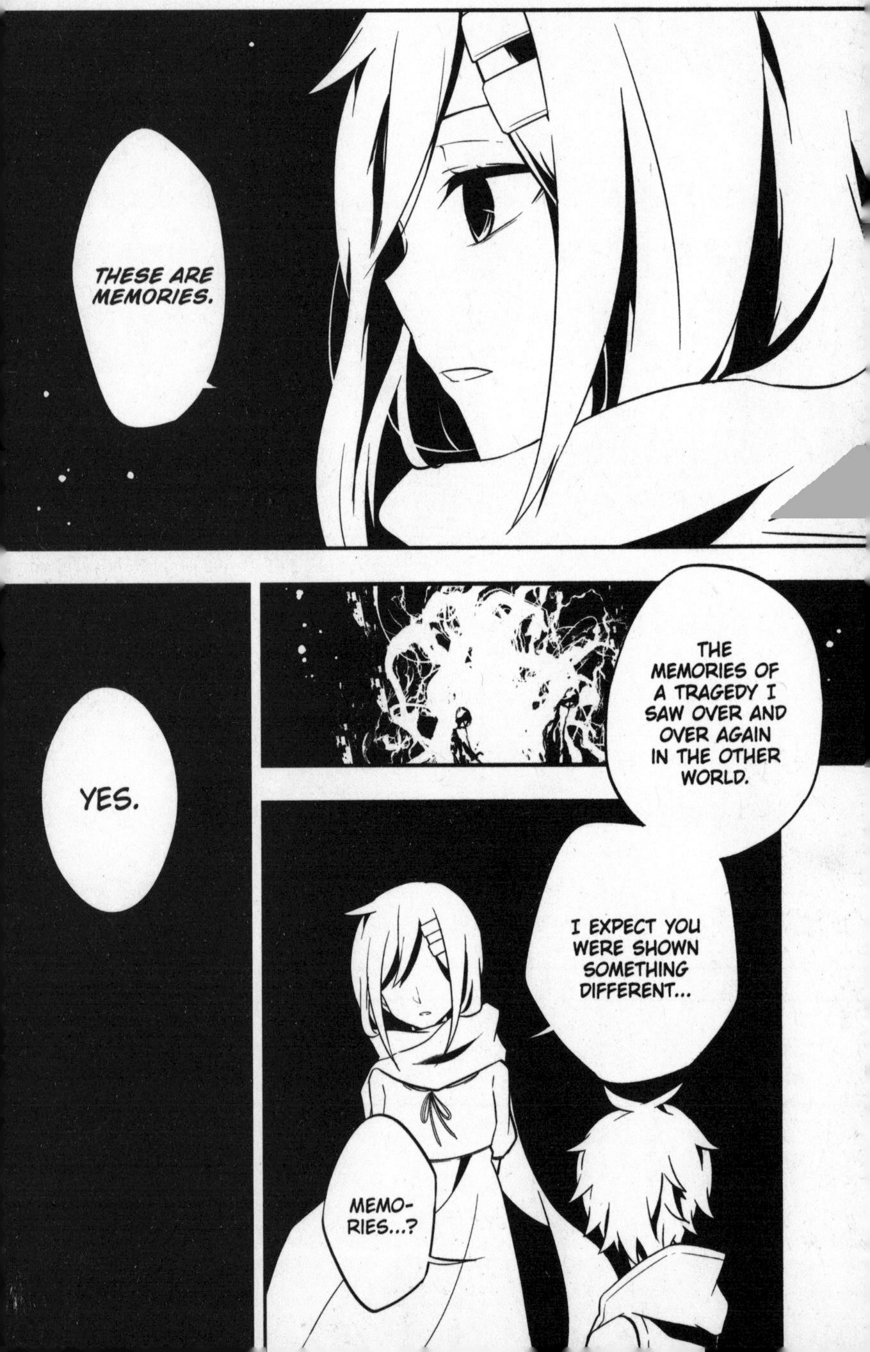
THESE ARE MEMORIES.
THE MEMORIES OF A TRAGEDY I SAW OVER AND OVER AGAIN IN THE OTHER WORLD.
I EXPECT YOU WERE SHOWN SOMETHING DIFFERENT...
MEMO-RIES...?
YES.

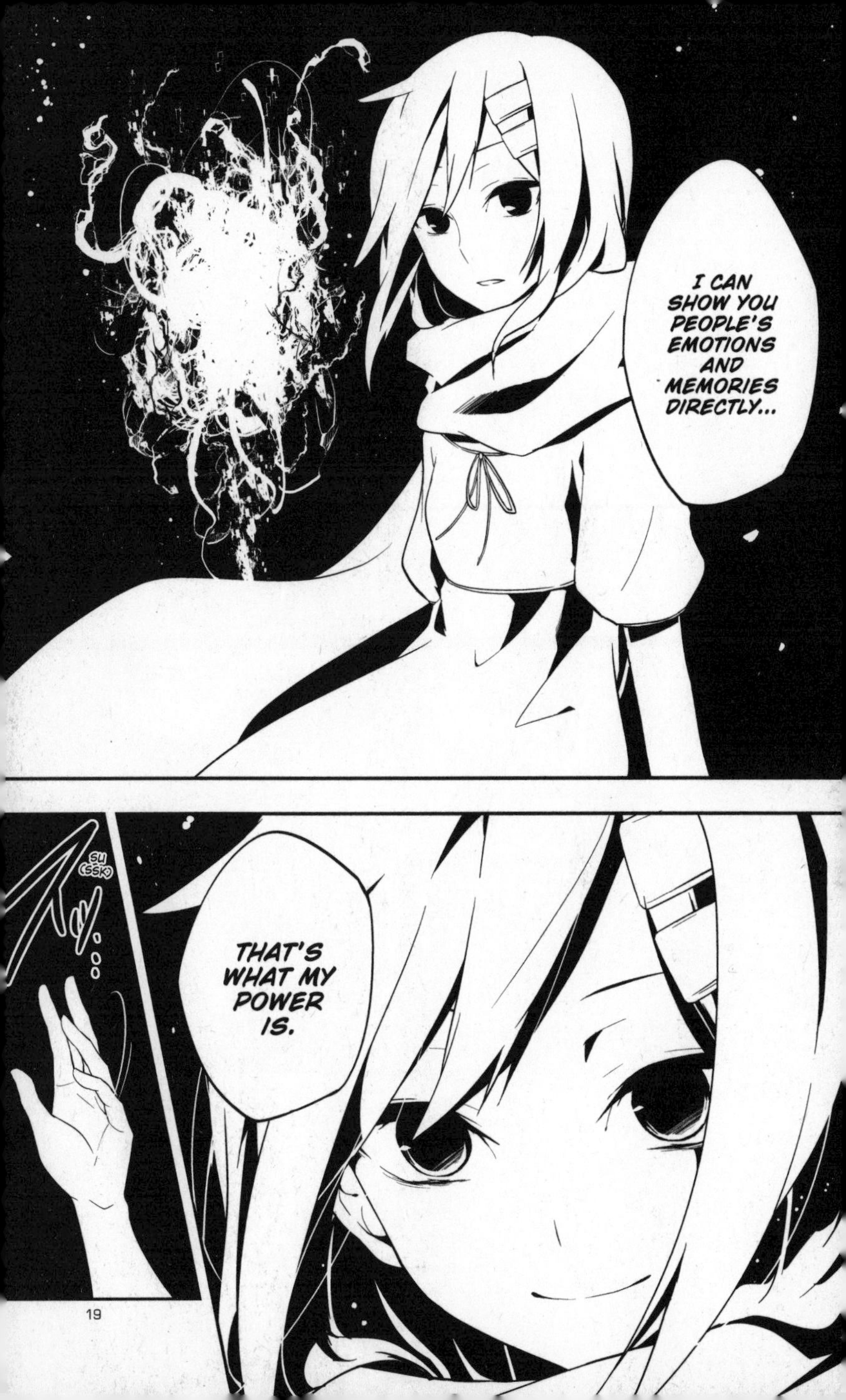
I CAN SHOW YOU PEOPLE'S EMOTIONS AND MEMORIES DIRECTLY...
THAT'S WHAT MY POWER IS.
SU (SSK)

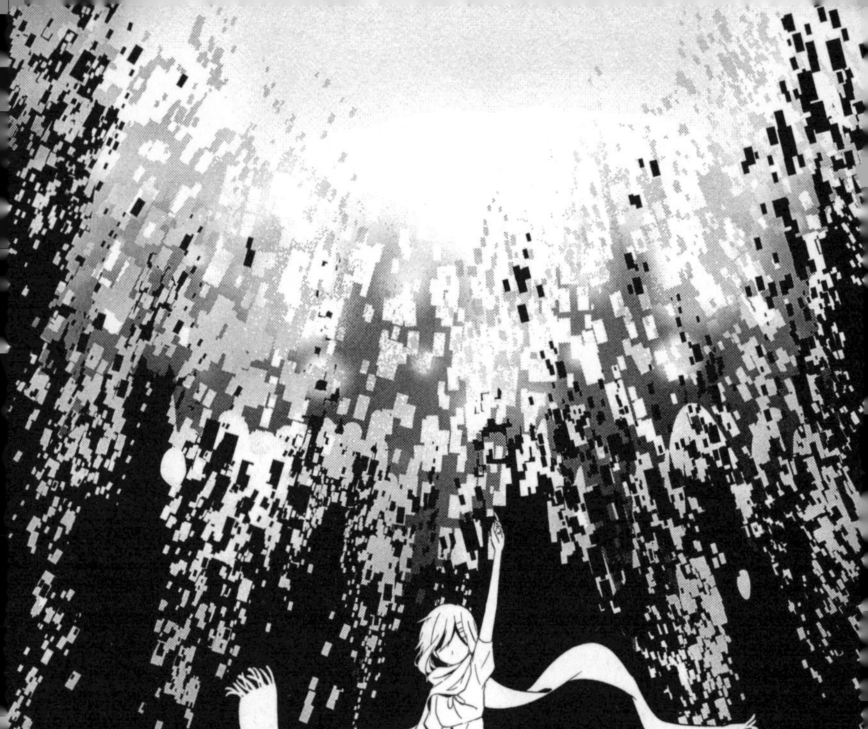
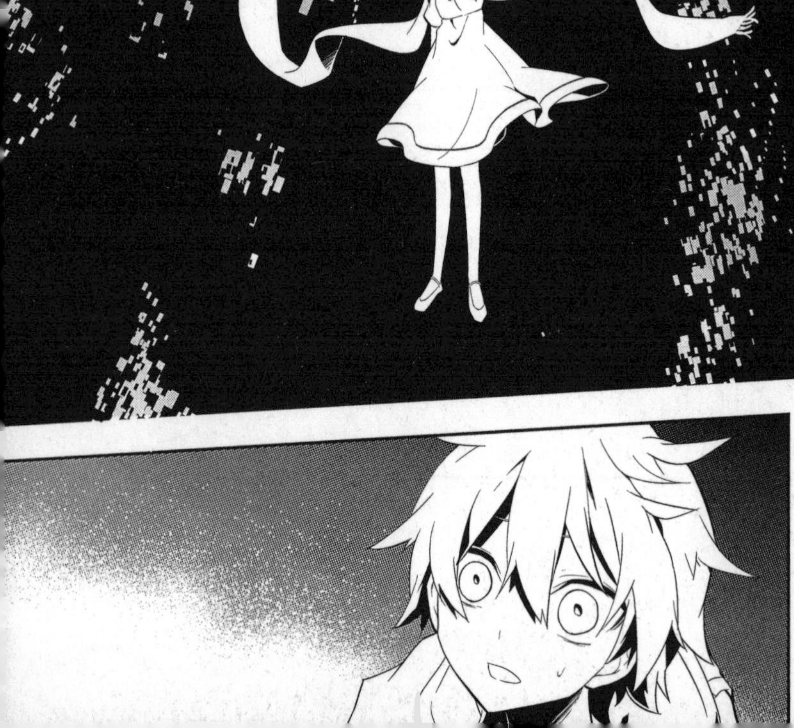

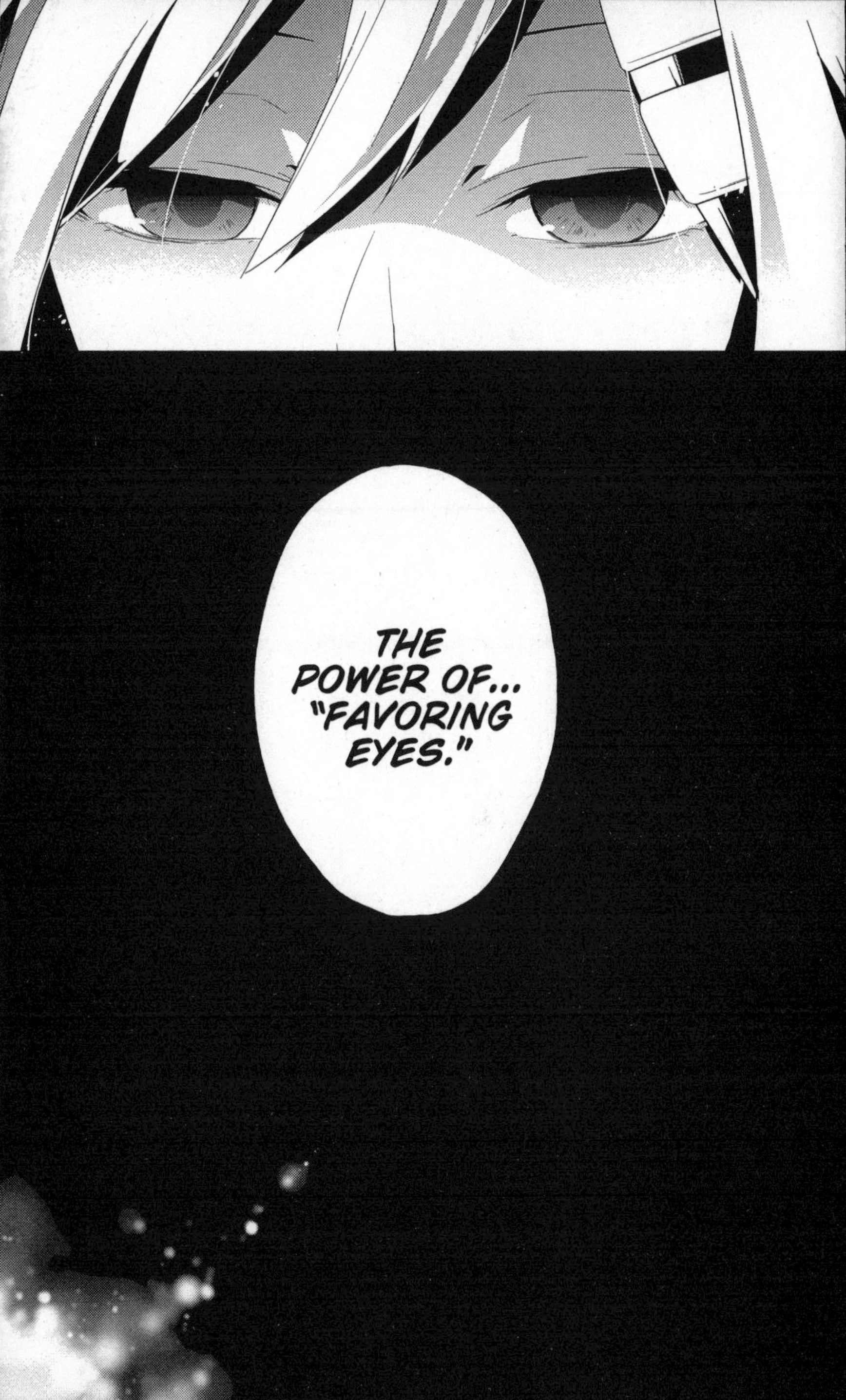
THE POWER OF... "FAVORING EYES."

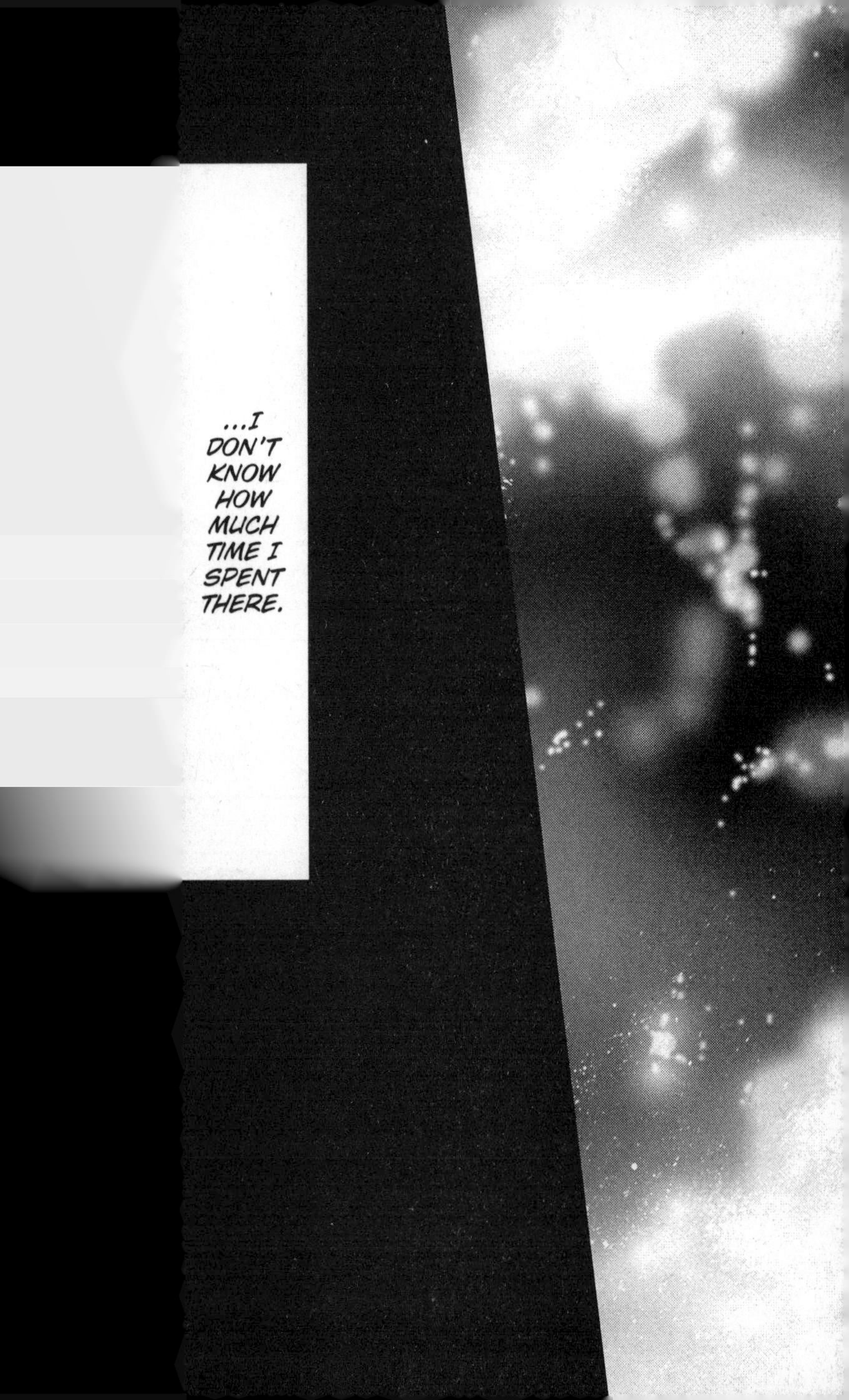
...I DON'T KNOW HOW MUCH TIME I SPENT THERE.

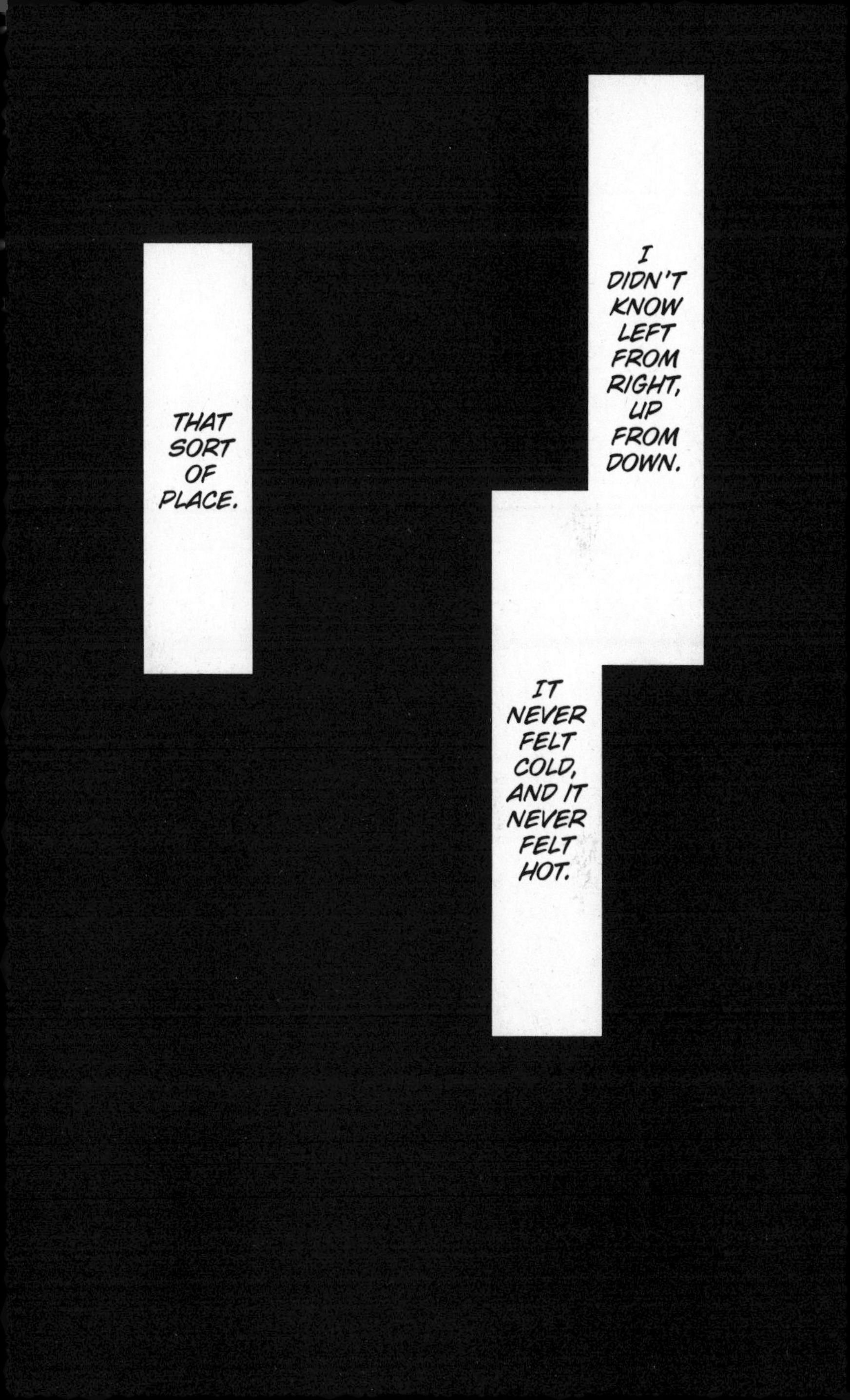
I DIDN'T KNOW LEFT FROM RIGHT, UP FROM DOWN.
IT NEVER FELT COLD, AND IT NEVER FELT HOT.
THAT SORT OF PLACE.

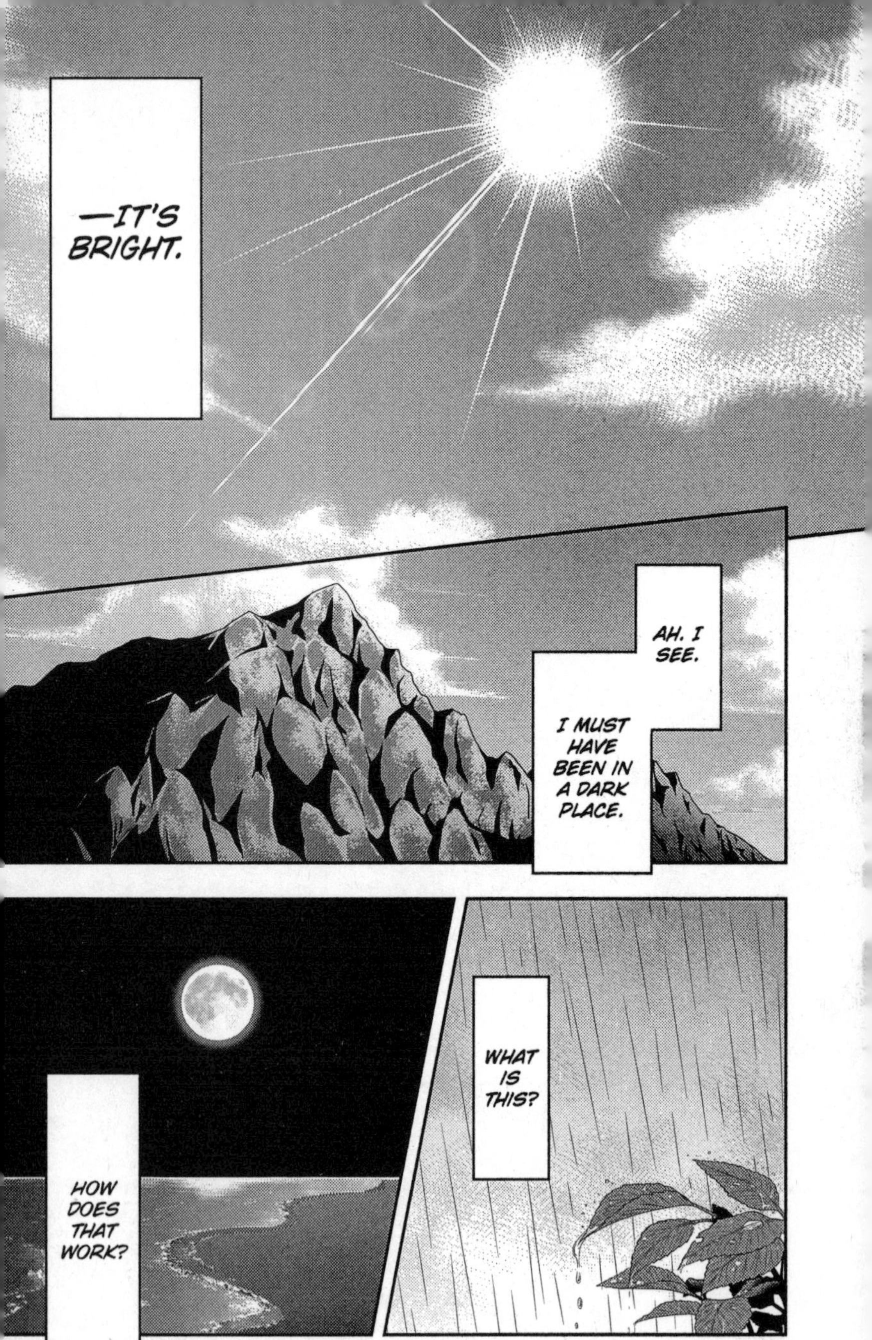
—IT'S BRIGHT.
AH. I SEE.
I MUST HAVE BEEN IN A DARK PLACE.
WHAT IS THIS?
HOW DOES THAT WORK?

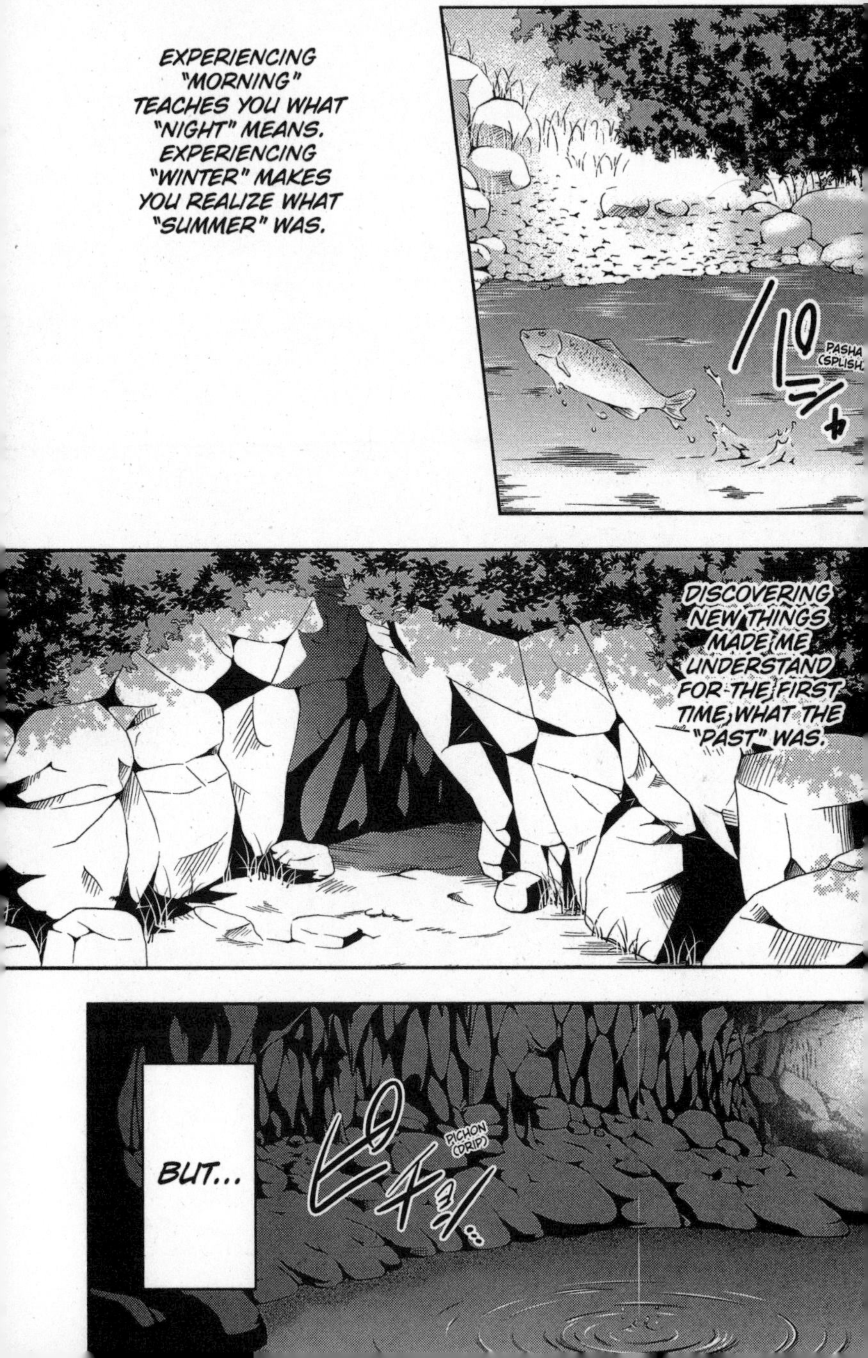
PASHA (SPLISH)
EXPERIENCING "MORNING" TEACHES YOU WHAT "NIGHT" MEANS. EXPERIENCING "WINTER" MAKES YOU REALIZE WHAT "SUMMER" WAS.
DISCOVERING NEW THINGS MADE ME UNDERSTAND FOR THE FIRST TIME WHAT THE "PAST" WAS.
PICHON (DRIP)
BUT...

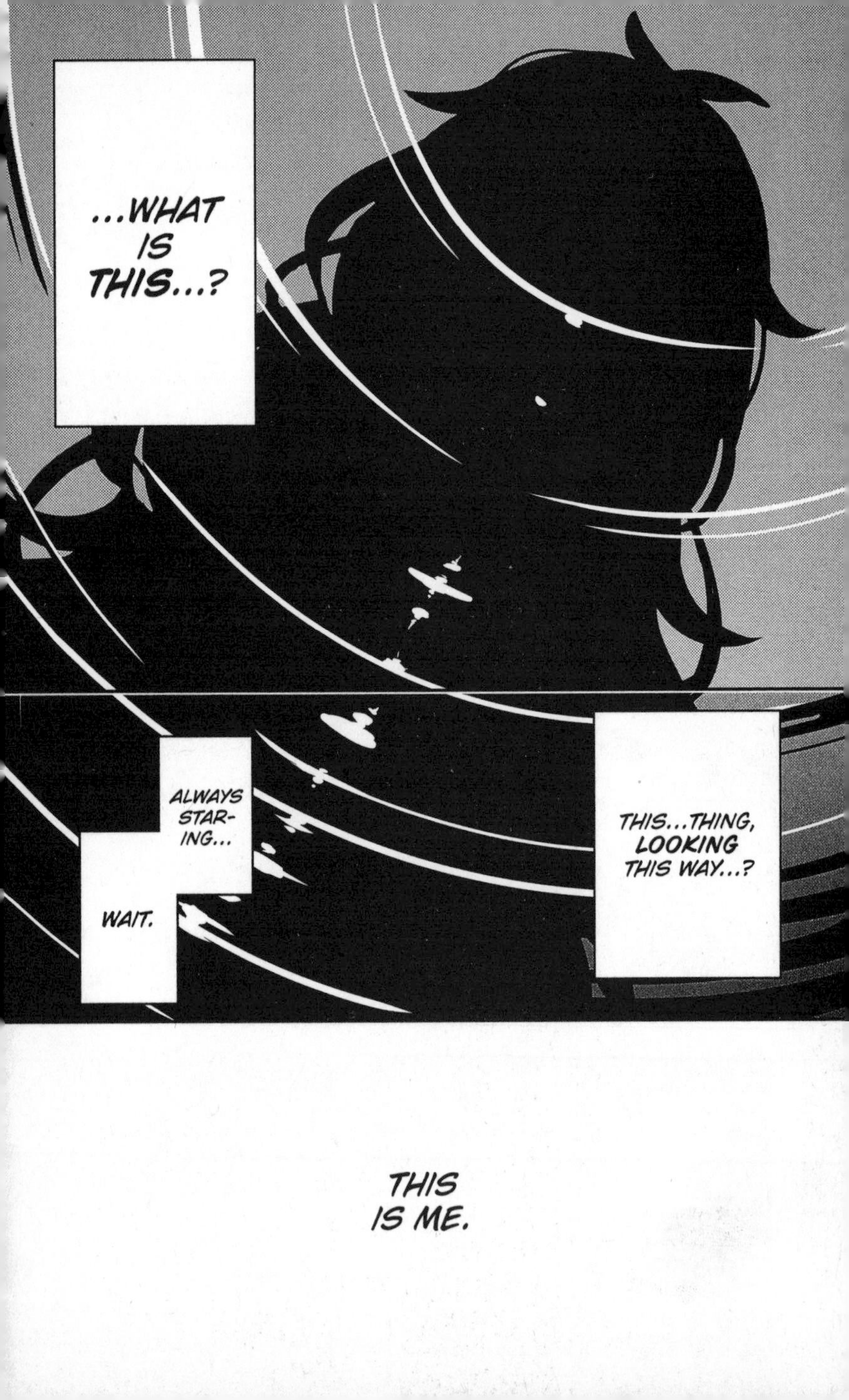
...WHAT IS THIS...?
THIS...THING, LOOKING THIS WAY...?
ALWAYS STARING...
WAIT.
THIS IS ME.

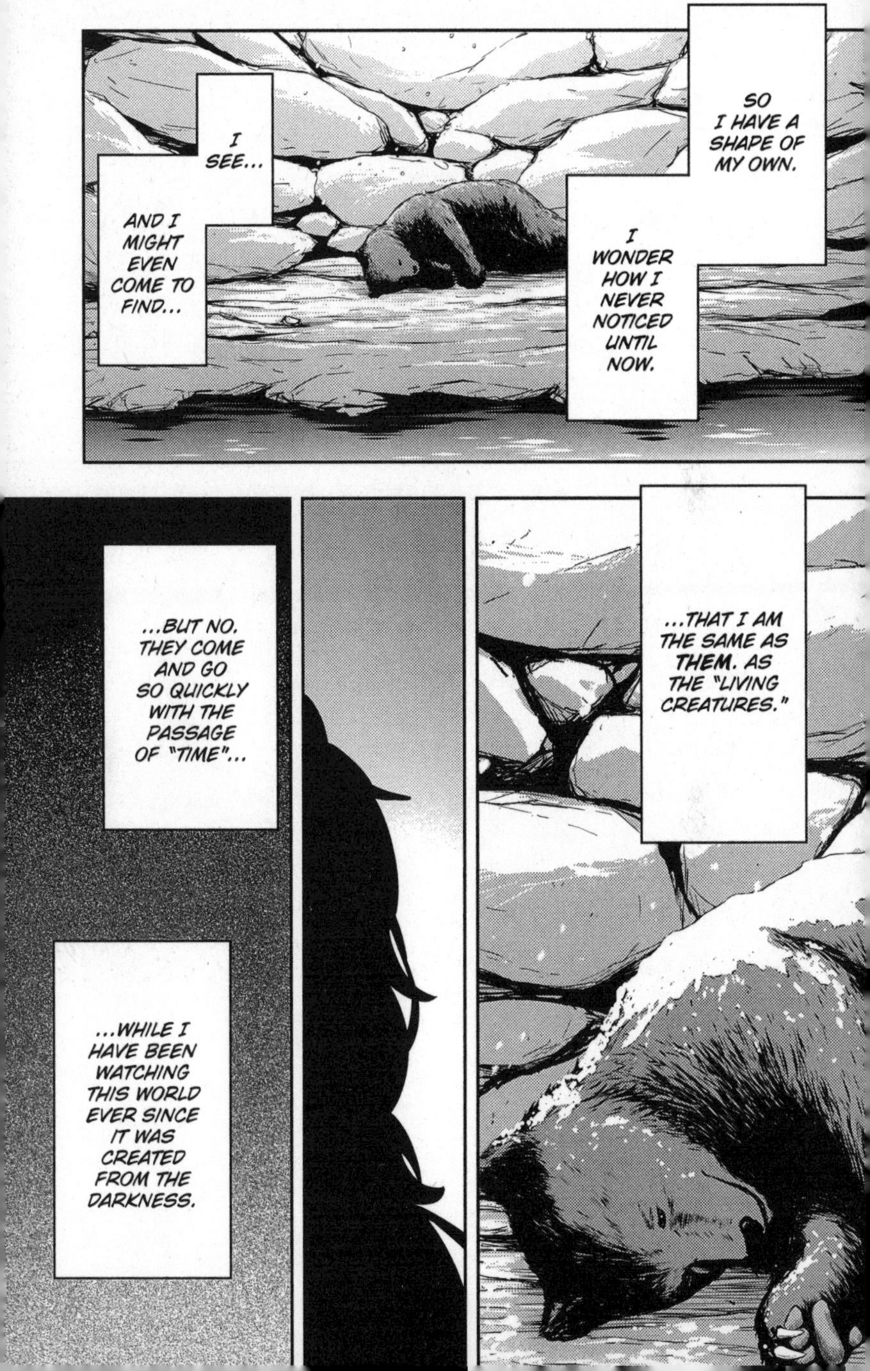
SO I HAVE A SHAPE OF MY OWN.
I WONDER HOW I NEVER NOTICED UNTIL NOW.
I SEE...
AND I MIGHT EVEN COME TO FIND...
...THAT I AM THE SAME AS THEM. AS THE "LIVING CREATURES."
...BUT NO. THEY COME AND GO SO QUICKLY WITH THE PASSAGE OF "TIME"...
...WHILE I HAVE BEEN WATCHING THIS WORLD EVER SINCE IT WAS CREATED FROM THE DARKNESS.

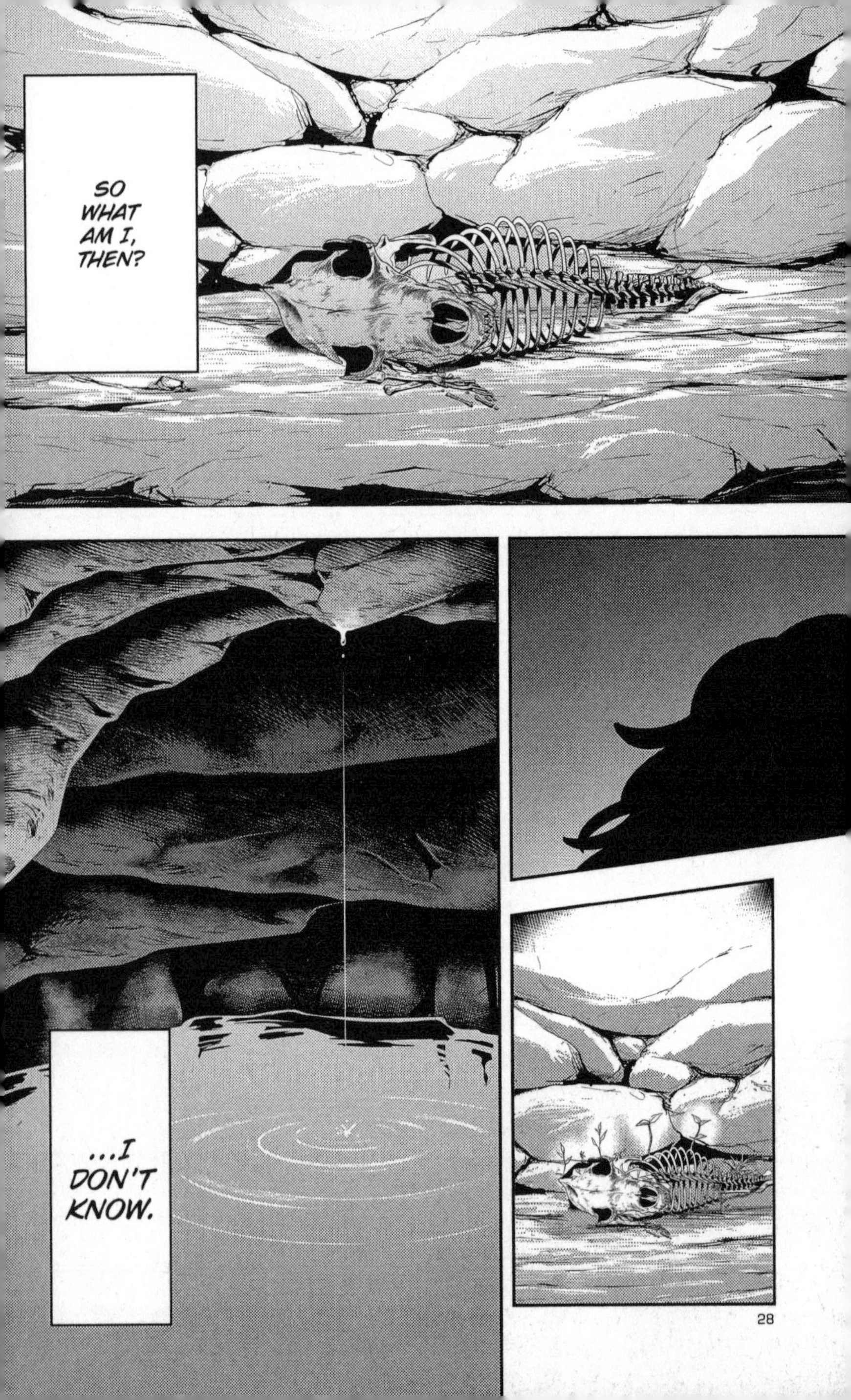
SO WHAT AM I, THEN?
...I DON'T KNOW.

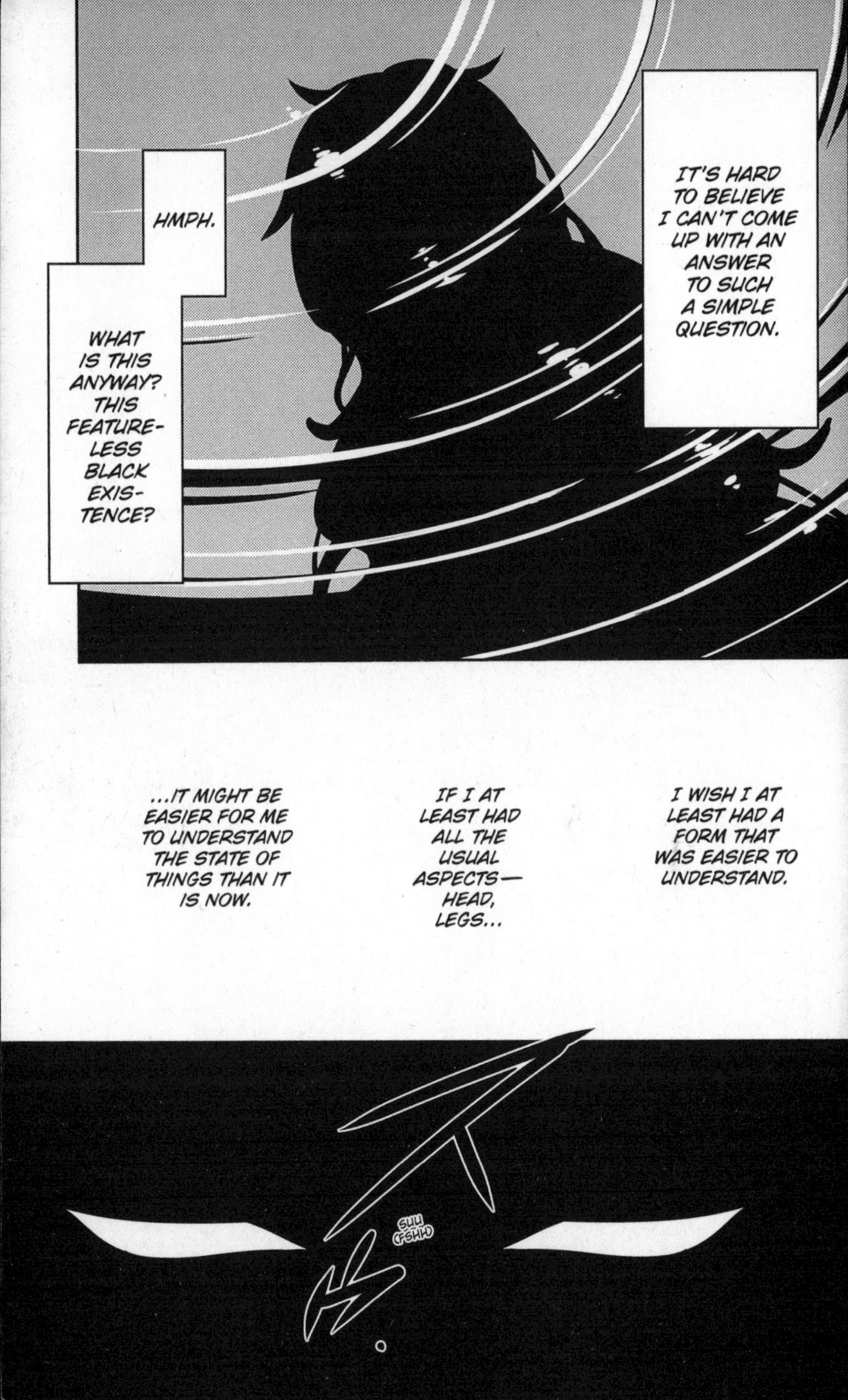
IT'S HARD TO BELIEVE I CAN'T COME UP WITH AN ANSWER TO SUCH A SIMPLE QUESTION.
HMPH.
WHAT IS THIS ANYWAY? THIS FEATURE-LESS BLACK EXIS-TENCE?
I WISH I AT LEAST HAD A FORM THAT WAS EASIER TO UNDERSTAND.
IF I AT LEAST HAD ALL THE USUAL ASPECTS— HEAD, LEGS...
...IT MIGHT BE EASIER FOR ME TO UNDERSTAND THE STATE OF THINGS THAN IT IS NOW.
SUU (FSHH)

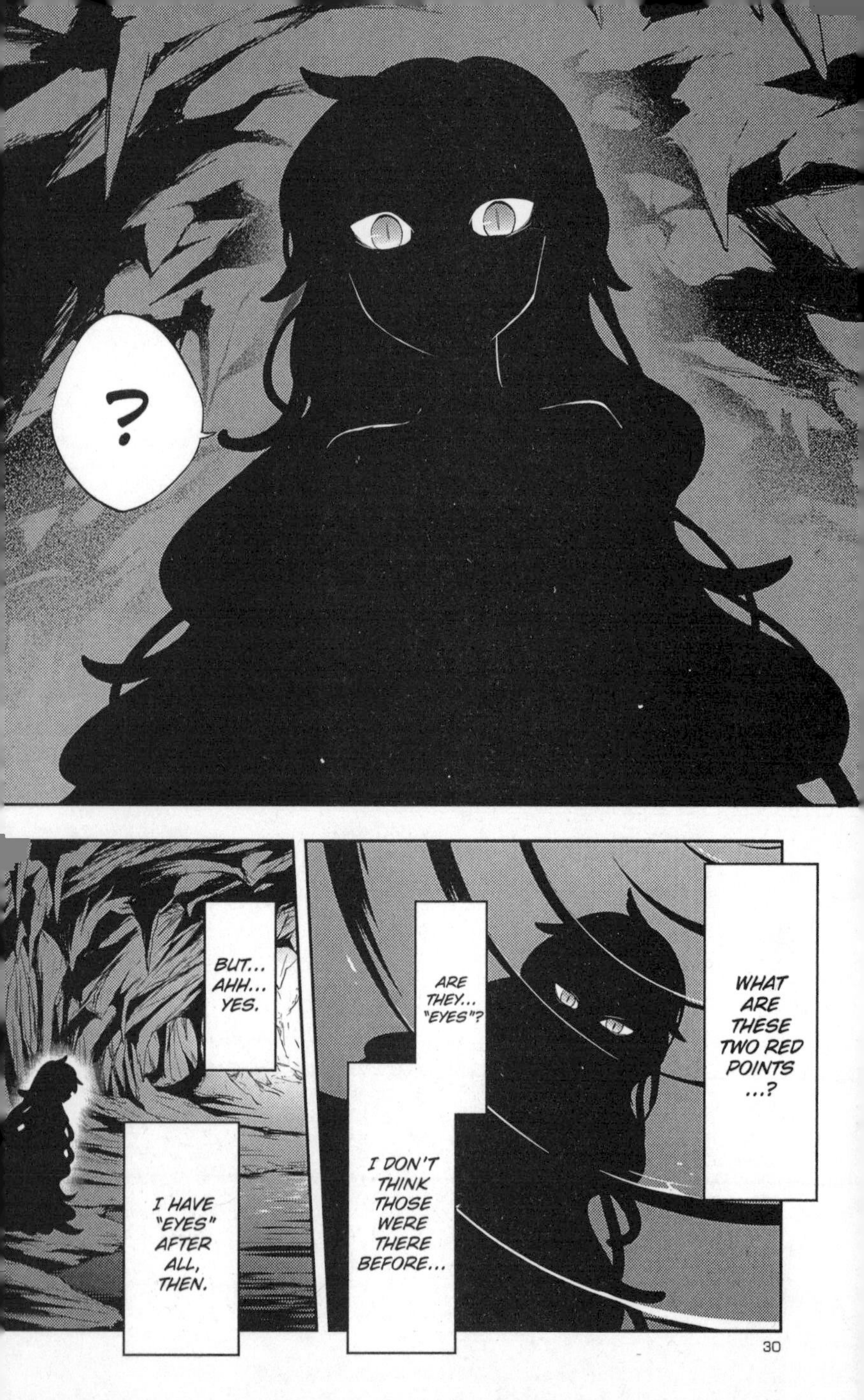
?
WHAT ARE THESE TWO RED POINTS ...?
ARE THEY... "EYES"?
I DON'T THINK THOSE WERE THERE BEFORE...
BUT... AHH... YES.
I HAVE "EYES" AFTER ALL, THEN.

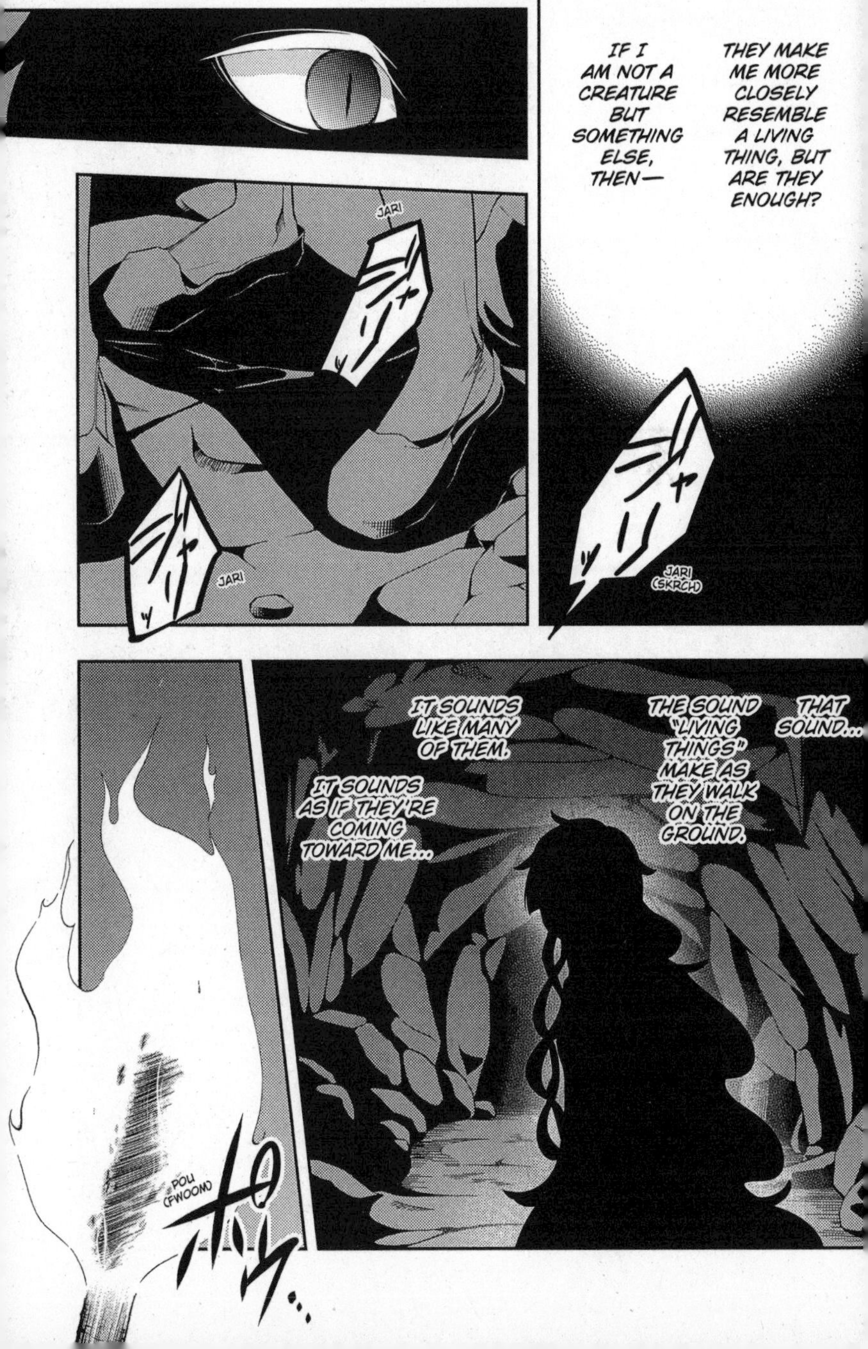
THEY MAKE ME MORE CLOSELY RESEMBLE A LIVING THING, BUT ARE THEY ENOUGH?
IF I AM NOT A CREATURE BUT SOMETHING ELSE, THEN—
JARI (SKRCH)
JARI
JARI
THAT SOUND...
THE SOUND "LIVING THINGS" MAKE AS THEY WALK ON THE GROUND.
IT SOUNDS LIKE MANY OF THEM.
IT SOUNDS AS IF THEY'RE COMING TOWARD ME...
POU (FWOOM)

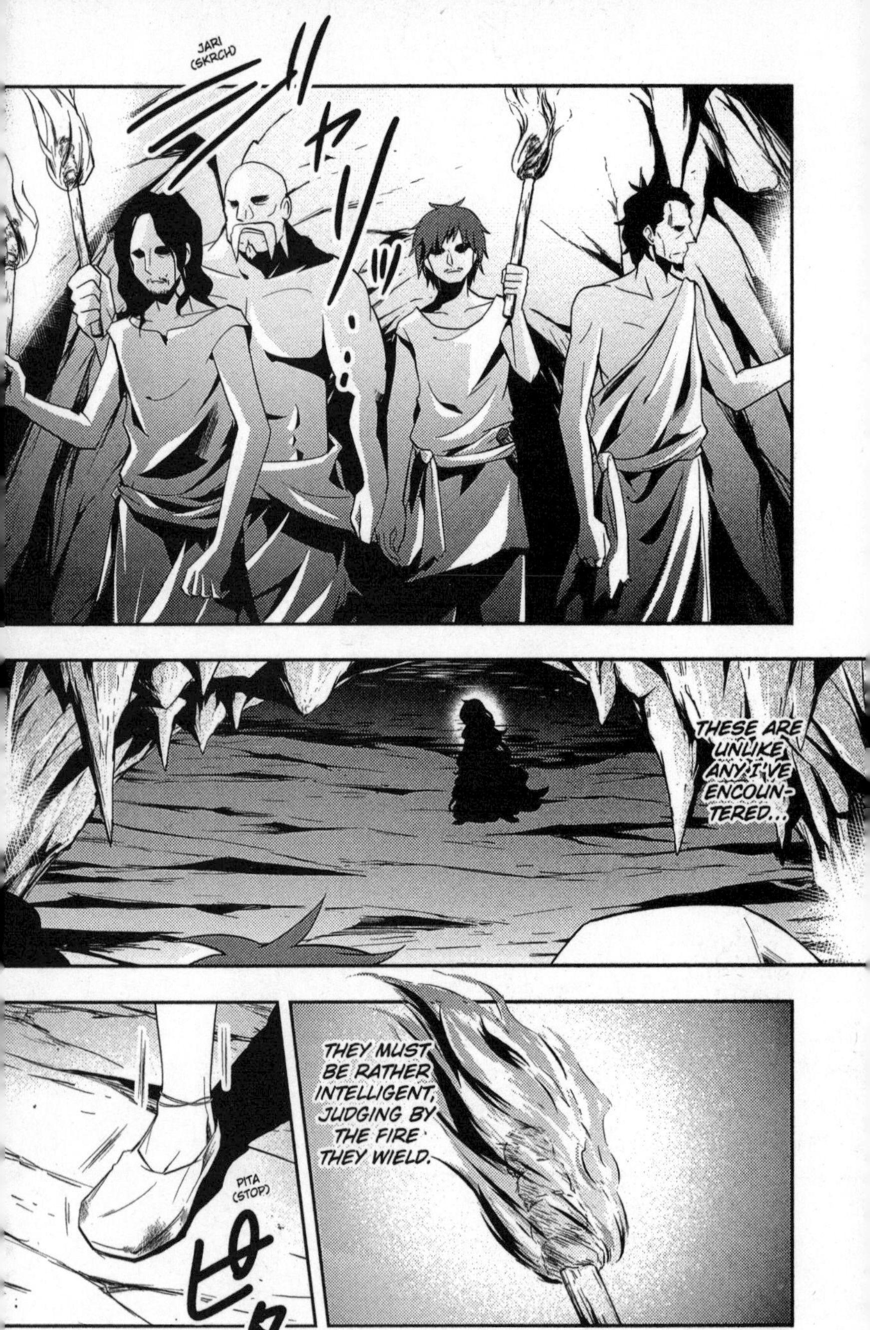
JARI (SKRCH)
THESE ARE UNLIKE ANY I'VE ENCOUNTERED...
THEY MUST BE RATHER INTELLIGENT, JUDGING BY THE FIRE THEY WIELD.
PITA (STOP)

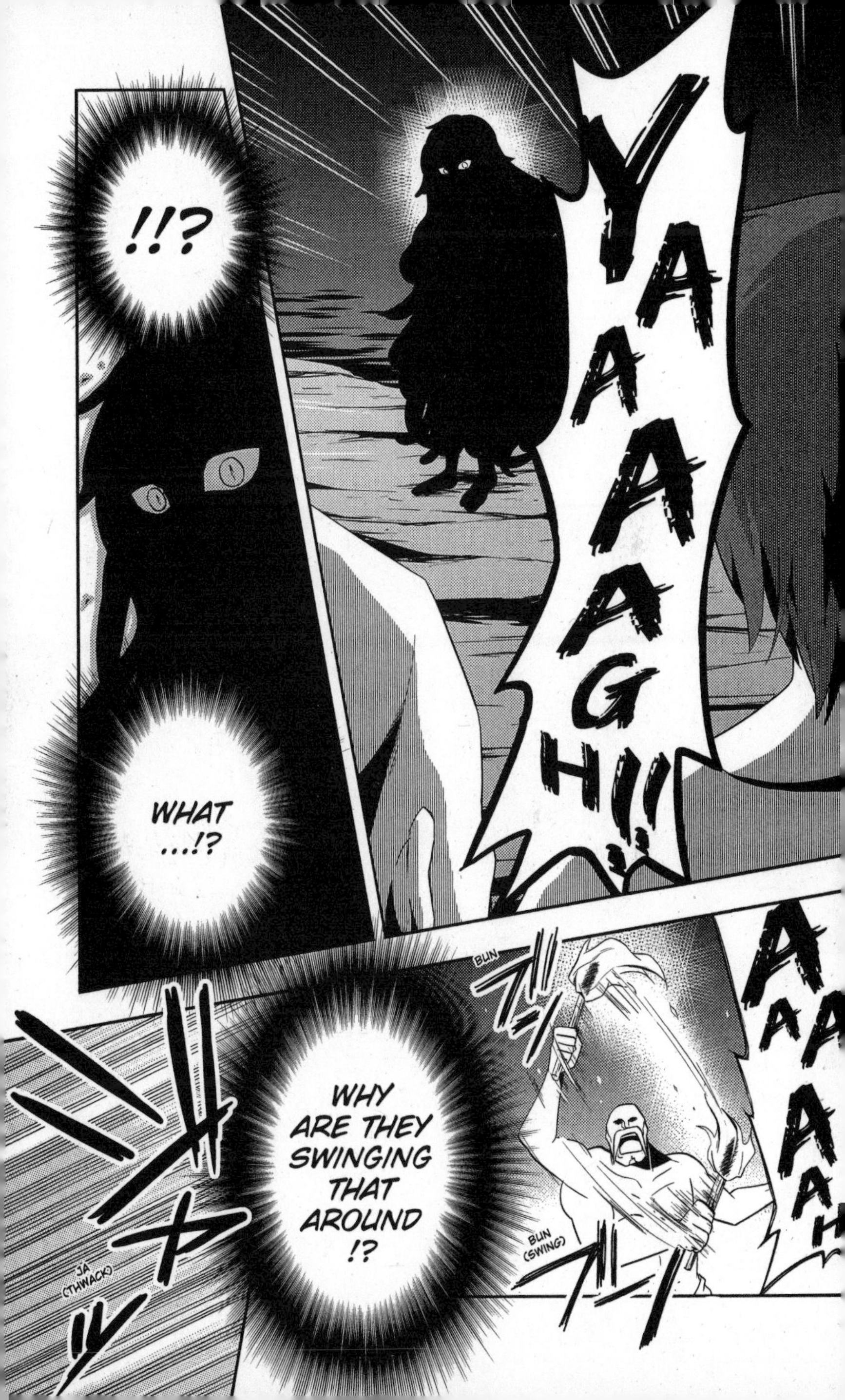
YAAAAAGH!!
!!?
WHAT ...!?
AAAAAAH
BUN
BUN (SWING)
WHY ARE THEY SWINGING THAT AROUND !?
JA (THWACK)

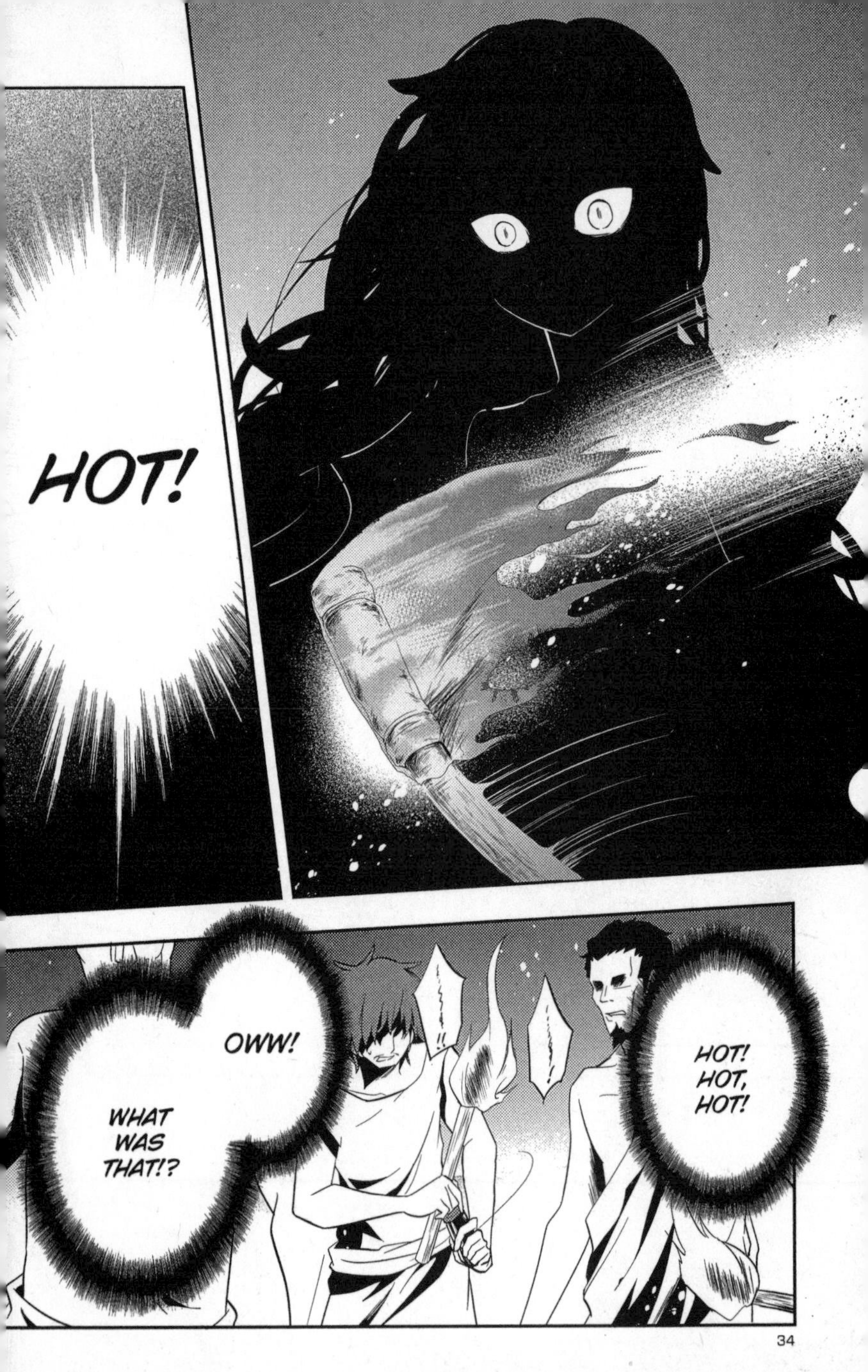
HOT!
HOT! HOT, HOT!
OWW!
WHAT WAS THAT!?

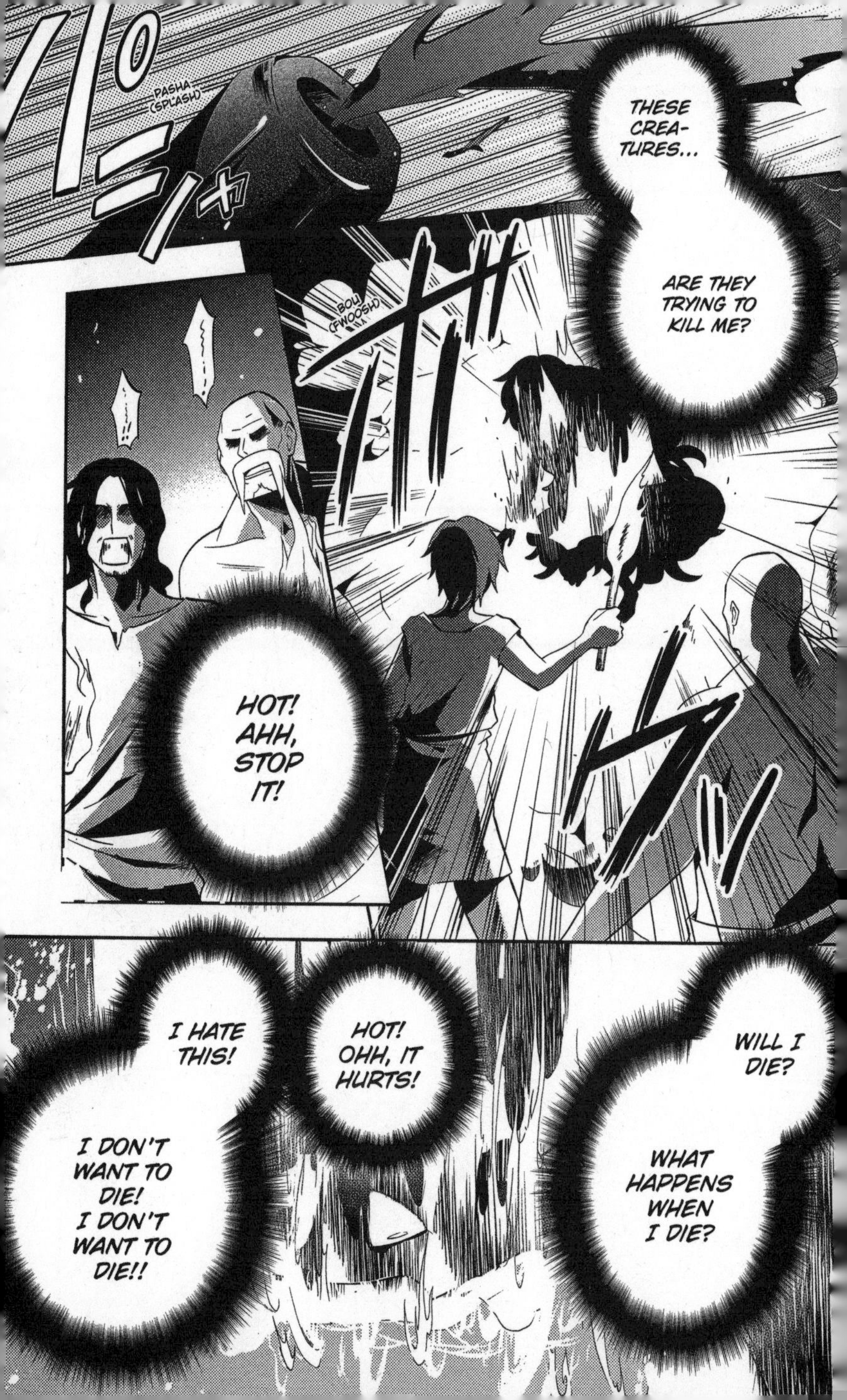
THESE CREA-TURES...
ARE THEY TRYING TO KILL ME?
PASHA (SPLASH)
BOU (FWOOSH)
HOT! AHH, STOP IT!
WILL I DIE?
WHAT HAPPENS WHEN I DIE?
HOT! OHH, IT HURTS!
I HATE THIS!
I DON'T WANT TO DIE! I DON'T WANT TO DIE!!

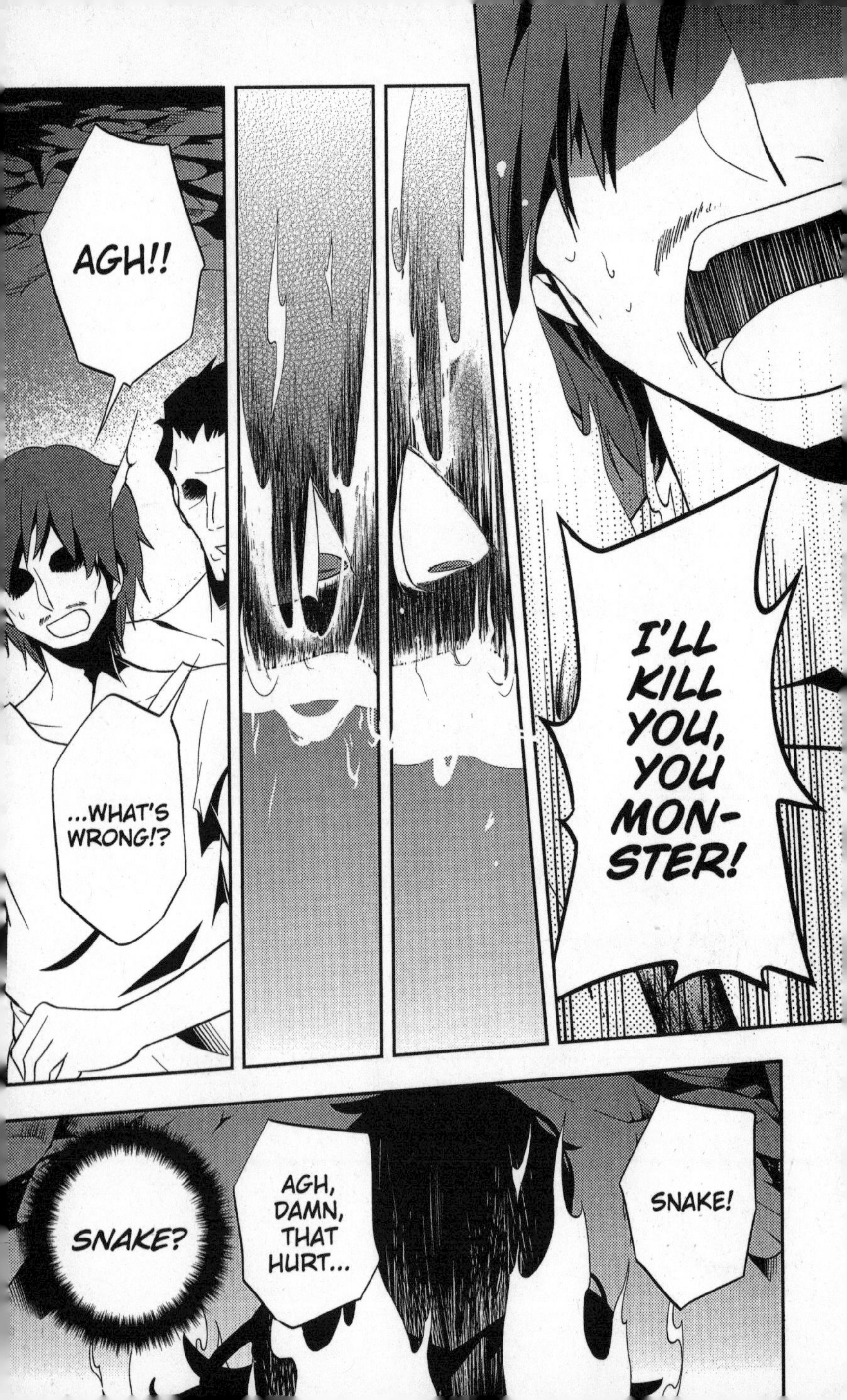
I'LL KILL YOU, YOU MONSTER!
AGH!!
...WHAT'S WRONG!?
SNAKE!
AGH, DAMN, THAT HURT...
SNAKE?

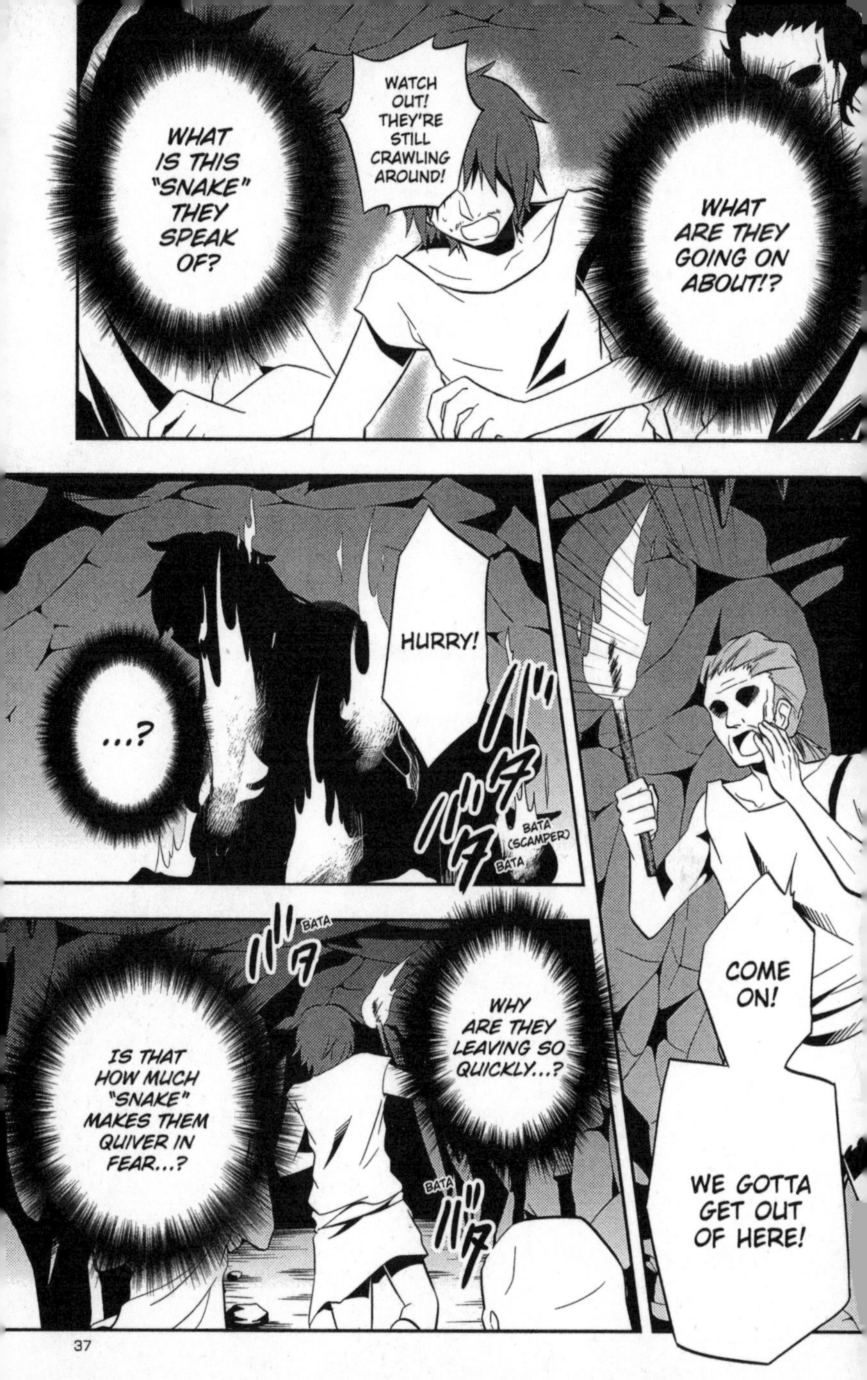
WATCH OUT! THEY'RE STILL CRAWLING AROUND!
WHAT ARE THEY GOING ON ABOUT!?
WHAT IS THIS "SNAKE" THEY SPEAK OF?
COME ON!
WE GOTTA GET OUT OF HERE!
HURRY!
BATA (SCAMPER) BATA
...?
BATA
WHY ARE THEY LEAVING SO QUICKLY...?
IS THAT HOW MUCH "SNAKE" MAKES THEM QUIVER IN FEAR...?
BATA

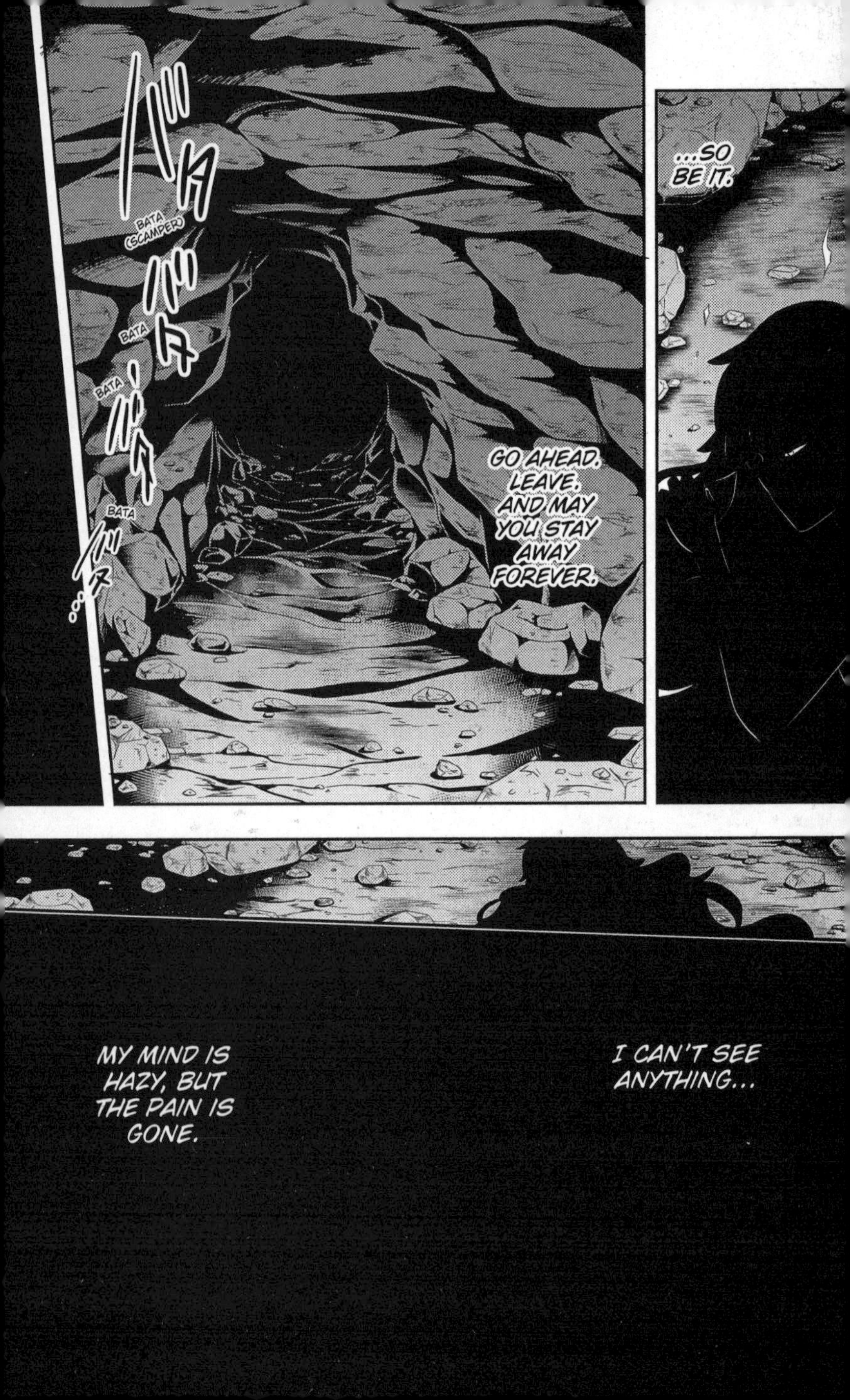
...SO BE IT.
GO AHEAD. LEAVE. AND MAY YOU STAY AWAY FOREVER.
BATA (SCAMPER)
BATA
BATA
BATA
I CAN'T SEE ANYTHING...
MY MIND IS HAZY, BUT THE PAIN IS GONE.

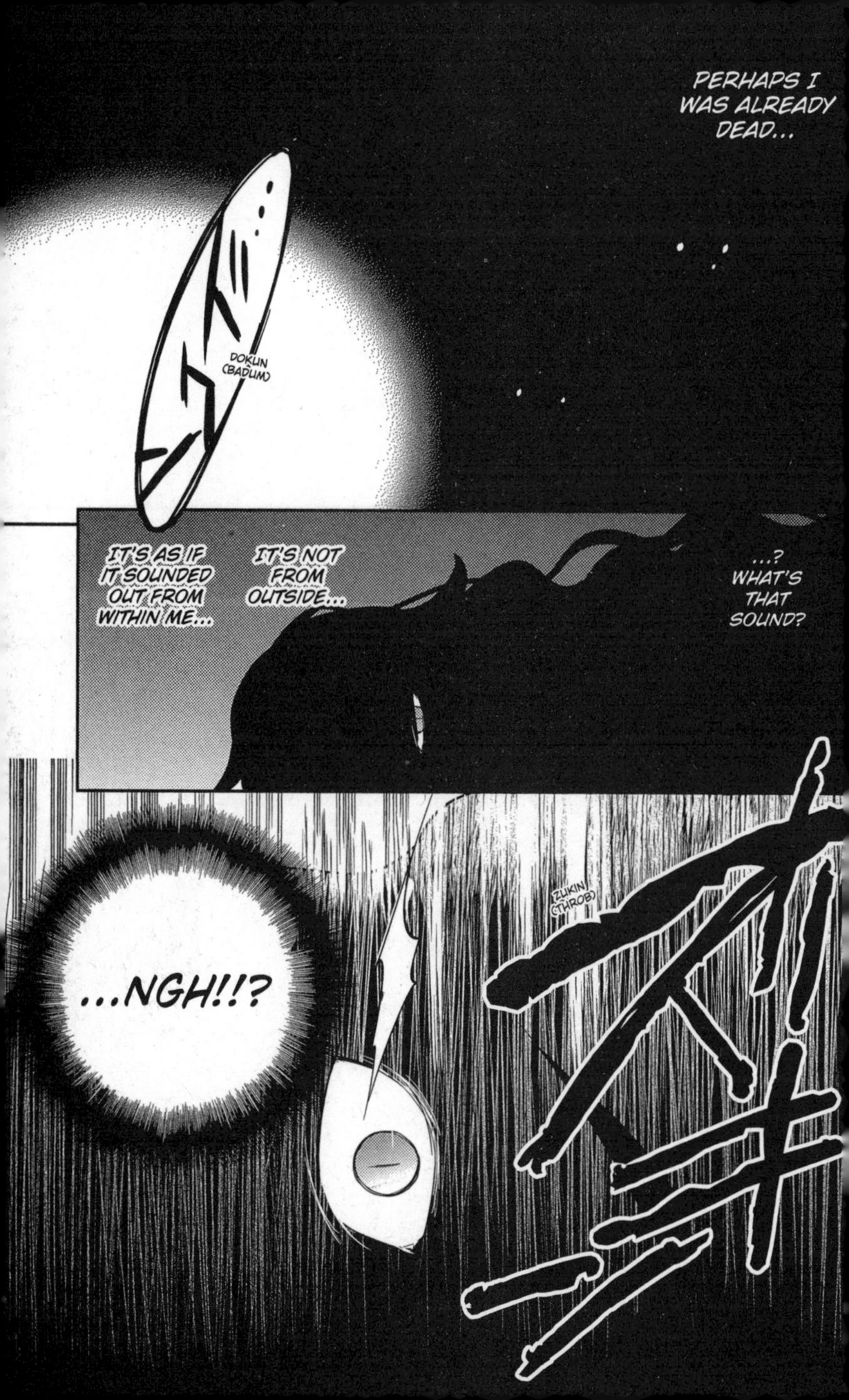
PERHAPS I WAS ALREADY DEAD...
DOKUN (BADUM)
...? WHAT'S THAT SOUND?
IT'S NOT FROM OUTSIDE...
IT'S AS IF IT SOUNDED OUT FROM WITHIN ME...
ZUKIN (THROB)
...NGH!!?

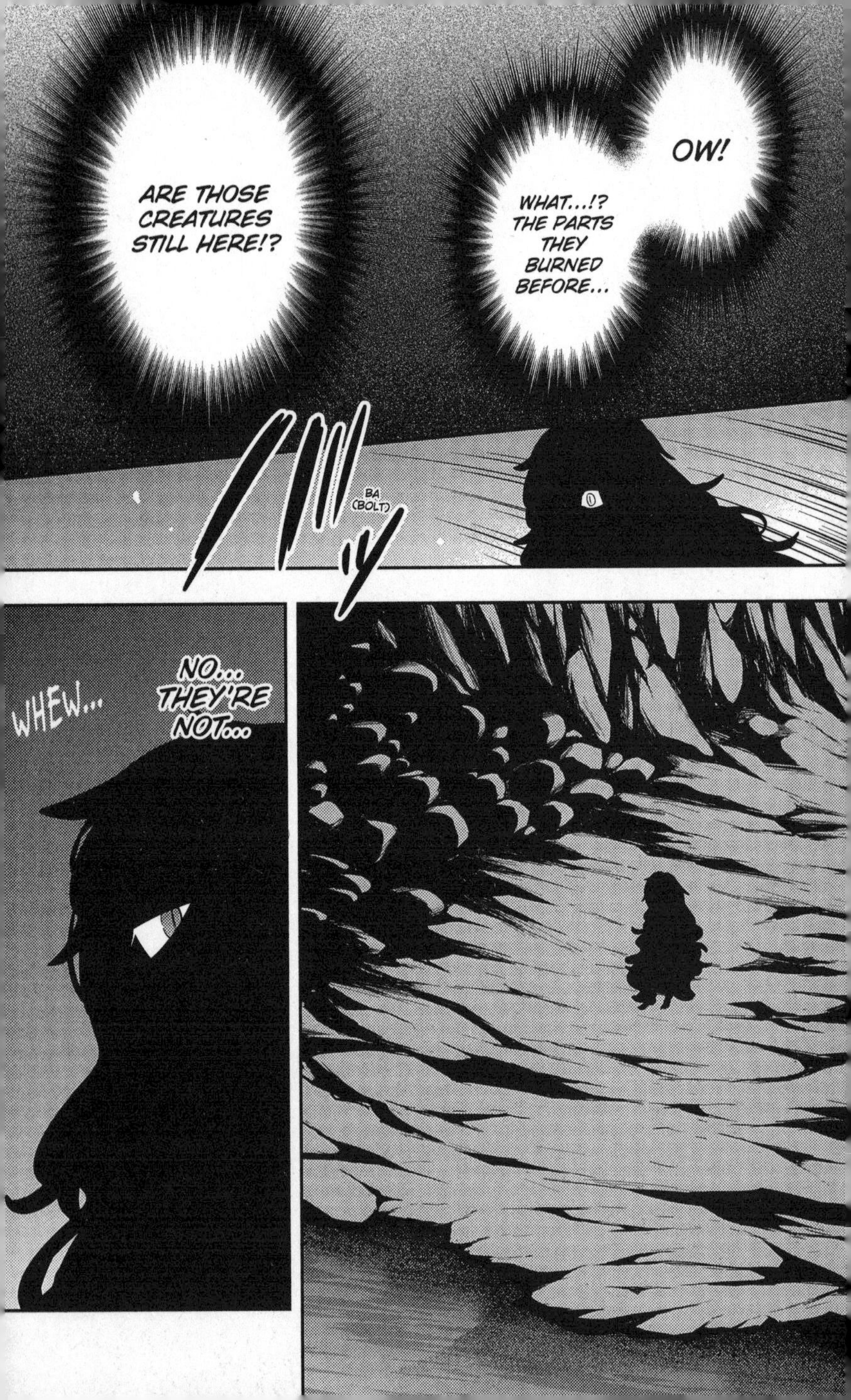
OW!
WHAT...!? THE PARTS THEY BURNED BEFORE...
ARE THOSE CREATURES STILL HERE!?
BA (BOLT)
NO... THEY'RE NOT...
WHEW...

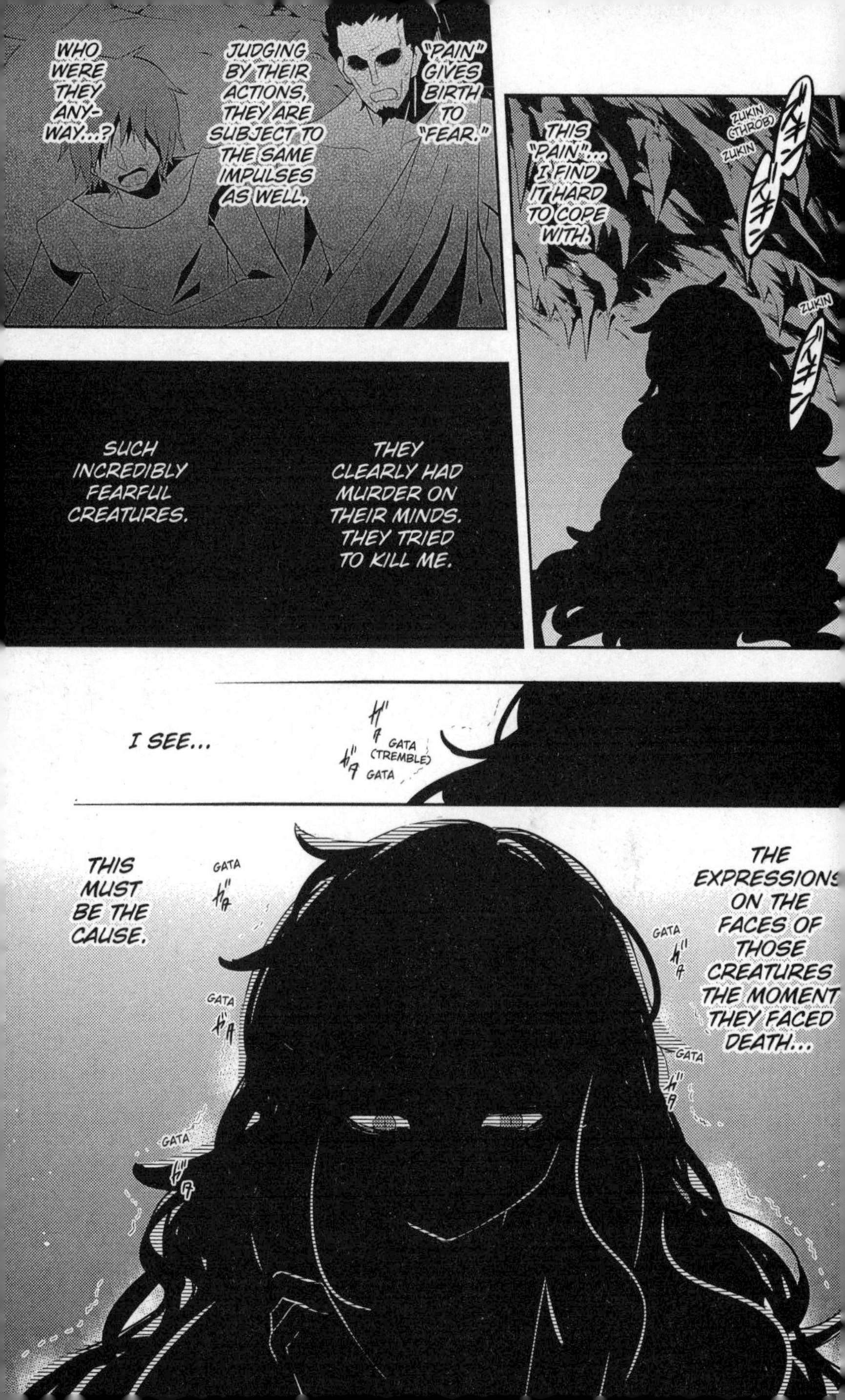
"PAIN" GIVES BIRTH TO "FEAR."
JUDGING BY THEIR ACTIONS, THEY ARE SUBJECT TO THE SAME IMPULSES AS WELL.
WHO WERE THEY ANY-WAY...?
ZUKIN (THROB) ZUKIN
THIS "PAIN"... I FIND IT HARD TO COPE WITH.
ZUKIN
THEY CLEARLY HAD MURDER ON THEIR MINDS. THEY TRIED TO KILL ME.
SUCH INCREDIBLY FEARFUL CREATURES.
GATA (TREMBLE) GATA
I SEE...
THE EXPRESSIONS ON THE FACES OF THOSE CREATURES THE MOMENT THEY FACED DEATH...
GATA
GATA
GATA
GATA
GATA
THIS MUST BE THE CAUSE.

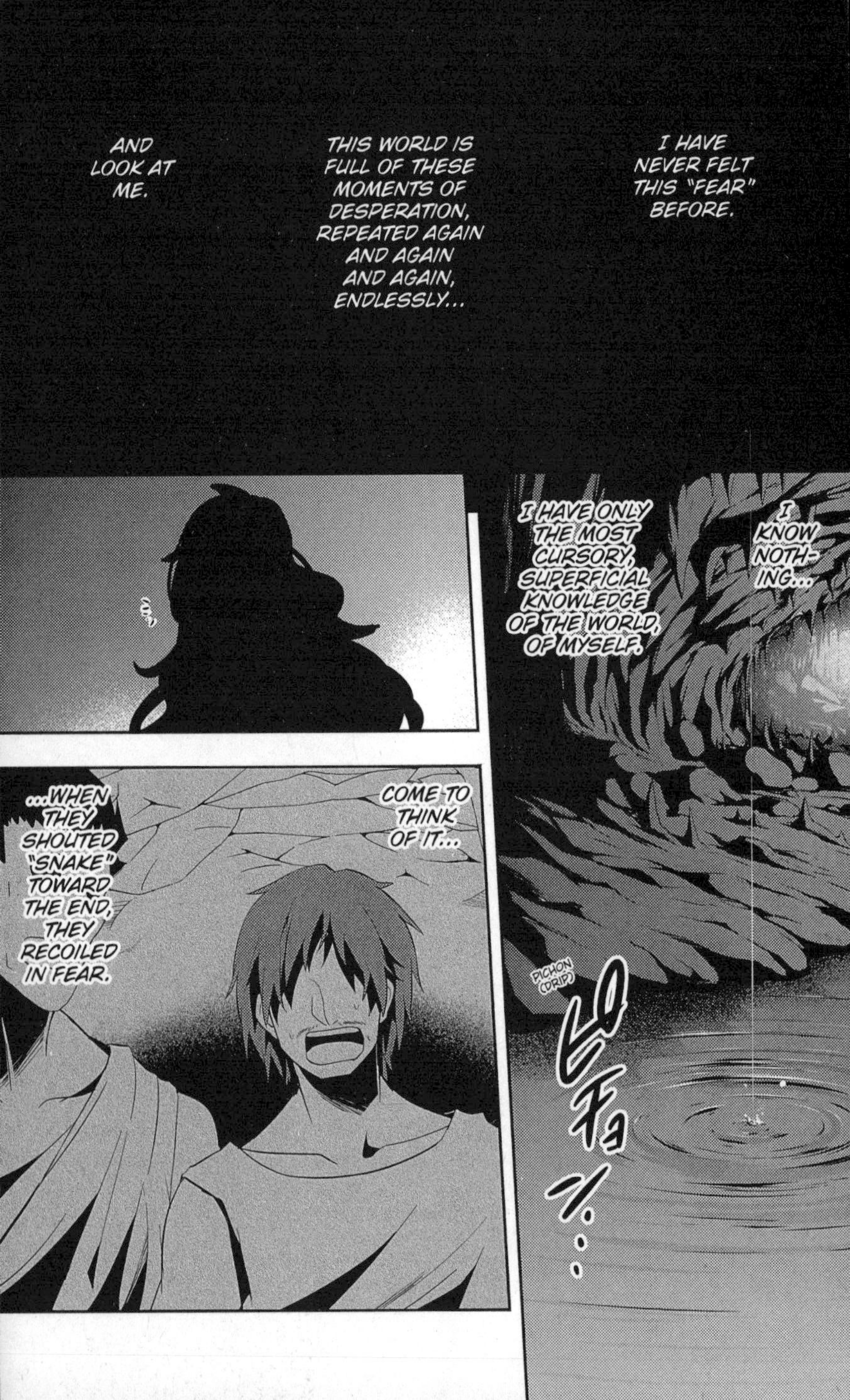
I HAVE NEVER FELT THIS "FEAR" BEFORE.
THIS WORLD IS FULL OF THESE MOMENTS OF DESPERATION, REPEATED AGAIN AND AGAIN AND AGAIN, ENDLESSLY...
AND LOOK AT ME.
I KNOW NOTHING...
I HAVE ONLY THE MOST CURSORY, SUPERFICIAL KNOWLEDGE OF THE WORLD, OF MYSELF.
PICHON (DRIP)
ピチョン...
COME TO THINK OF IT...
...WHEN THEY SHOUTED "SNAKE" TOWARD THE END, THEY RECOILED IN FEAR.

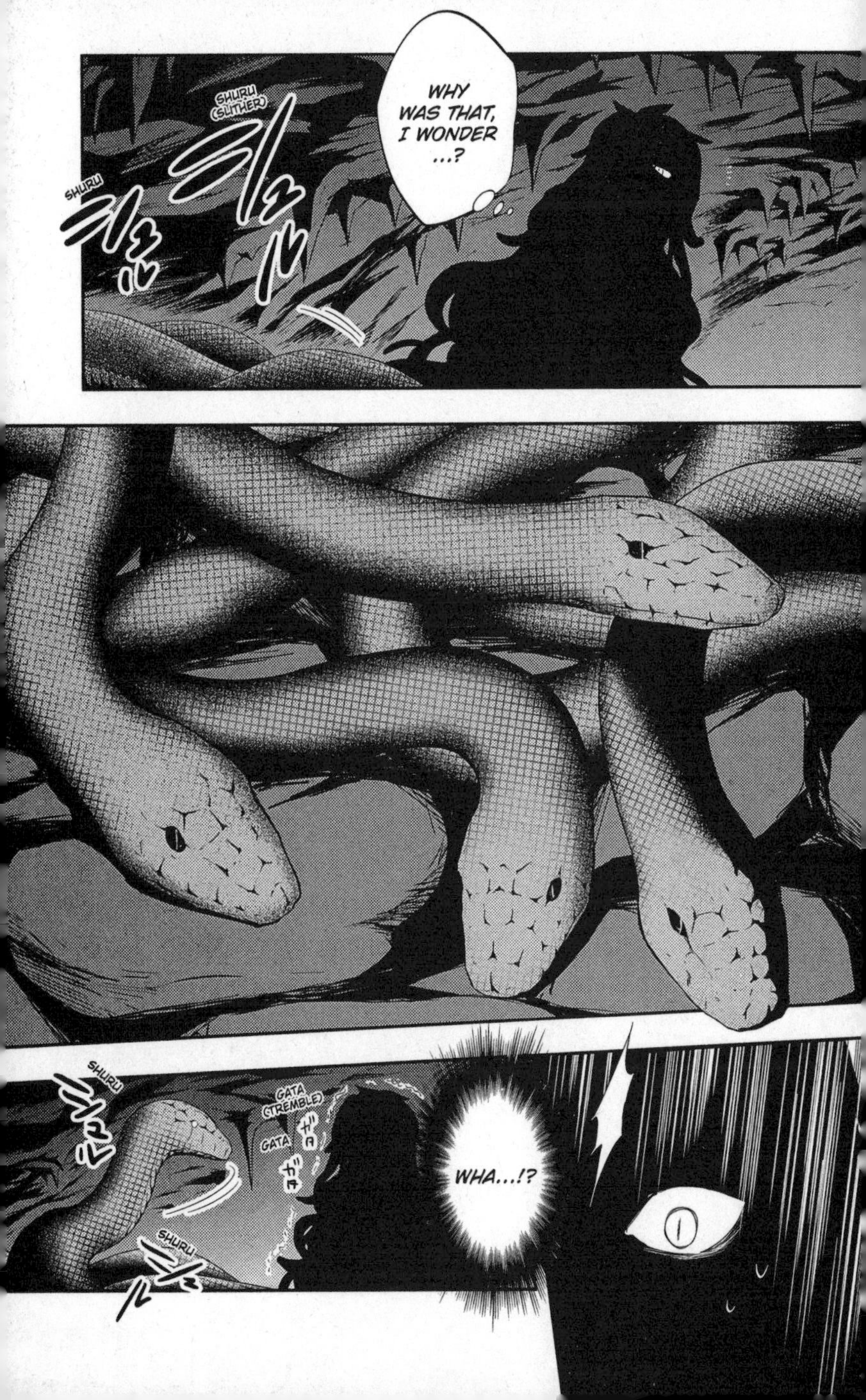
WHY WAS THAT, I WONDER ...?
SHURU (SLITHER)
SHURU
WHA...!?
GATA (TREMBLE)
GATA
SHURU
SHURU

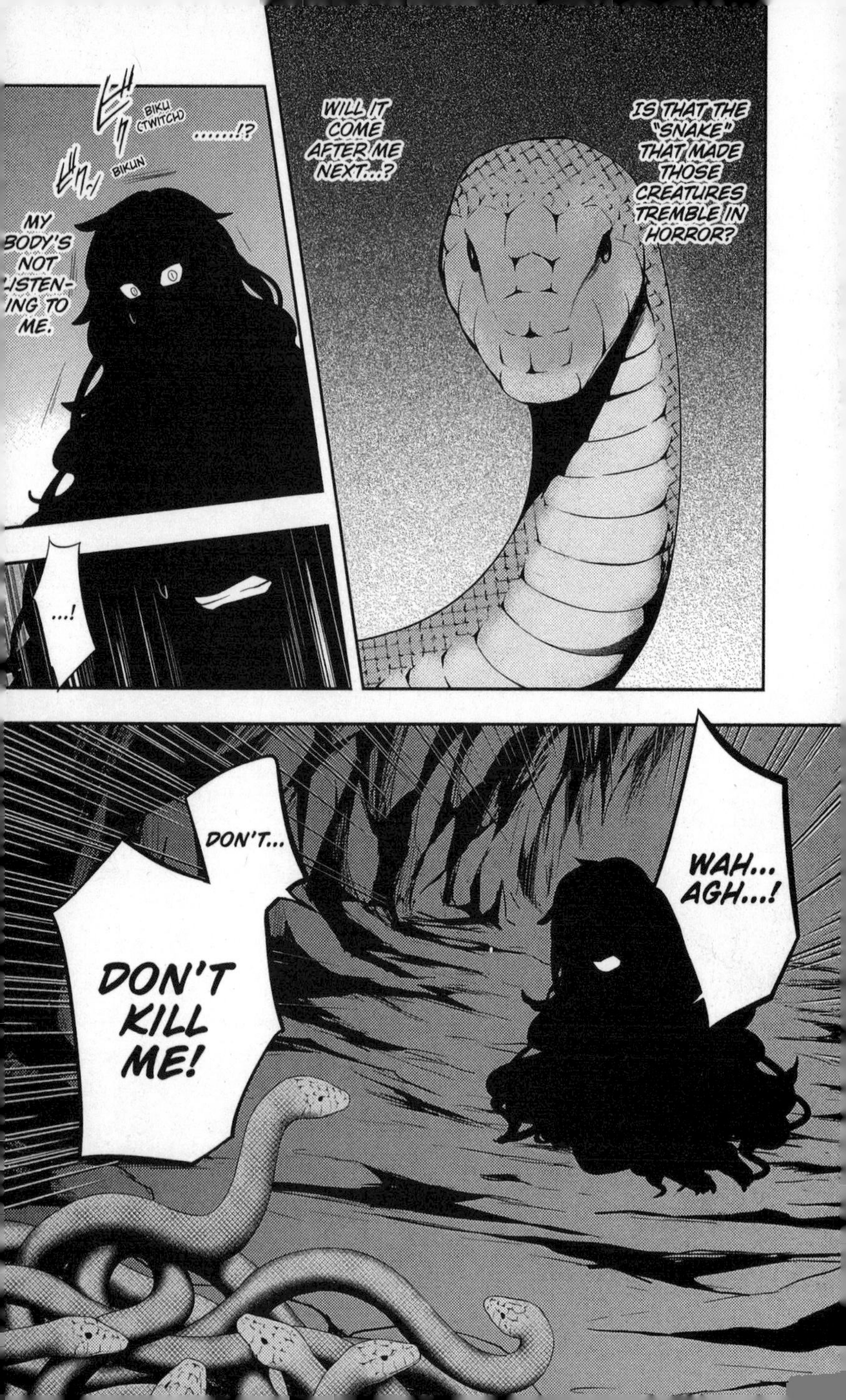
IS THAT THE "SNAKE" THAT MADE THOSE CREATURES TREMBLE IN HORROR?
WILL IT COME AFTER ME NEXT...?
BIKU (TWITCH)
......!?
BIKUN
MY BODY'S NOT LISTENING TO ME.
...!
WAH... AGH...!
DON'T...
DON'T KILL ME!

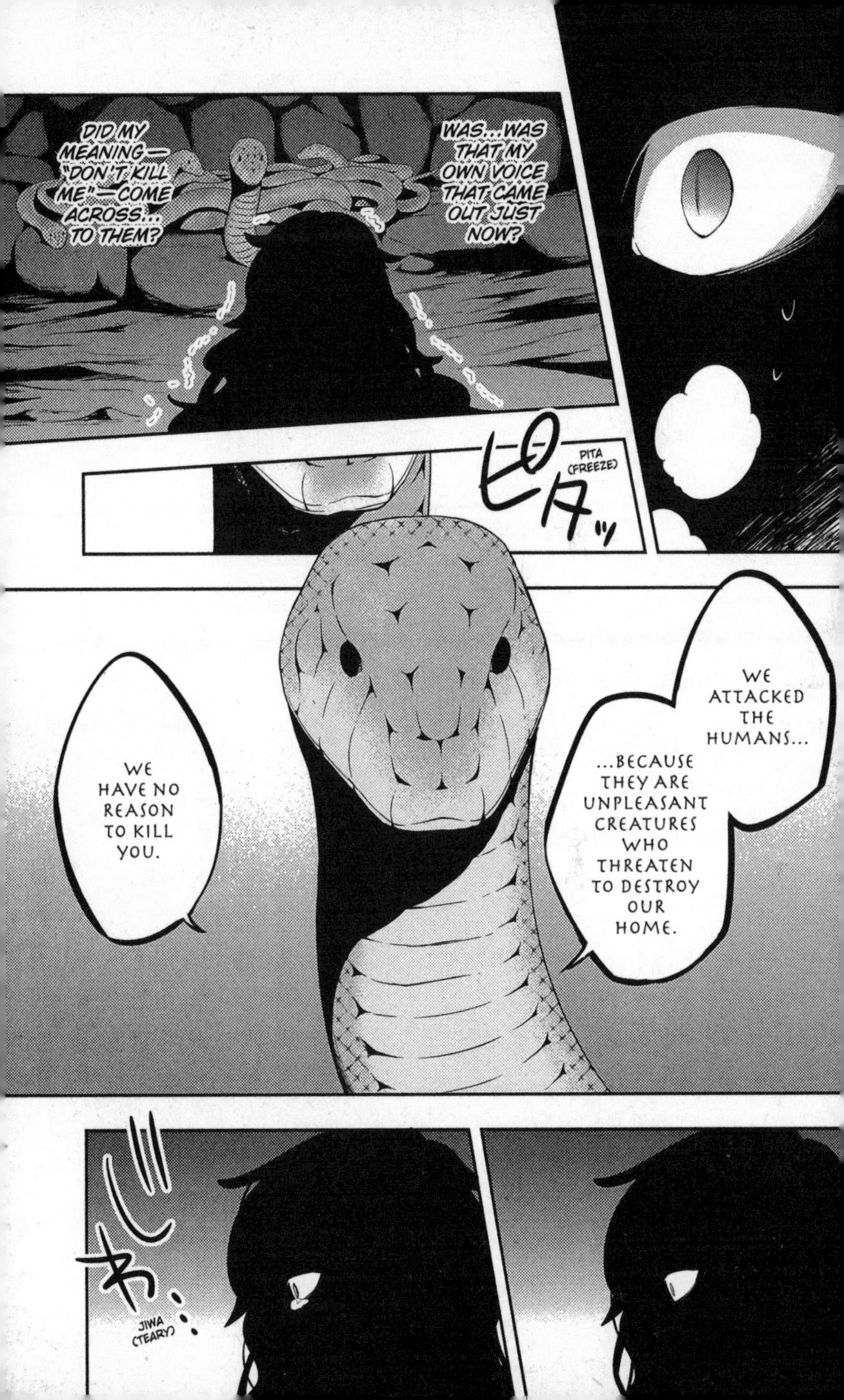
WAS...WAS THAT MY OWN VOICE THAT CAME OUT JUST NOW?
DID MY MEANING—"DON'T KILL ME"—COME ACROSS... TO THEM?
ピタッ
PITA (FREEZE)
WE ATTACKED THE HUMANS...
...BECAUSE THEY ARE UNPLEASANT CREATURES WHO THREATEN TO DESTROY OUR HOME.
WE HAVE NO REASON TO KILL YOU.
じわ…
JIWA (TEARY)

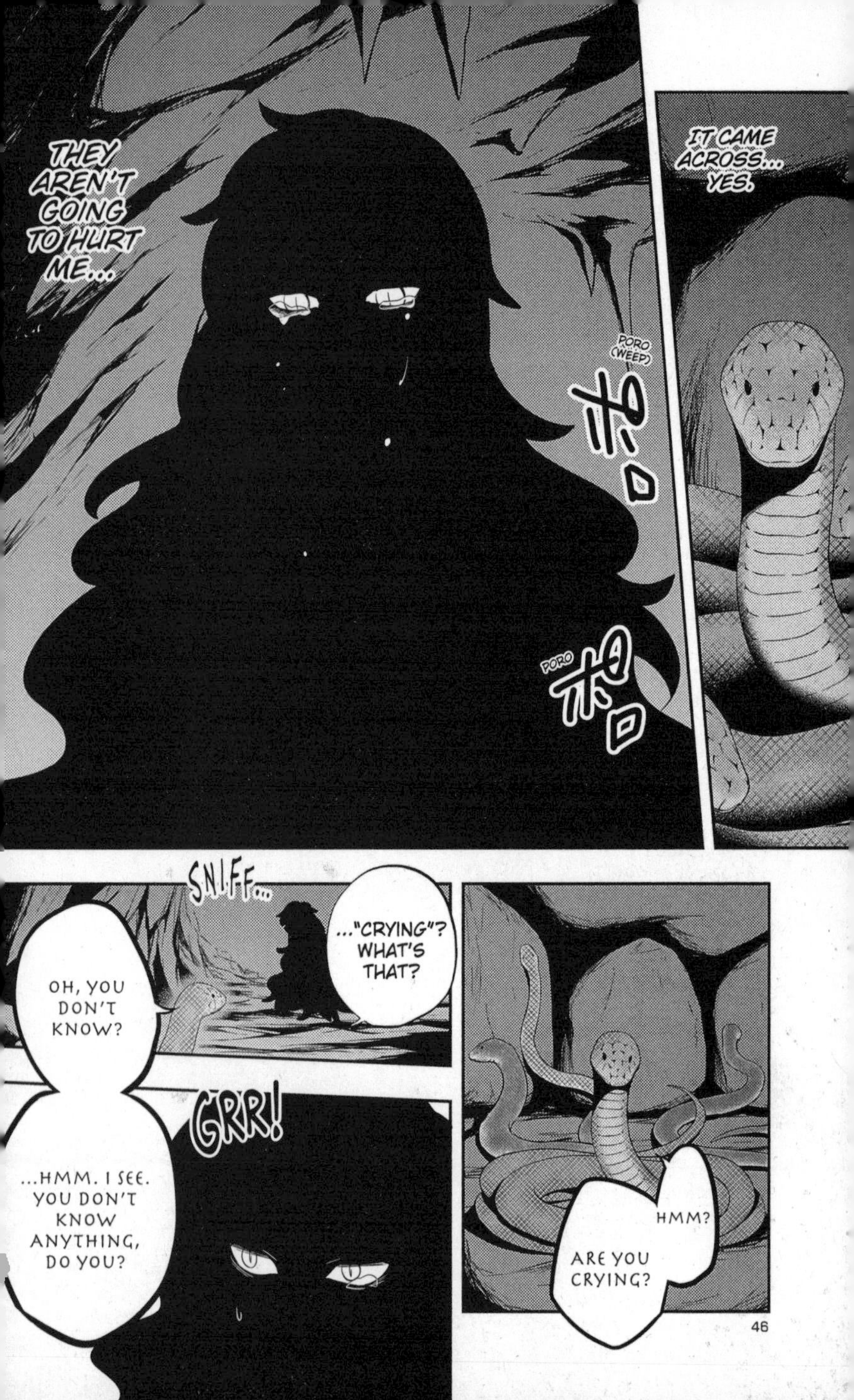
IT CAME ACROSS... YES.
THEY AREN'T GOING TO HURT ME...
PORO (WEEP)
PORO
HMM?
ARE YOU CRYING?
SNIFF...
..."CRYING"? WHAT'S THAT?
OH, YOU DON'T KNOW?
GRR!
...HMM. I SEE. YOU DON'T KNOW ANYTHING, DO YOU?

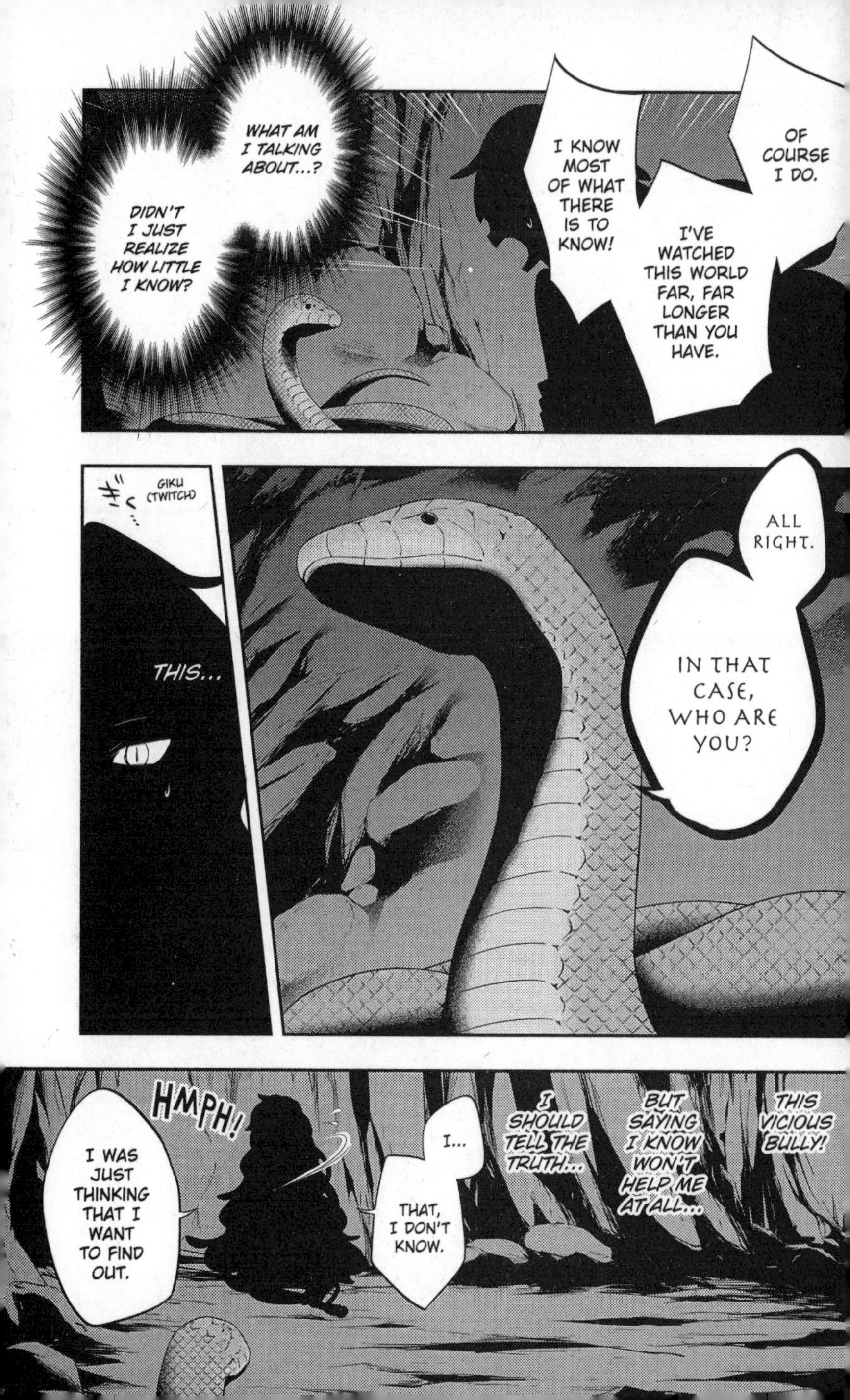
OF COURSE I DO.
I KNOW MOST OF WHAT THERE IS TO KNOW!
I'VE WATCHED THIS WORLD FAR, FAR LONGER THAN YOU HAVE.
WHAT AM I TALKING ABOUT...?
DIDN'T I JUST REALIZE HOW LITTLE I KNOW?
ALL RIGHT.
IN THAT CASE, WHO ARE YOU?
GIKU (TWITCH)
THIS...
THIS VICIOUS BULLY!
BUT SAYING I KNOW WON'T HELP ME AT ALL...
I SHOULD TELL THE TRUTH...
I...
THAT, I DON'T KNOW.
HMPH!
I WAS JUST THINKING THAT I WANT TO FIND OUT.

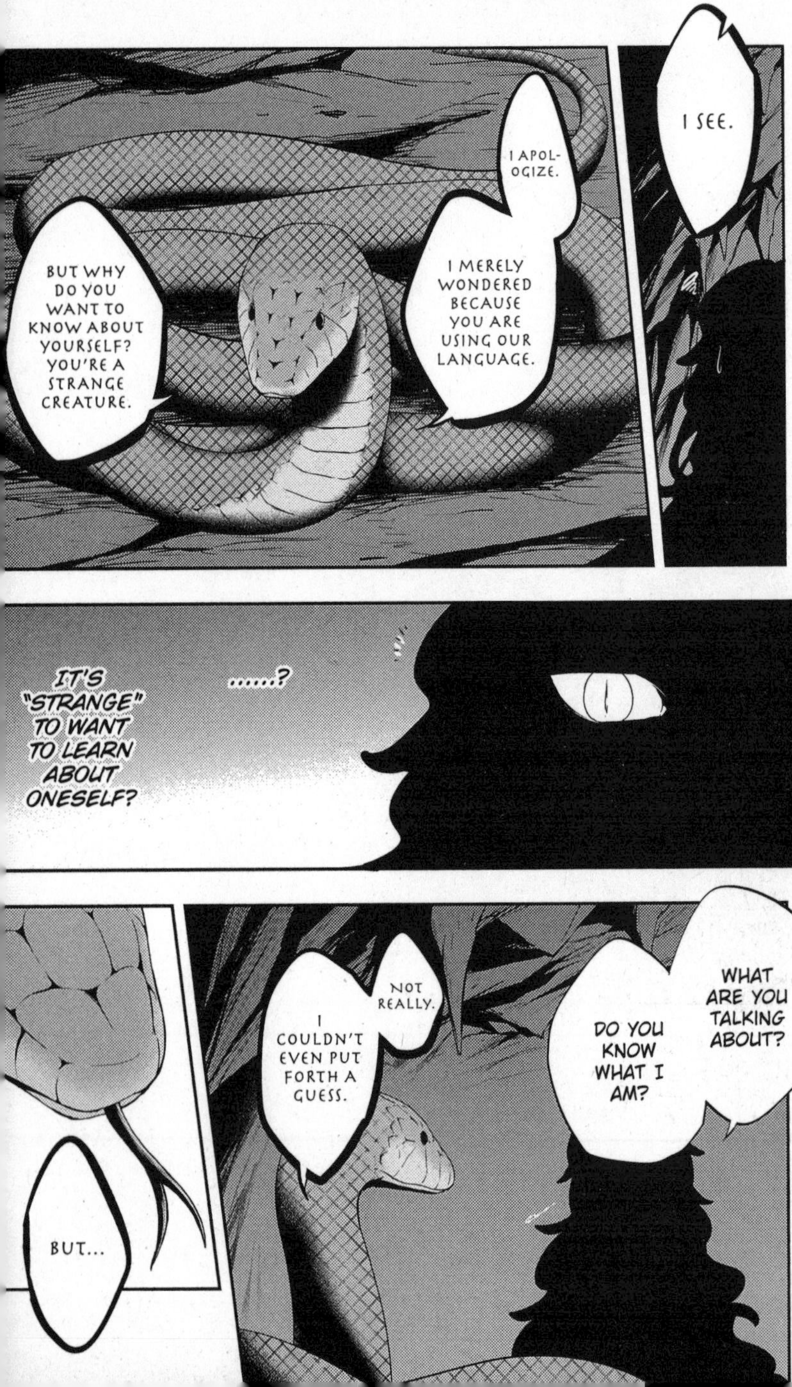
I SEE.
I APOLOGIZE.
I MERELY WONDERED BECAUSE YOU ARE USING OUR LANGUAGE.
BUT WHY DO YOU WANT TO KNOW ABOUT YOURSELF? YOU'RE A STRANGE CREATURE.
......?
IT'S "STRANGE" TO WANT TO LEARN ABOUT ONESELF?
WHAT ARE YOU TALKING ABOUT?
DO YOU KNOW WHAT I AM?
NOT REALLY.
I COULDN'T EVEN PUT FORTH A GUESS.
BUT...

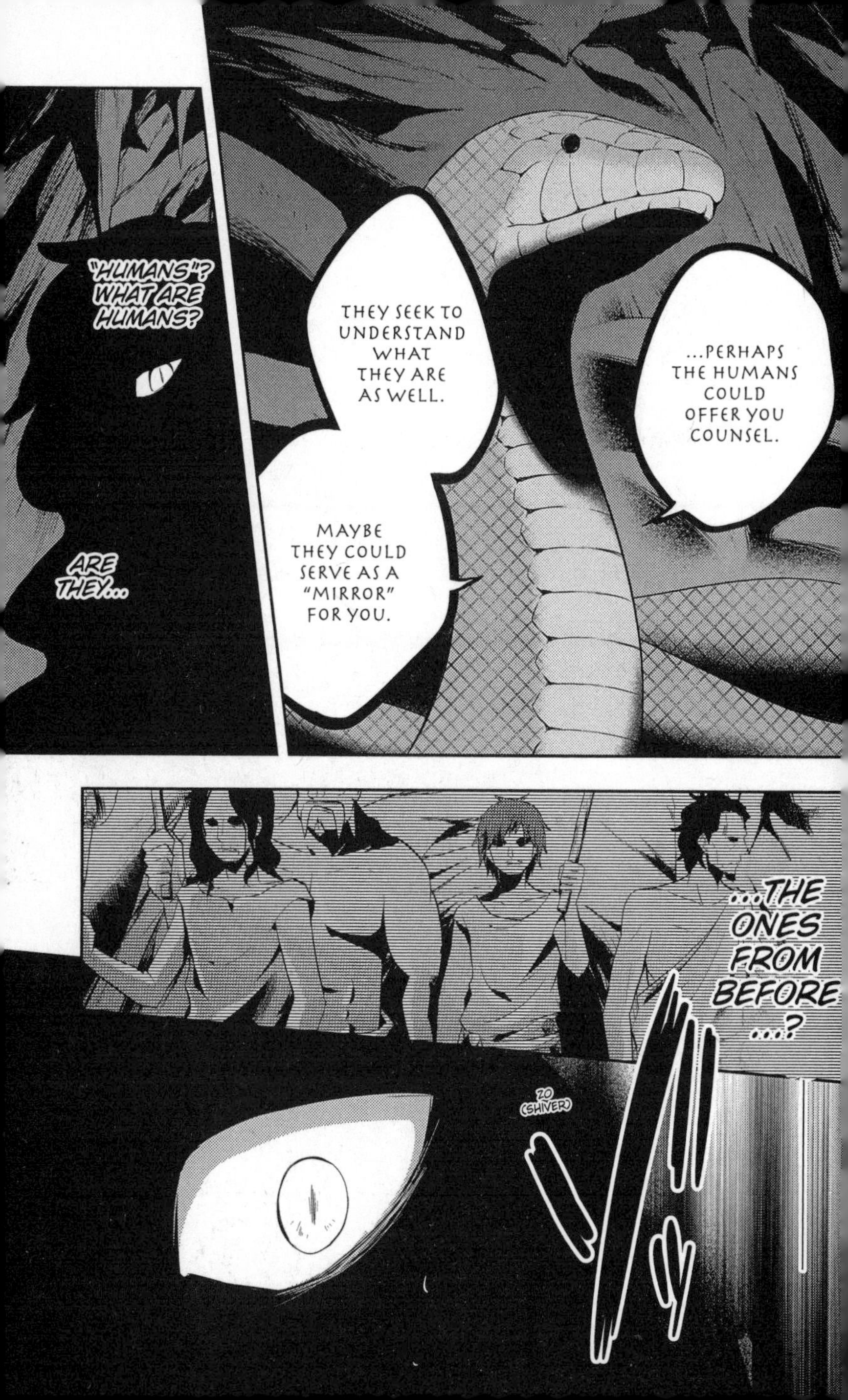
...PERHAPS THE HUMANS COULD OFFER YOU COUNSEL.
THEY SEEK TO UNDERSTAND WHAT THEY ARE AS WELL.
MAYBE THEY COULD SERVE AS A "MIRROR" FOR YOU.
"HUMANS"? WHAT ARE HUMANS?
ARE THEY...
...THE ONES FROM BEFORE...?
ZO (SHIVER)

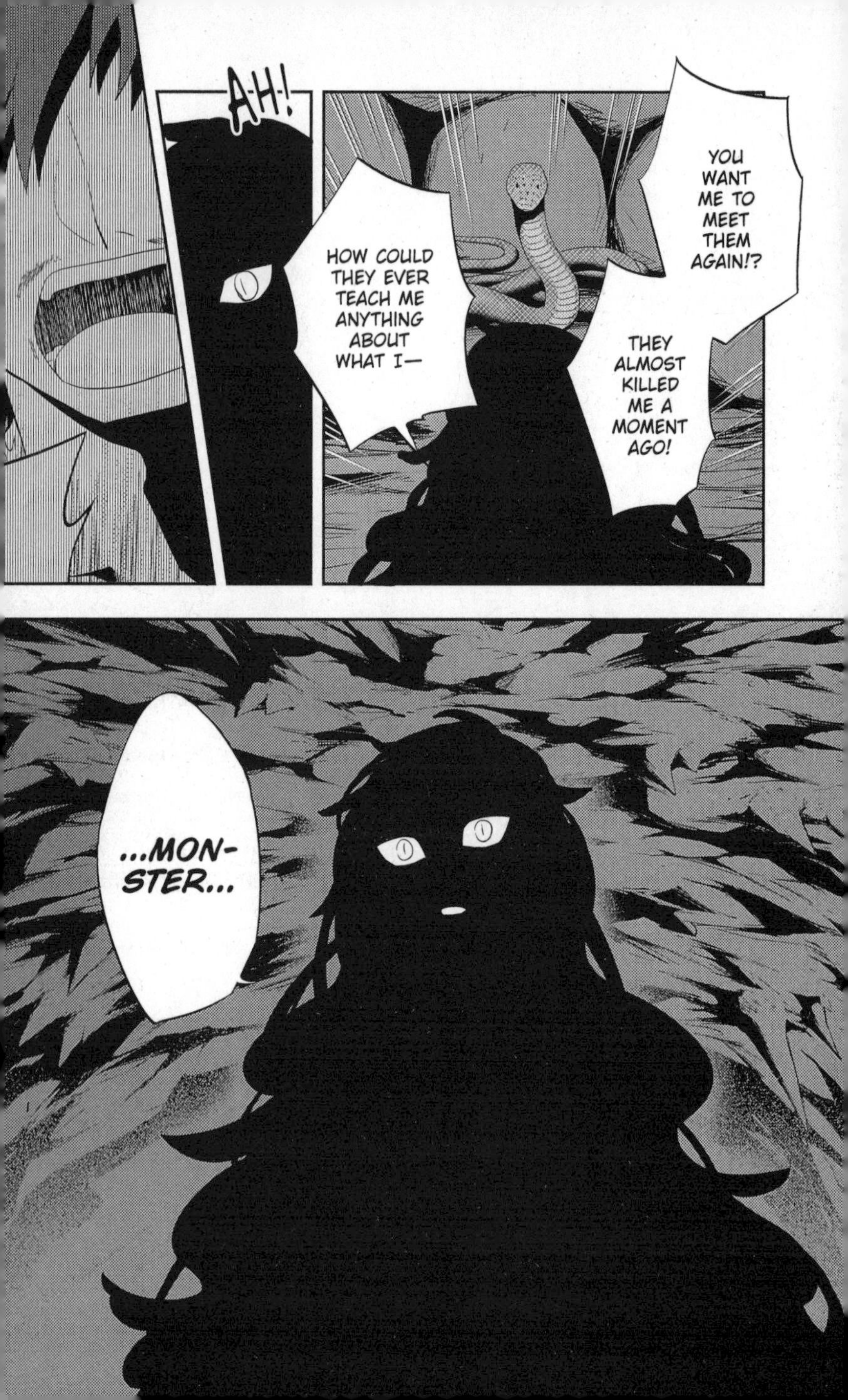
YOU WANT ME TO MEET THEM AGAIN!?
THEY ALMOST KILLED ME A MOMENT AGO!
HOW COULD THEY EVER TEACH ME ANYTHING ABOUT WHAT I—
AH!
...MON-STER...

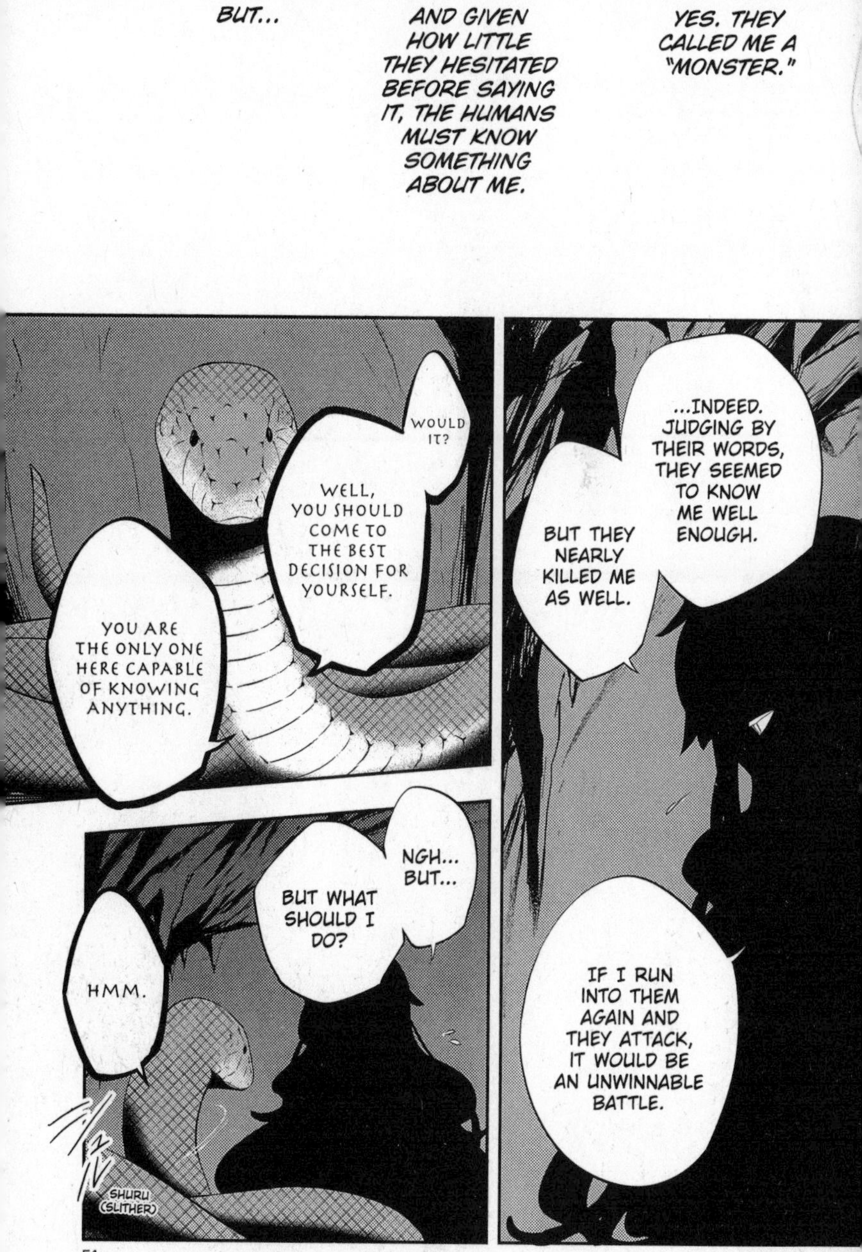
YES. THEY CALLED ME A "MONSTER."
AND GIVEN HOW LITTLE THEY HESITATED BEFORE SAYING IT, THE HUMANS MUST KNOW SOMETHING ABOUT ME.
BUT...
...INDEED. JUDGING BY THEIR WORDS, THEY SEEMED TO KNOW ME WELL ENOUGH.
BUT THEY NEARLY KILLED ME AS WELL.
IF I RUN INTO THEM AGAIN AND THEY ATTACK, IT WOULD BE AN UNWINNABLE BATTLE.
WOULD IT?
WELL, YOU SHOULD COME TO THE BEST DECISION FOR YOURSELF.
YOU ARE THE ONLY ONE HERE CAPABLE OF KNOWING ANYTHING.
NGH... BUT...
BUT WHAT SHOULD I DO?
HMM.
SHURU (SLITHER)

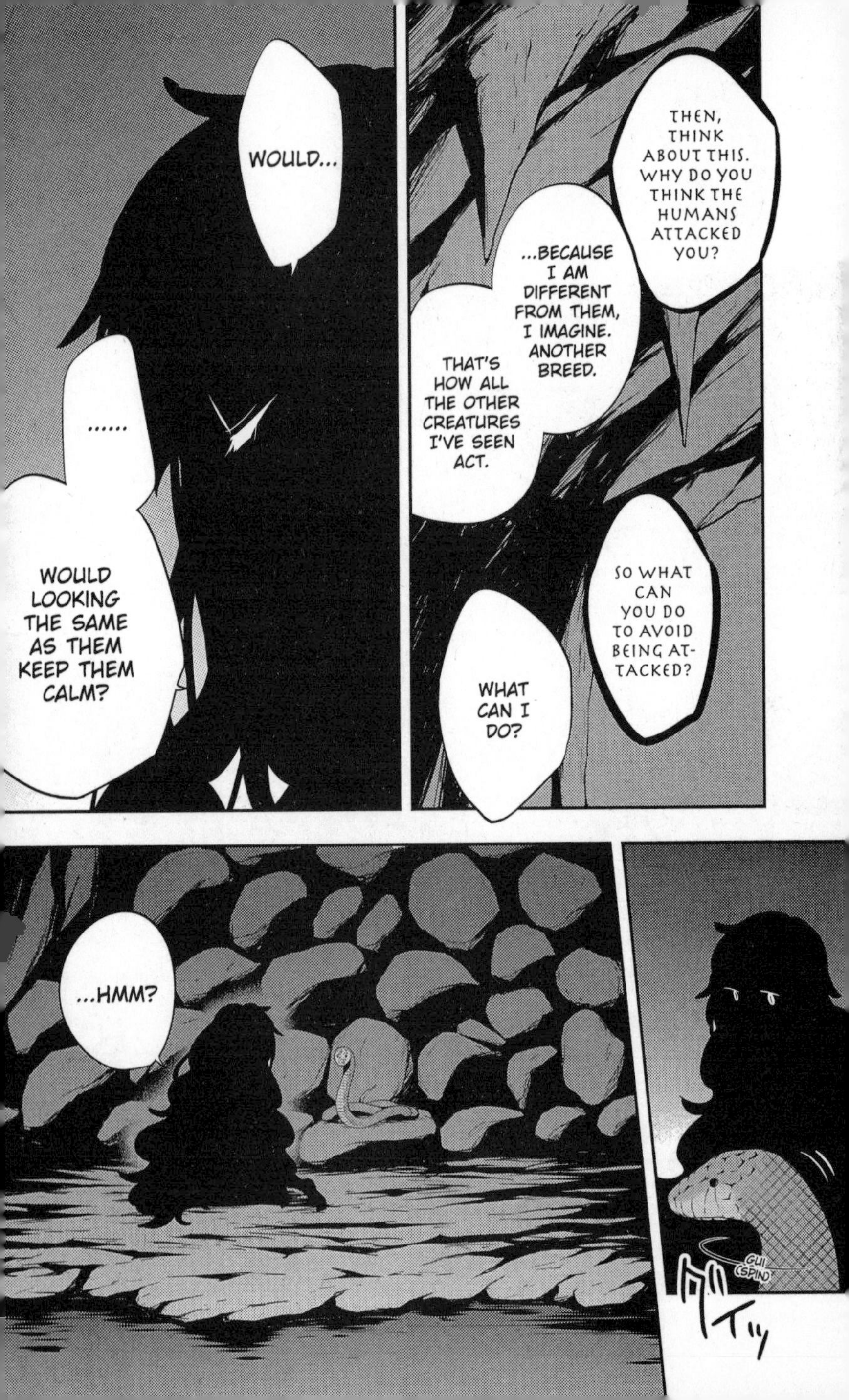
THEN, THINK ABOUT THIS. WHY DO YOU THINK THE HUMANS ATTACKED YOU?
...BECAUSE I AM DIFFERENT FROM THEM, I IMAGINE. ANOTHER BREED.
THAT'S HOW ALL THE OTHER CREATURES I'VE SEEN ACT.
SO WHAT CAN YOU DO TO AVOID BEING ATTACKED?
WHAT CAN I DO?
WOULD...
......
WOULD LOOKING THE SAME AS THEM KEEP THEM CALM?
GUI (SPIN)
...HMM?

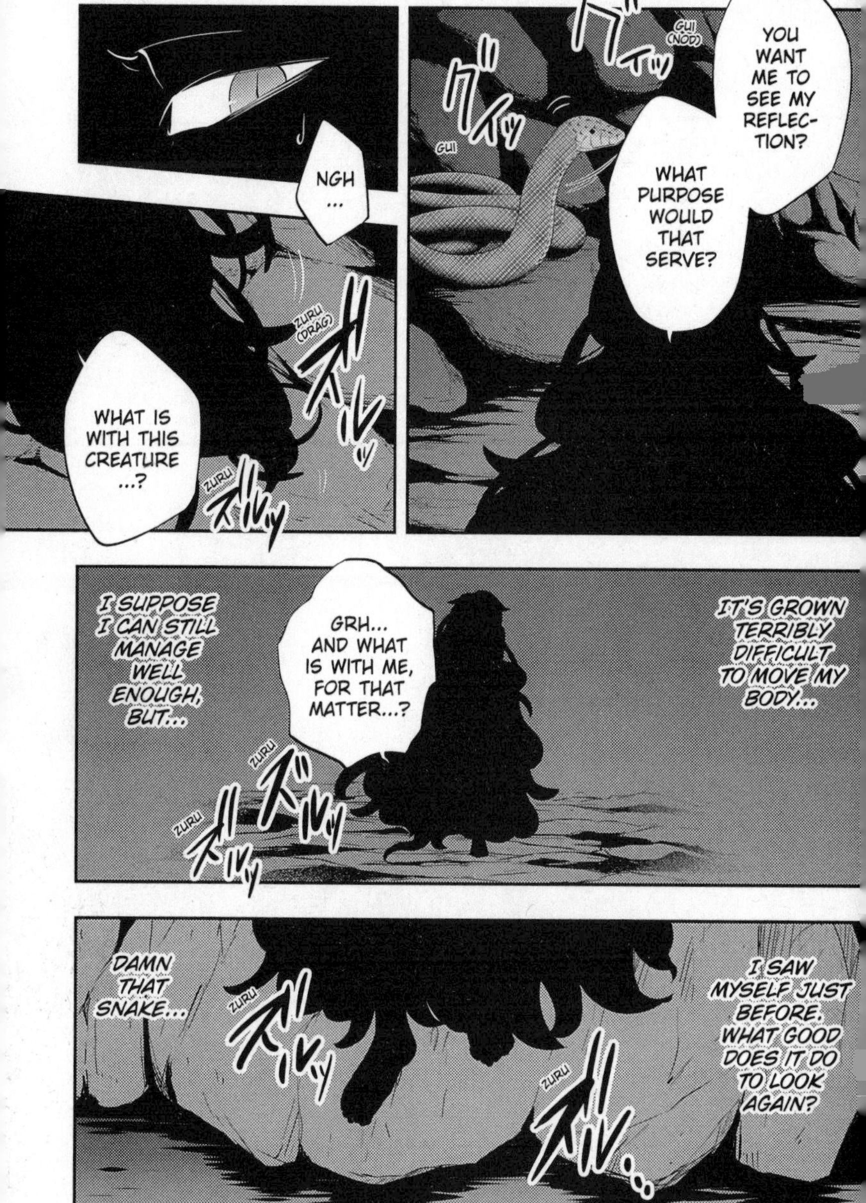
GUI (NOD)
YOU WANT ME TO SEE MY REFLECTION?
GUI
WHAT PURPOSE WOULD THAT SERVE?
NGH...
ZURU (DRAG)
WHAT IS WITH THIS CREATURE...?
ZURU
IT'S GROWN TERRIBLY DIFFICULT TO MOVE MY BODY...
GRH... AND WHAT IS WITH ME, FOR THAT MATTER...?
I SUPPOSE I CAN STILL MANAGE WELL ENOUGH, BUT...
ZURU
ZURU
I SAW MYSELF JUST BEFORE. WHAT GOOD DOES IT DO TO LOOK AGAIN?
ZURU
DAMN THAT SNAKE...
ZURU

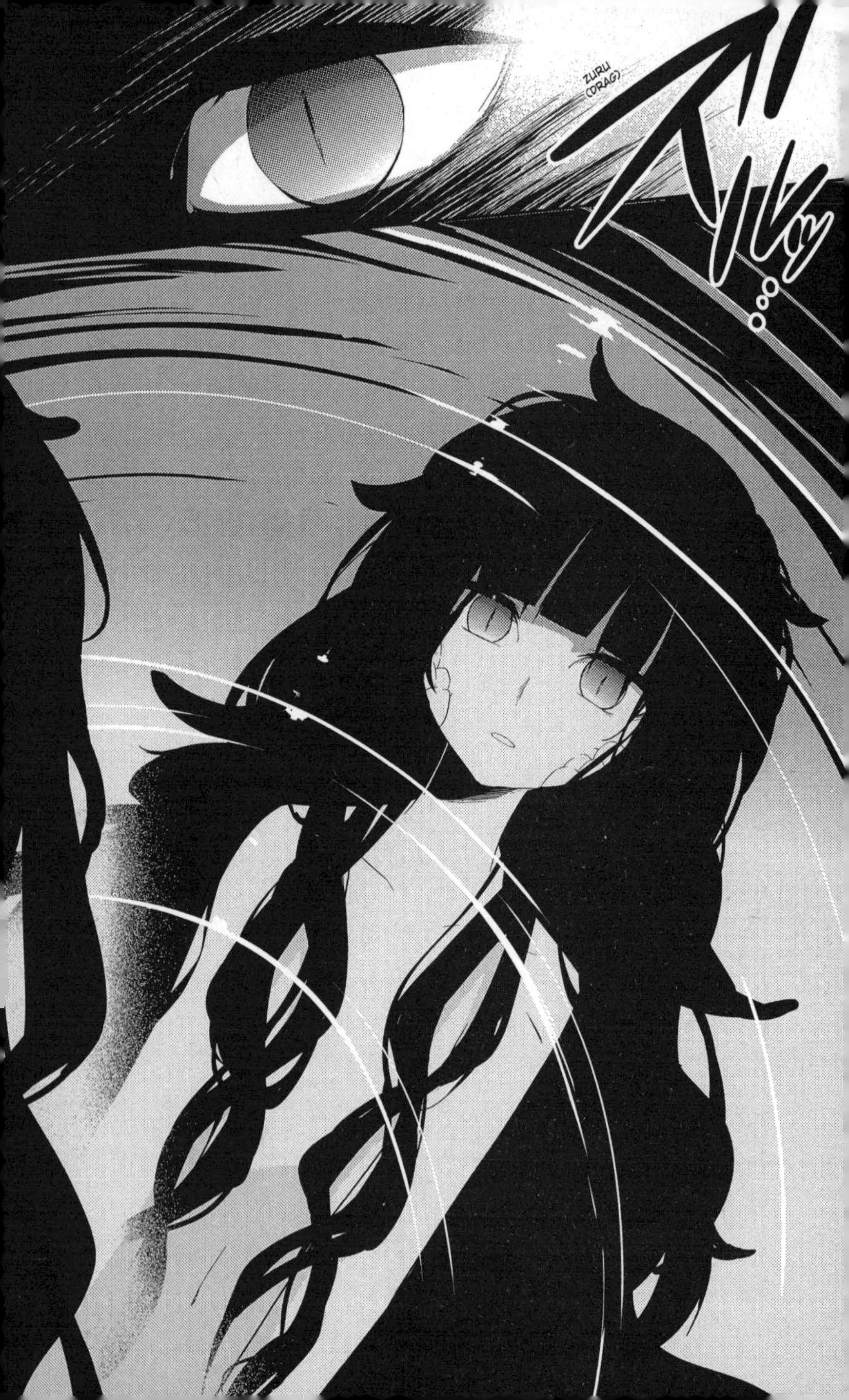
ZURU
(DRAG)

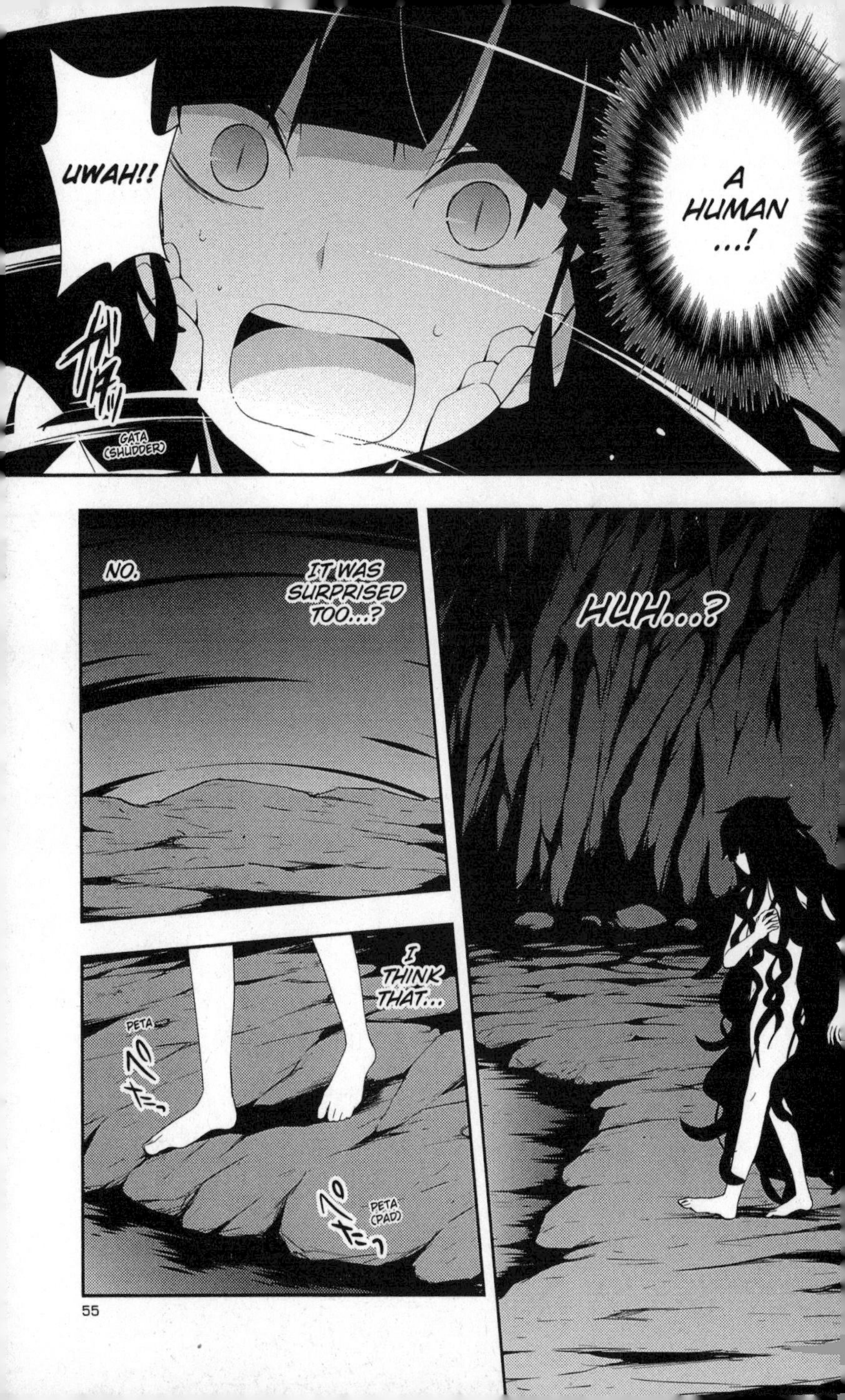
A HUMAN ...!
UWAH!!
GATA (SHUDDER)
HUH...?
IT WAS SURPRISED TOO...?
NO.
I THINK THAT...
PETA
PETA (PAD)

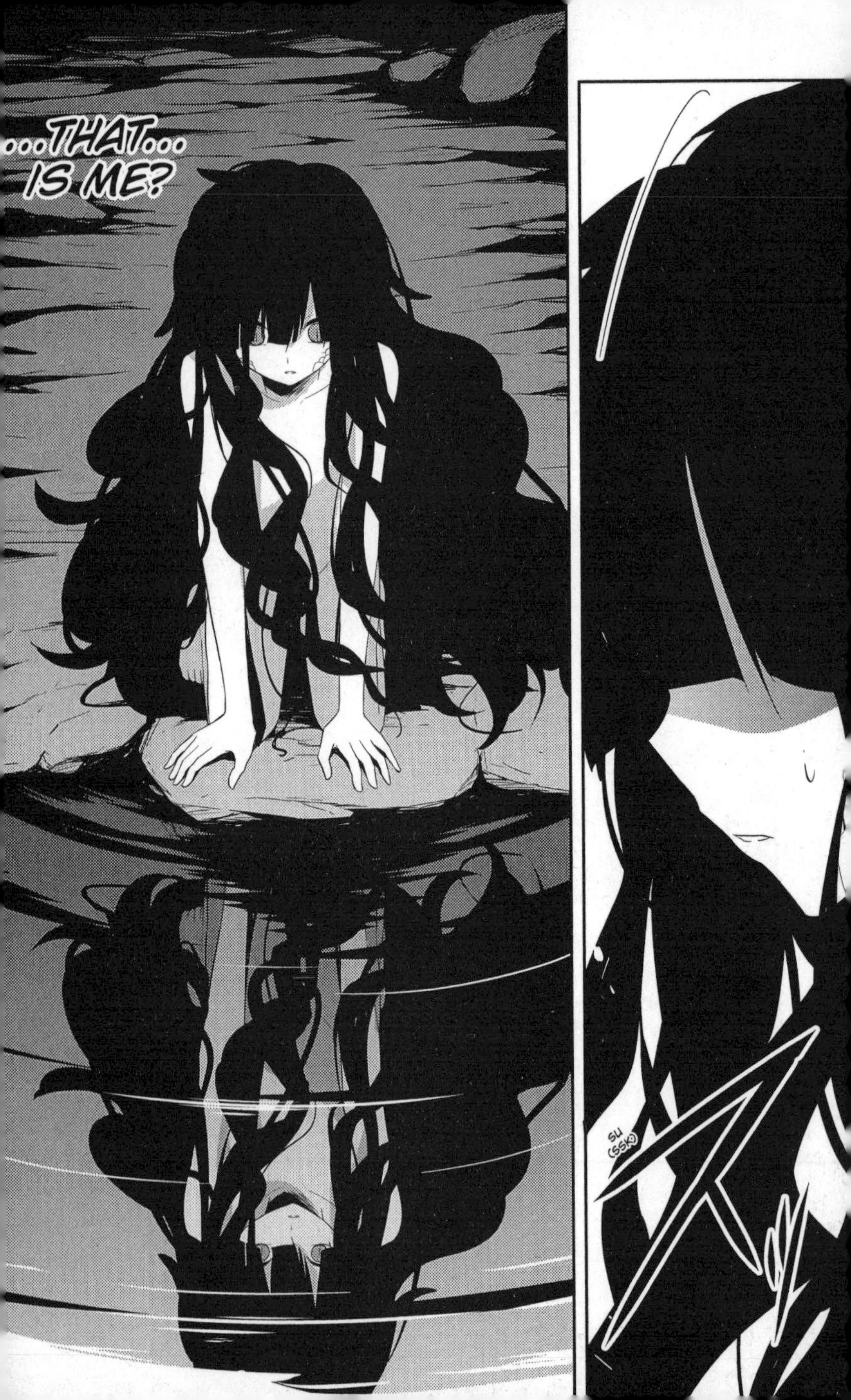
SU (SSK)
...THAT... IS ME?

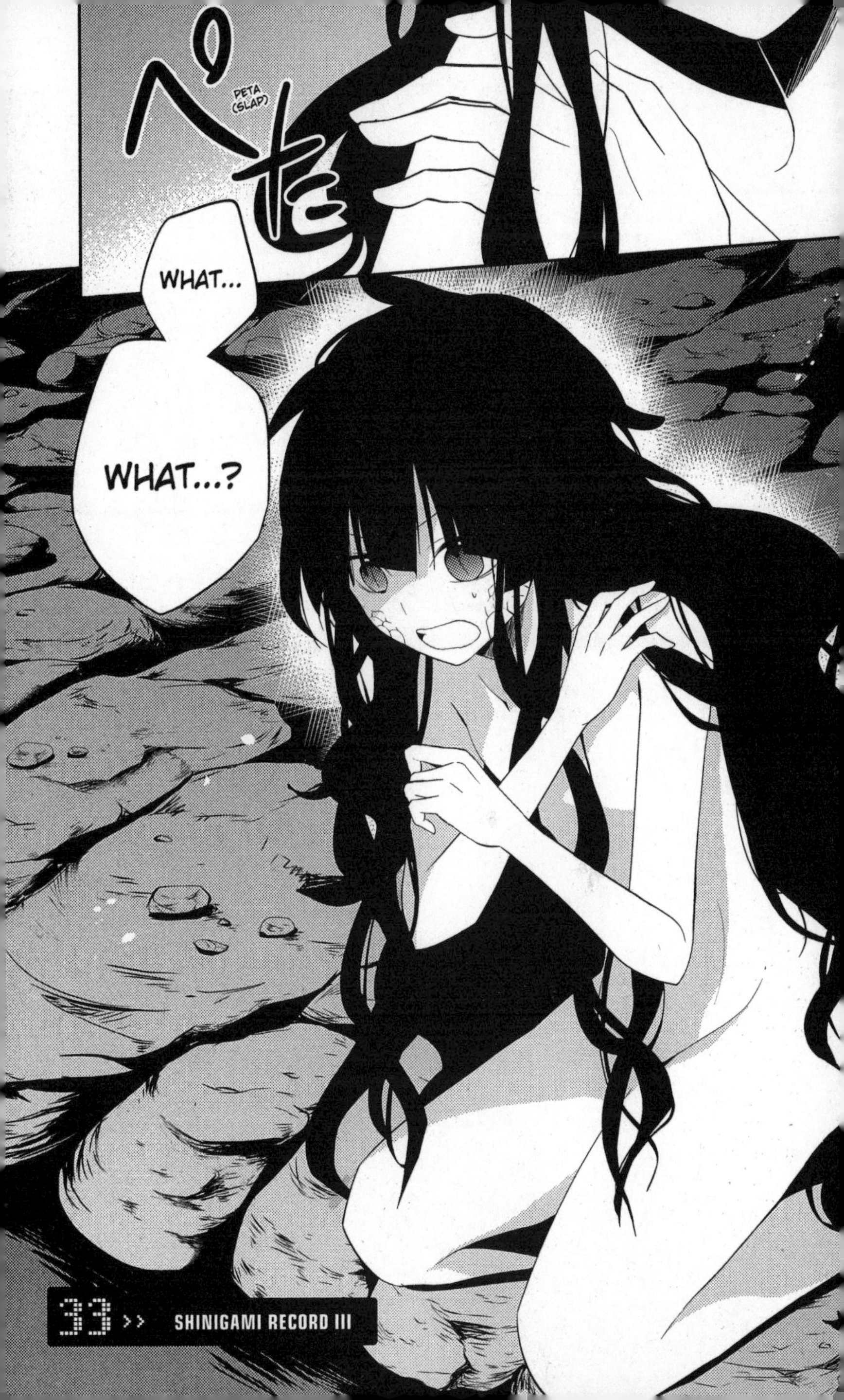
ぺた
PETA (SLAP)
WHAT...
WHAT...?
33 >> SHINIGAMI RECORD III

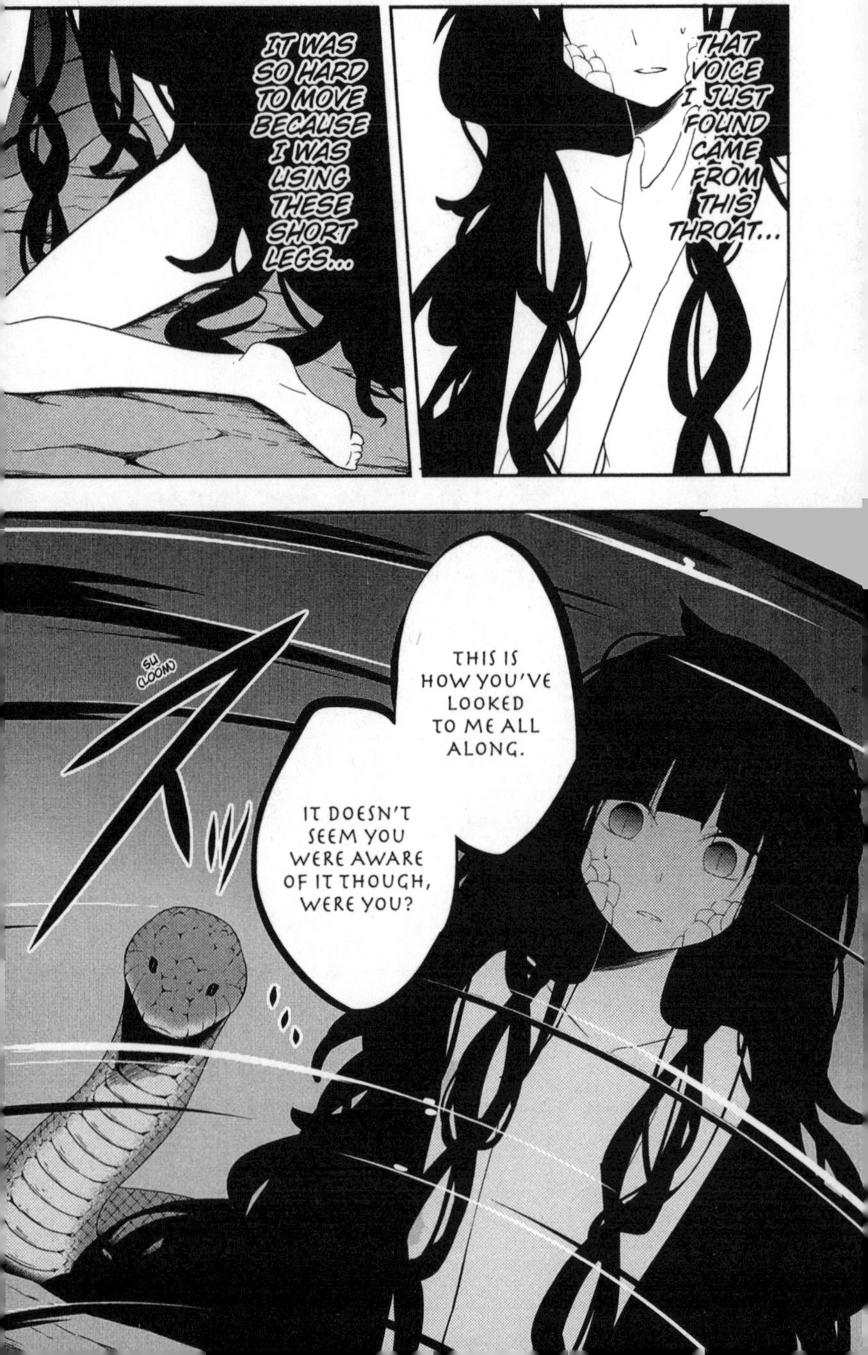
THAT VOICE I JUST FOUND CAME FROM THIS THROAT...
IT WAS SO HARD TO MOVE BECAUSE I WAS USING THESE SHORT LEGS...
THIS IS HOW YOU'VE LOOKED TO ME ALL ALONG.
IT DOESN'T SEEM YOU WERE AWARE OF IT THOUGH, WERE YOU?
SU (LOOM)

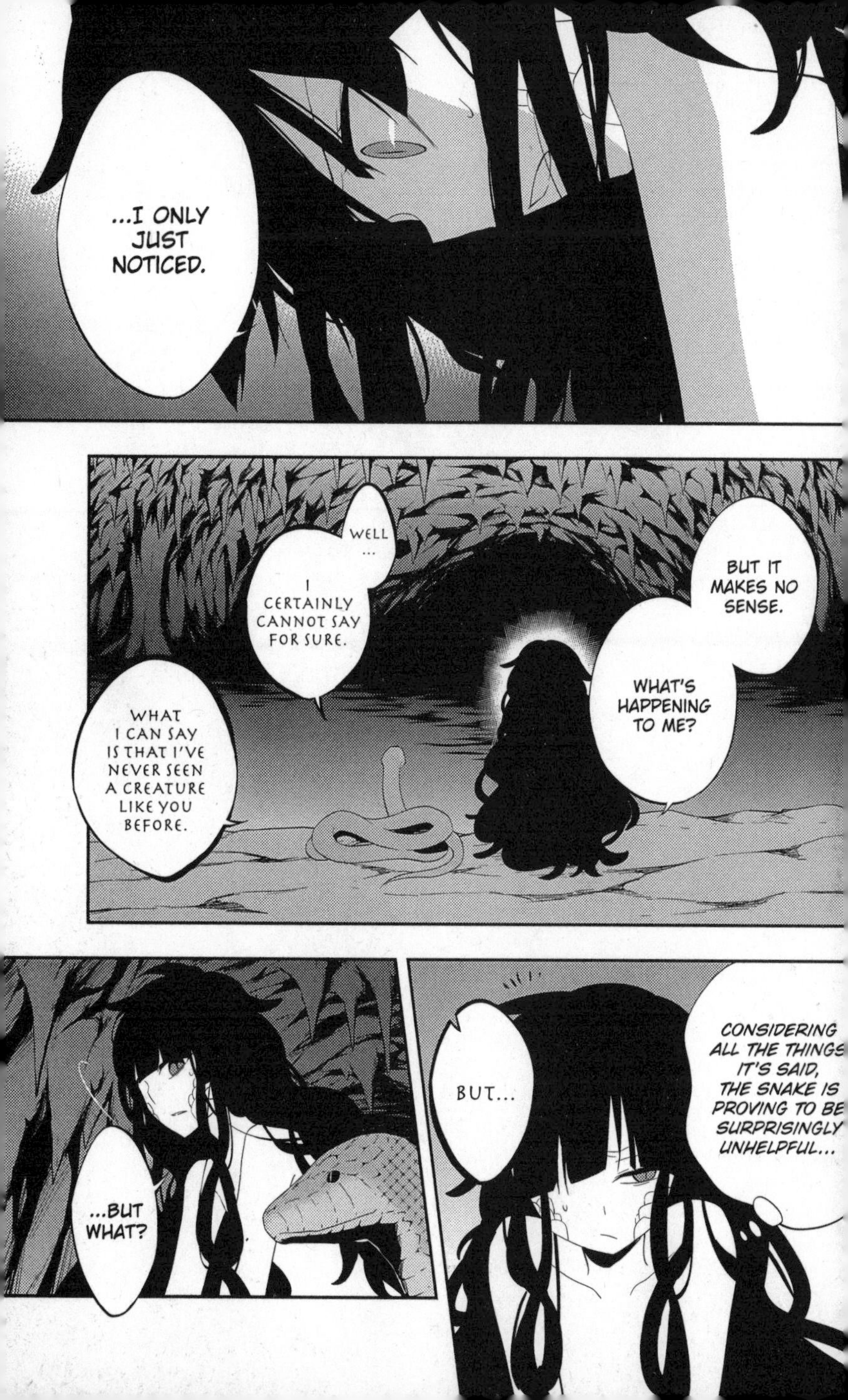
...I ONLY JUST NOTICED.
BUT IT MAKES NO SENSE.
WHAT'S HAPPENING TO ME?
WELL...
I CERTAINLY CANNOT SAY FOR SURE.
WHAT I CAN SAY IS THAT I'VE NEVER SEEN A CREATURE LIKE YOU BEFORE.
CONSIDERING ALL THE THINGS IT'S SAID, THE SNAKE IS PROVING TO BE SURPRISINGLY UNHELPFUL...
BUT...
...BUT WHAT?

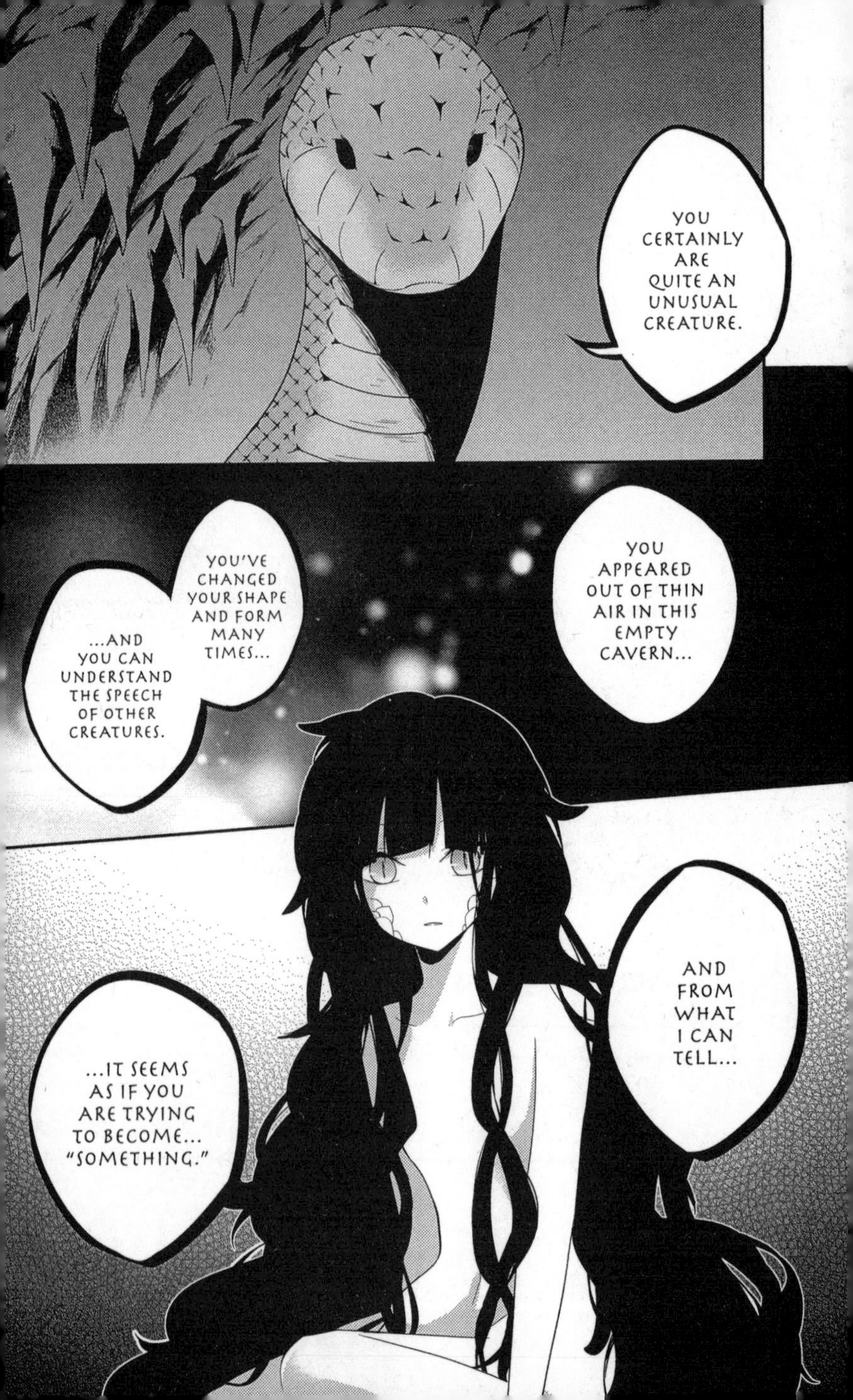
YOU CERTAINLY ARE QUITE AN UNUSUAL CREATURE.
YOU APPEARED OUT OF THIN AIR IN THIS EMPTY CAVERN...
YOU'VE CHANGED YOUR SHAPE AND FORM MANY TIMES...
...AND YOU CAN UNDERSTAND THE SPEECH OF OTHER CREATURES.
AND FROM WHAT I CAN TELL...
...IT SEEMS AS IF YOU ARE TRYING TO BECOME... "SOMETHING."

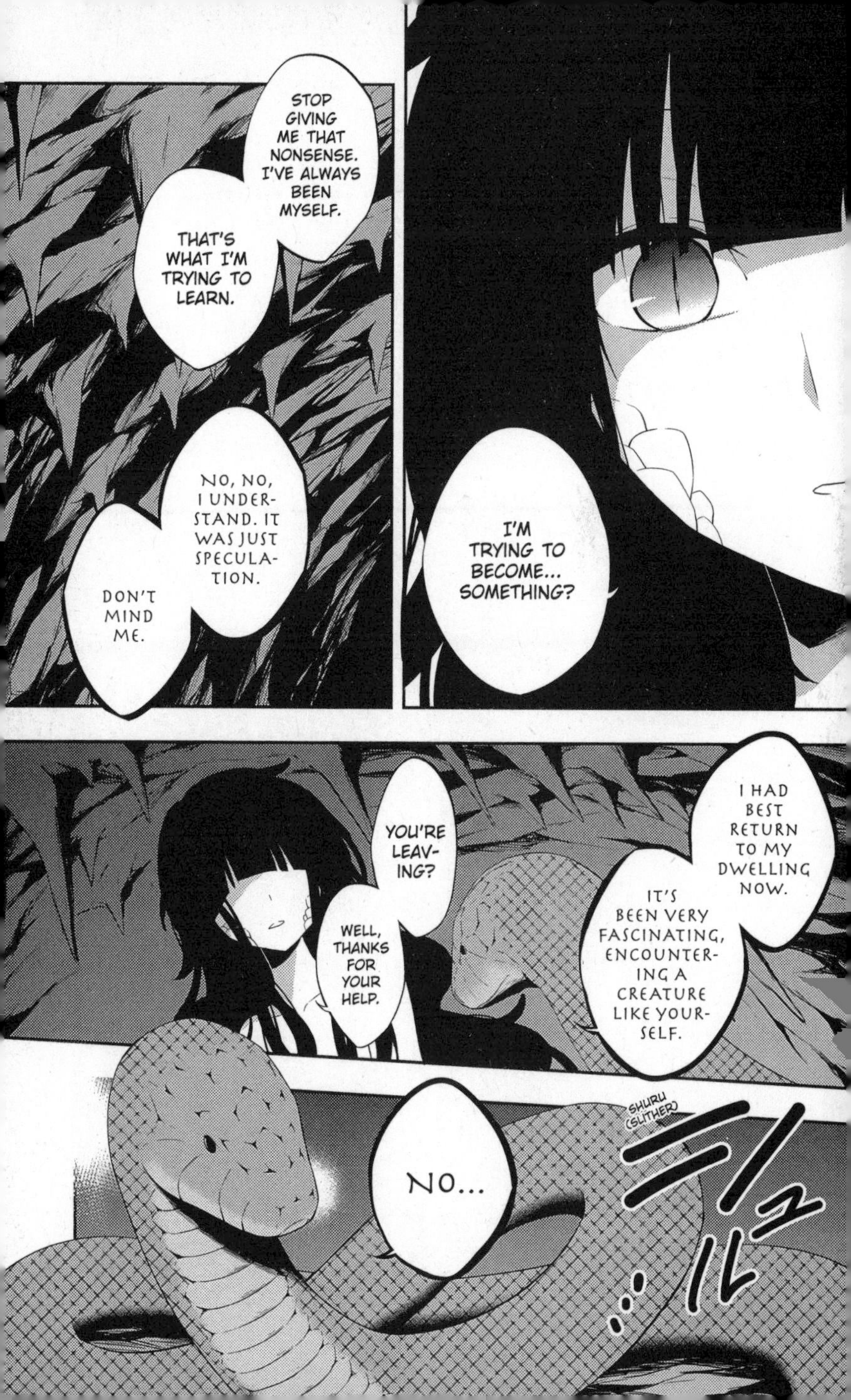
I'M TRYING TO BECOME... SOMETHING?
STOP GIVING ME THAT NONSENSE. I'VE ALWAYS BEEN MYSELF.
THAT'S WHAT I'M TRYING TO LEARN.
NO, NO, I UNDERSTAND. IT WAS JUST SPECULATION.
DON'T MIND ME.
I HAD BEST RETURN TO MY DWELLING NOW.
IT'S BEEN VERY FASCINATING, ENCOUNTERING A CREATURE LIKE YOURSELF.
YOU'RE LEAVING?
WELL, THANKS FOR YOUR HELP.
SHURU (SLITHER)
NO...

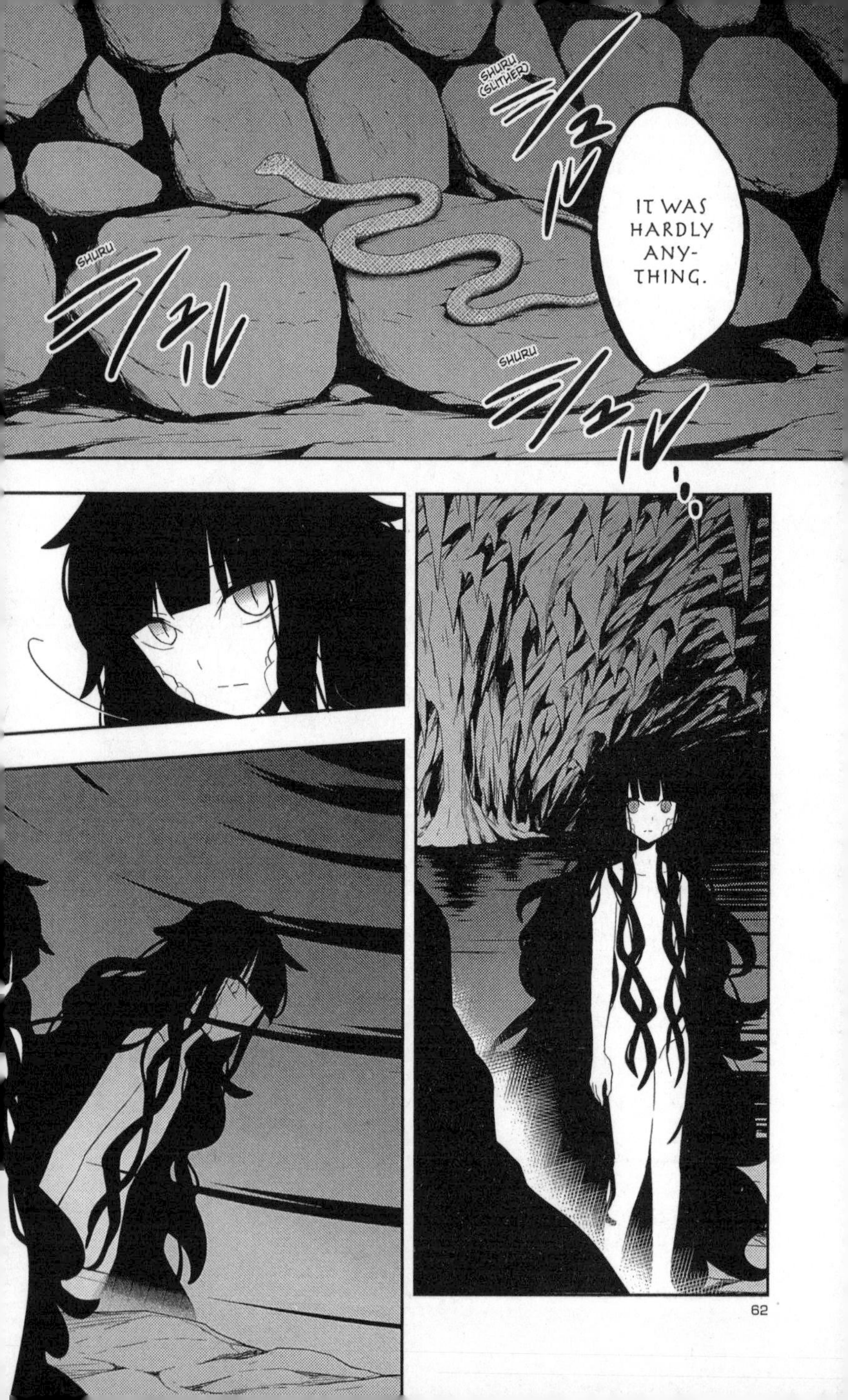
SHURU (SLITHER)
IT WAS HARDLY ANY-THING.
SHURU
SHURU
...

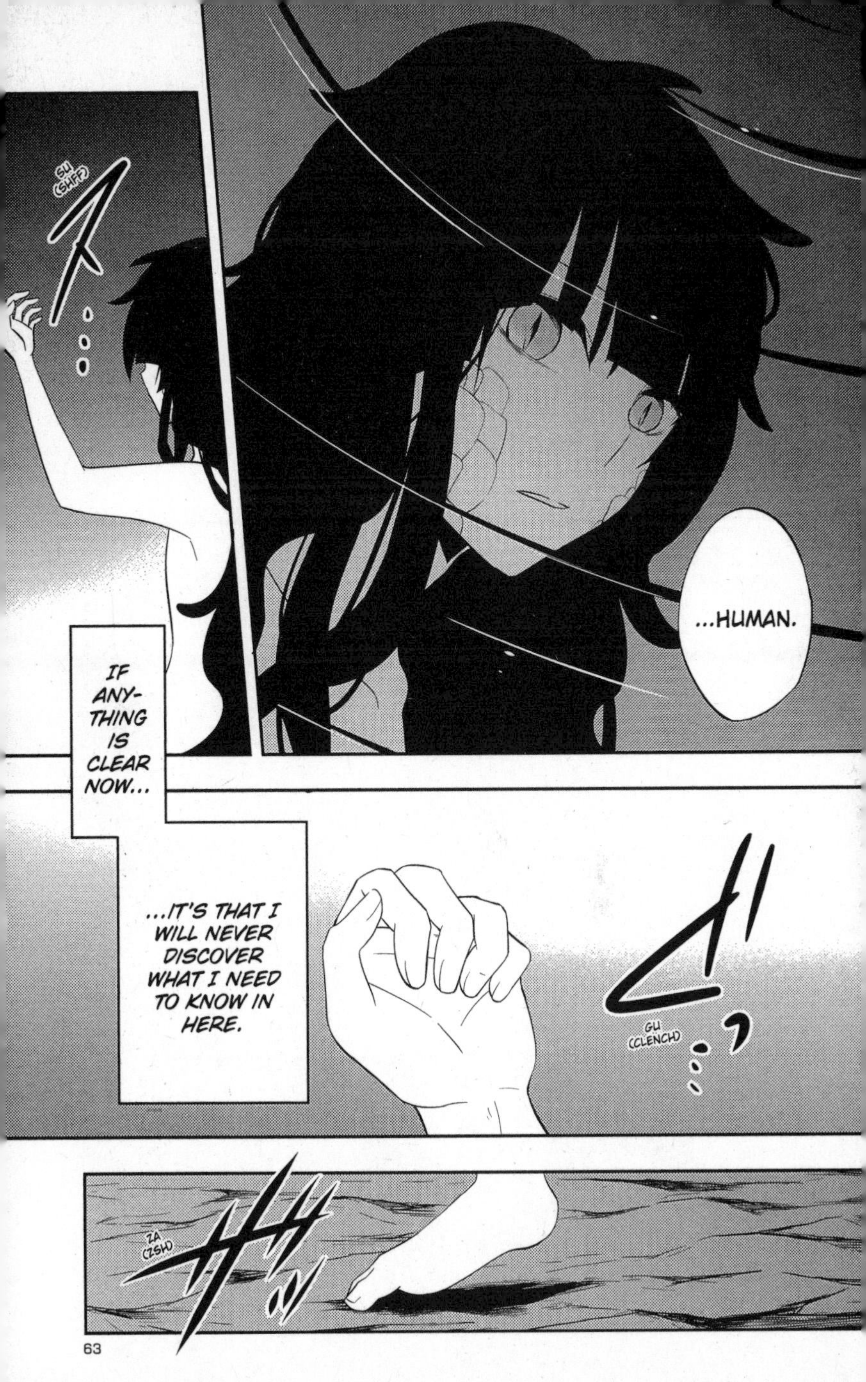
...HUMAN.
SU (SHFF)
IF ANY-THING IS CLEAR NOW...
...IT'S THAT I WILL NEVER DISCOVER WHAT I NEED TO KNOW IN HERE.
GU (CLENCH)
ZA (ZSH)

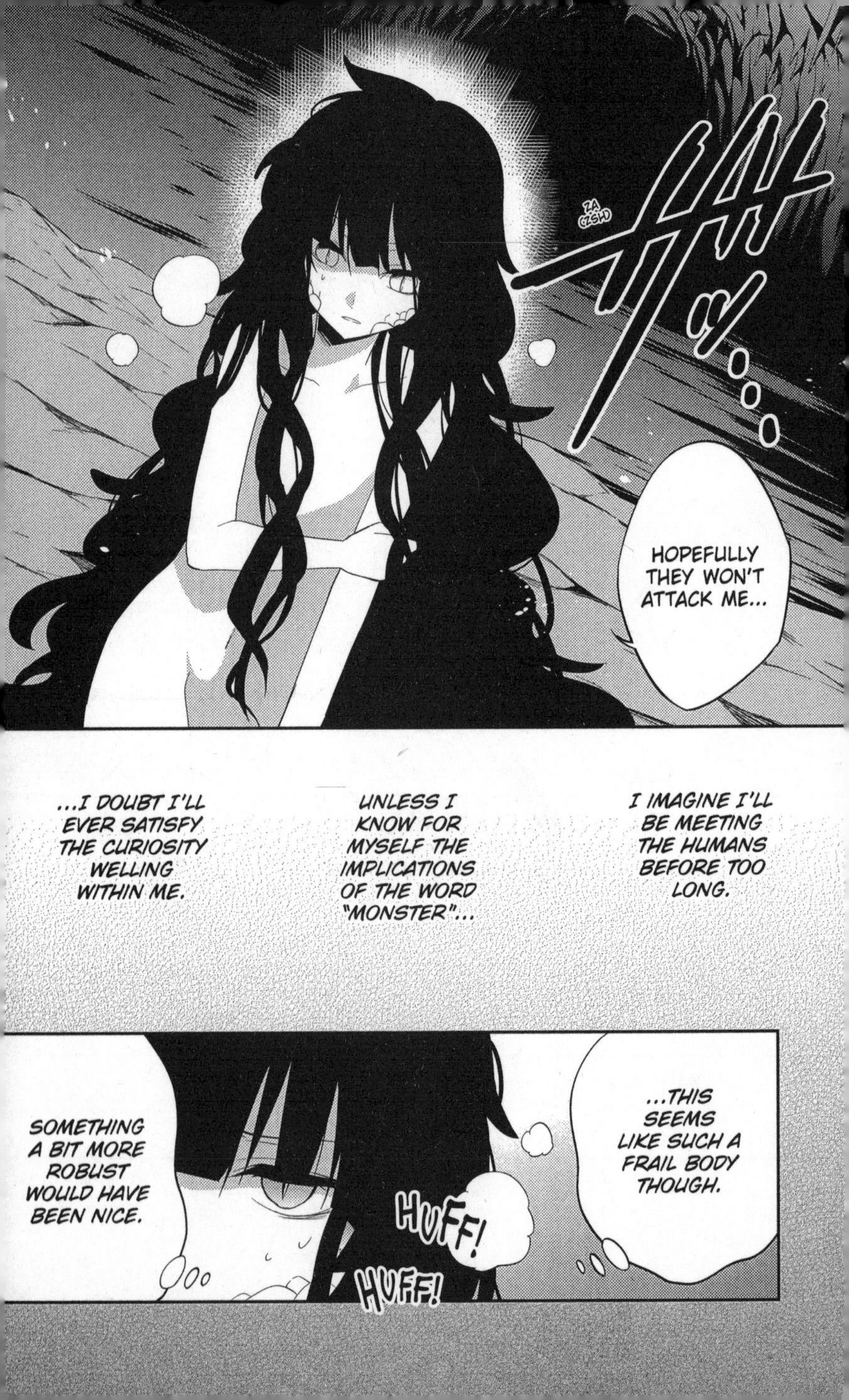
HOPEFULLY THEY WON'T ATTACK ME...
I IMAGINE I'LL BE MEETING THE HUMANS BEFORE TOO LONG.
UNLESS I KNOW FOR MYSELF THE IMPLICATIONS OF THE WORD "MONSTER"...
...I DOUBT I'LL EVER SATISFY THE CURIOSITY WELLING WITHIN ME.
...THIS SEEMS LIKE SUCH A FRAIL BODY THOUGH.
HUFF!
HUFF!
SOMETHING A BIT MORE ROBUST WOULD HAVE BEEN NICE.

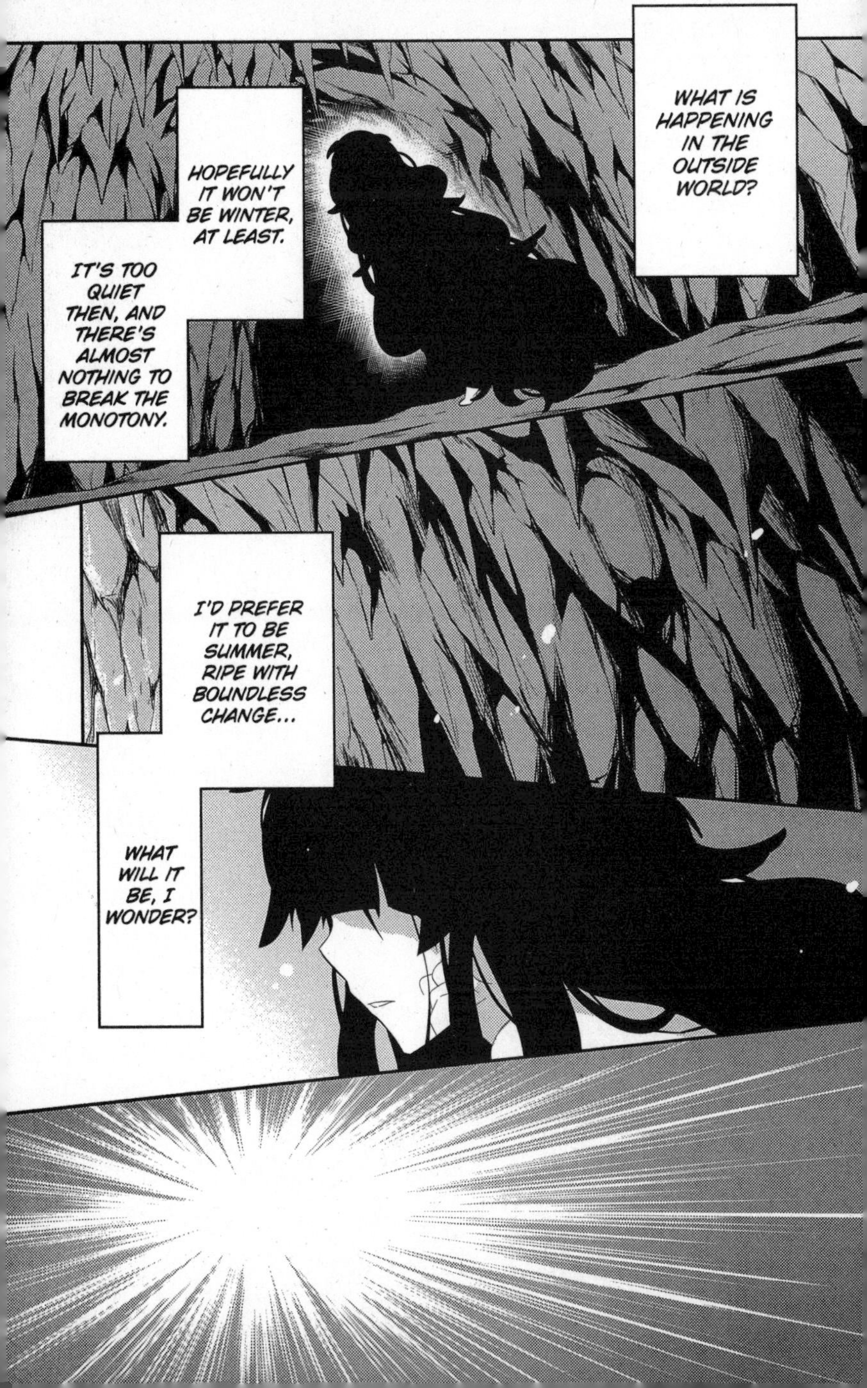
WHAT IS HAPPENING IN THE OUTSIDE WORLD?
HOPEFULLY IT WON'T BE WINTER, AT LEAST.
IT'S TOO QUIET THEN, AND THERE'S ALMOST NOTHING TO BREAK THE MONOTONY.
I'D PREFER IT TO BE SUMMER, RIPE WITH BOUNDLESS CHANGE...
WHAT WILL IT BE, I WONDER?

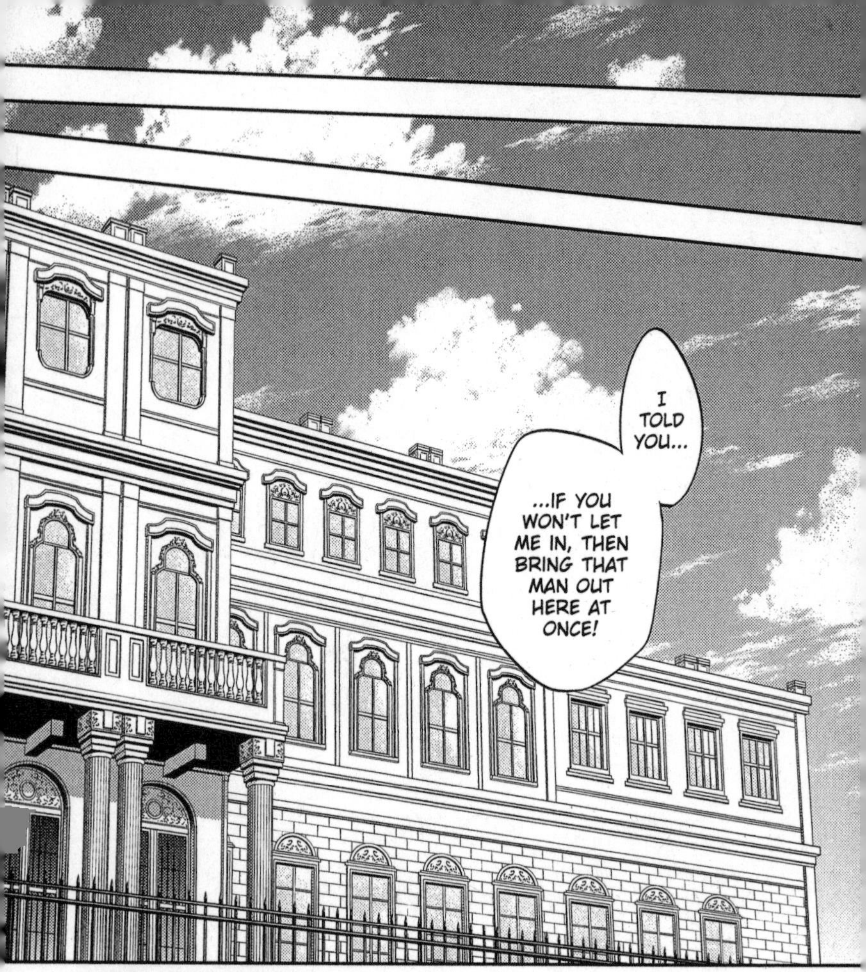
I TOLD YOU...
...IF YOU WON'T LET ME IN, THEN BRING THAT MAN OUT HERE AT ONCE!

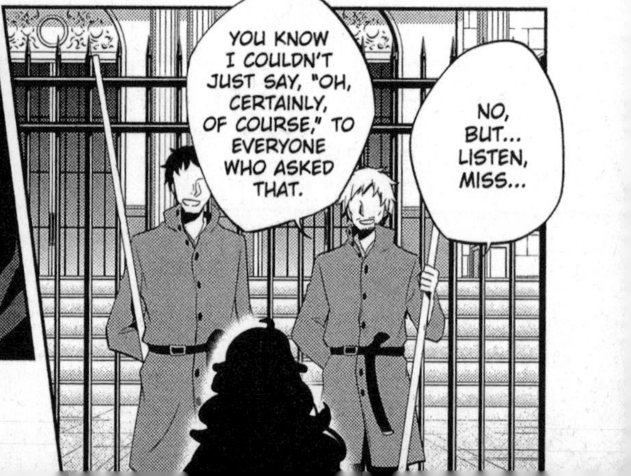
NO, BUT... LISTEN, MISS...
YOU KNOW I COULDN'T JUST SAY, "OH, CERTAINLY, OF COURSE," TO EVERYONE WHO ASKED THAT.

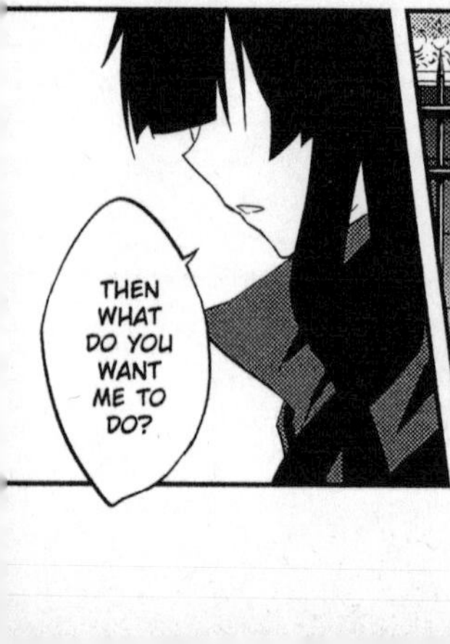
THEN WHAT DO YOU WANT ME TO DO?

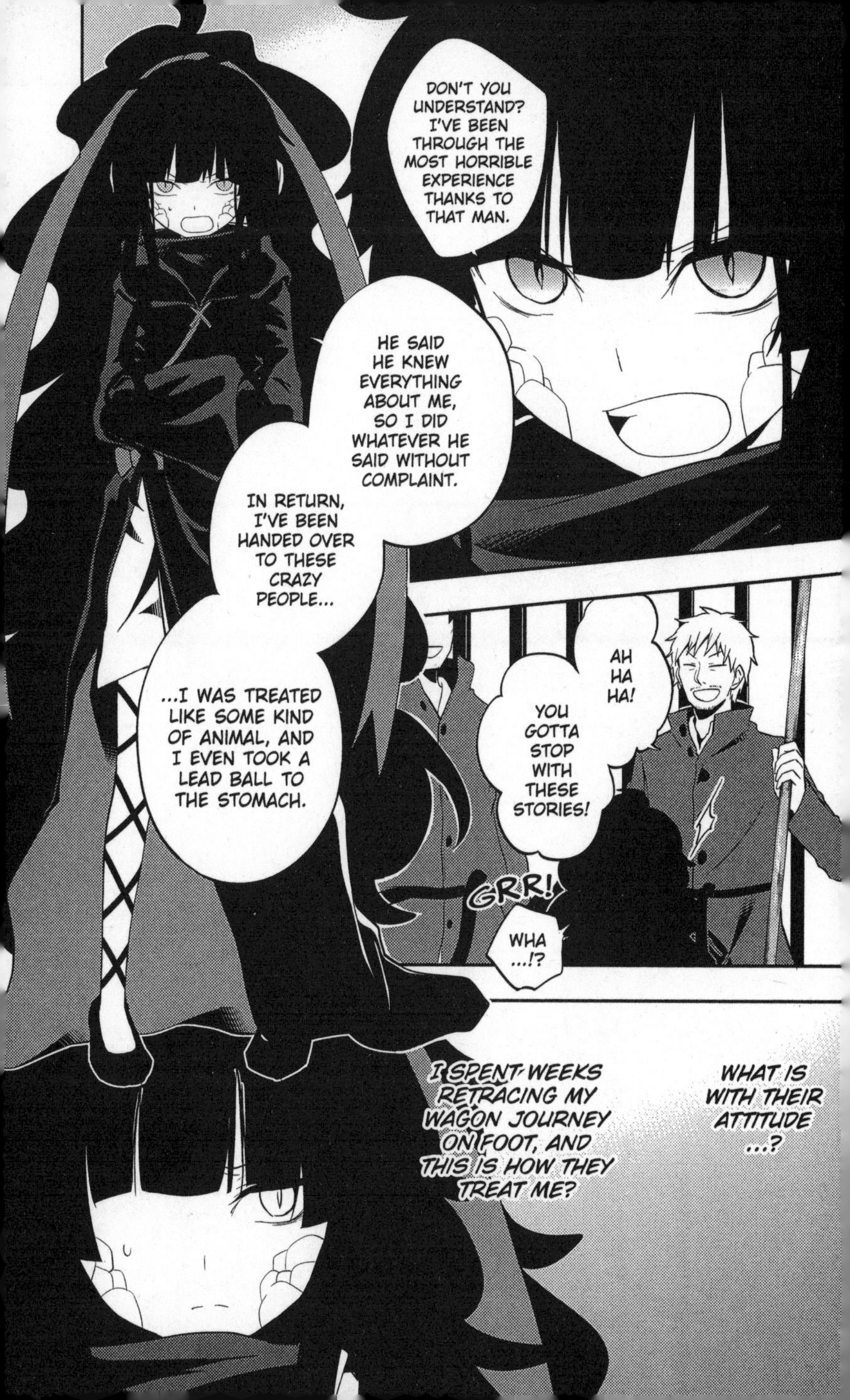
DON'T YOU UNDERSTAND? I'VE BEEN THROUGH THE MOST HORRIBLE EXPERIENCE THANKS TO THAT MAN.
HE SAID HE KNEW EVERYTHING ABOUT ME, SO I DID WHATEVER HE SAID WITHOUT COMPLAINT.
IN RETURN, I'VE BEEN HANDED OVER TO THESE CRAZY PEOPLE...
...I WAS TREATED LIKE SOME KIND OF ANIMAL, AND I EVEN TOOK A LEAD BALL TO THE STOMACH.
AH HA HA!
YOU GOTTA STOP WITH THESE STORIES!
GRR!
WHA ...!?
WHAT IS WITH THEIR ATTITUDE ...?
I SPENT WEEKS RETRACING MY WAGON JOURNEY ON FOOT, AND THIS IS HOW THEY TREAT ME?

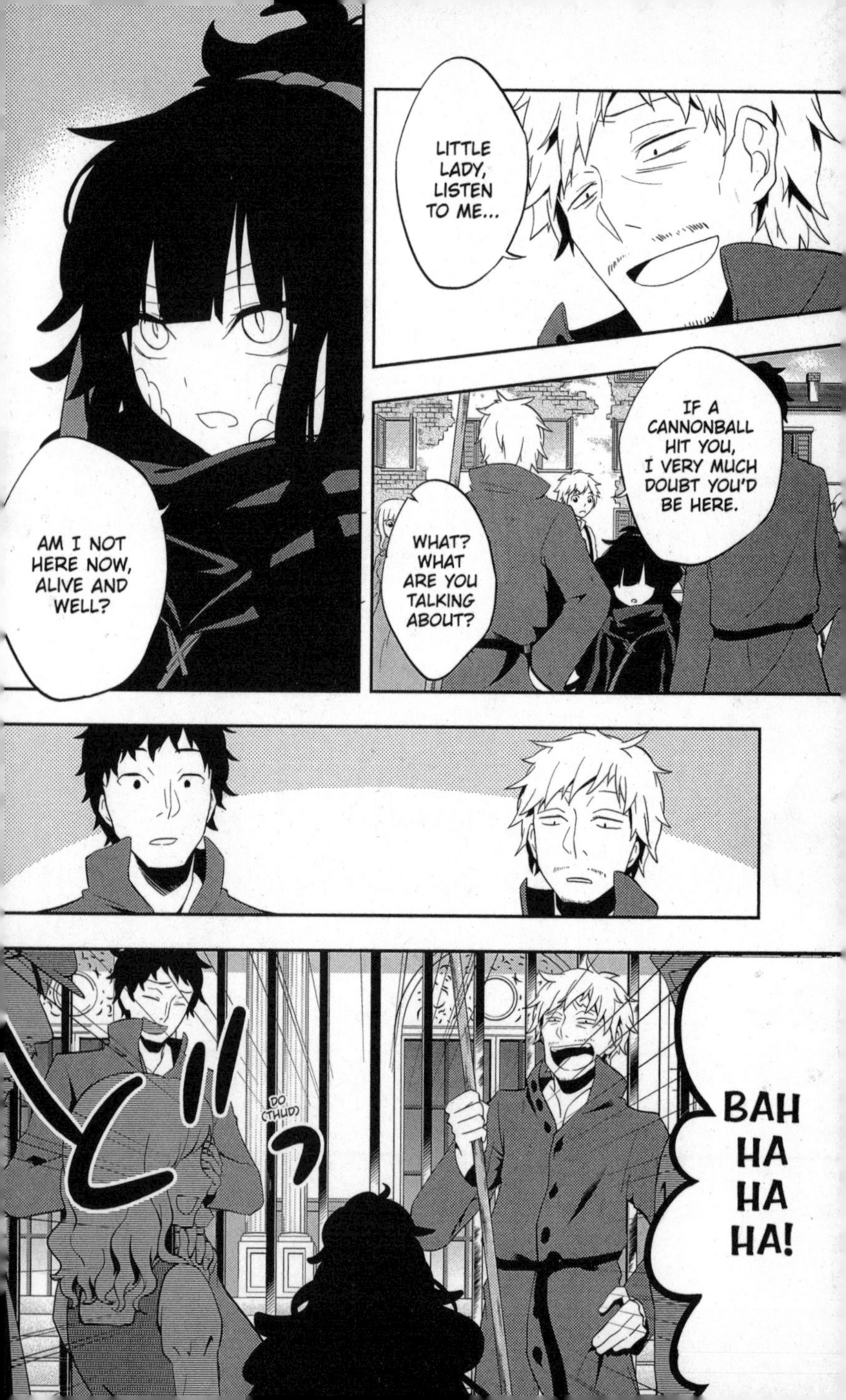
LITTLE LADY, LISTEN TO ME...
IF A CANNONBALL HIT YOU, I VERY MUCH DOUBT YOU'D BE HERE.
WHAT? WHAT ARE YOU TALKING ABOUT?
AM I NOT HERE NOW, ALIVE AND WELL?
BAH HA HA HA!
DO (THUD)

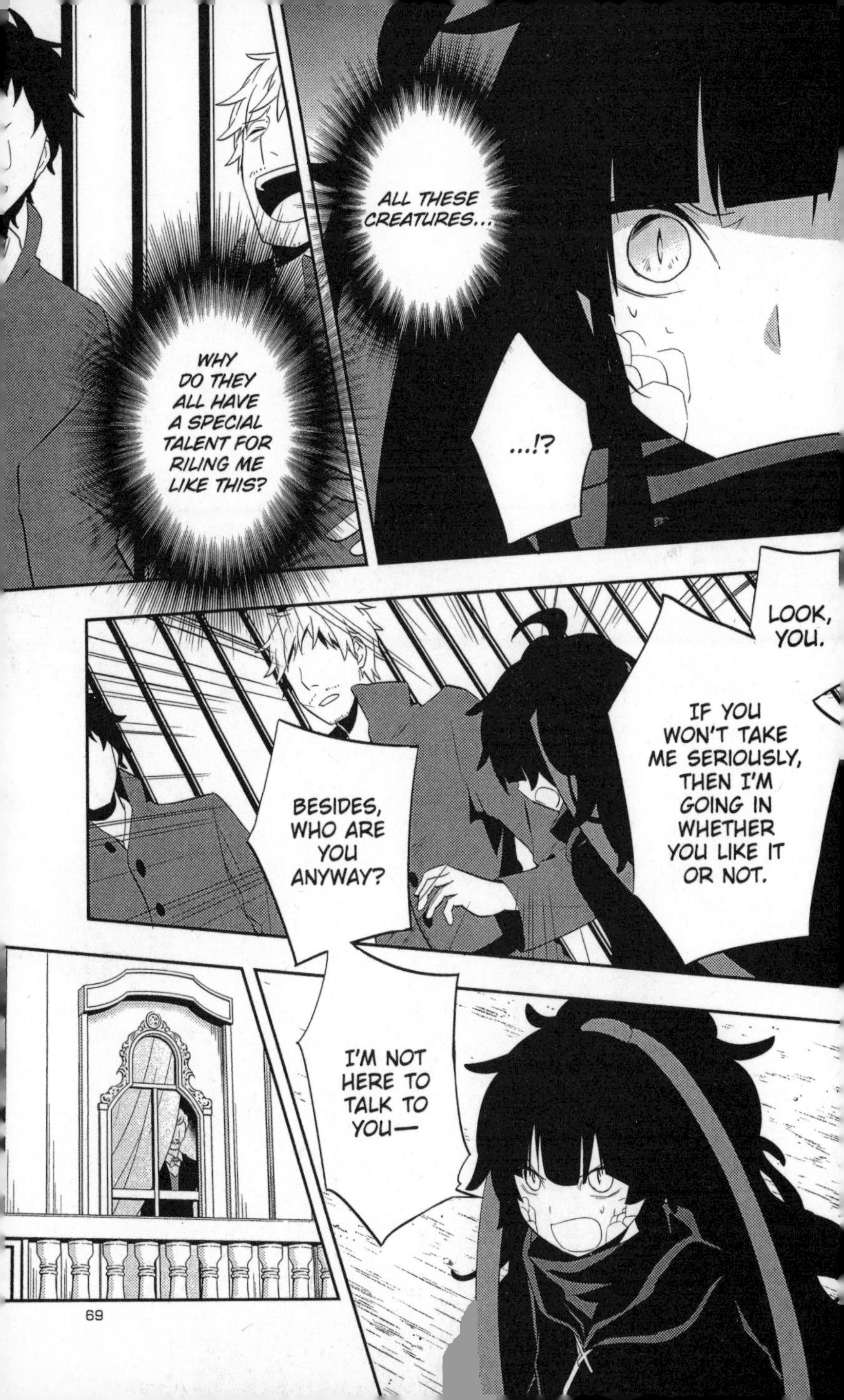
...!?
ALL THESE CREATURES...
WHY DO THEY ALL HAVE A SPECIAL TALENT FOR RILING ME LIKE THIS?
LOOK, YOU.
IF YOU WON'T TAKE ME SERIOUSLY, THEN I'M GOING IN WHETHER YOU LIKE IT OR NOT.
BESIDES, WHO ARE YOU ANYWAY?
I'M NOT HERE TO TALK TO YOU—

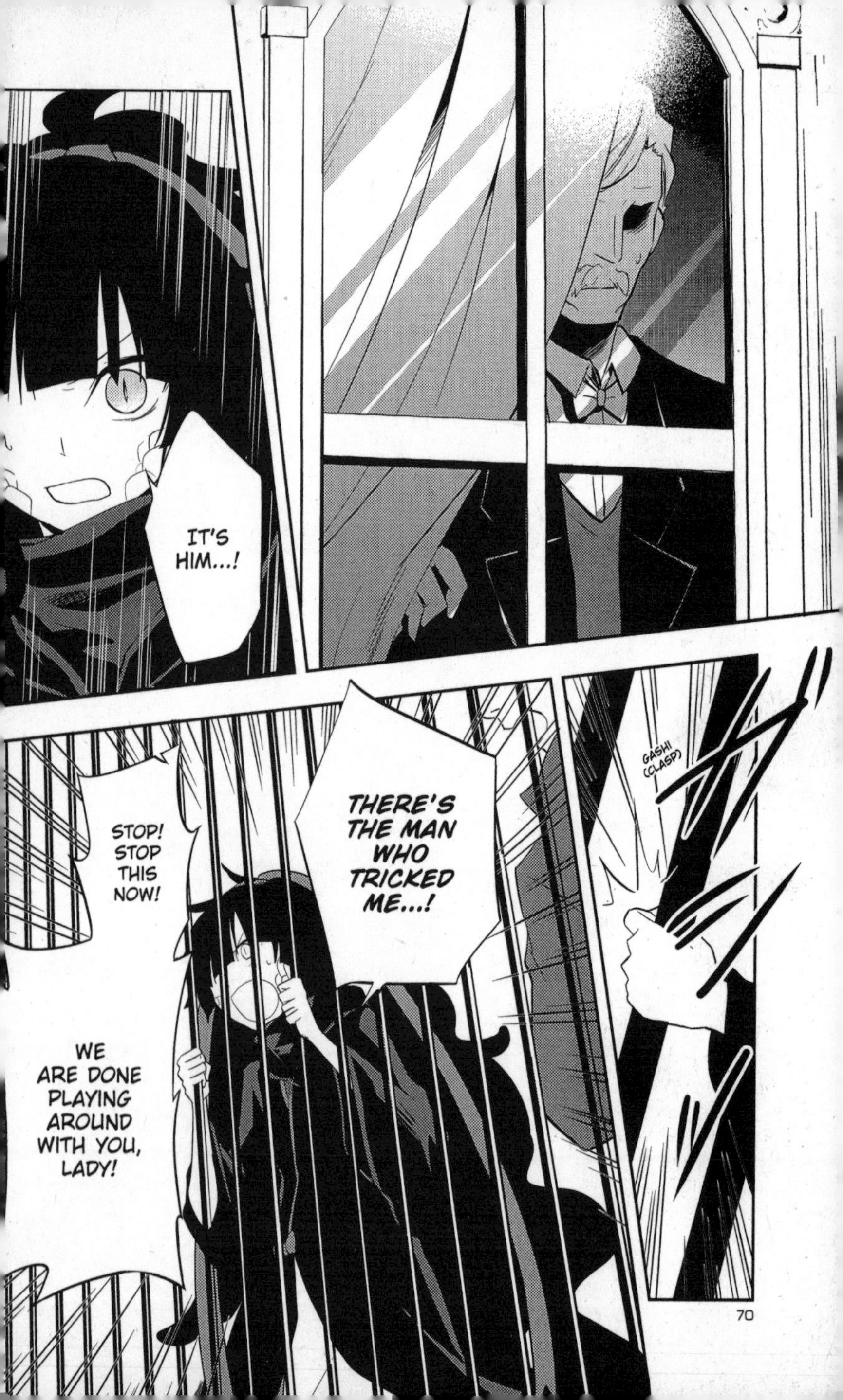
IT'S HIM...!
GASHI (CLASP)
THERE'S THE MAN WHO TRICKED ME...!
STOP! STOP THIS NOW!
WE ARE DONE PLAYING AROUND WITH YOU, LADY!

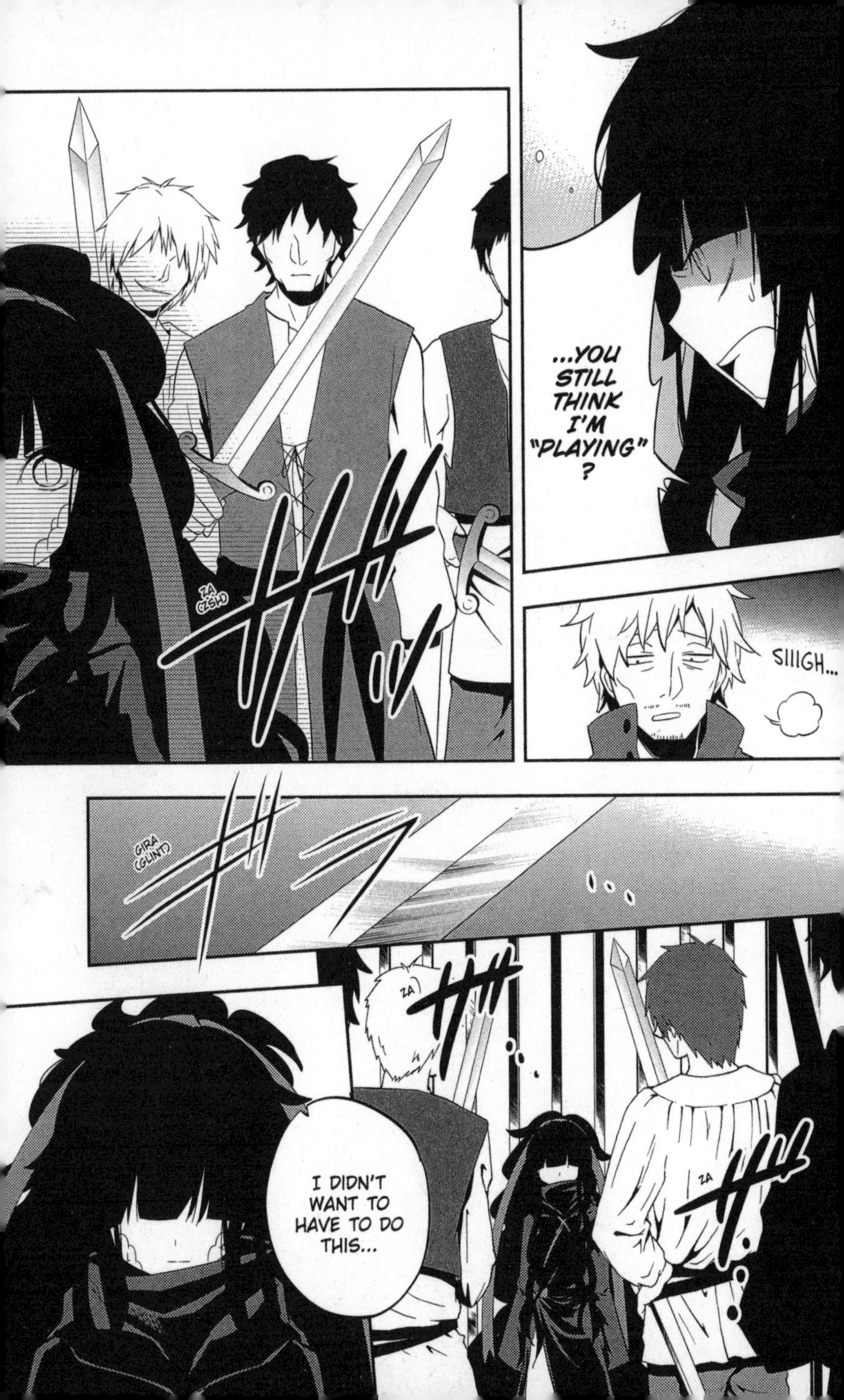
...YOU STILL THINK I'M "PLAYING" ?
SIIIGH...
ZA (ZSH)
GIRA (GLINT)
...
ZA
ZA
I DIDN'T WANT TO HAVE TO DO THIS...

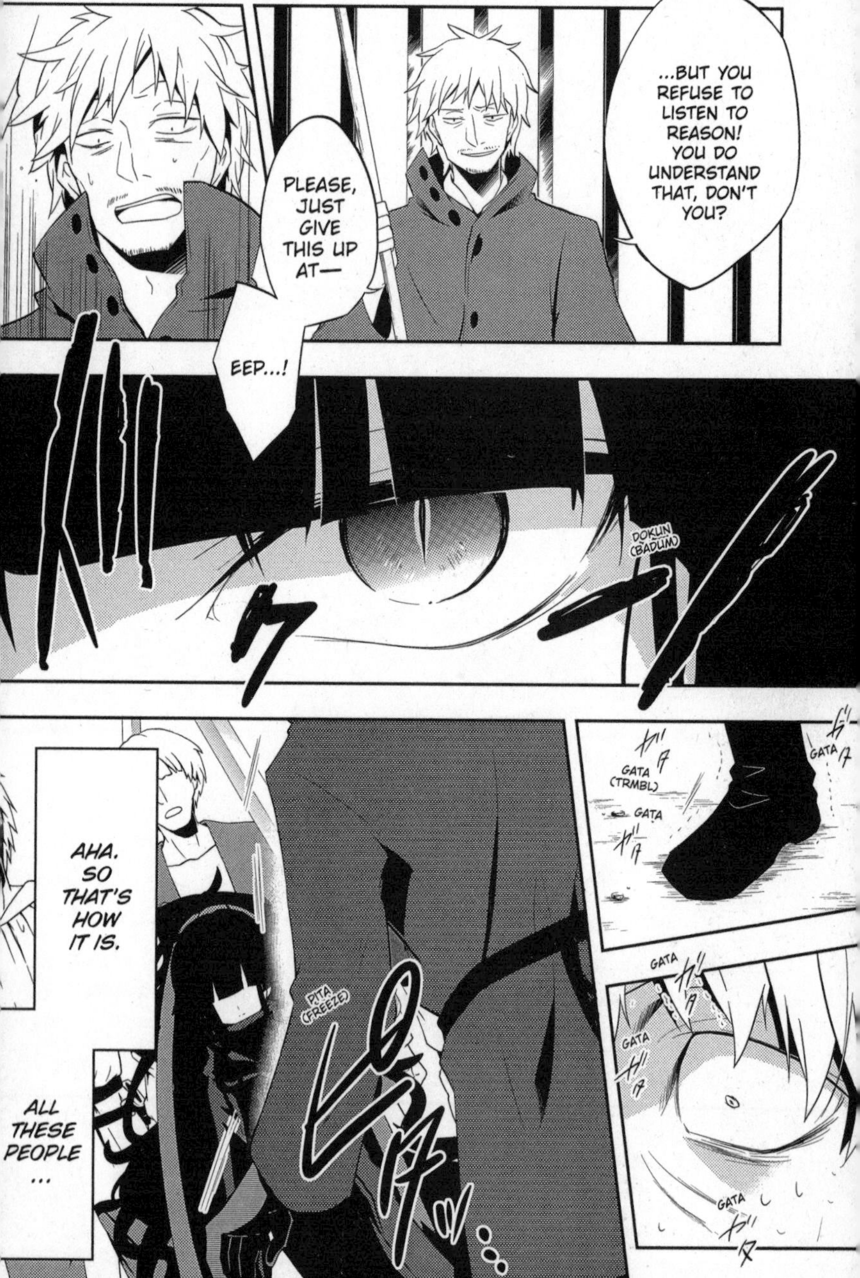
...BUT YOU REFUSE TO LISTEN TO REASON! YOU DO UNDERSTAND THAT, DON'T YOU?
PLEASE, JUST GIVE THIS UP AT—
EEP...!
DOKUN (BADUM)
GATA
GATA (TRMBL)
GATA
GATA
GATA
GATA
PITA (FREEZE)
AHA. SO THAT'S HOW IT IS.
ALL THESE PEOPLE ...

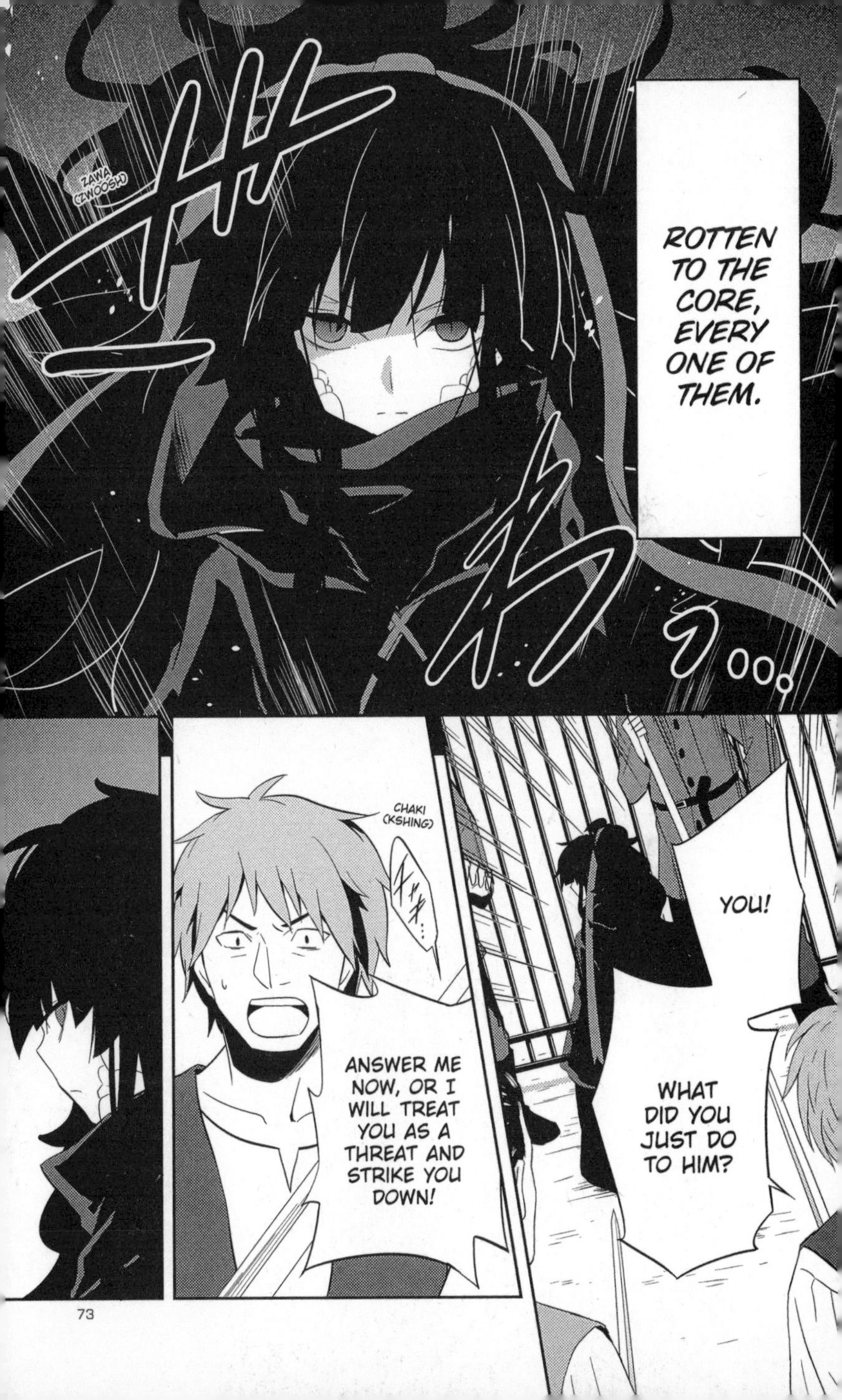
ZAWA (ZWOOSH)
ROTTEN TO THE CORE, EVERY ONE OF THEM.
YOU!
WHAT DID YOU JUST DO TO HIM?
CHAKI (KSHING)
ANSWER ME NOW, OR I WILL TREAT YOU AS A THREAT AND STRIKE YOU DOWN!

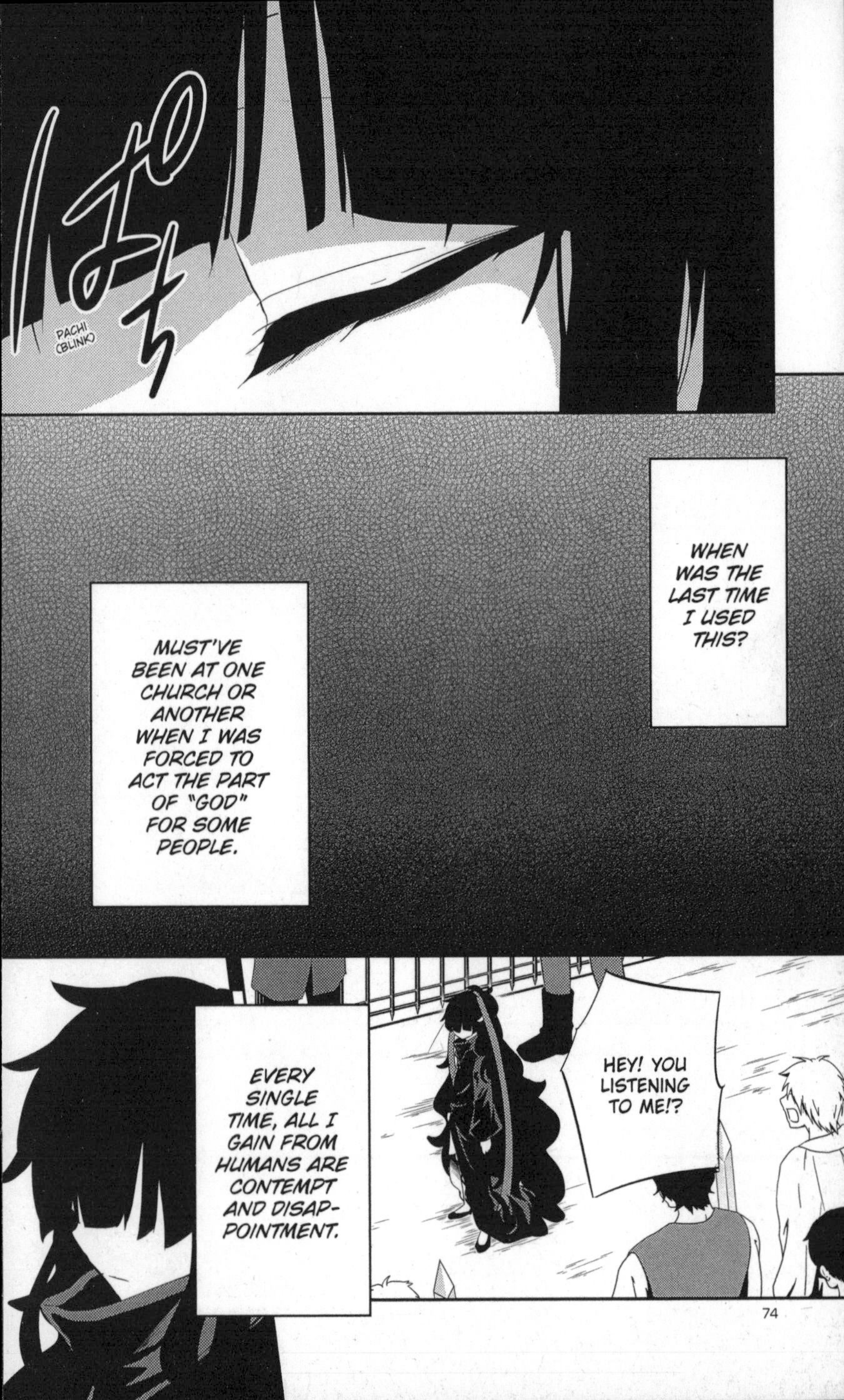
PACHI (BLINK)
WHEN WAS THE LAST TIME I USED THIS?
MUST'VE BEEN AT ONE CHURCH OR ANOTHER WHEN I WAS FORCED TO ACT THE PART OF "GOD" FOR SOME PEOPLE.
HEY! YOU LISTENING TO ME!?
EVERY SINGLE TIME, ALL I GAIN FROM HUMANS ARE CONTEMPT AND DISAP-POINTMENT.

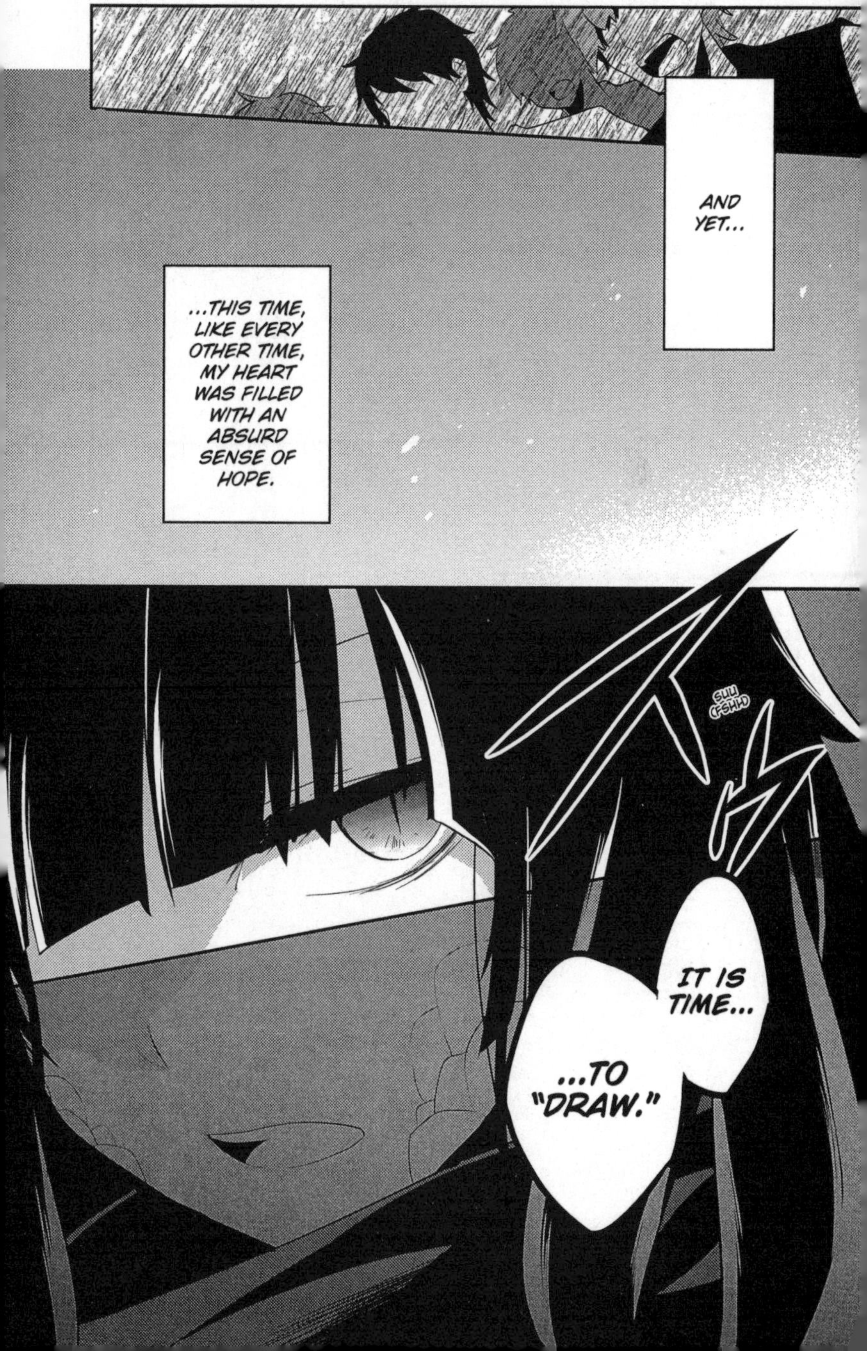
AND YET...
...THIS TIME, LIKE EVERY OTHER TIME, MY HEART WAS FILLED WITH AN ABSURD SENSE OF HOPE.
IT IS TIME...
...TO "DRAW."

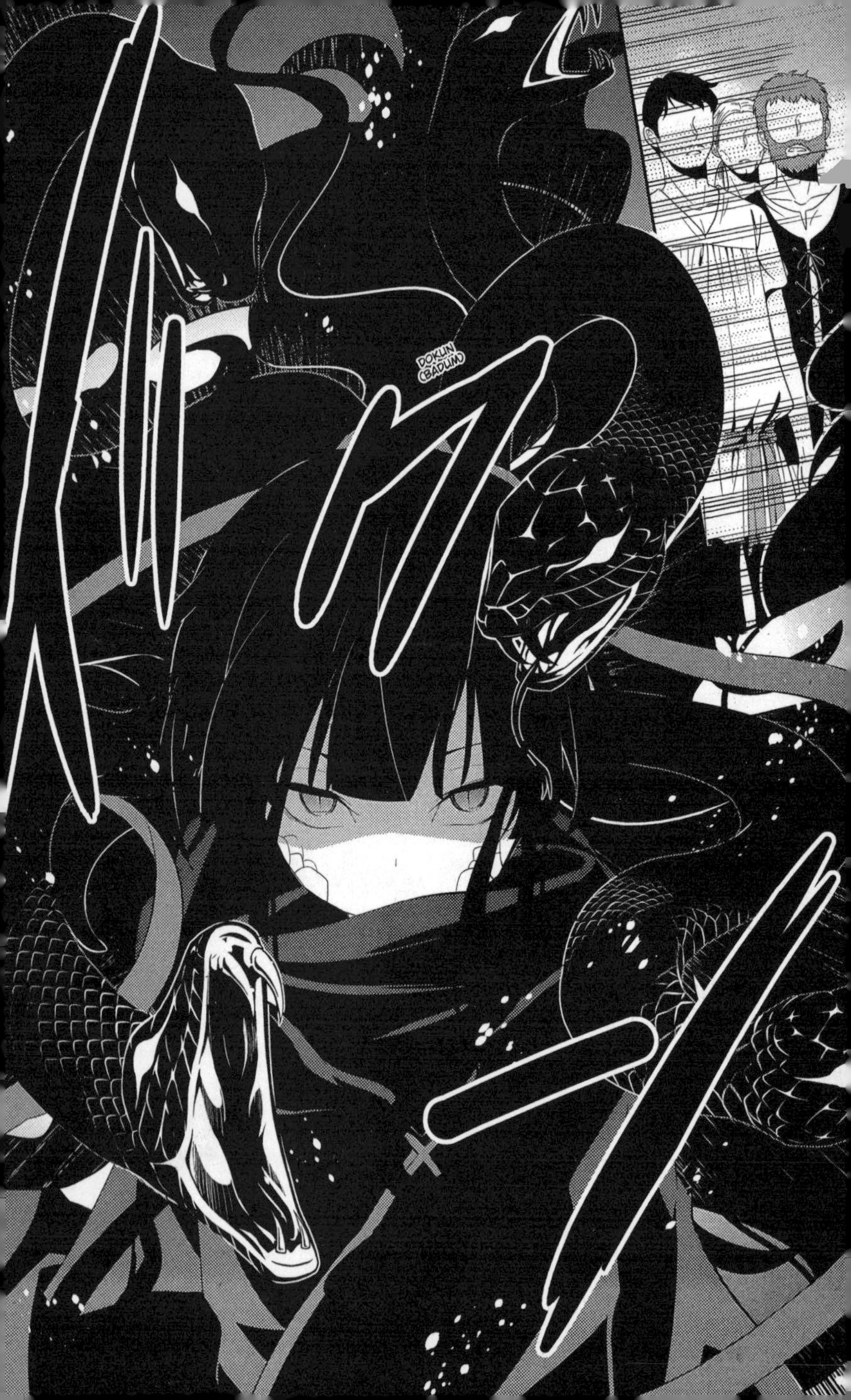
DOKUN
(BADUM)

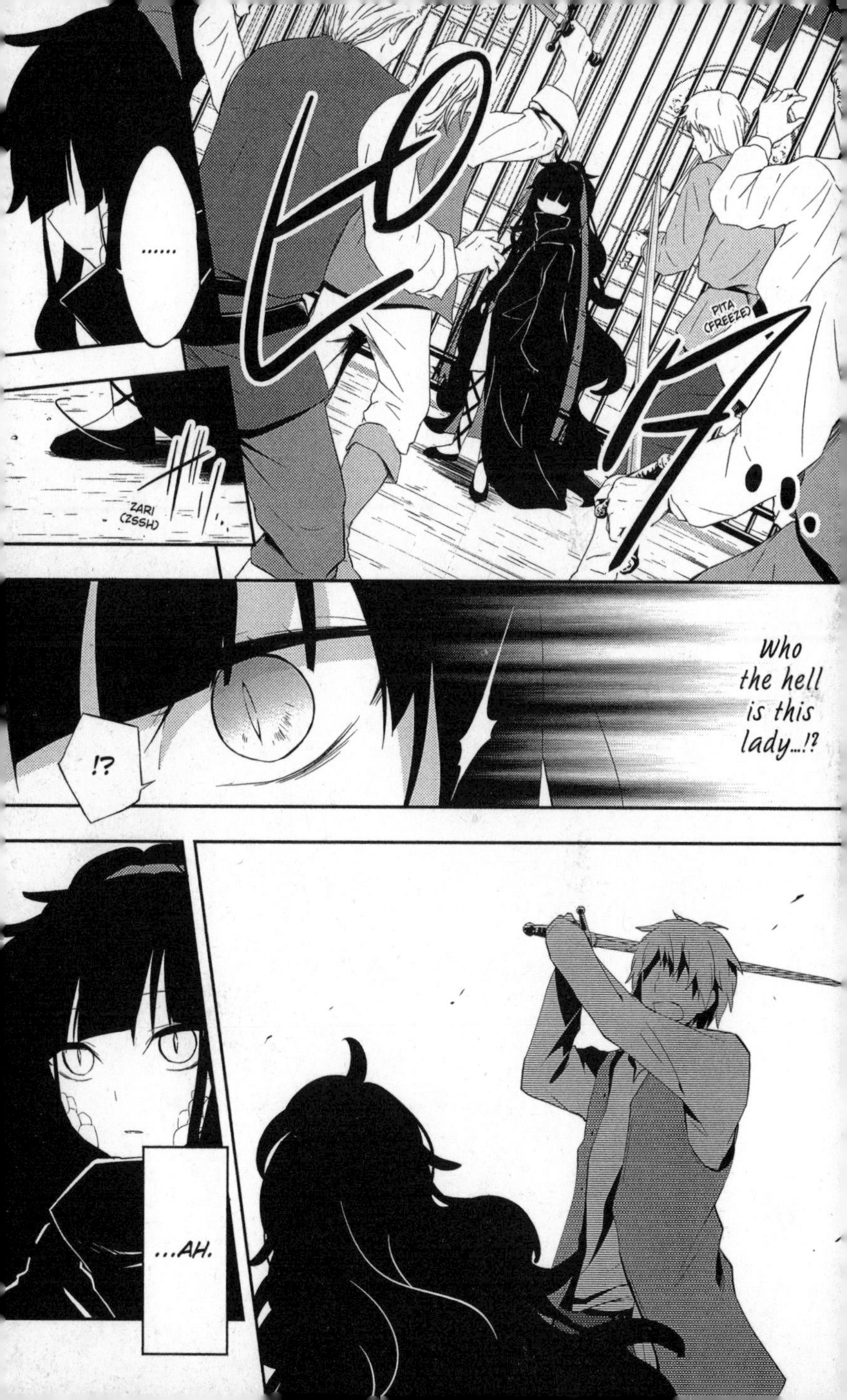
......
PITA (FREEZE)
ZARI (ZSSH)
!?
Who the hell is this lady...!?
...AH.

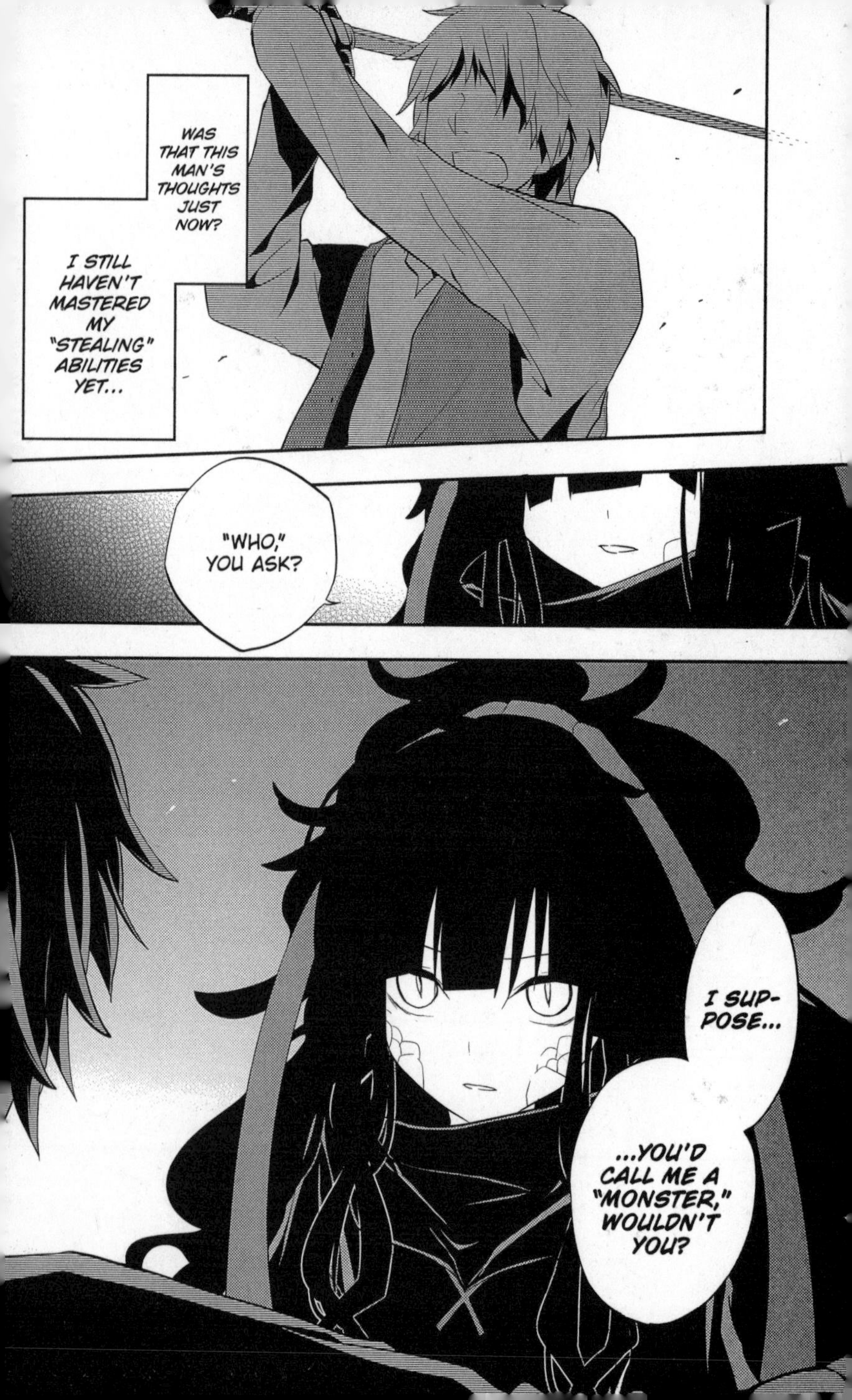
WAS THAT THIS MAN'S THOUGHTS JUST NOW?
I STILL HAVEN'T MASTERED MY "STEALING" ABILITIES YET...
"WHO," YOU ASK?
I SUP-POSE...
...YOU'D CALL ME A "MONSTER," WOULDN'T YOU?

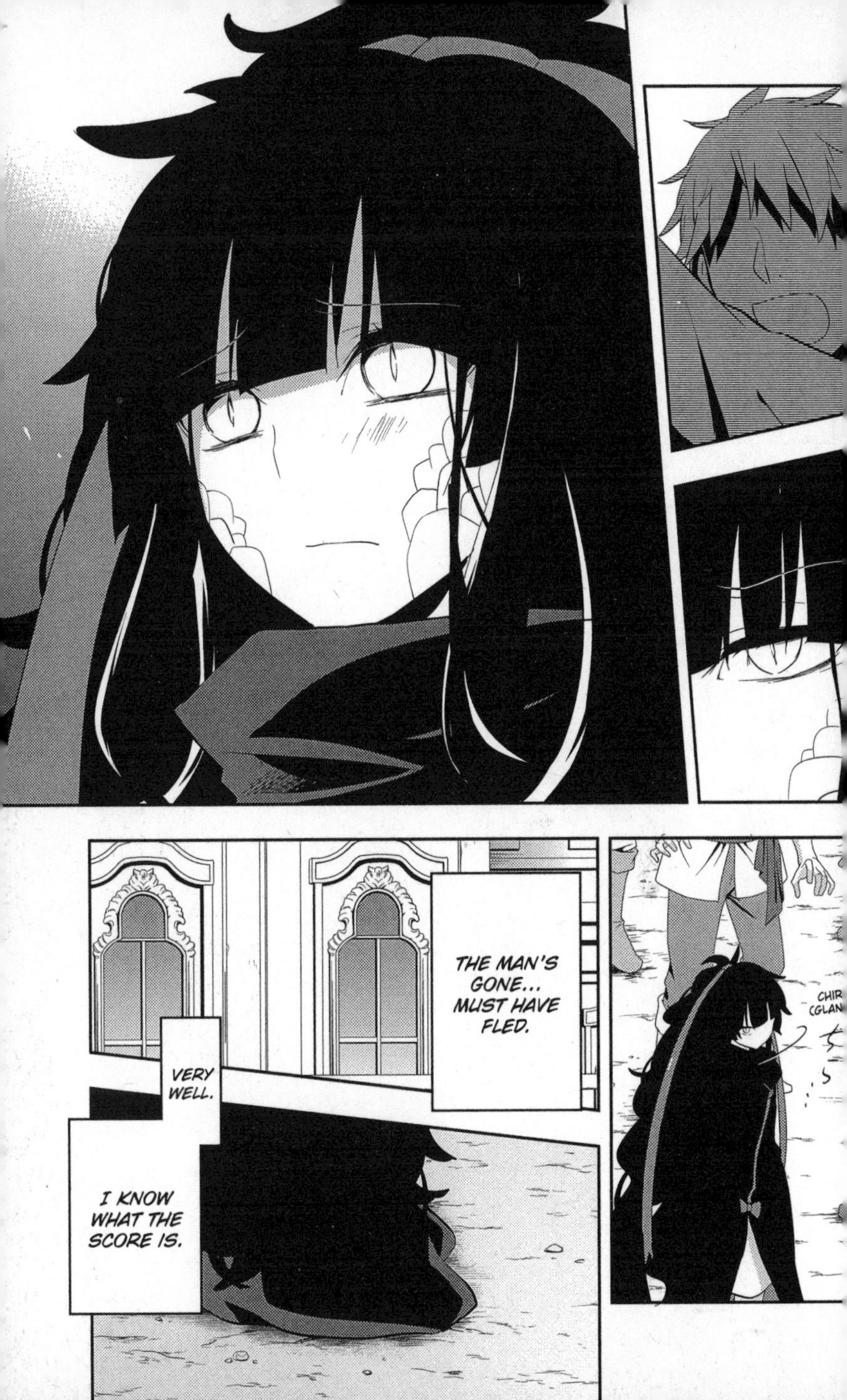
THE MAN'S GONE... MUST HAVE FLED.
VERY WELL.
I KNOW WHAT THE SCORE IS.

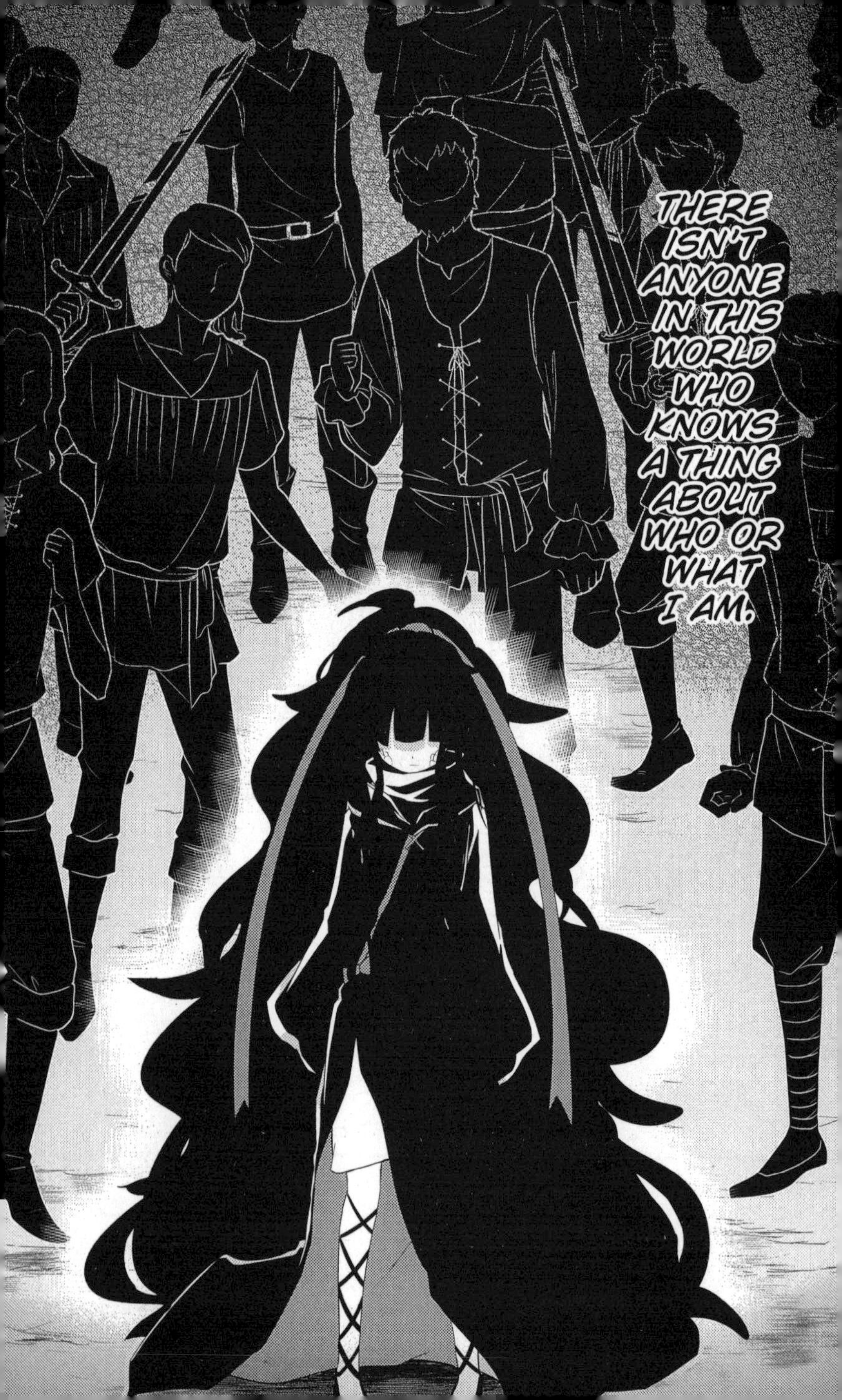
THERE ISN'T ANYONE IN THIS WORLD WHO KNOWS A THING ABOUT WHO OR WHAT I AM.

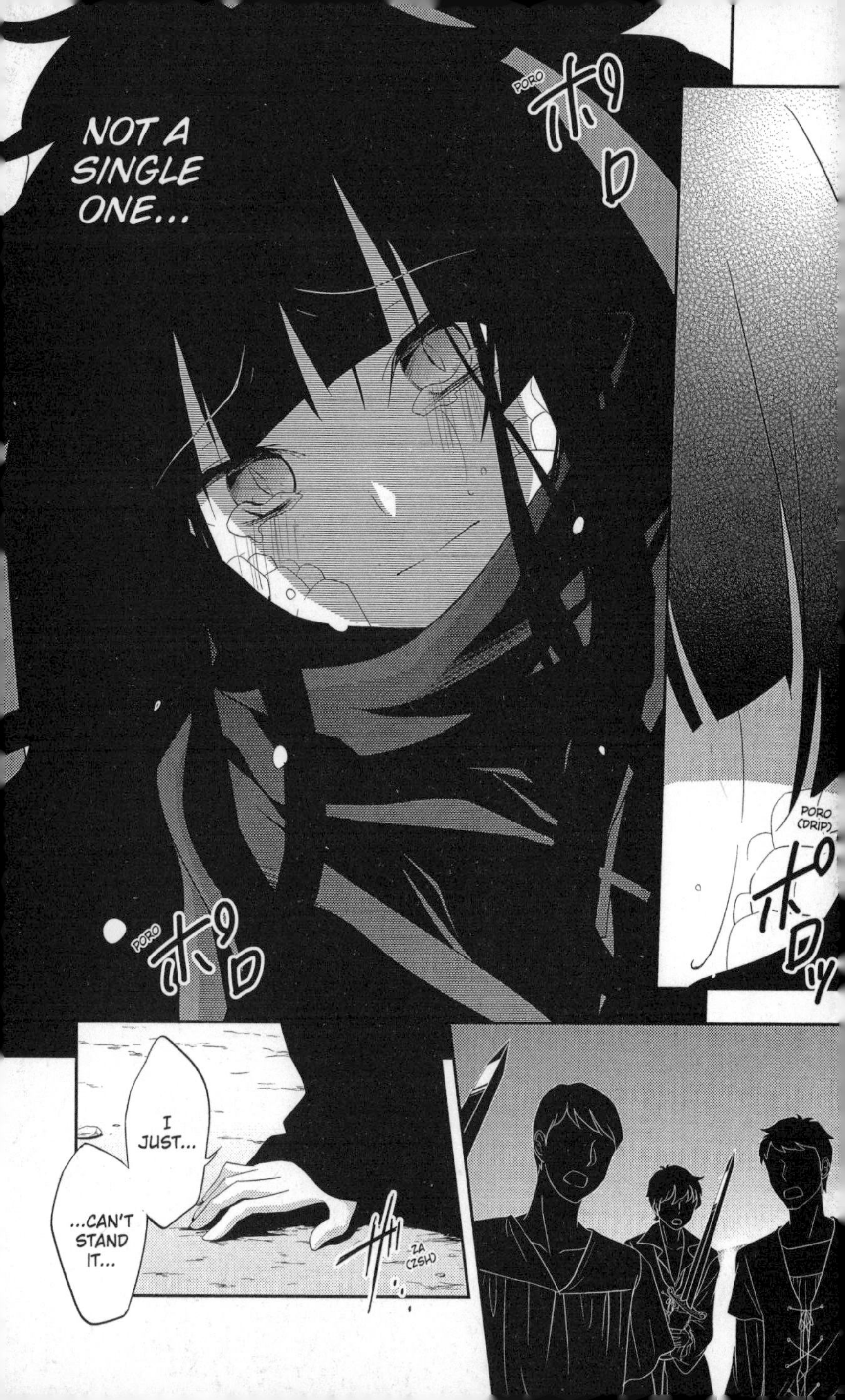
PORO (DRIP)
NOT A SINGLE ONE...
PORO
PORO
I JUST...
...CAN'T STAND IT...
ZA (ZSH)

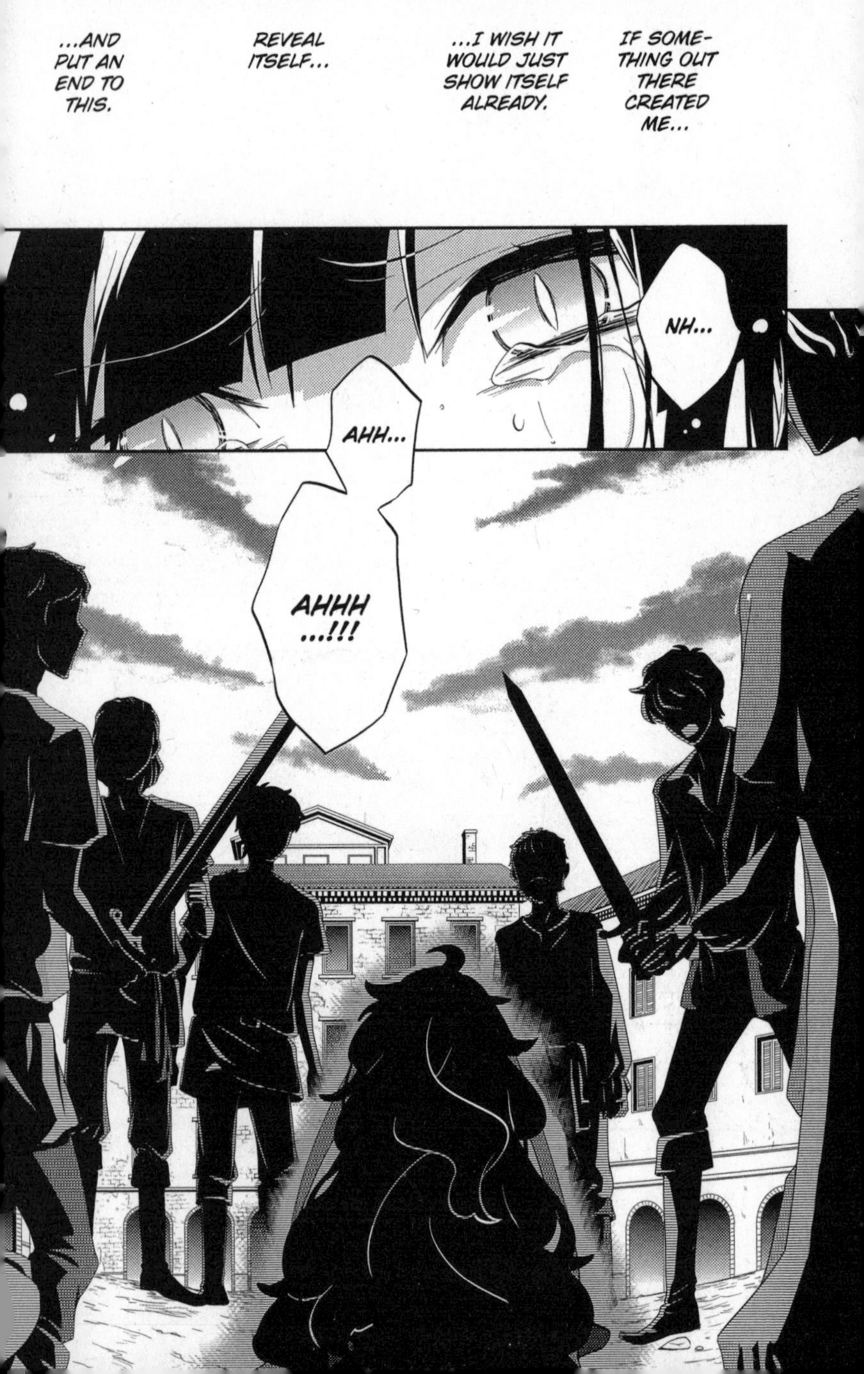
IF SOMETHING OUT THERE CREATED ME...
...I WISH IT WOULD JUST SHOW ITSELF ALREADY.
REVEAL ITSELF...
...AND PUT AN END TO THIS.
NH...
AHH...
AHHH ...!!!

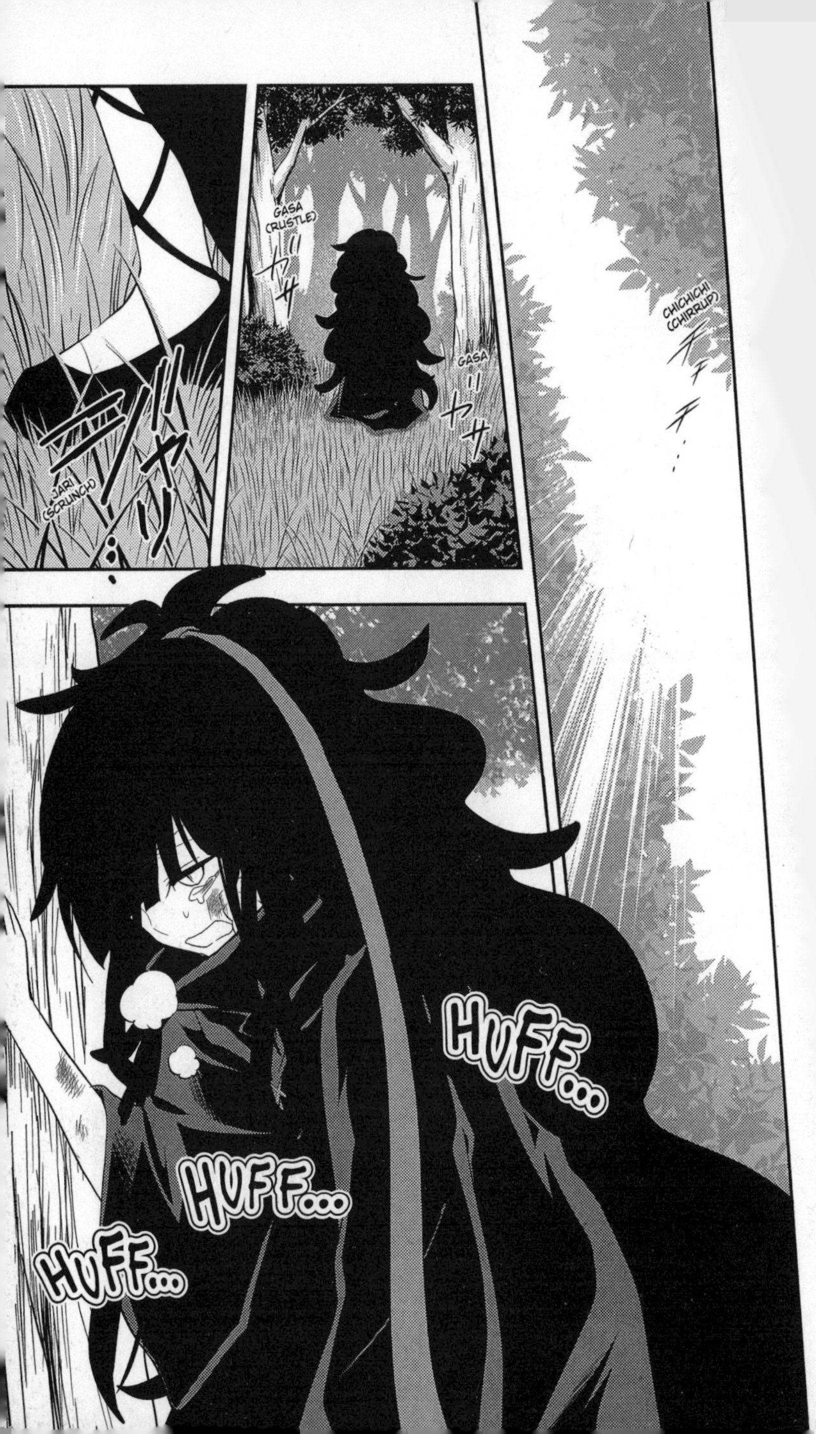
CHICHICHI (CHIRRUP)
GASA (RUSTLE)
GASA
JARI (SCRUNCH)
HUFF...
HUFF...
HUFF...

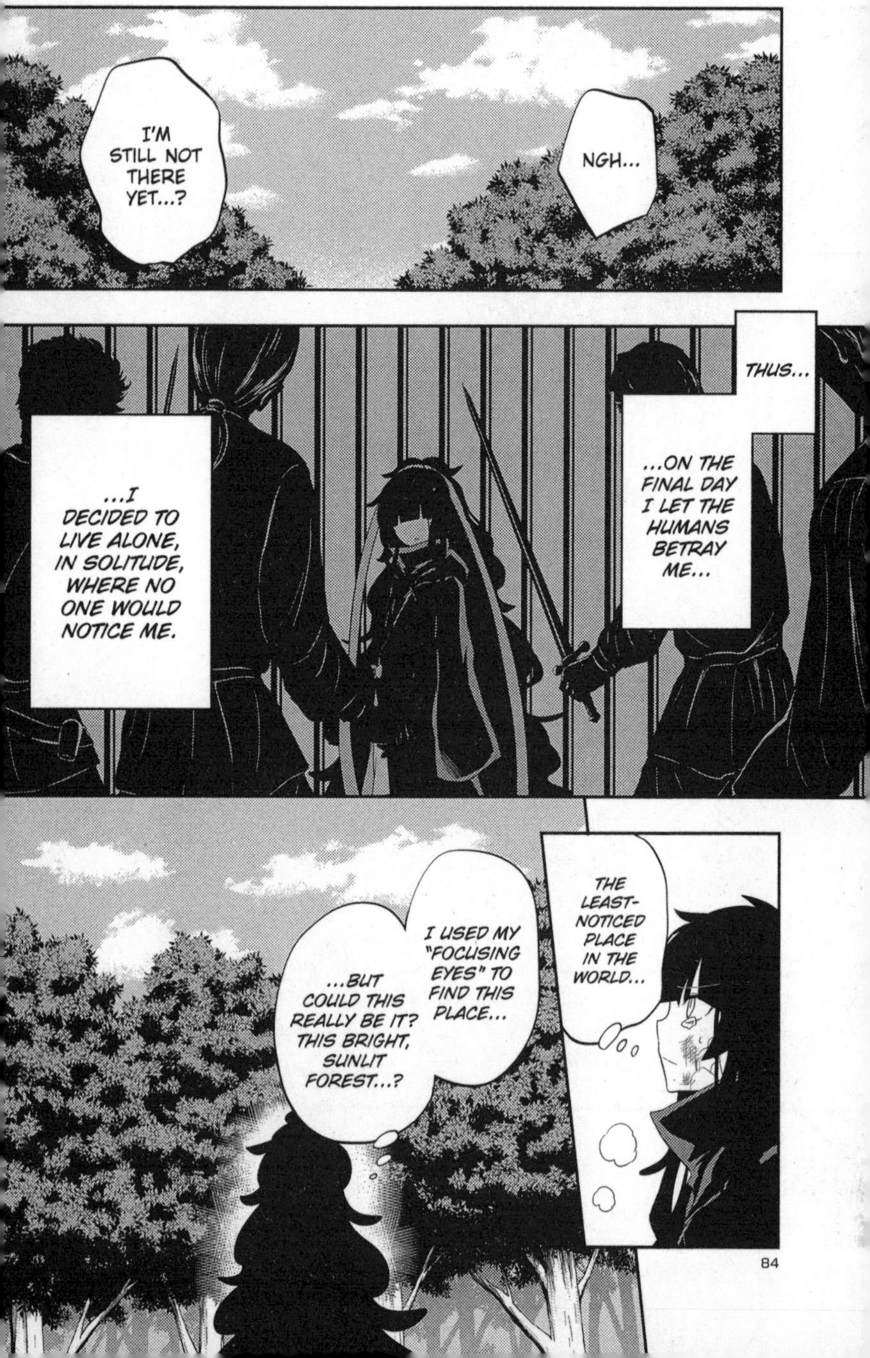
NGH...
I'M STILL NOT THERE YET...?
THUS...
...ON THE FINAL DAY I LET THE HUMANS BETRAY ME...
...I DECIDED TO LIVE ALONE, IN SOLITUDE, WHERE NO ONE WOULD NOTICE ME.
THE LEAST-NOTICED PLACE IN THE WORLD...
I USED MY "FOCUSING EYES" TO FIND THIS PLACE...
...BUT COULD THIS REALLY BE IT? THIS BRIGHT, SUNLIT FOREST...?

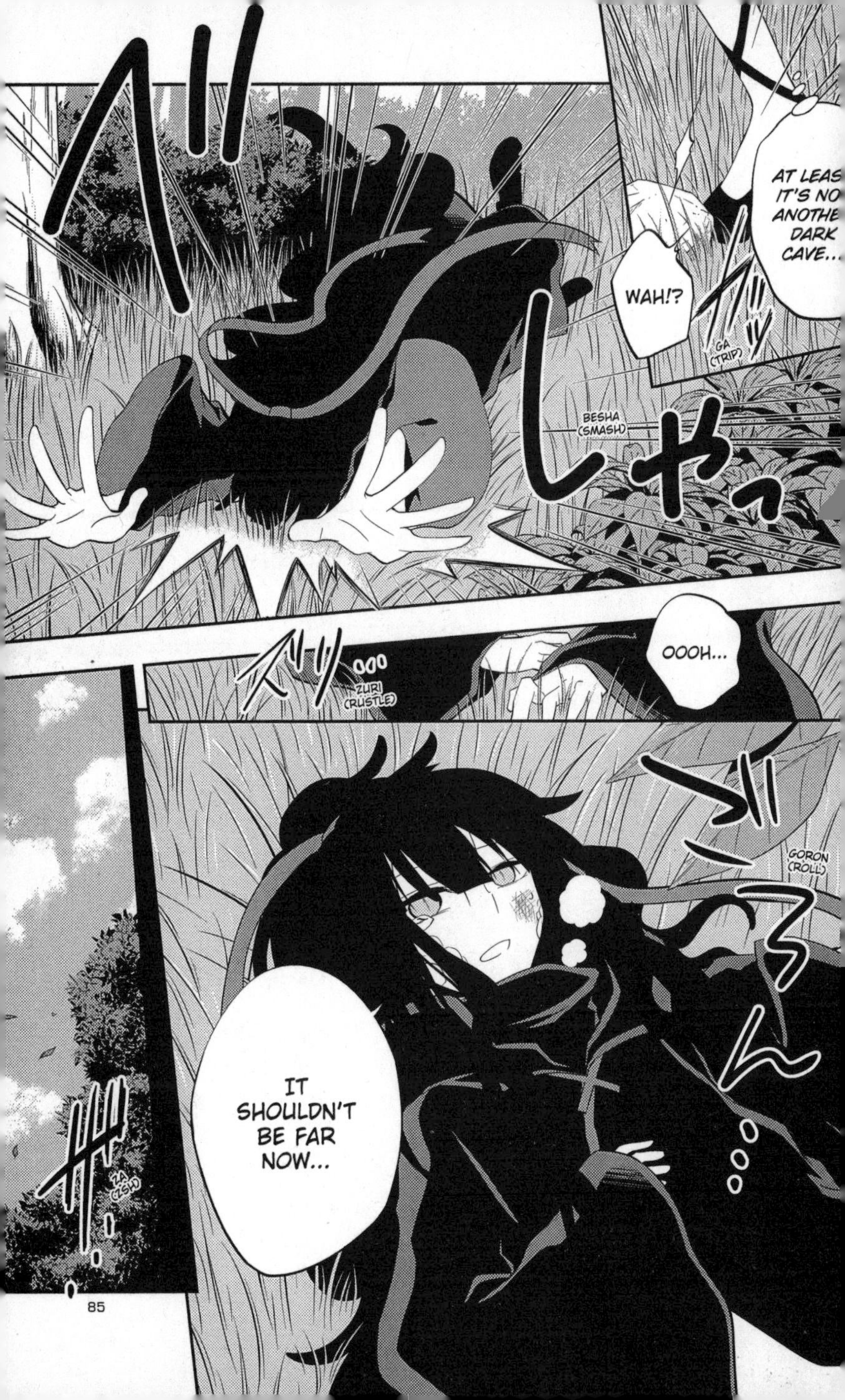
AT LEAS IT'S NO ANOTHE DARK CAVE...
WAH!?
GA (TRIP)
BESHA (SMASH)
OOOH...
ZURI (RUSTLE)
GORON (ROLL)
IT SHOULDN'T BE FAR NOW...
ZA (ZSH)

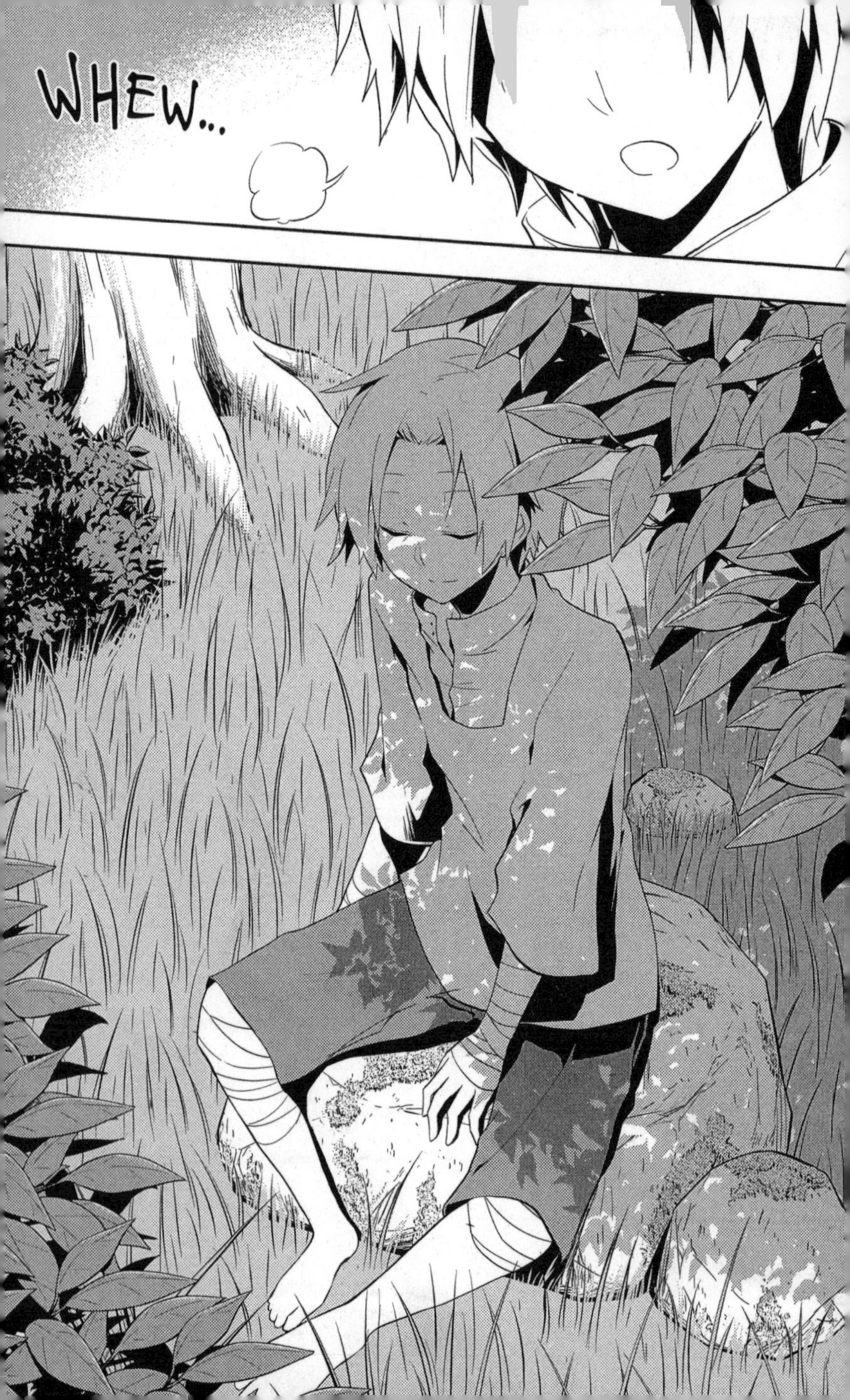
WHEW...

34 >> SHINIGAMI RECORD IV

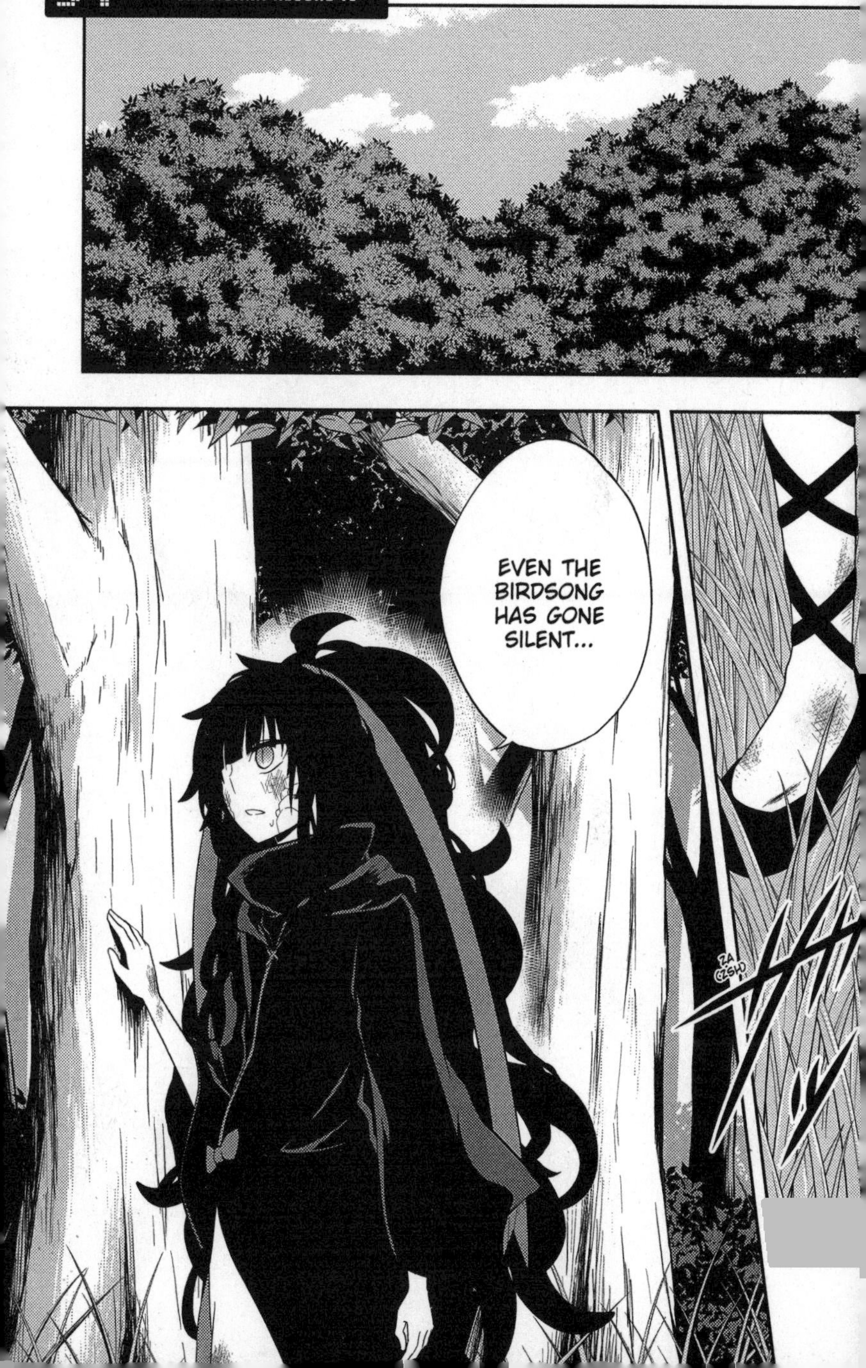
EVEN THE BIRDSONG HAS GONE SILENT...
ZA (ZSH)

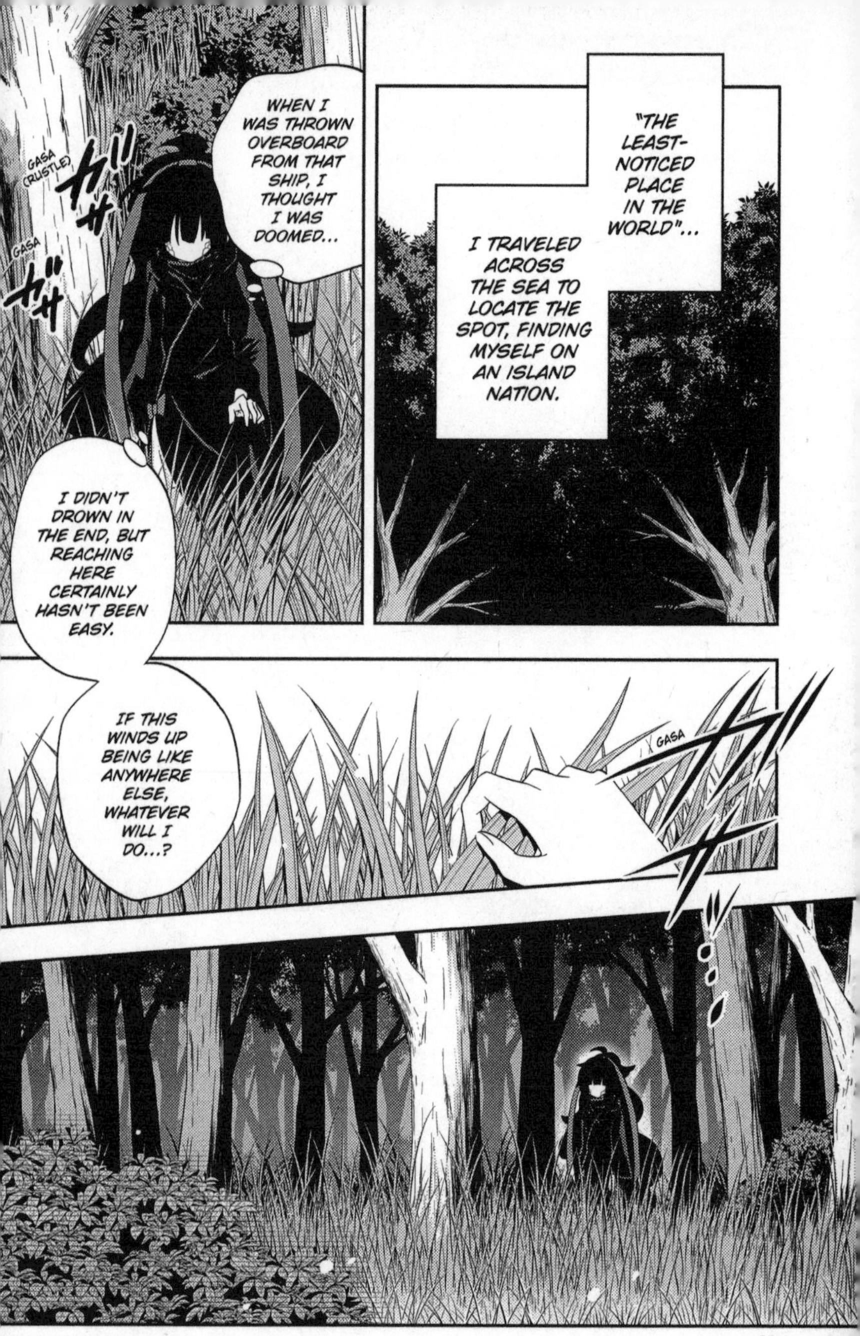
"THE LEAST-NOTICED PLACE IN THE WORLD"...
I TRAVELED ACROSS THE SEA TO LOCATE THE SPOT, FINDING MYSELF ON AN ISLAND NATION.
GASA (RUSTLE)
GASA
WHEN I WAS THROWN OVERBOARD FROM THAT SHIP, I THOUGHT I WAS DOOMED...
I DIDN'T DROWN IN THE END, BUT REACHING HERE CERTAINLY HASN'T BEEN EASY.
GASA
IF THIS WINDS UP BEING LIKE ANYWHERE ELSE, WHATEVER WILL I DO...?

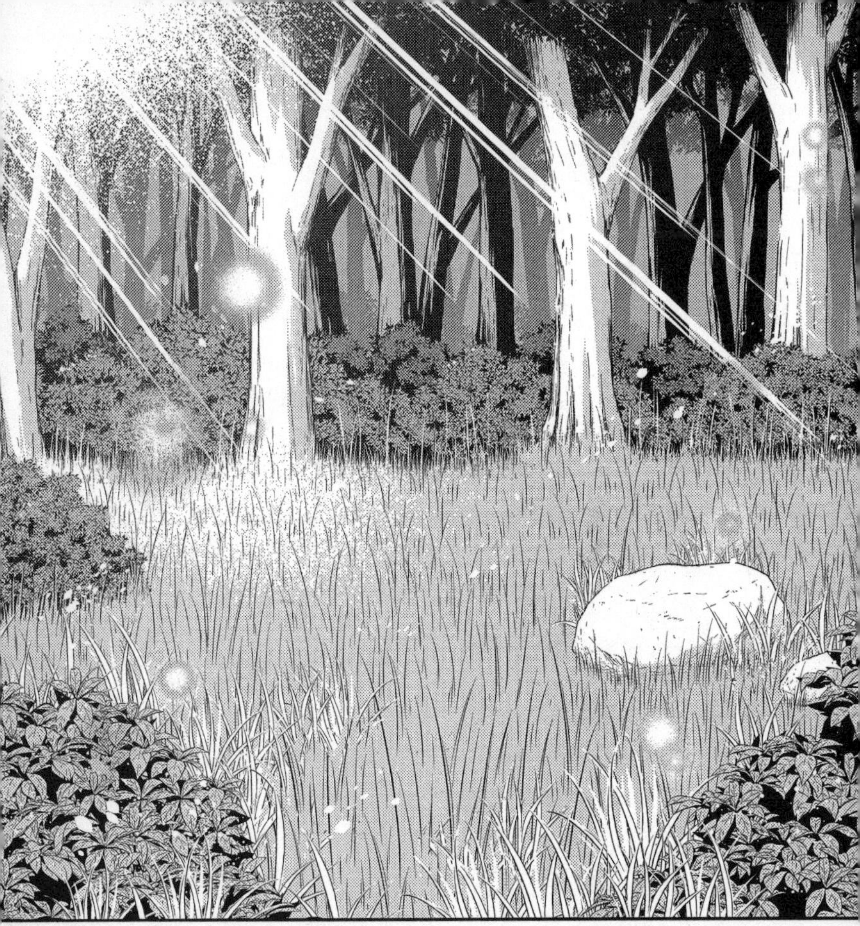

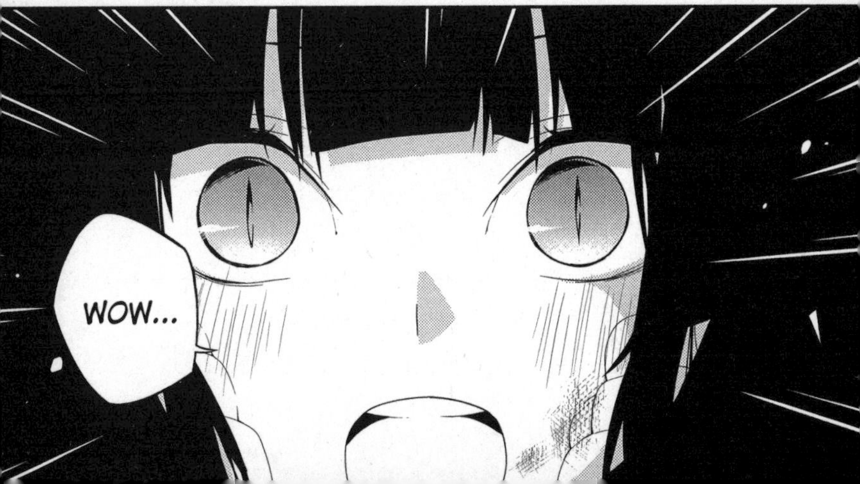
WOW...

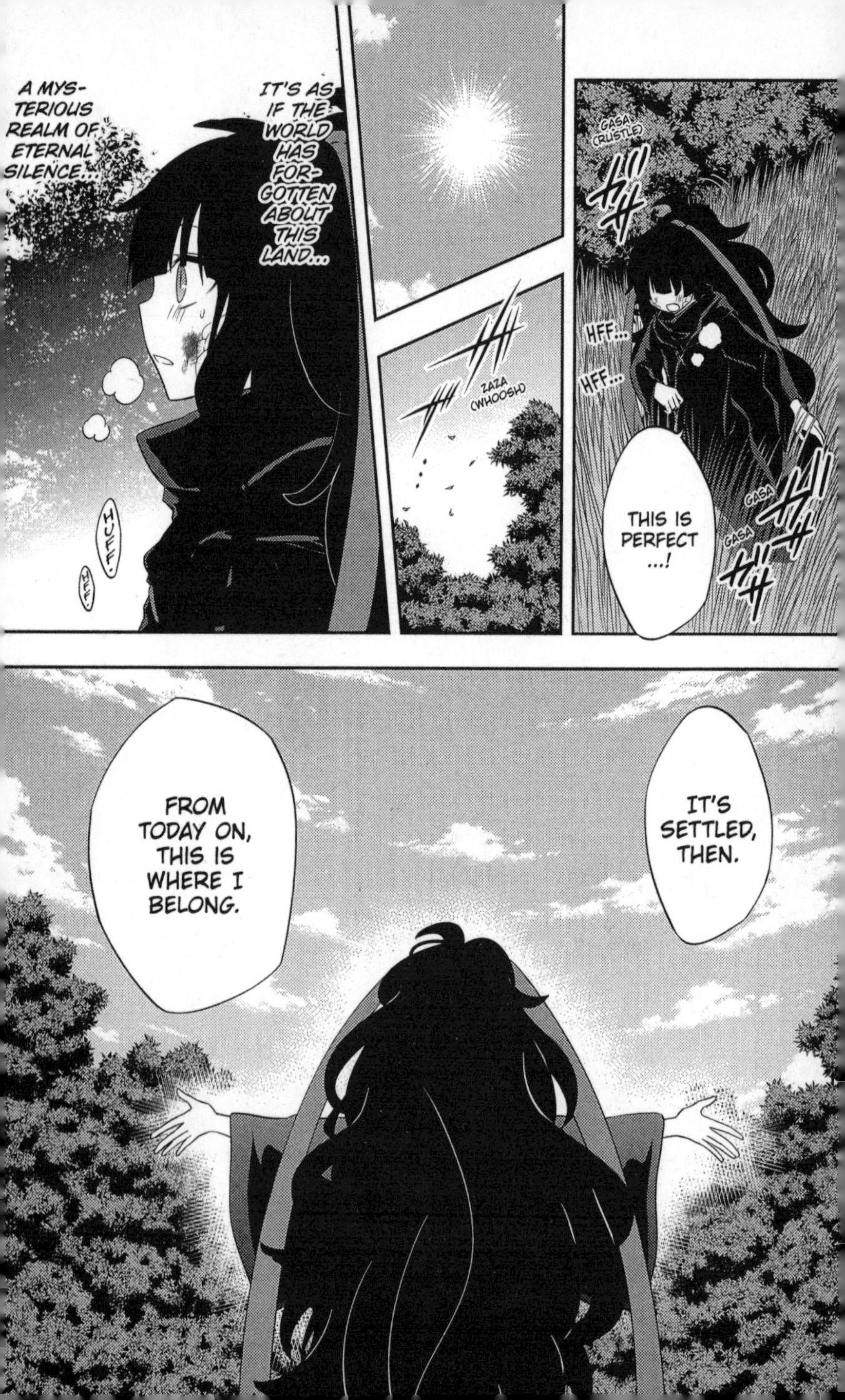
GASA (RUSTLE)
HFF... HFF...
THIS IS PERFECT...!
GASA GASA
ZAZA (WHOOSH)
IT'S AS IF THE WORLD HAS FORGOTTEN ABOUT THIS LAND...
A MYSTERIOUS REALM OF ETERNAL SILENCE...
HUFF. HFF.
IT'S SETTLED, THEN.
FROM TODAY ON, THIS IS WHERE I BELONG.

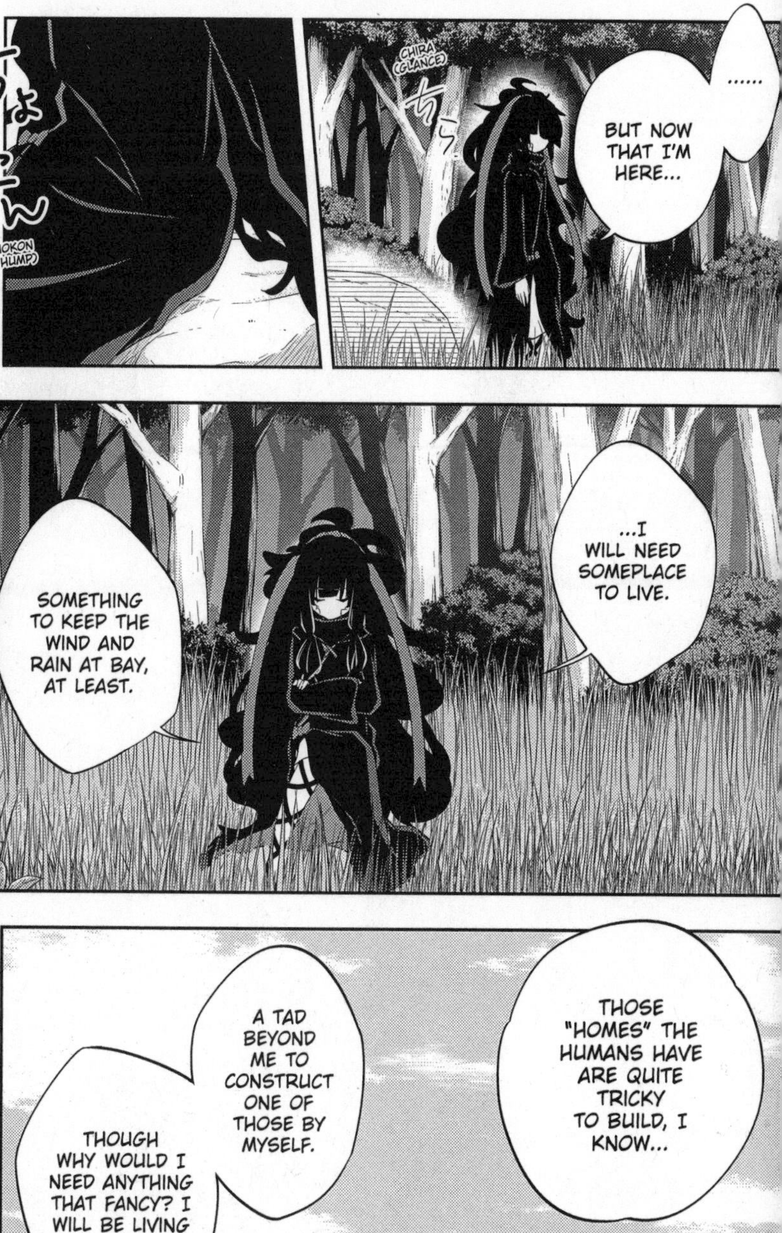
......
BUT NOW THAT I'M HERE...
ちら
CHIRA (GLANCE)
ちょこん
CHOKON (WHUMP)
...I WILL NEED SOMEPLACE TO LIVE.
SOMETHING TO KEEP THE WIND AND RAIN AT BAY, AT LEAST.
THOSE "HOMES" THE HUMANS HAVE ARE QUITE TRICKY TO BUILD, I KNOW...
A TAD BEYOND ME TO CONSTRUCT ONE OF THOSE BY MYSELF.
THOUGH WHY WOULD I NEED ANYTHING THAT FANCY? I WILL BE LIVING ALONE.

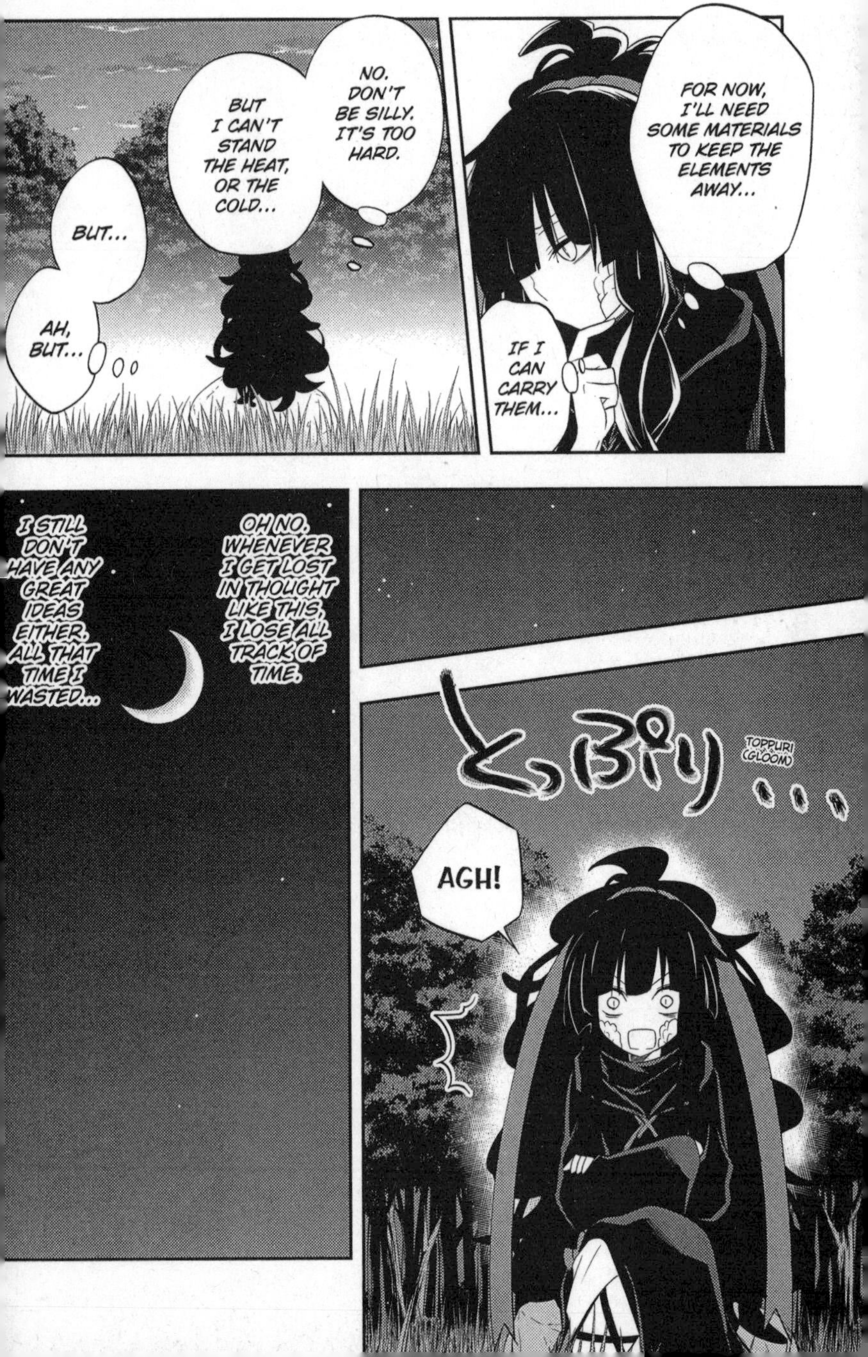
FOR NOW, I'LL NEED SOME MATERIALS TO KEEP THE ELEMENTS AWAY...
IF I CAN CARRY THEM...
NO. DON'T BE SILLY. IT'S TOO HARD.
BUT I CAN'T STAND THE HEAT, OR THE COLD...
BUT...
AH, BUT...
とっぷり・・・
TOPPURI (GLOOM)
AGH!
OH NO. WHENEVER I GET LOST IN THOUGHT LIKE THIS, I LOSE ALL TRACK OF TIME.
I STILL DON'T HAVE ANY GREAT IDEAS EITHER. ALL THAT TIME I WASTED...

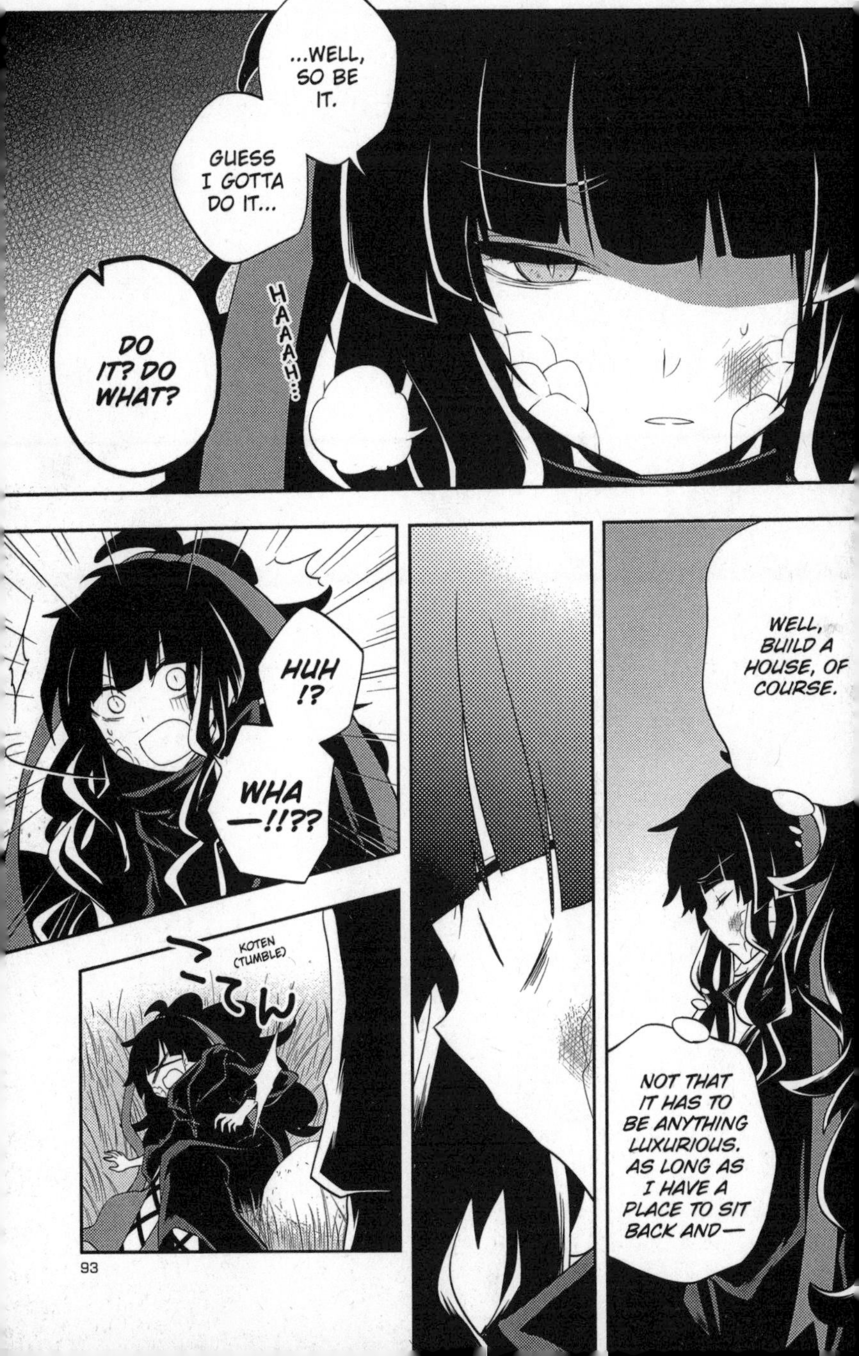

...WELL, SO BE IT.
GUESS I GOTTA DO IT...
HAAAAH..
DO IT? DO WHAT?
WELL, BUILD A HOUSE, OF COURSE.
NOT THAT IT HAS TO BE ANYTHING LUXURIOUS. AS LONG AS I HAVE A PLACE TO SIT BACK AND—
HUH!?
WHA—!!??
こてん
KOTEN (TUMBLE)

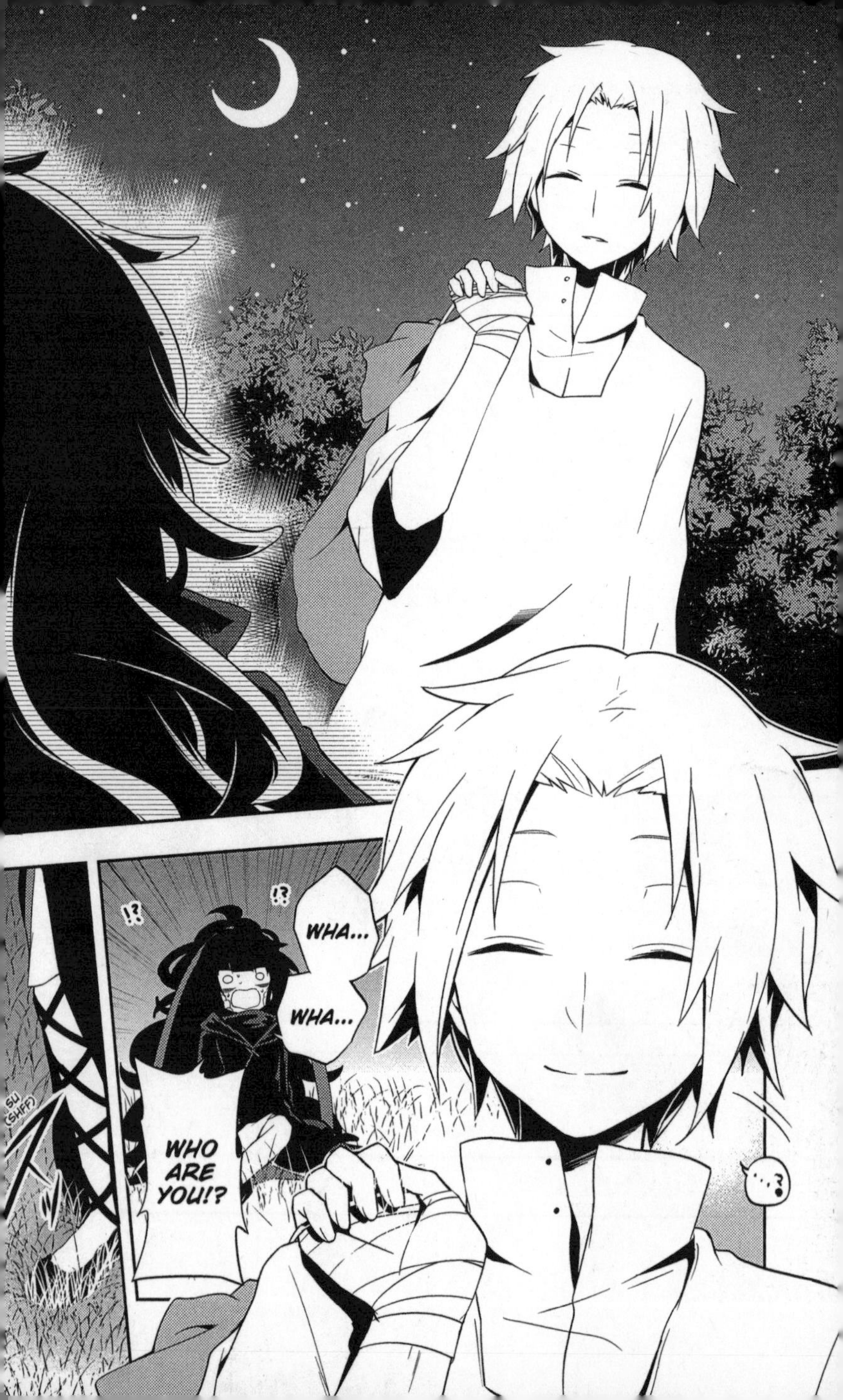
...?
!?
!?
WHA...
WHA...
WHO ARE YOU!?
SU (SHFF)

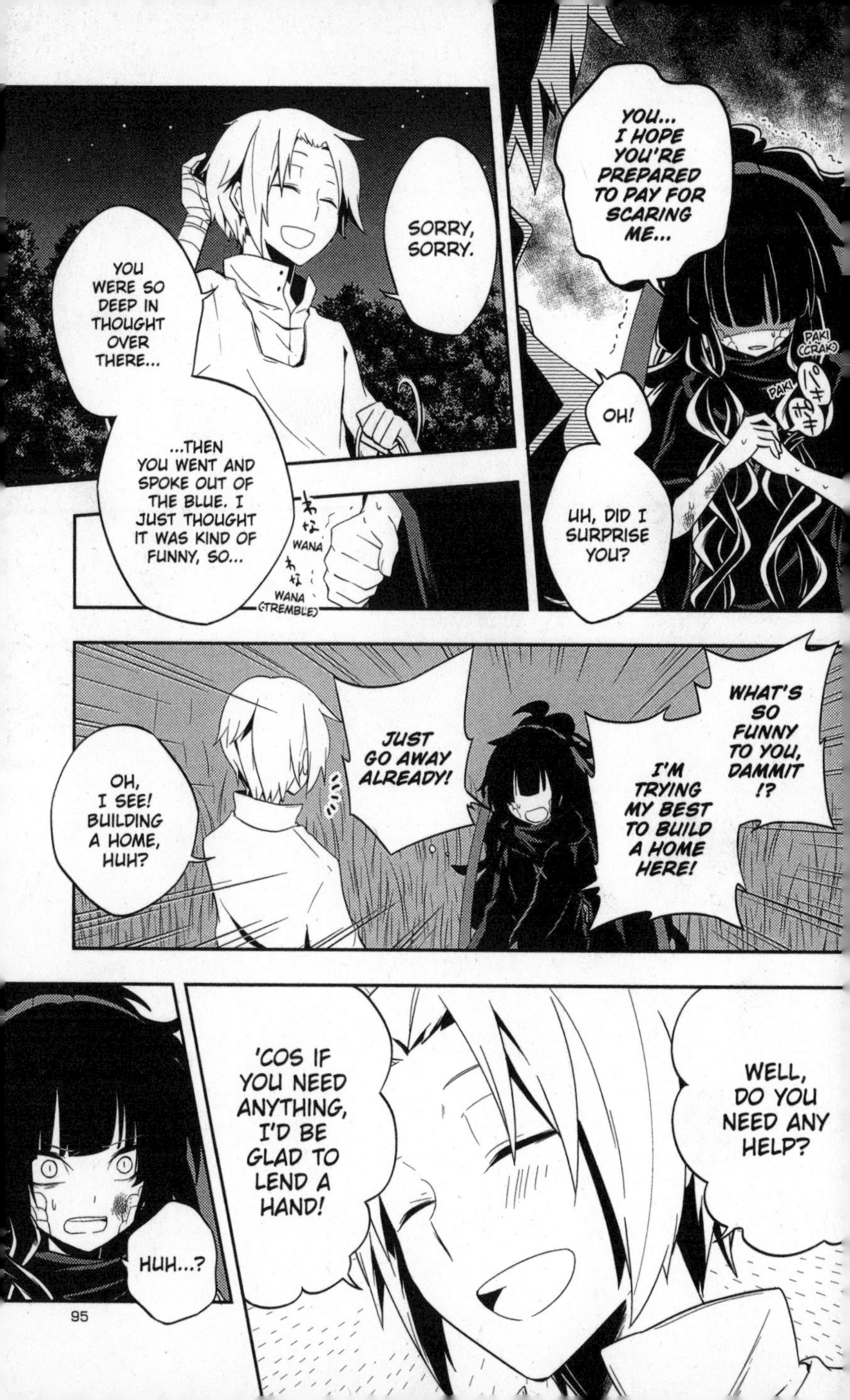
YOU... I HOPE YOU'RE PREPARED TO PAY FOR SCARING ME...
PAKI (CRAK)
PAKI
OH!
UH, DID I SURPRISE YOU?
SORRY, SORRY.
YOU WERE SO DEEP IN THOUGHT OVER THERE...
...THEN YOU WENT AND SPOKE OUT OF THE BLUE. I JUST THOUGHT IT WAS KIND OF FUNNY, SO...
WANA
WANA (TREMBLE)
WHAT'S SO FUNNY TO YOU, DAMMIT!?
I'M TRYING MY BEST TO BUILD A HOME HERE!
JUST GO AWAY ALREADY!
OH, I SEE! BUILDING A HOME, HUH?
WELL, DO YOU NEED ANY HELP?
'COS IF YOU NEED ANYTHING, I'D BE GLAD TO LEND A HAND!
HUH...?

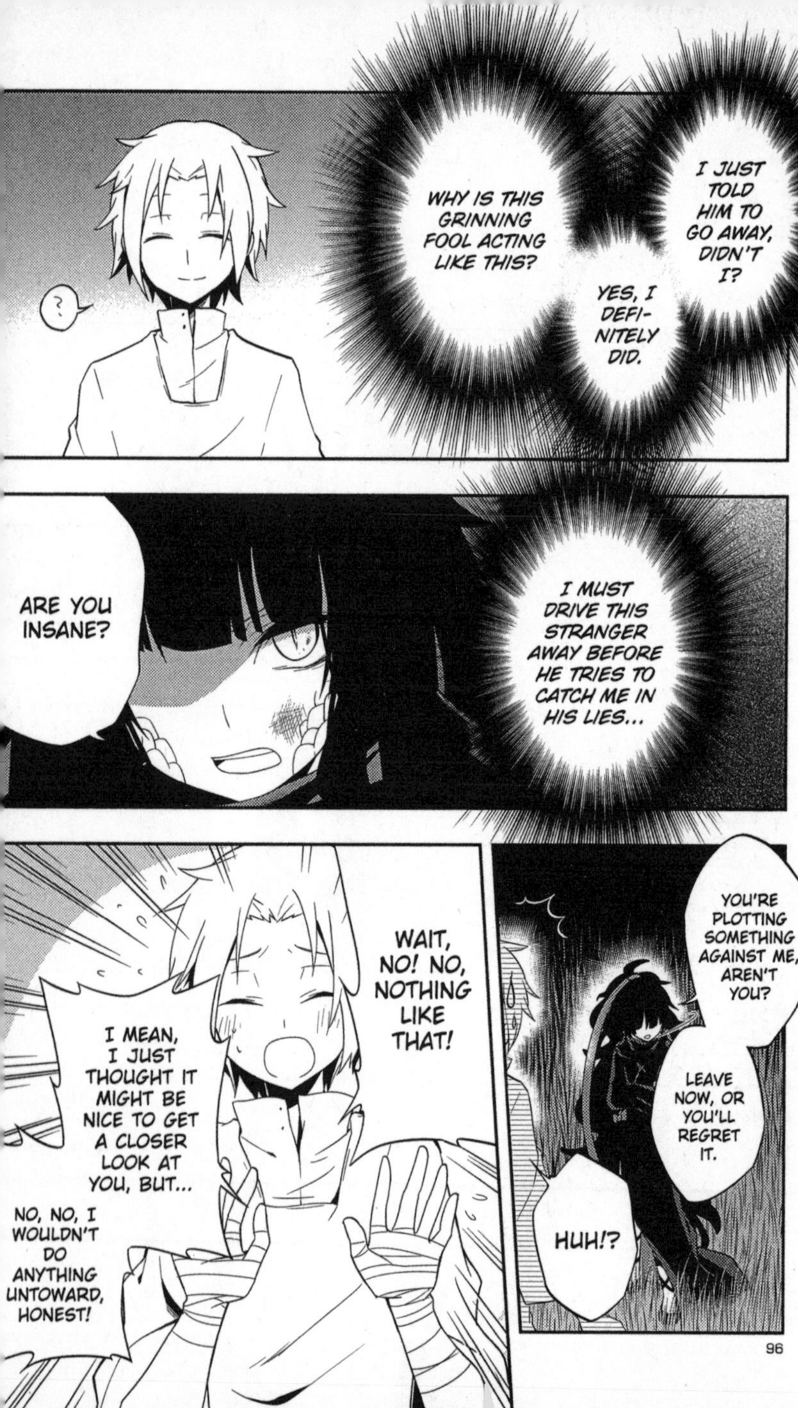
I JUST TOLD HIM TO GO AWAY, DIDN'T I?
YES, I DEFINITELY DID.
WHY IS THIS GRINNING FOOL ACTING LIKE THIS?
?
I MUST DRIVE THIS STRANGER AWAY BEFORE HE TRIES TO CATCH ME IN HIS LIES...
ARE YOU INSANE?
YOU'RE PLOTTING SOMETHING AGAINST ME, AREN'T YOU?
LEAVE NOW, OR YOU'LL REGRET IT.
HUH!?
WAIT, NO! NO, NOTHING LIKE THAT!
I MEAN, I JUST THOUGHT IT MIGHT BE NICE TO GET A CLOSER LOOK AT YOU, BUT...
NO, NO, I WOULDN'T DO ANYTHING UNTOWARD, HONEST!

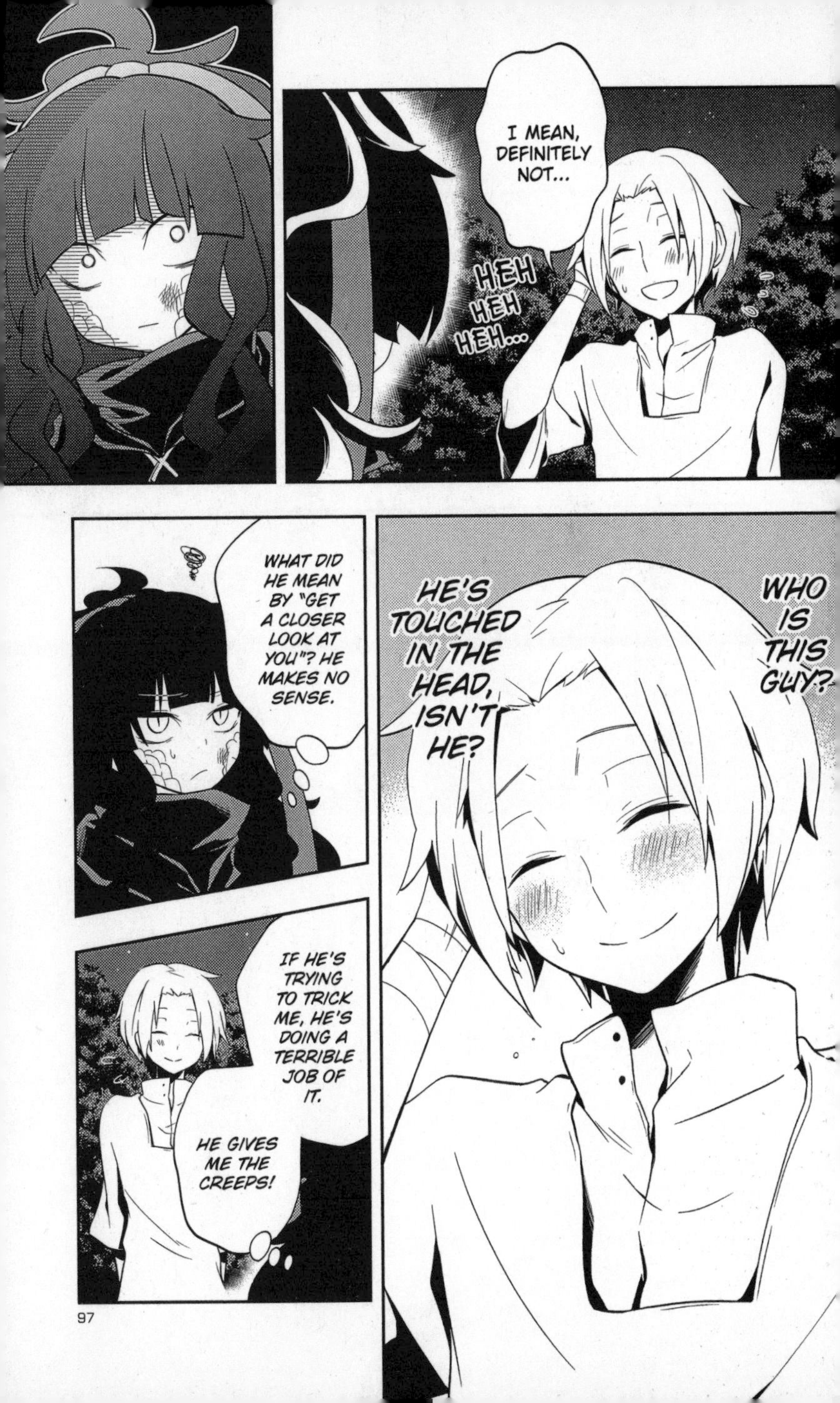
I MEAN, DEFINITELY NOT...
HEH HEH HEH...
WHO IS THIS GUY?
HE'S TOUCHED IN THE HEAD, ISN'T HE?
WHAT DID HE MEAN BY "GET A CLOSER LOOK AT YOU"? HE MAKES NO SENSE.
IF HE'S TRYING TO TRICK ME, HE'S DOING A TERRIBLE JOB OF IT.
HE GIVES ME THE CREEPS!

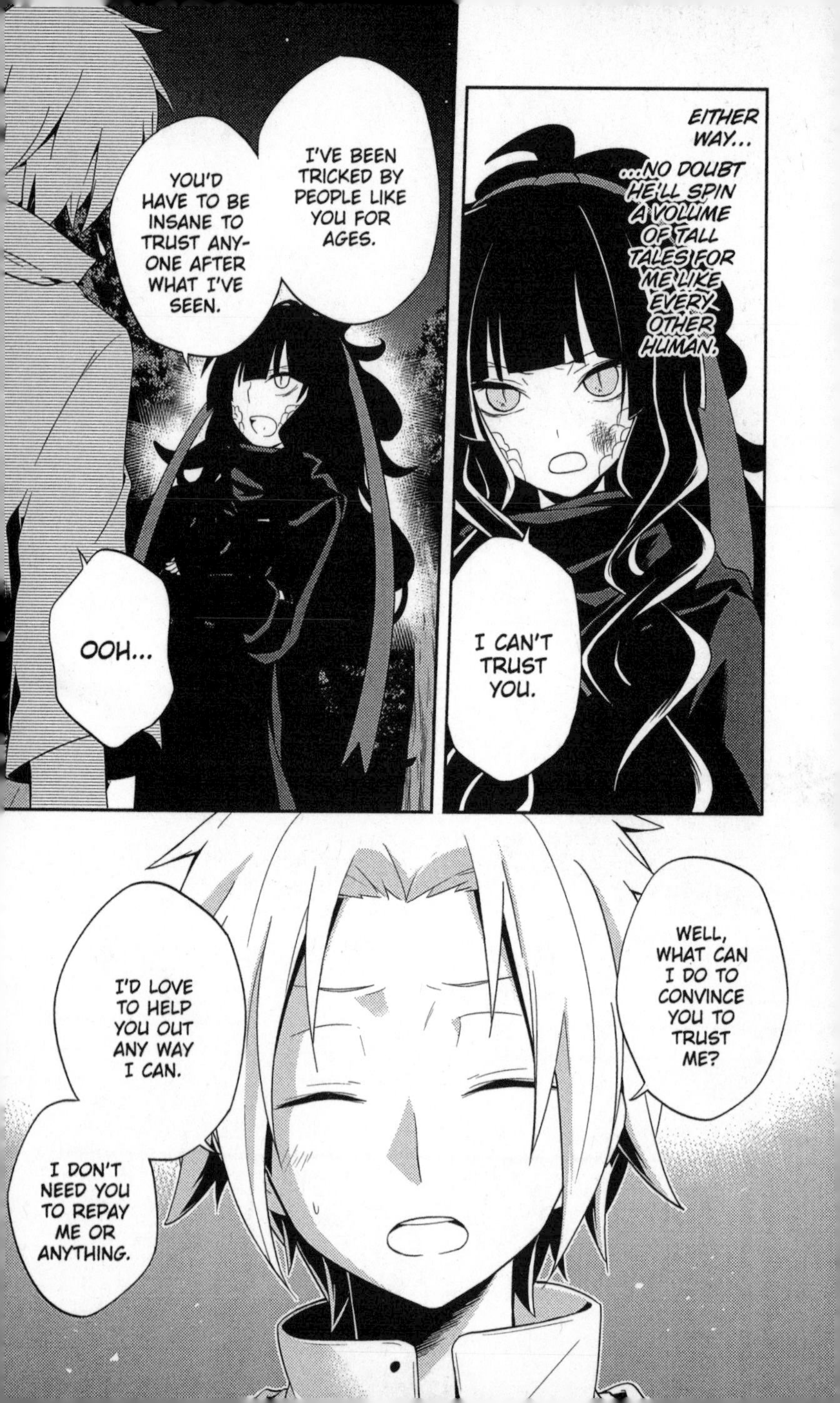
EITHER WAY...
...NO DOUBT HE'LL SPIN A VOLUME OF TALL TALES FOR ME LIKE EVERY OTHER HUMAN.
I CAN'T TRUST YOU.
I'VE BEEN TRICKED BY PEOPLE LIKE YOU FOR AGES.
YOU'D HAVE TO BE INSANE TO TRUST ANY-ONE AFTER WHAT I'VE SEEN.
OOH...
WELL, WHAT CAN I DO TO CONVINCE YOU TO TRUST ME?
I'D LOVE TO HELP YOU OUT ANY WAY I CAN.
I DON'T NEED YOU TO REPAY ME OR ANYTHING.

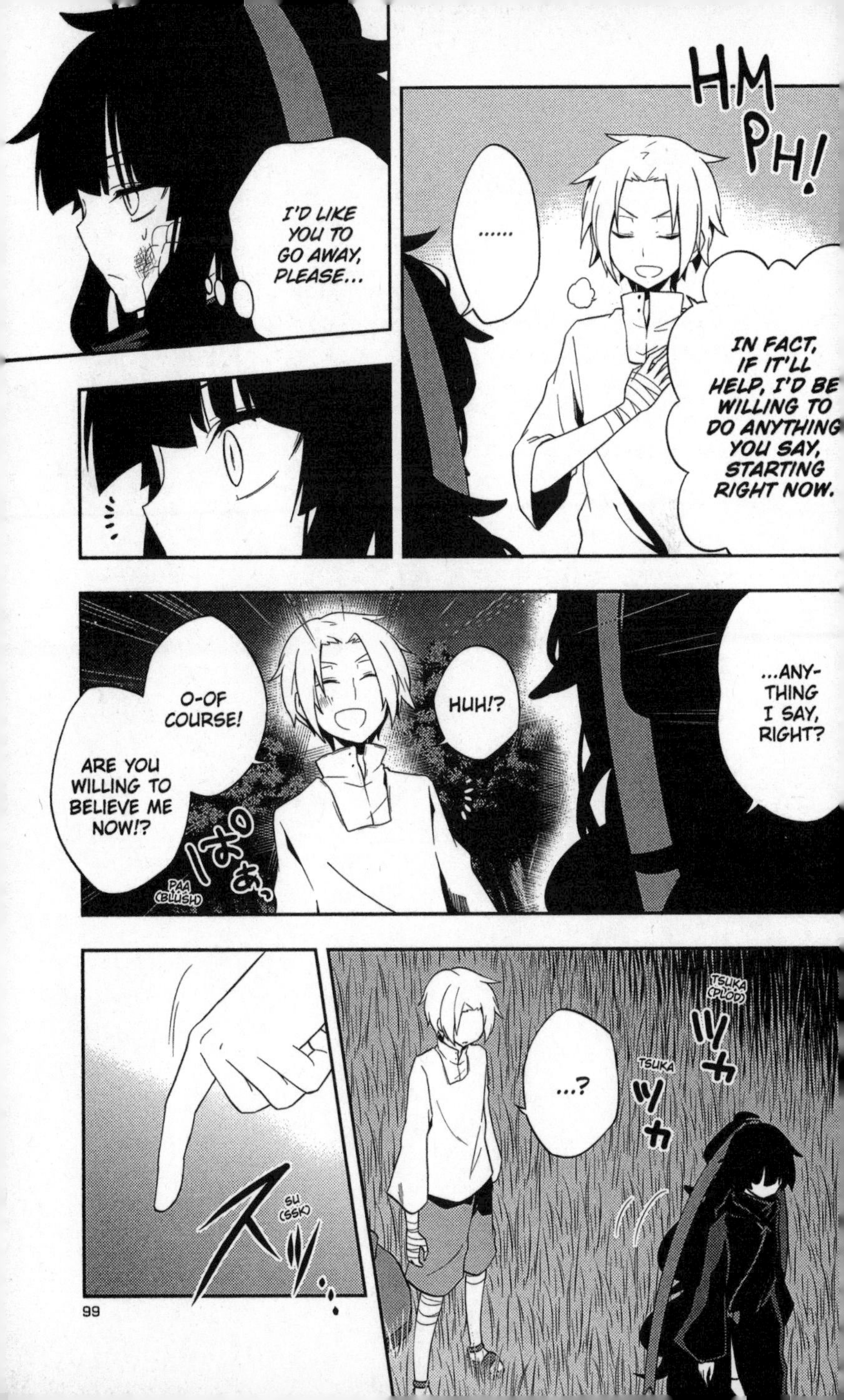
HMPH!
......
IN FACT, IF IT'LL HELP, I'D BE WILLING TO DO ANYTHING YOU SAY, STARTING RIGHT NOW.
I'D LIKE YOU TO GO AWAY, PLEASE...
...ANY-THING I SAY, RIGHT?
HUH!?
O-OF COURSE!
ARE YOU WILLING TO BELIEVE ME NOW!?
ぱぁっ
PAA (BLUSH)
ツカ
TSUKA (PLOD)
ツカ
TSUKA
...?
スッ
SU (SSK)

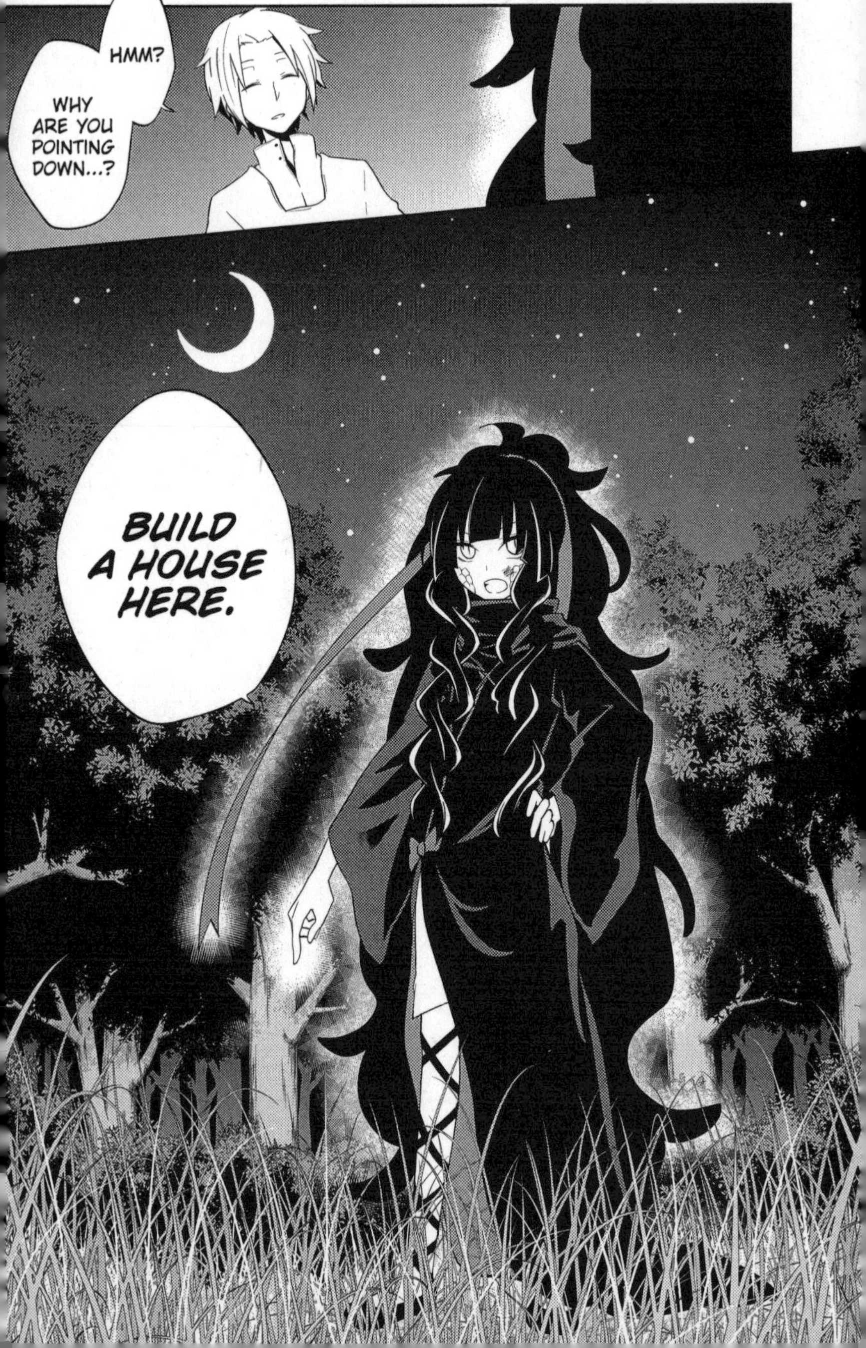
HMM?
WHY ARE YOU POINTING DOWN...?
BUILD A HOUSE HERE.

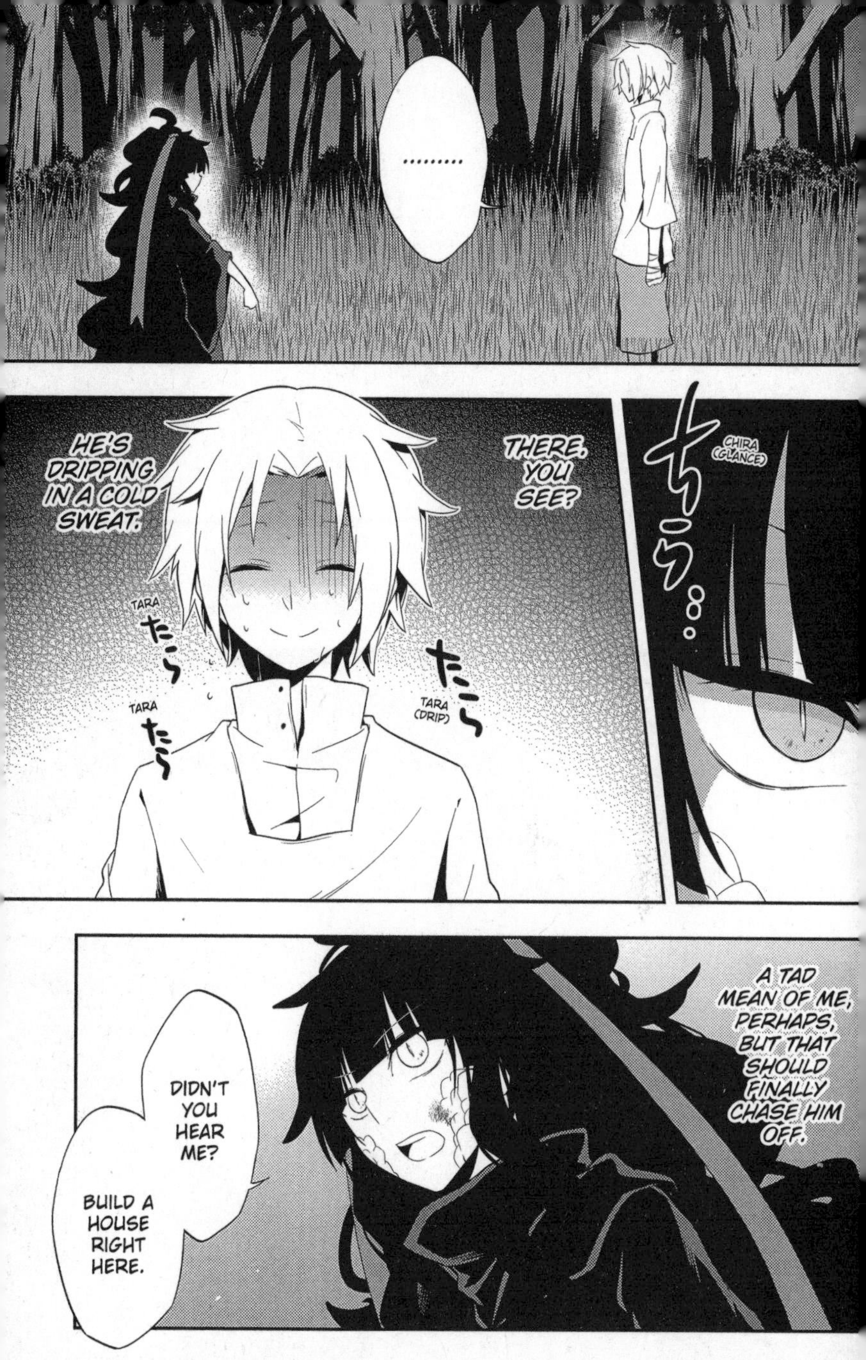
....
ちら
CHIRA (GLANCE)
THERE. YOU SEE?
HE'S DRIPPING IN A COLD SWEAT.
たら
TARA (DRIP)
たら
TARA
たら
TARA
A TAD MEAN OF ME, PERHAPS, BUT THAT SHOULD FINALLY CHASE HIM OFF.
DIDN'T YOU HEAR ME?
BUILD A HOUSE RIGHT HERE.

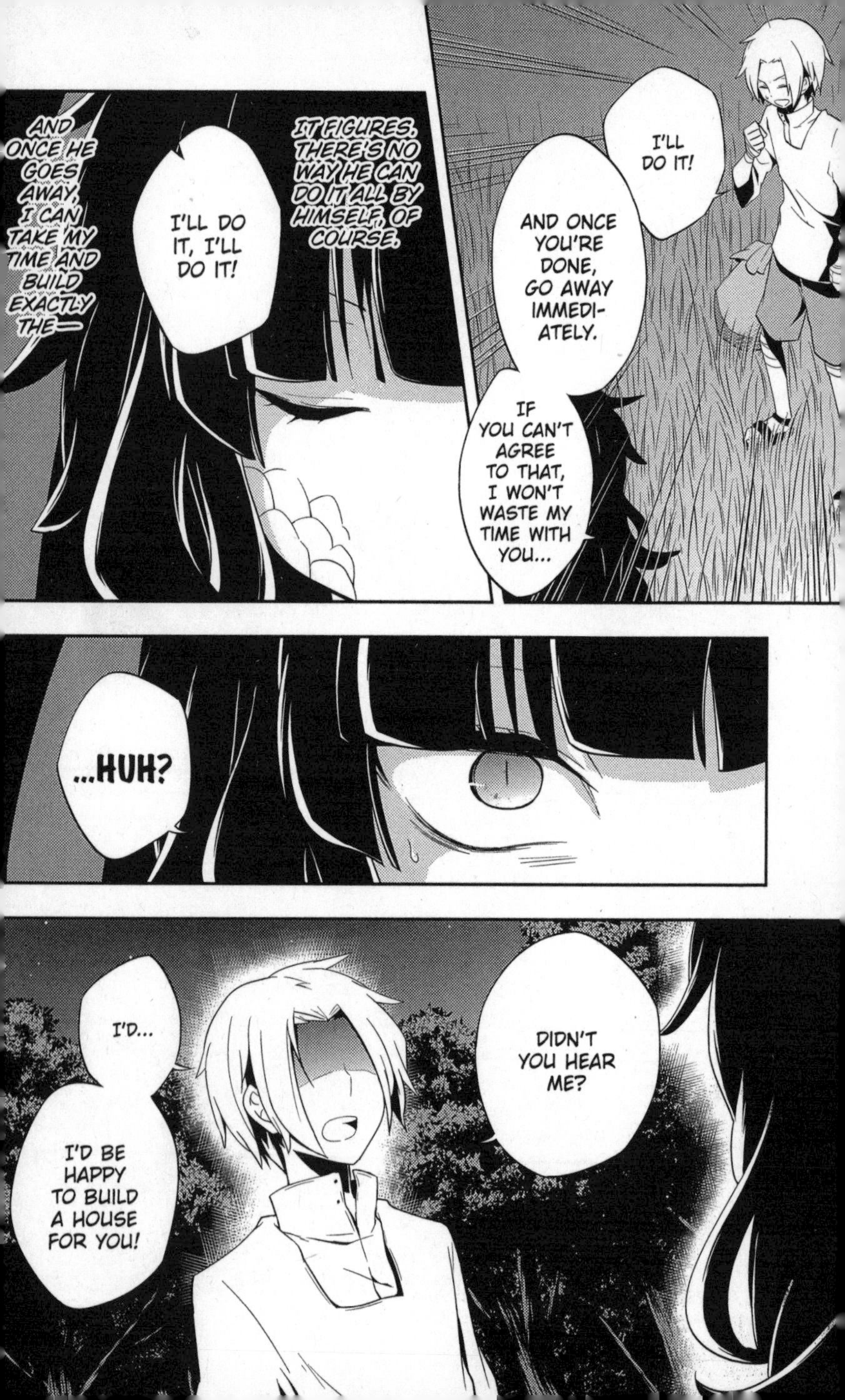
I'LL DO IT!
AND ONCE YOU'RE DONE, GO AWAY IMMEDIATELY.
IF YOU CAN'T AGREE TO THAT, I WON'T WASTE MY TIME WITH YOU...
IT FIGURES. THERE'S NO WAY HE CAN DO IT ALL BY HIMSELF, OF COURSE.
I'LL DO IT, I'LL DO IT!
AND ONCE HE GOES AWAY, I CAN TAKE MY TIME AND BUILD EXACTLY THE—
...HUH?
DIDN'T YOU HEAR ME?
I'D...
I'D BE HAPPY TO BUILD A HOUSE FOR YOU!

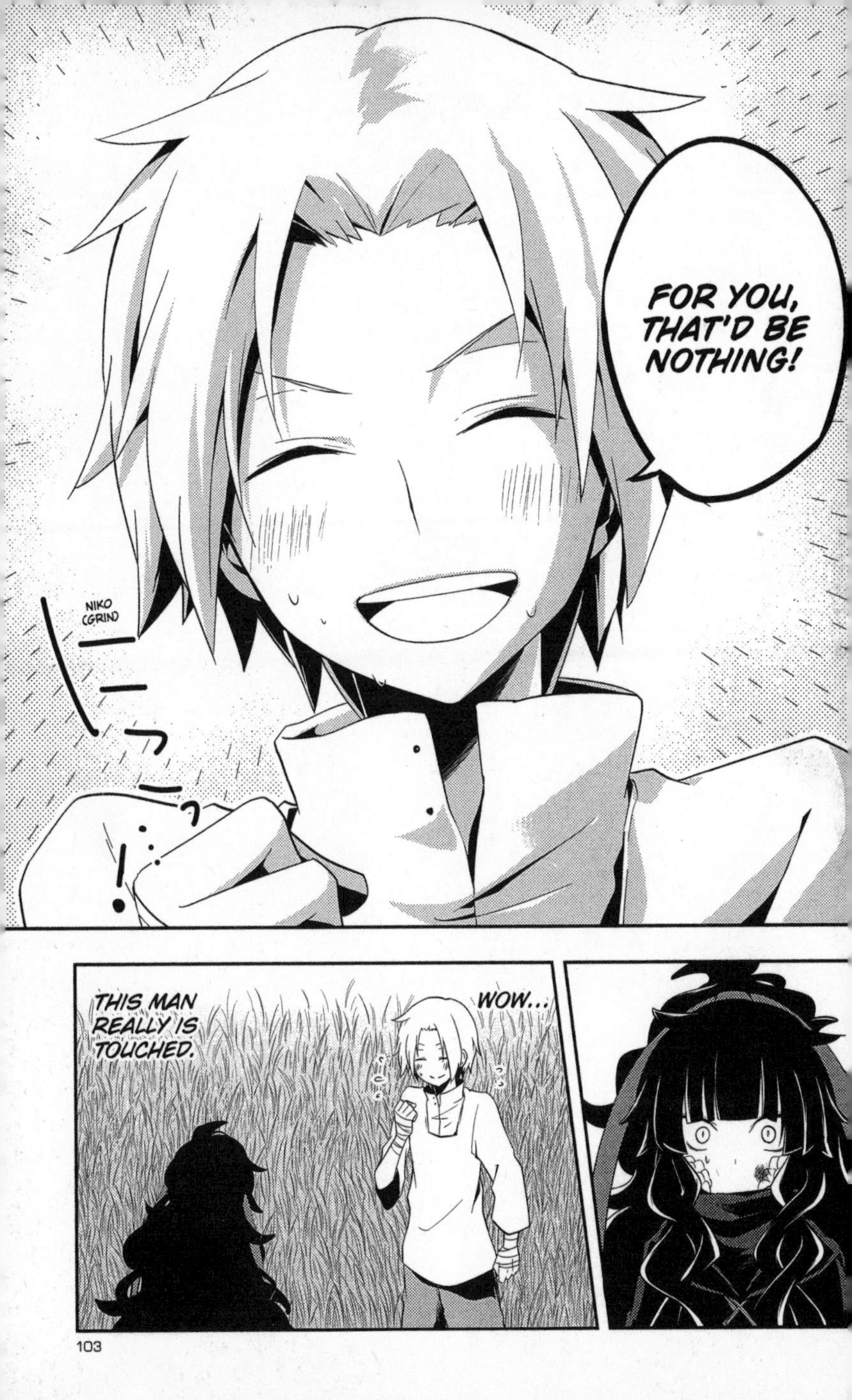
FOR YOU, THAT'D BE NOTHING!
NIKO (GRIN)
WOW...
THIS MAN REALLY IS TOUCHED.

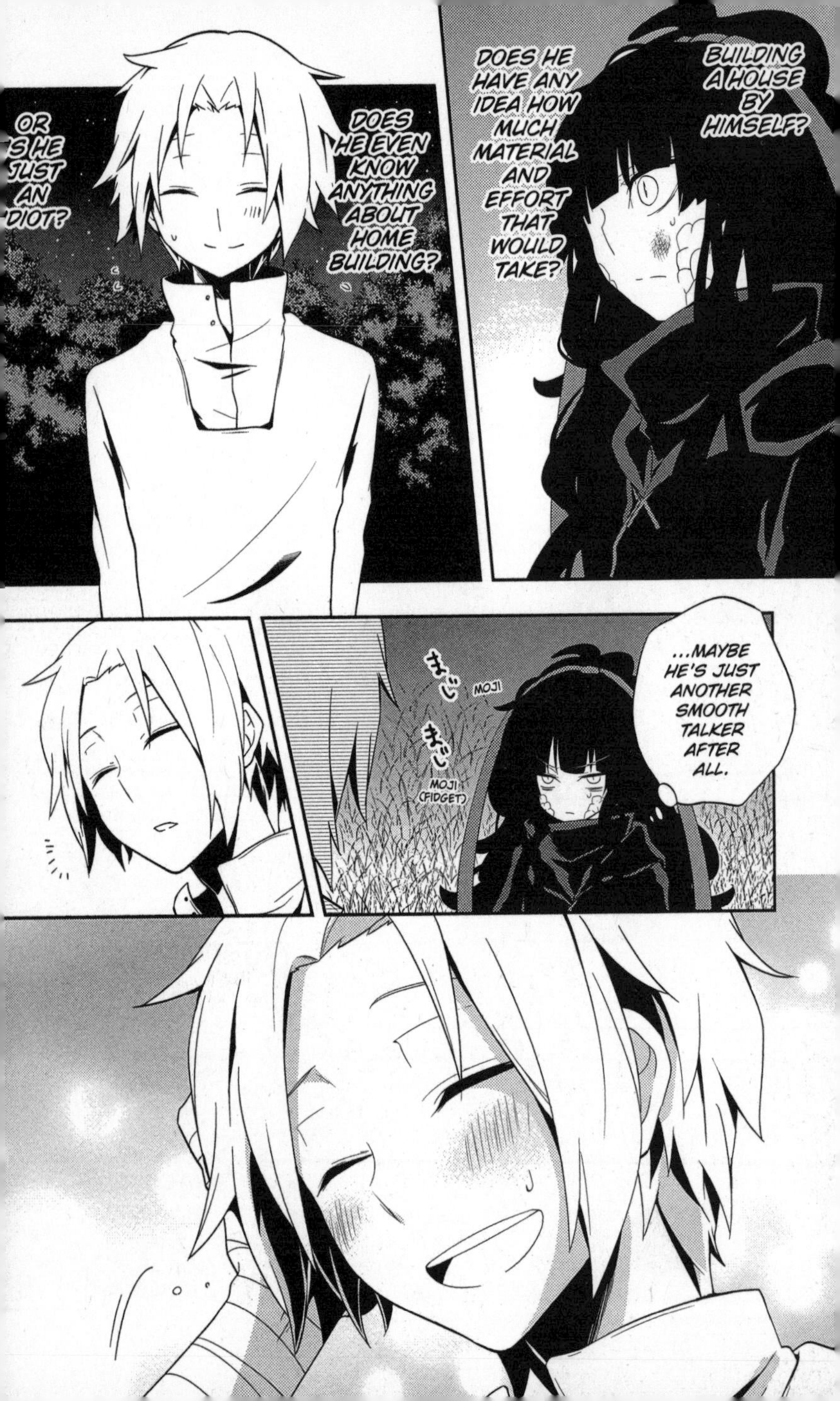
BUILDING A HOUSE BY HIMSELF?
DOES HE HAVE ANY IDEA HOW MUCH MATERIAL AND EFFORT THAT WOULD TAKE?
DOES HE EVEN KNOW ANYTHING ABOUT HOME BUILDING?
OR S HE JUST AN DIOT?
...MAYBE HE'S JUST ANOTHER SMOOTH TALKER AFTER ALL.
もじ
MOJI
もじ
MOJI (FIDGET)

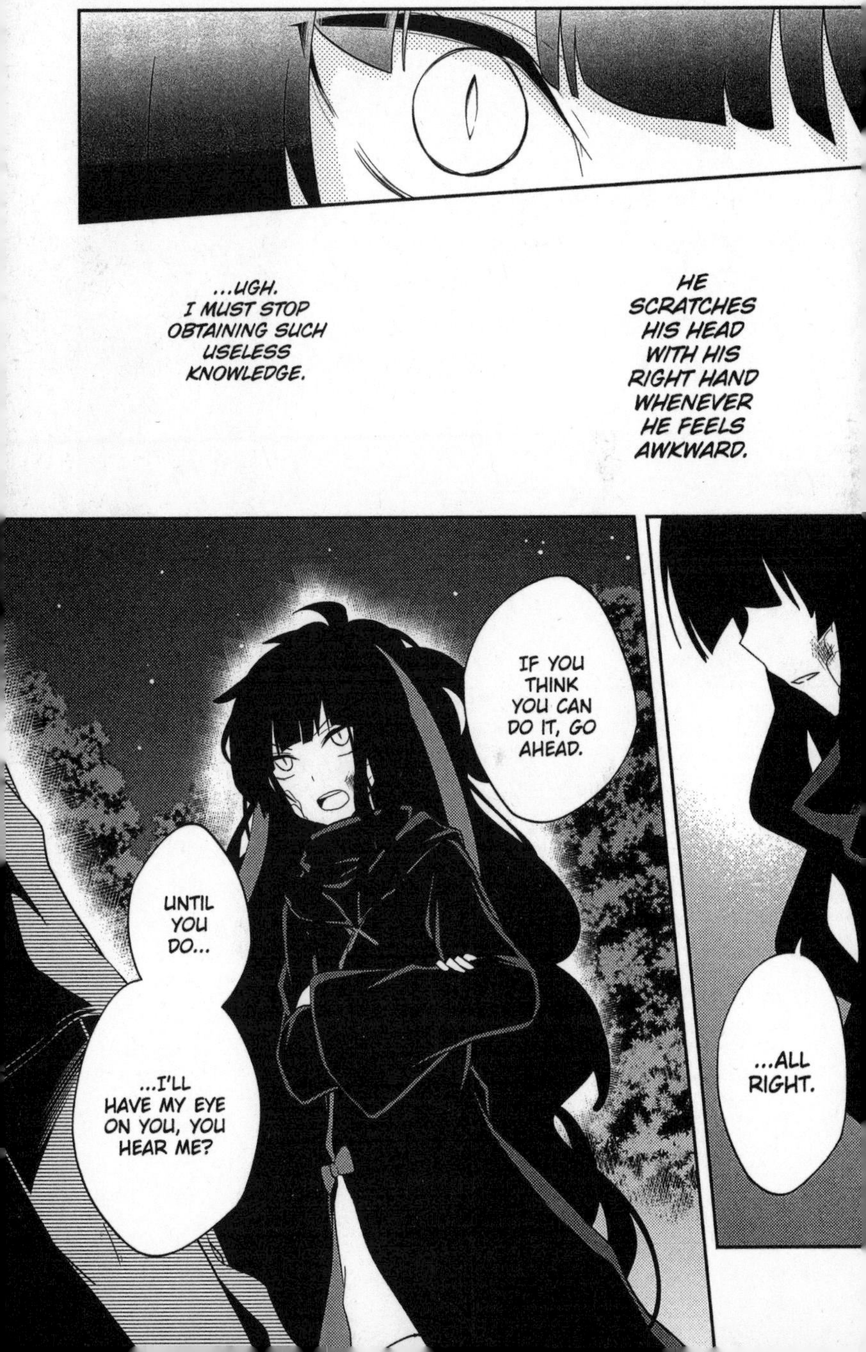
HE SCRATCHES HIS HEAD WITH HIS RIGHT HAND WHENEVER HE FEELS AWKWARD.
...UGH. I MUST STOP OBTAINING SUCH USELESS KNOWLEDGE.
...ALL RIGHT.
IF YOU THINK YOU CAN DO IT, GO AHEAD.
UNTIL YOU DO...
...I'LL HAVE MY EYE ON YOU, YOU HEAR ME?

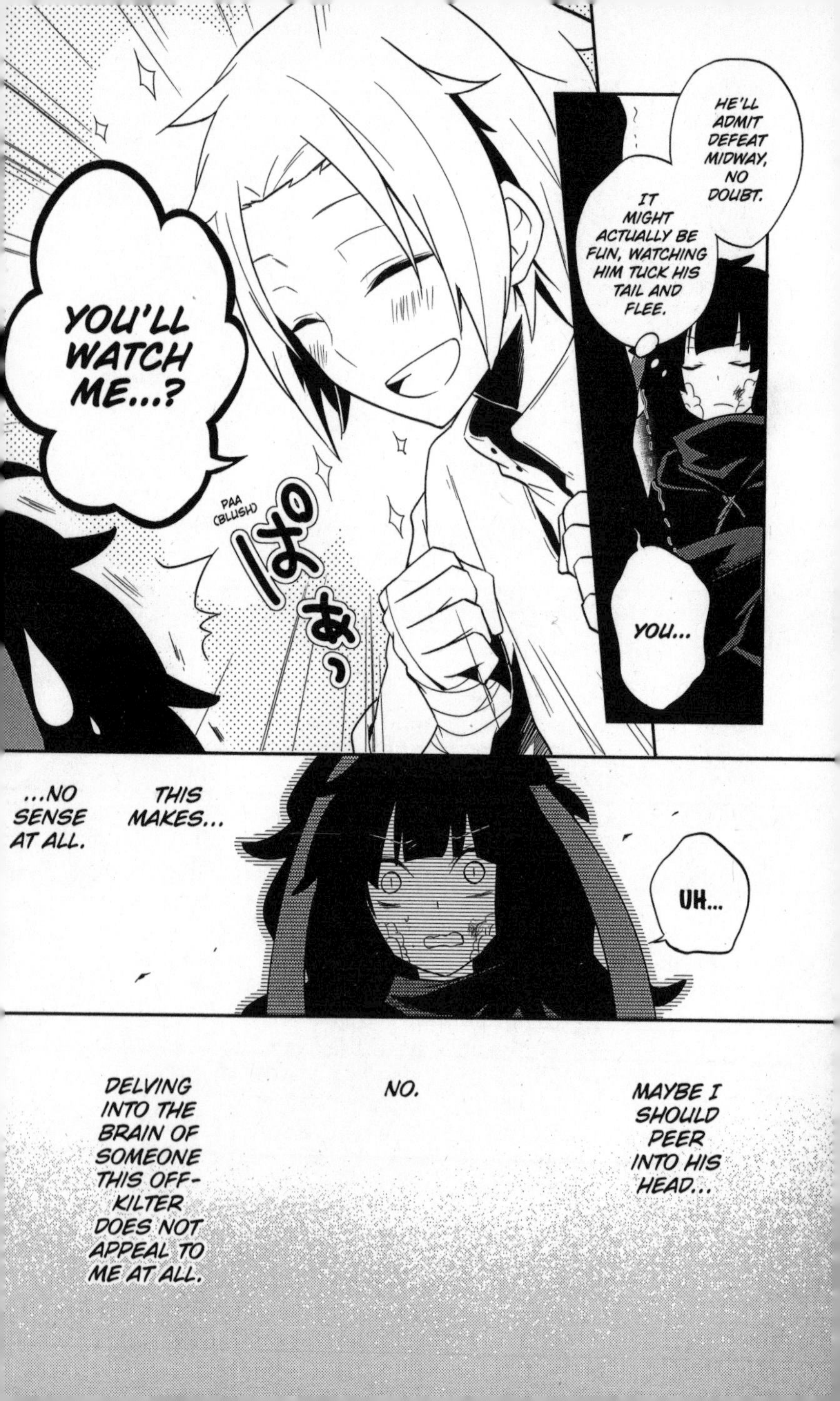
HE'LL ADMIT DEFEAT MIDWAY, NO DOUBT.
IT MIGHT ACTUALLY BE FUN, WATCHING HIM TUCK HIS TAIL AND FLEE.
YOU...
YOU'LL WATCH ME...?
PAA (BLUSH)
ぱあっ
UH...
THIS MAKES...
...NO SENSE AT ALL.
MAYBE I SHOULD PEER INTO HIS HEAD...
NO.
DELVING INTO THE BRAIN OF SOMEONE THIS OFF-KILTER DOES NOT APPEAL TO ME AT ALL.

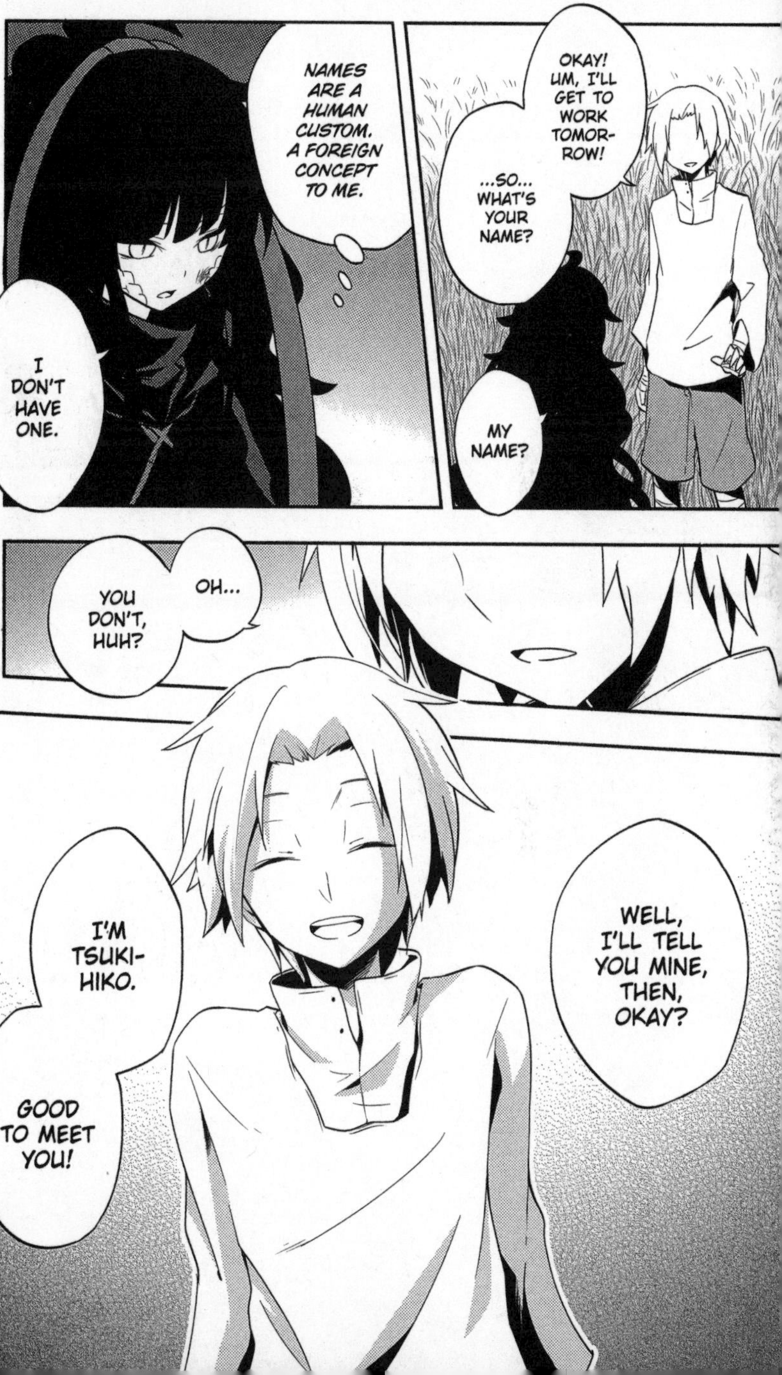
OKAY! UM, I'LL GET TO WORK TOMOR-ROW!
...SO... WHAT'S YOUR NAME?
MY NAME?
NAMES ARE A HUMAN CUSTOM. A FOREIGN CONCEPT TO ME.
I DON'T HAVE ONE.
OH...
YOU DON'T, HUH?
WELL, I'LL TELL YOU MINE, THEN, OKAY?
I'M TSUKI-HIKO.
GOOD TO MEET YOU!

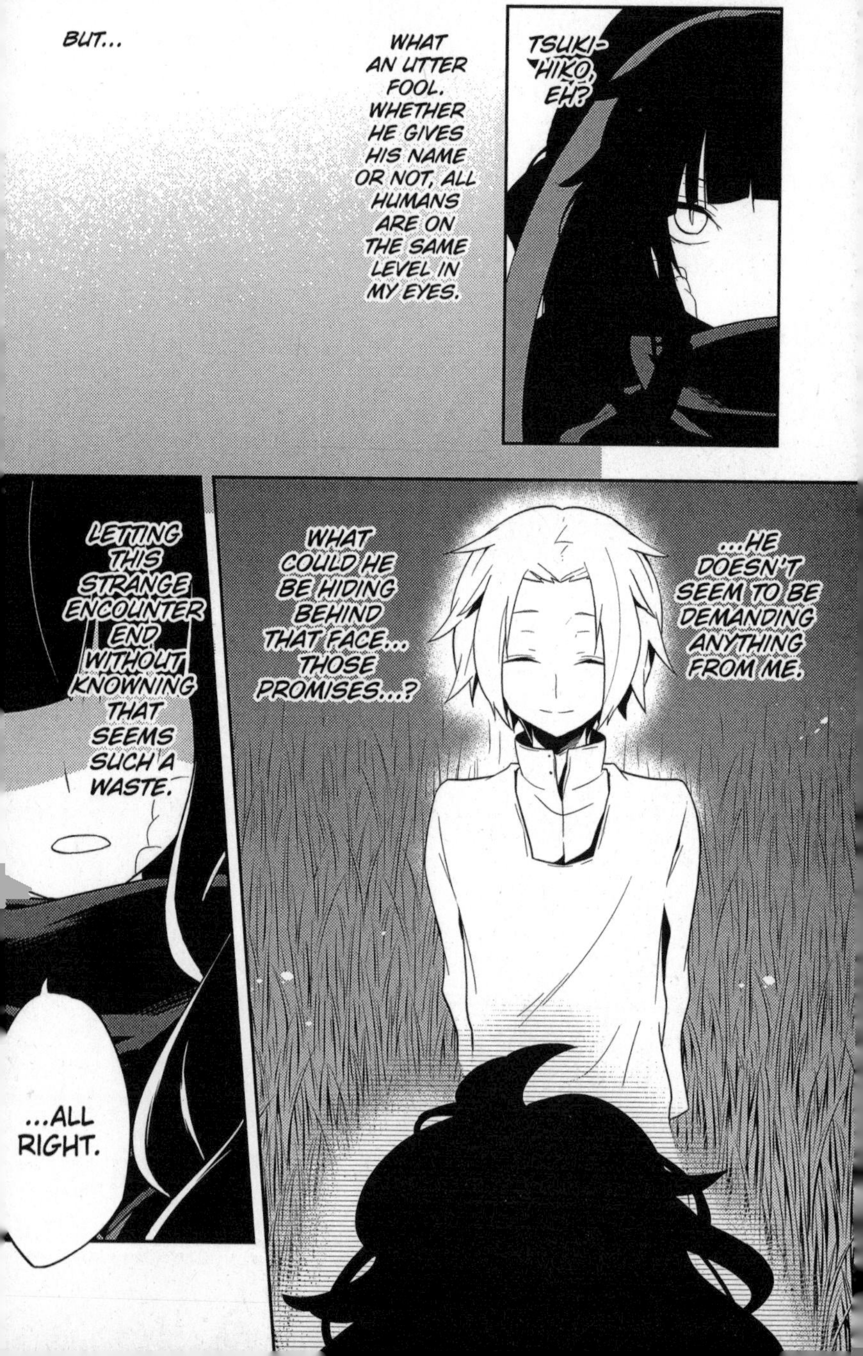
TSUKIHIKO, EH?
WHAT AN UTTER FOOL. WHETHER HE GIVES HIS NAME OR NOT, ALL HUMANS ARE ON THE SAME LEVEL IN MY EYES.
BUT...
...HE DOESN'T SEEM TO BE DEMANDING ANYTHING FROM ME.
WHAT COULD HE BE HIDING BEHIND THAT FACE... THOSE PROMISES...?
LETTING THIS STRANGE ENCOUNTER END WITHOUT KNOWNING THAT SEEMS SUCH A WASTE.
...ALL RIGHT.

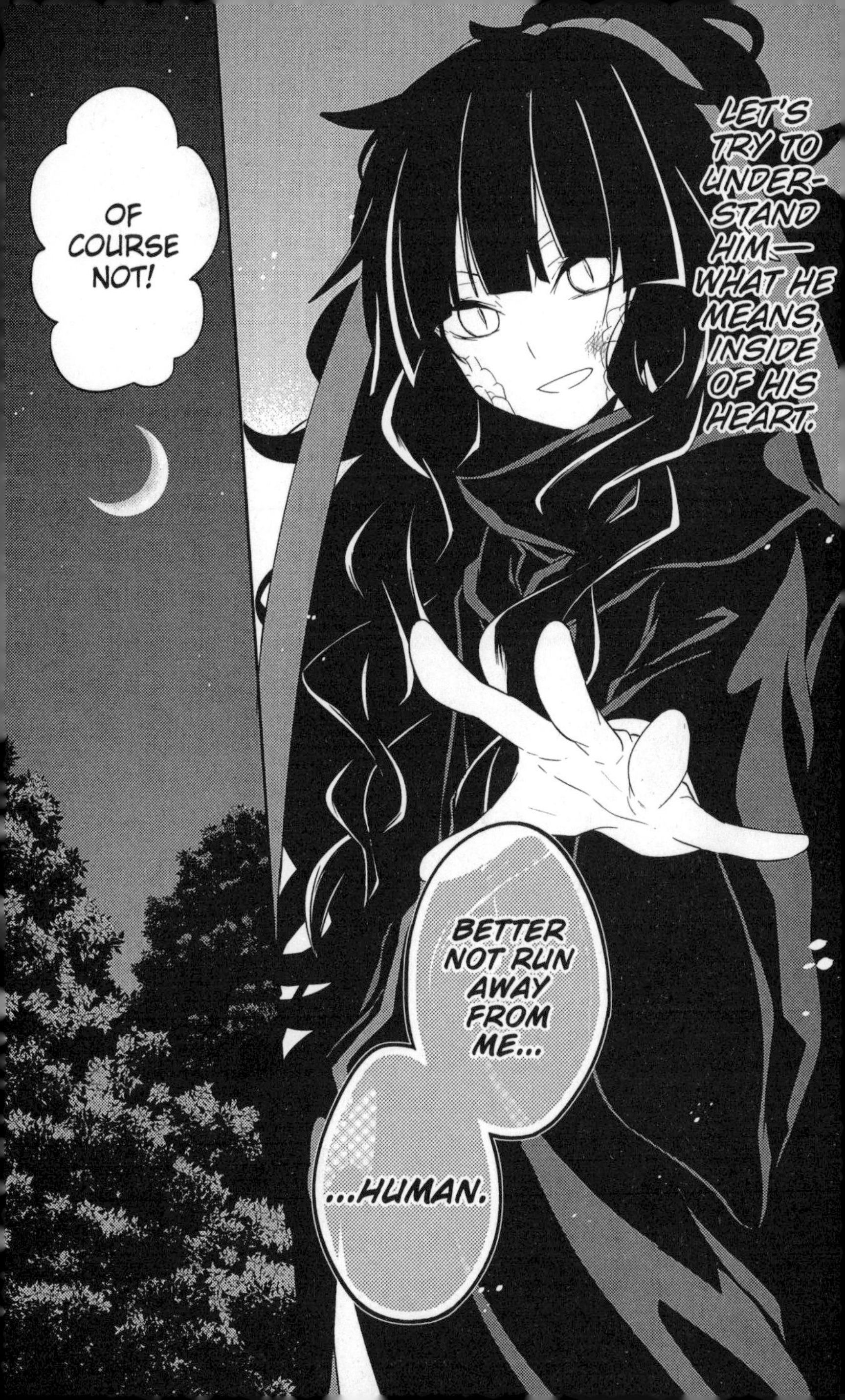
LET'S TRY TO UNDER-STAND HIM—WHAT HE MEANS, INSIDE OF HIS HEART.
OF COURSE NOT!
BETTER NOT RUN AWAY FROM ME...
...HUMAN.

KAGEROU
DAZE

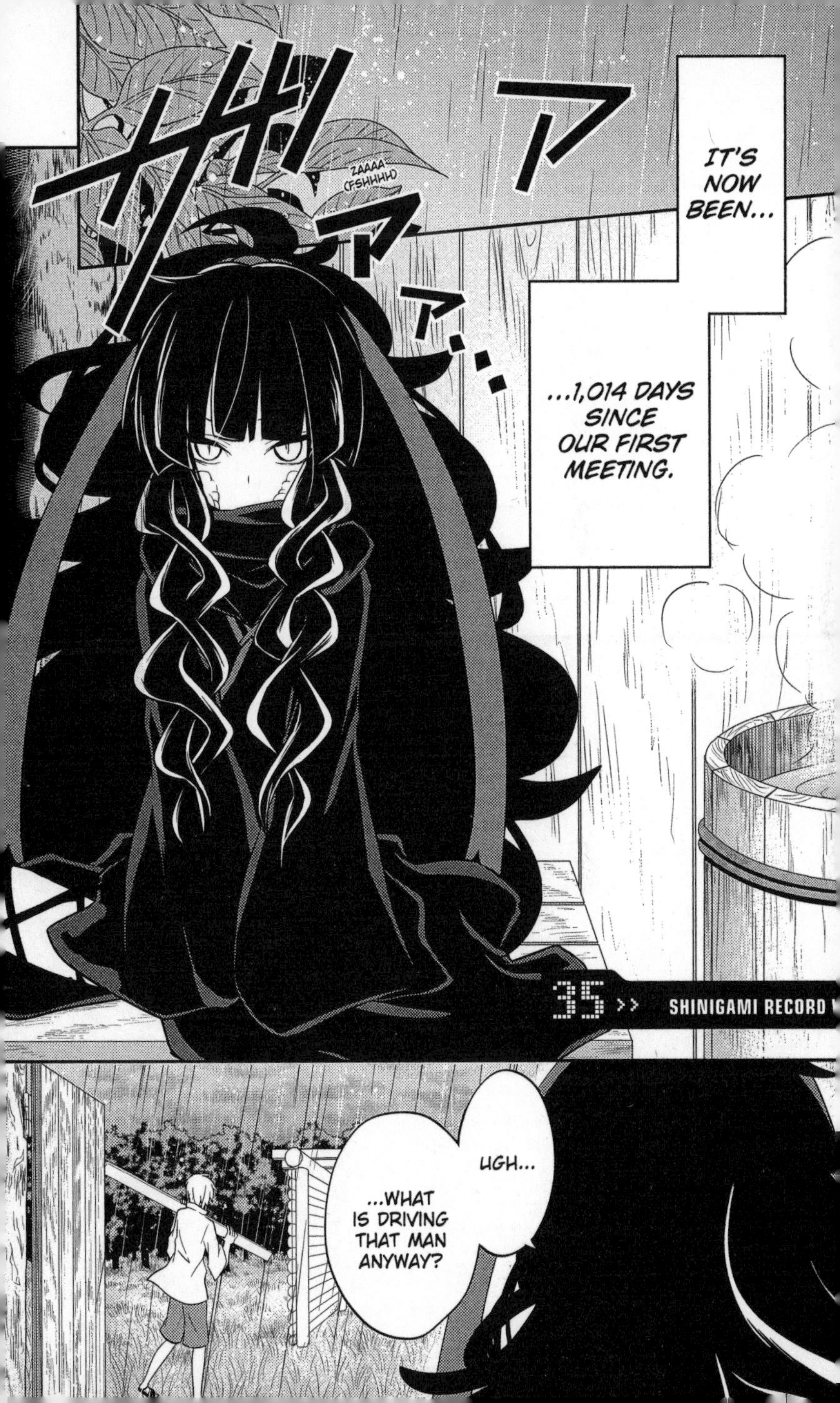
IT'S NOW BEEN...
ZAAAA (FSHHHH)
...1,014 DAYS SINCE OUR FIRST MEETING.
35 >> SHINIGAMI RECORD
UGH...
...WHAT IS DRIVING THAT MAN ANYWAY?

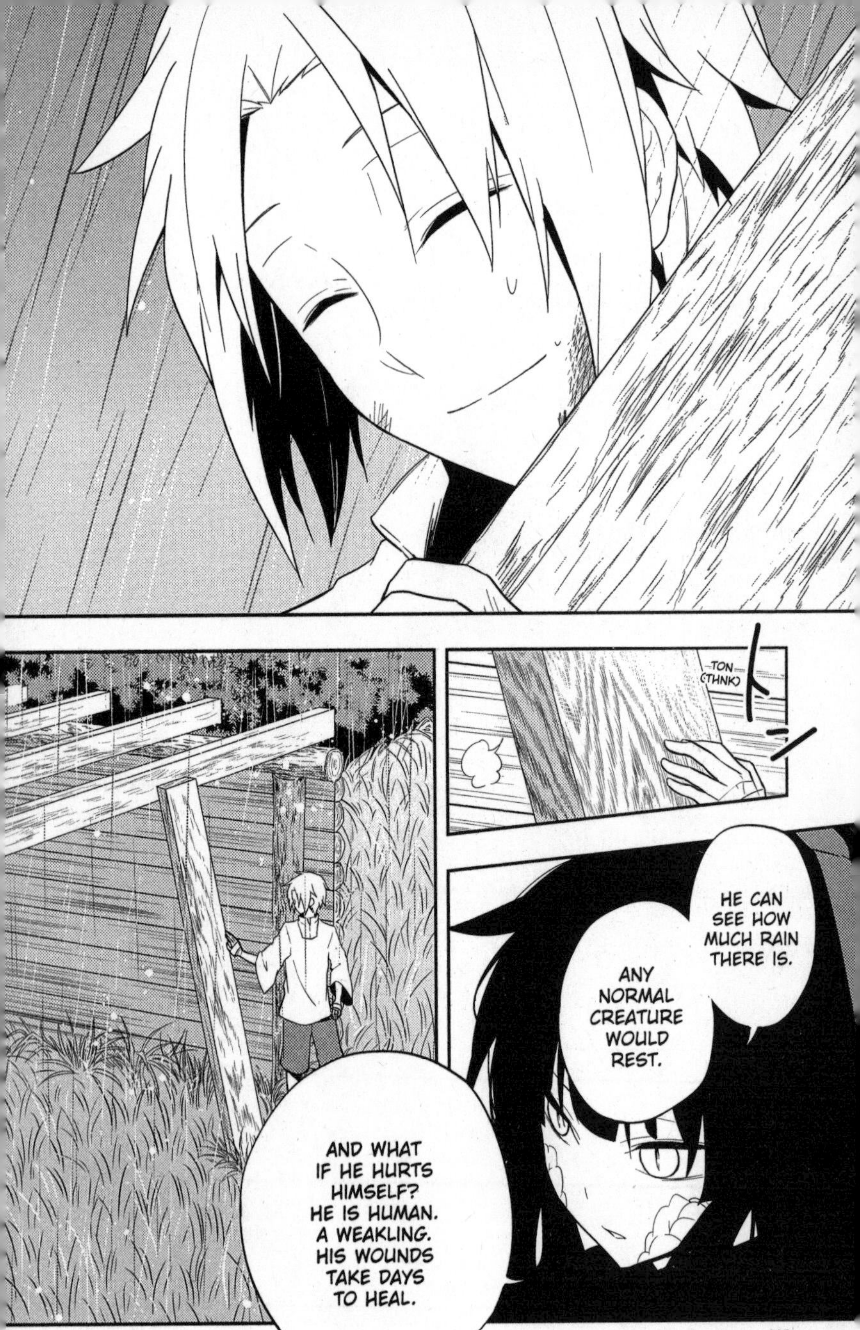
TON
(THNK)
HE CAN SEE HOW MUCH RAIN THERE IS.
ANY NORMAL CREATURE WOULD REST.
AND WHAT IF HE HURTS HIMSELF? HE IS HUMAN. A WEAKLING. HIS WOUNDS TAKE DAYS TO HEAL.

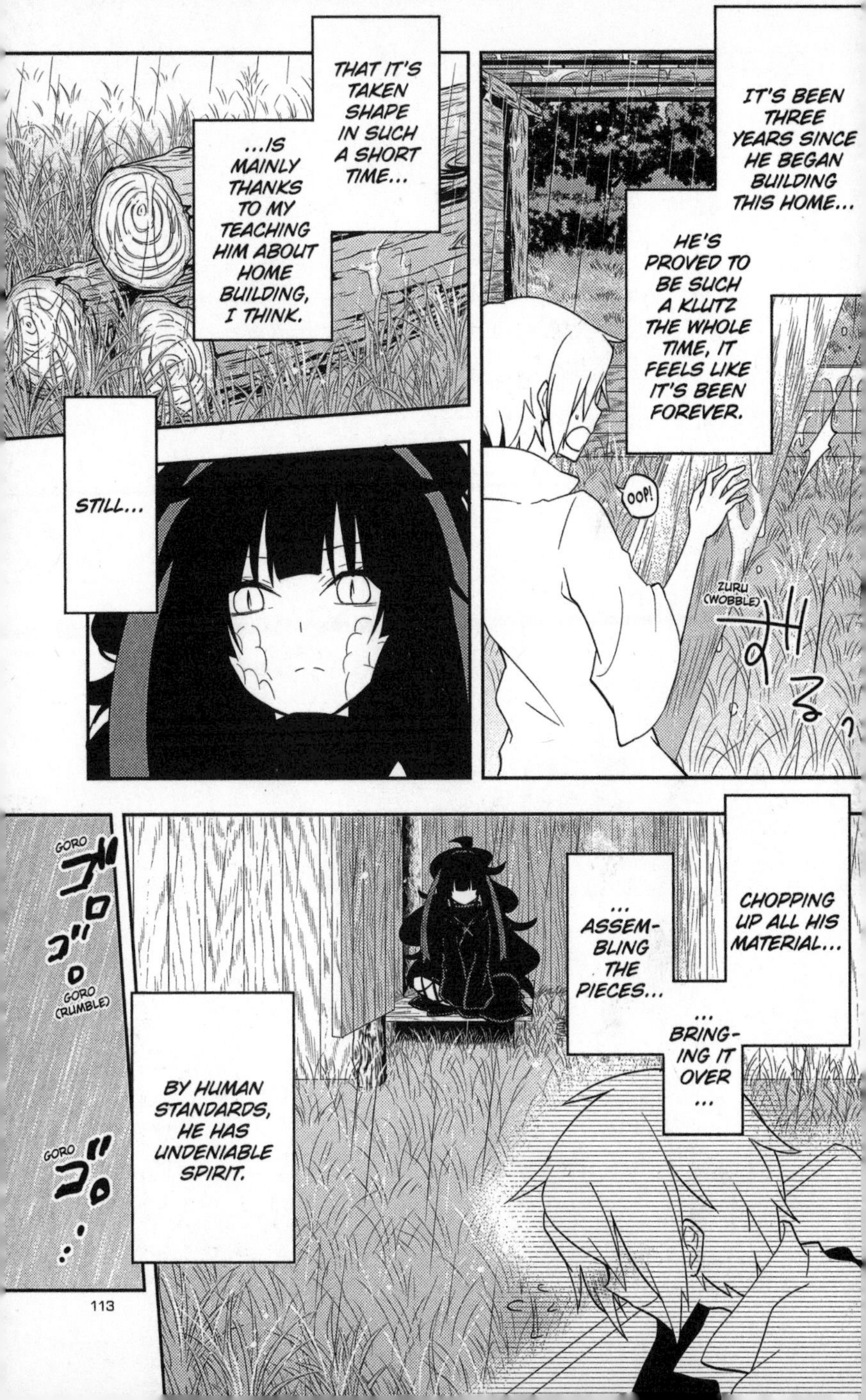
IT'S BEEN THREE YEARS SINCE HE BEGAN BUILDING THIS HOME...
HE'S PROVED TO BE SUCH A KLUTZ THE WHOLE TIME, IT FEELS LIKE IT'S BEEN FOREVER.
OOP!
ZURU (WOBBLE)
THAT IT'S TAKEN SHAPE IN SUCH A SHORT TIME...
...IS MAINLY THANKS TO MY TEACHING HIM ABOUT HOME BUILDING, I THINK.
STILL...
CHOPPING UP ALL HIS MATERIAL...
...ASSEM-BLING THE PIECES...
...BRING-ING IT OVER...
BY HUMAN STANDARDS, HE HAS UNDENIABLE SPIRIT.
GORO GORO (RUMBLE)
GORO

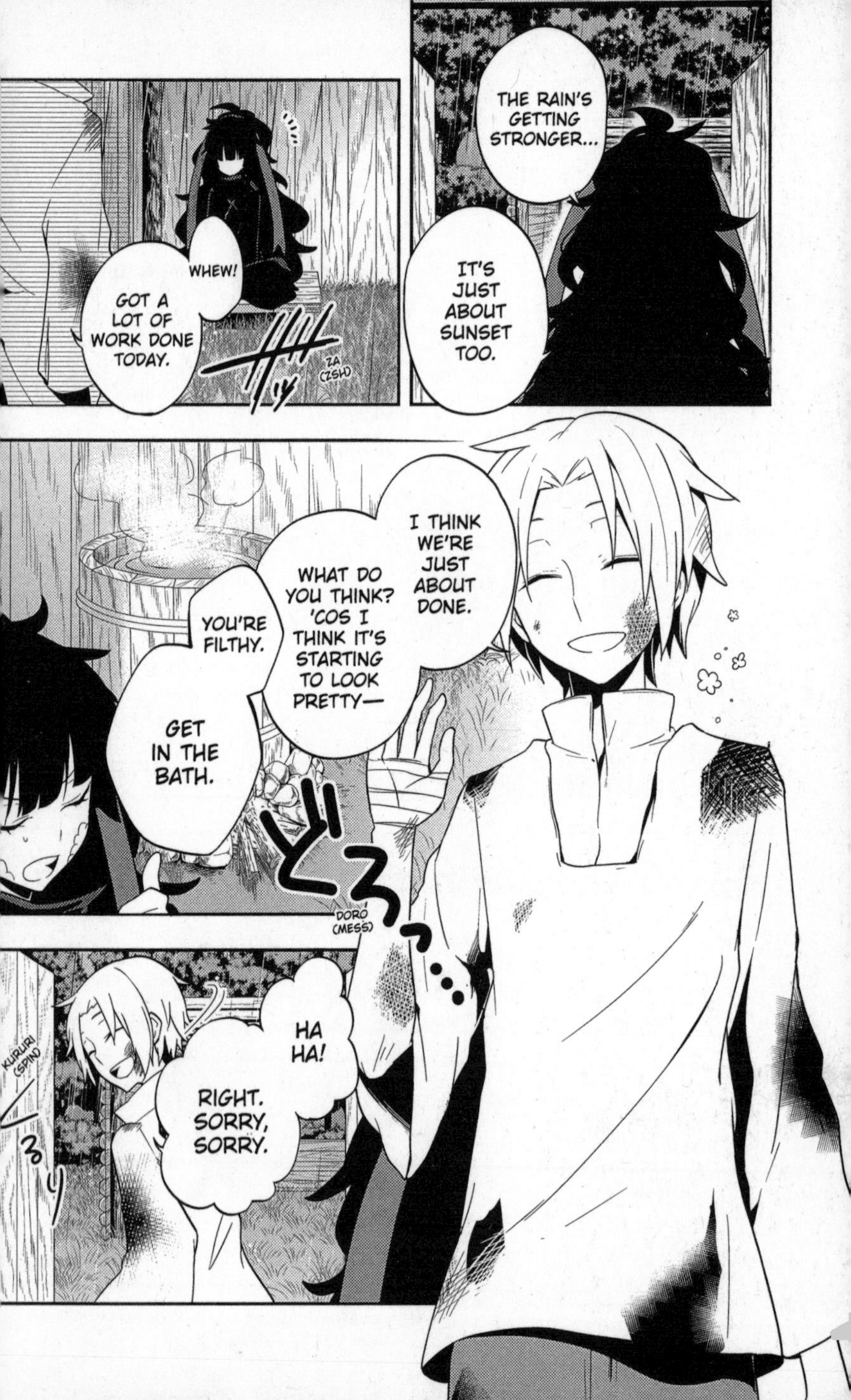
THE RAIN'S GETTING STRONGER...
IT'S JUST ABOUT SUNSET TOO.
WHEW!
GOT A LOT OF WORK DONE TODAY.
ZA (ZSH)
I THINK WE'RE JUST ABOUT DONE.
WHAT DO YOU THINK? 'COS I THINK IT'S STARTING TO LOOK PRETTY—
YOU'RE FILTHY.
GET IN THE BATH.
DORO (MESS)
HA HA!
RIGHT. SORRY, SORRY.
KURURI (SPIN)

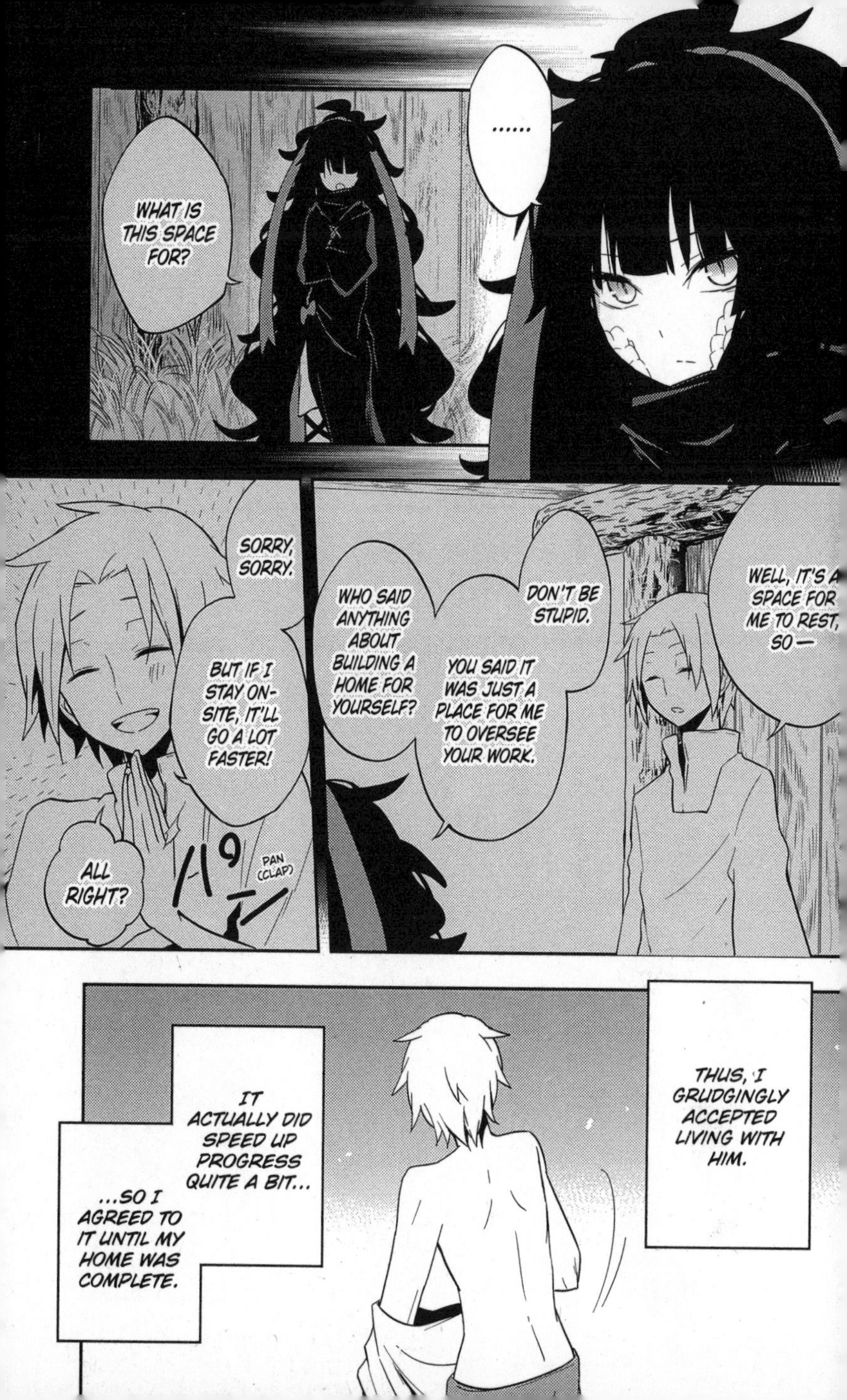
......
WHAT IS THIS SPACE FOR?
WELL, IT'S A SPACE FOR ME TO REST, SO—
DON'T BE STUPID.
WHO SAID ANYTHING ABOUT BUILDING A HOME FOR YOURSELF?
YOU SAID IT WAS JUST A PLACE FOR ME TO OVERSEE YOUR WORK.
SORRY, SORRY.
BUT IF I STAY ON-SITE, IT'LL GO A LOT FASTER!
PAN (CLAP)
ALL RIGHT?
THUS, I GRUDGINGLY ACCEPTED LIVING WITH HIM.
IT ACTUALLY DID SPEED UP PROGRESS QUITE A BIT...
...SO I AGREED TO IT UNTIL MY HOME WAS COMPLETE.

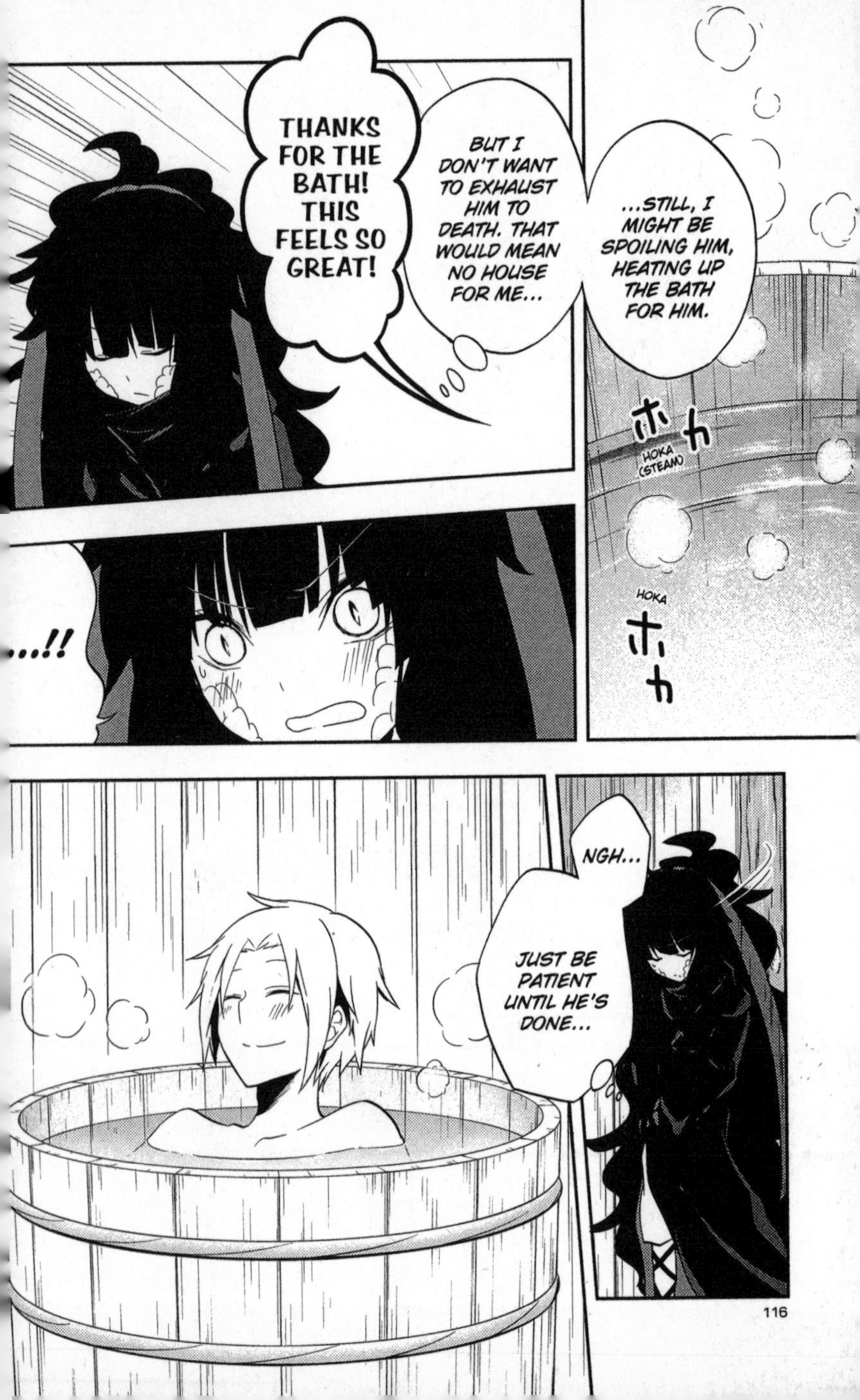
...STILL, I MIGHT BE SPOILING HIM, HEATING UP THE BATH FOR HIM.
ホカ
HOKA (STEAM)
HOKA
ホカ
BUT I DON'T WANT TO EXHAUST HIM TO DEATH. THAT WOULD MEAN NO HOUSE FOR ME...
THANKS FOR THE BATH! THIS FEELS SO GREAT!
...!!
NGH...
JUST BE PATIENT UNTIL HE'S DONE...

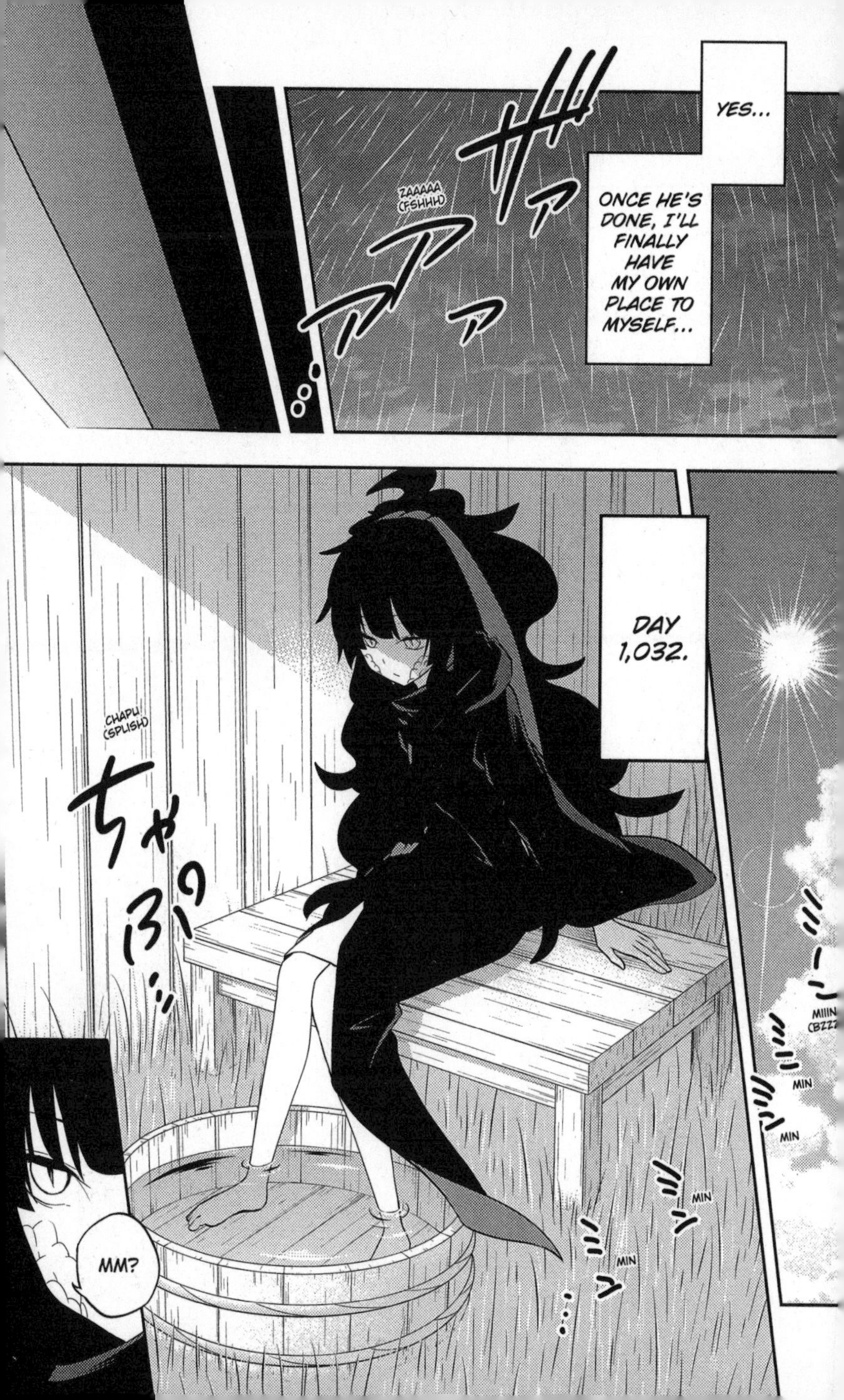
YES...
ONCE HE'S DONE, I'LL FINALLY HAVE MY OWN PLACE TO MYSELF...
ZAAAAA (FSHHH)
DAY 1,032.
MIIIN (BZZZ)
MIN
MIN
MIN
MIN
CHAPU (SPLISH)
MM?

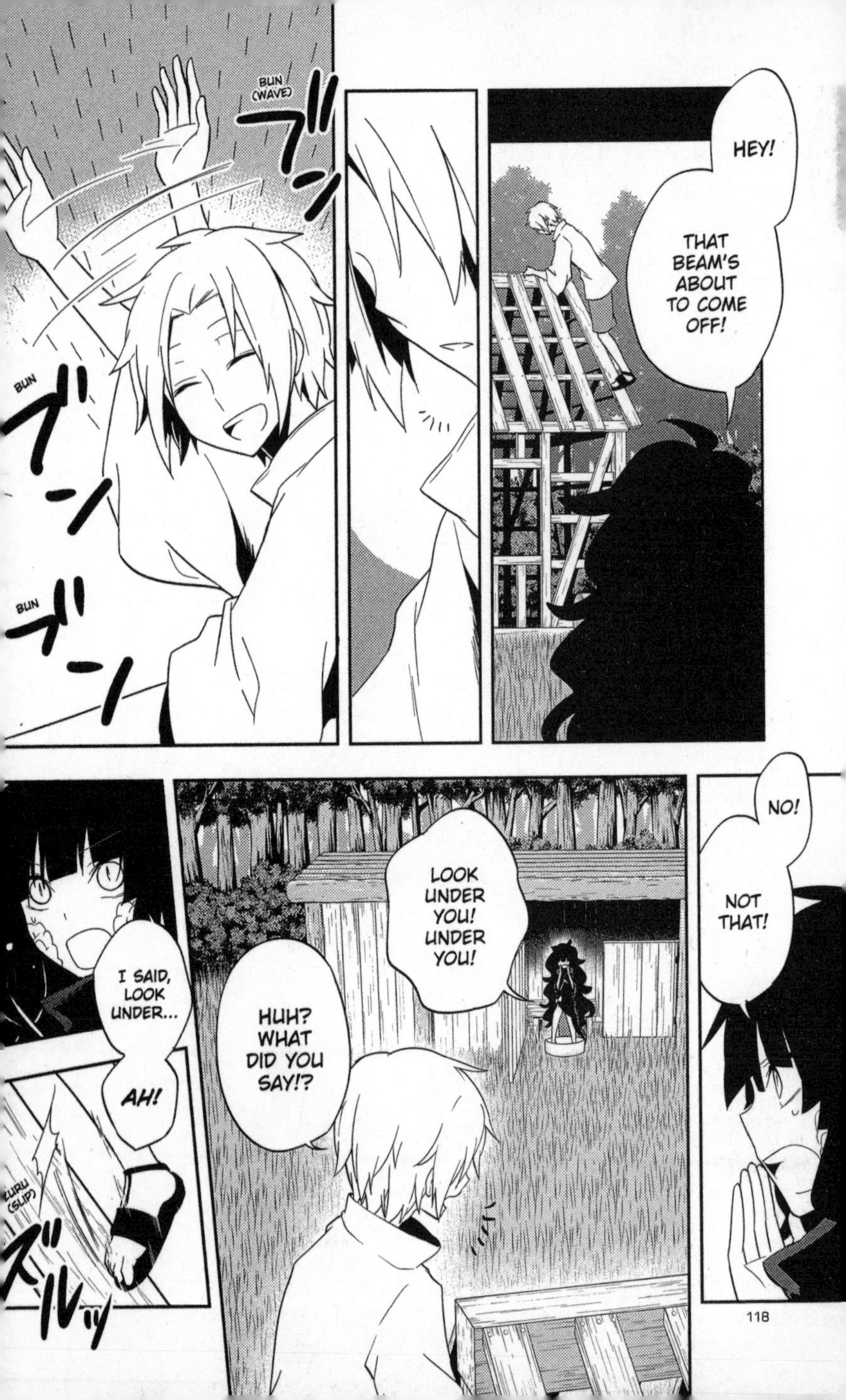

HEY!
THAT BEAM'S ABOUT TO COME OFF!
BUN (WAVE)
BUN
BUN
NO!
NOT THAT!
LOOK UNDER YOU! UNDER YOU!
HUH? WHAT DID YOU SAY!?
I SAID, LOOK UNDER...
AH!
ZURU (SLIP)

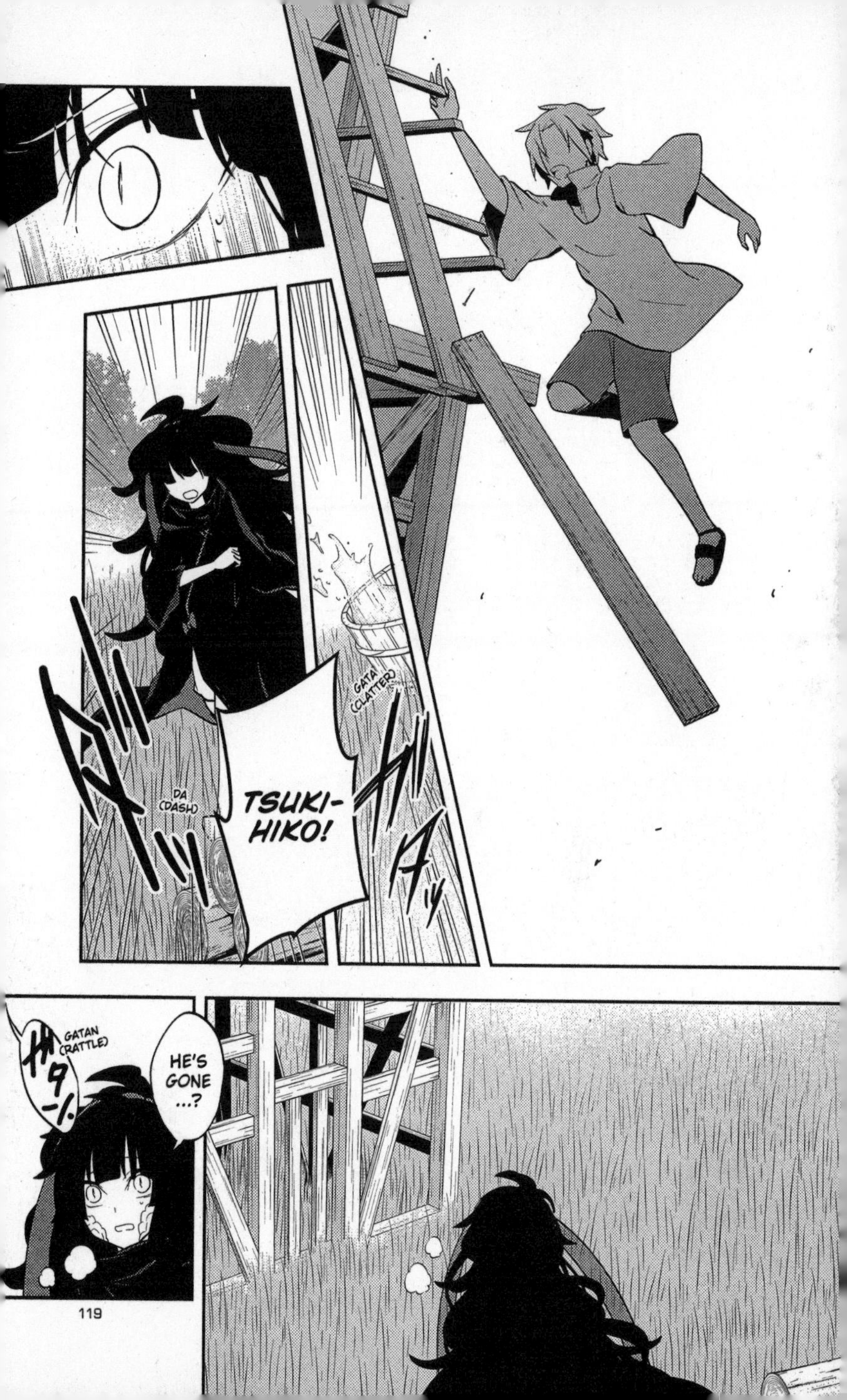
GATA (CLATTER)
TSUKI-HIKO!
DA (DASH)
HE'S GONE ...?
GATAN (RATTLE)

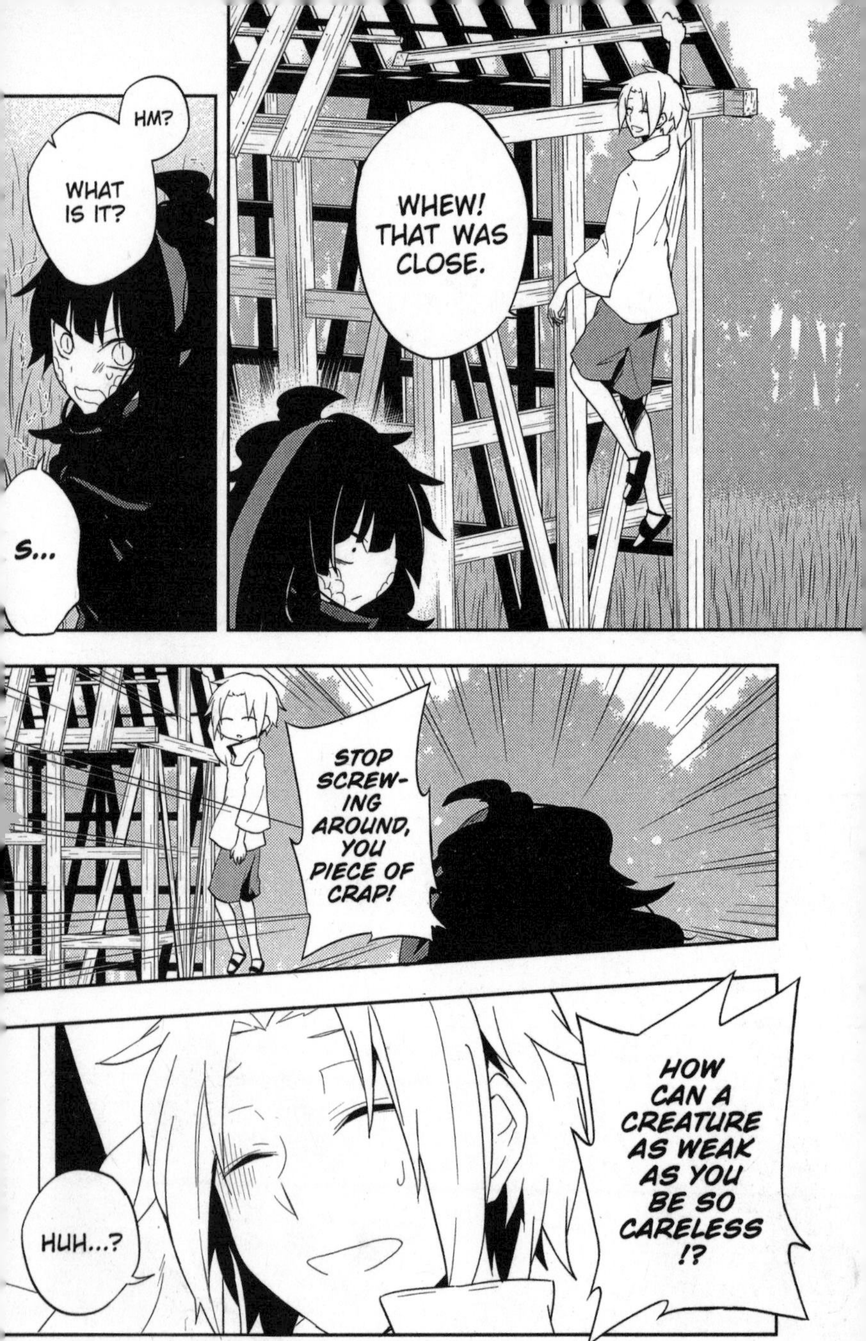
WHEW! THAT WAS CLOSE.
HM?
WHAT IS IT?
S...
STOP SCREWING-ING AROUND, YOU PIECE OF CRAP!
HOW CAN A CREATURE AS WEAK AS YOU BE SO CARELESS!?
HUH...?

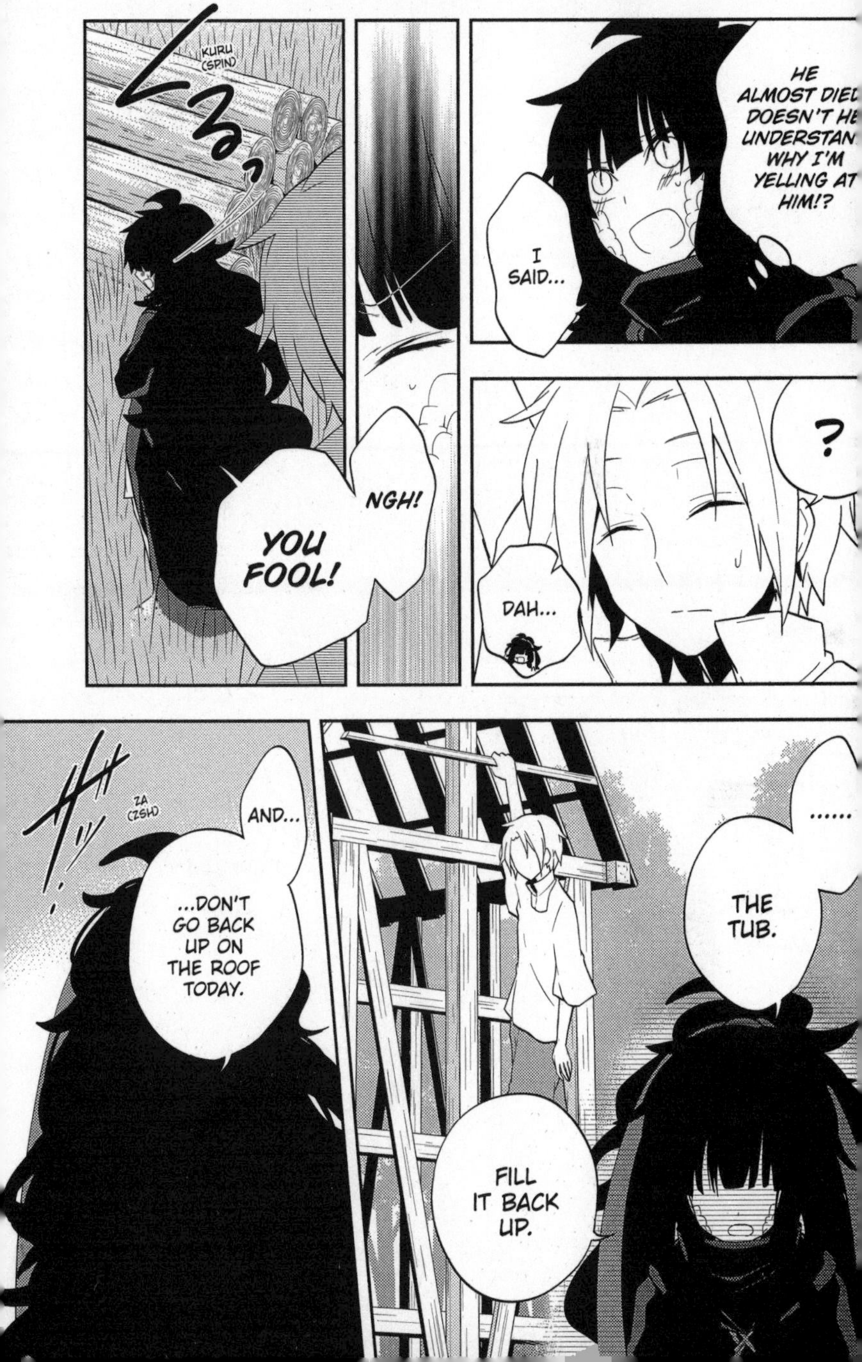
HE ALMOST DIED DOESN'T HE UNDERSTAN WHY I'M YELLING AT HIM!?
I SAID...
?
DAH...
NGH!
YOU FOOL!
KURU (SPIN)
......
THE TUB.
FILL IT BACK UP.
AND...
...DON'T GO BACK UP ON THE ROOF TODAY.
ZA (ZSH)

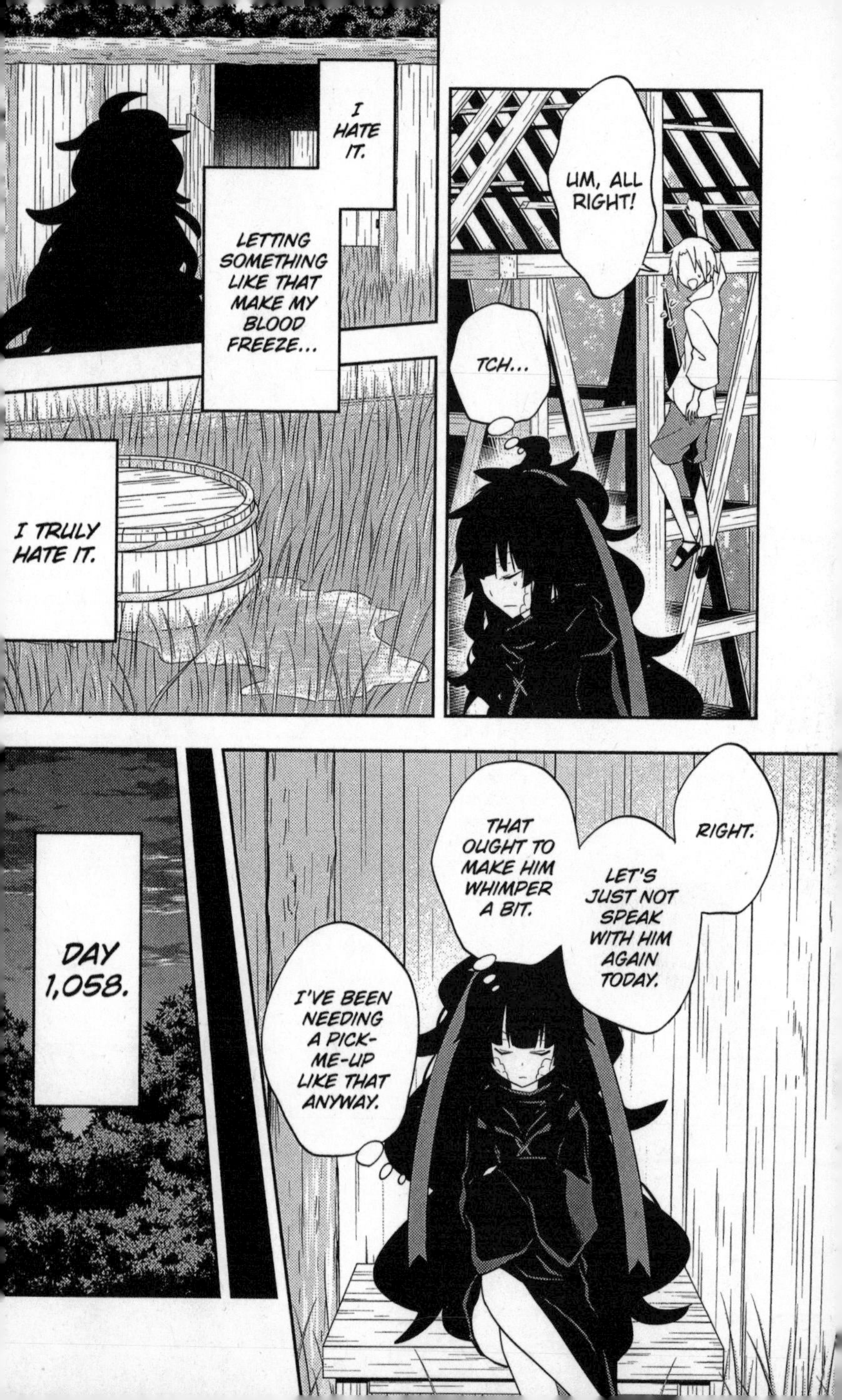
UM, ALL RIGHT!
TCH...
I HATE IT.
LETTING SOMETHING LIKE THAT MAKE MY BLOOD FREEZE...
I TRULY HATE IT.
RIGHT.
LET'S JUST NOT SPEAK WITH HIM AGAIN TODAY.
THAT OUGHT TO MAKE HIM WHIMPER A BIT.
I'VE BEEN NEEDING A PICK-ME-UP LIKE THAT ANYWAY.
DAY 1,058.

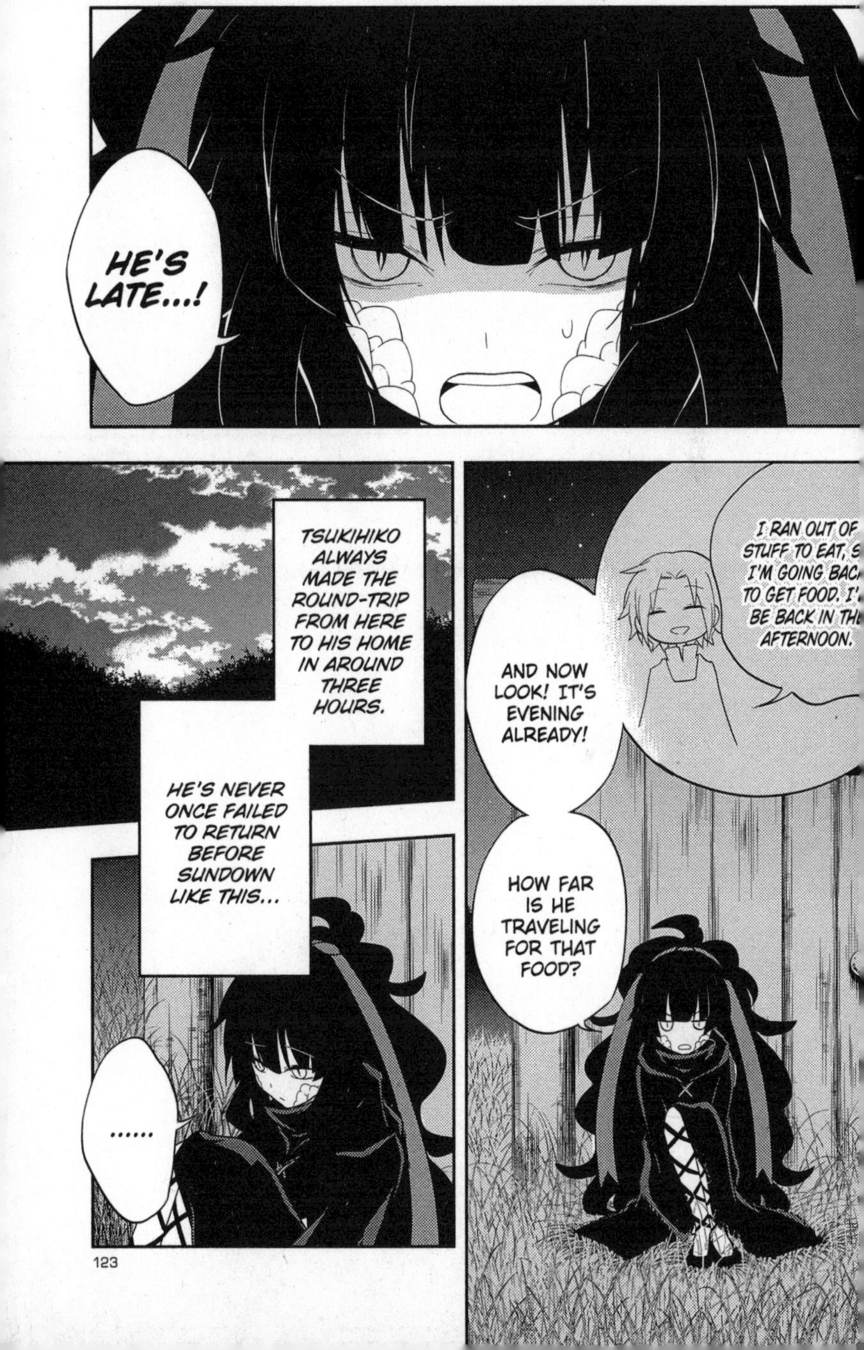
HE'S LATE...!
I RAN OUT OF STUFF TO EAT, S I'M GOING BAC TO GET FOOD. I' BE BACK IN TH AFTERNOON.
AND NOW LOOK! IT'S EVENING ALREADY!
HOW FAR IS HE TRAVELING FOR THAT FOOD?
TSUKIHIKO ALWAYS MADE THE ROUND-TRIP FROM HERE TO HIS HOME IN AROUND THREE HOURS.
HE'S NEVER ONCE FAILED TO RETURN BEFORE SUNDOWN LIKE THIS...
......

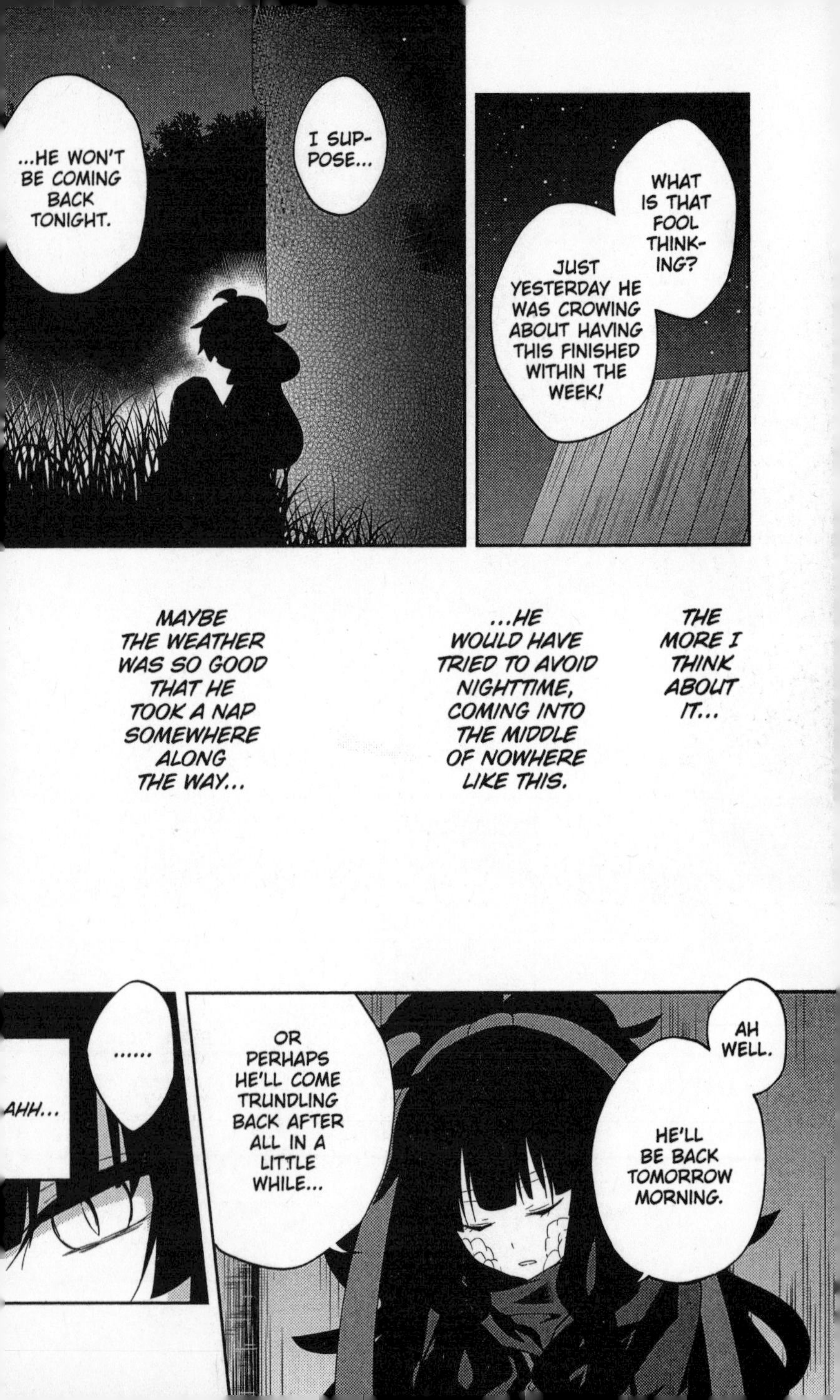
WHAT IS THAT FOOL THINKING?
JUST YESTERDAY HE WAS CROWING ABOUT HAVING THIS FINISHED WITHIN THE WEEK!
I SUPPOSE...
...HE WON'T BE COMING BACK TONIGHT.
THE MORE I THINK ABOUT IT...
...HE WOULD HAVE TRIED TO AVOID NIGHTTIME, COMING INTO THE MIDDLE OF NOWHERE LIKE THIS.
MAYBE THE WEATHER WAS SO GOOD THAT HE TOOK A NAP SOMEWHERE ALONG THE WAY...
AH WELL.
HE'LL BE BACK TOMORROW MORNING.
OR PERHAPS HE'LL COME TRUNDLING BACK AFTER ALL IN A LITTLE WHILE...
......
AHH...

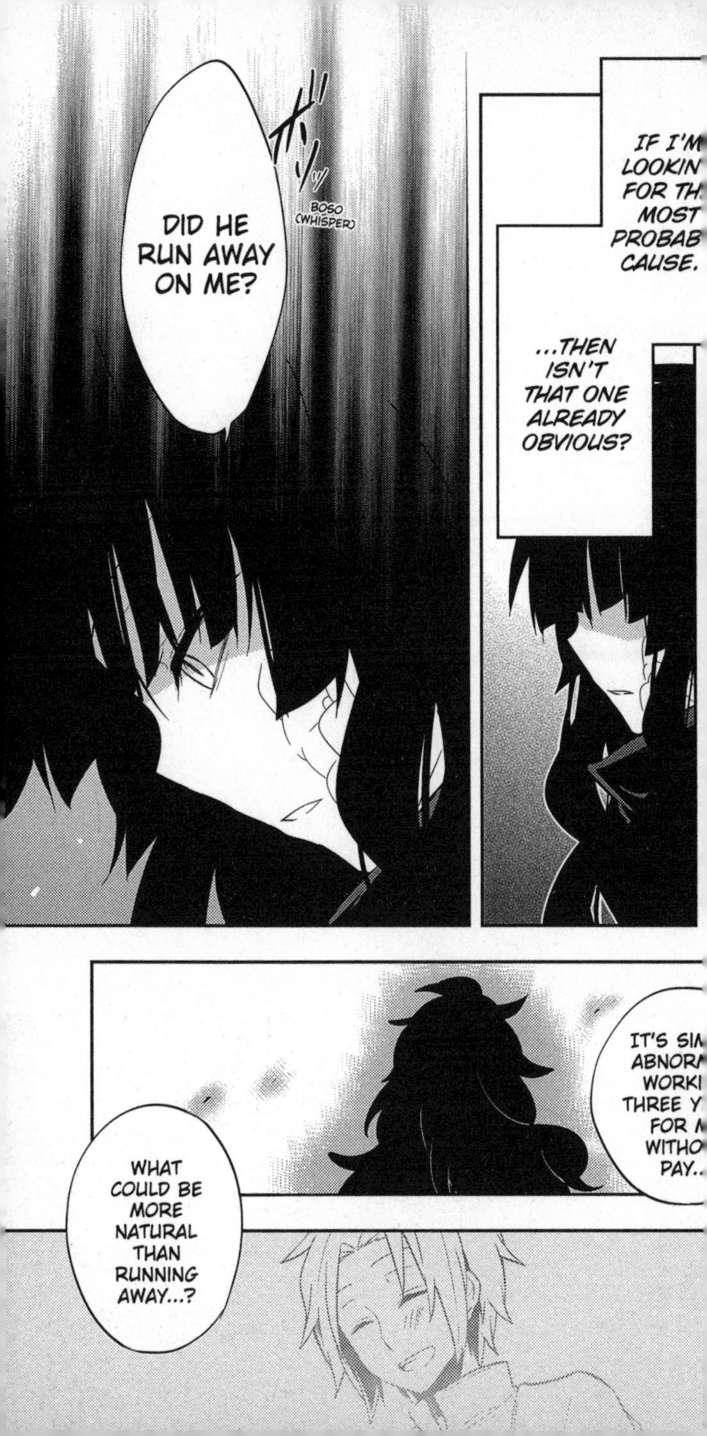
IF I'M LOOKIN FOR TH MOST PROBAB CAUSE.
...THEN ISN'T THAT ONE ALREADY OBVIOUS?
BOSO (WHISPER)
DID HE RUN AWAY ON ME?
IT'S SIM ABNORM WORKI THREE Y FOR M WITHO PAY..
WHAT COULD BE MORE NATURAL THAN RUNNING AWAY...?

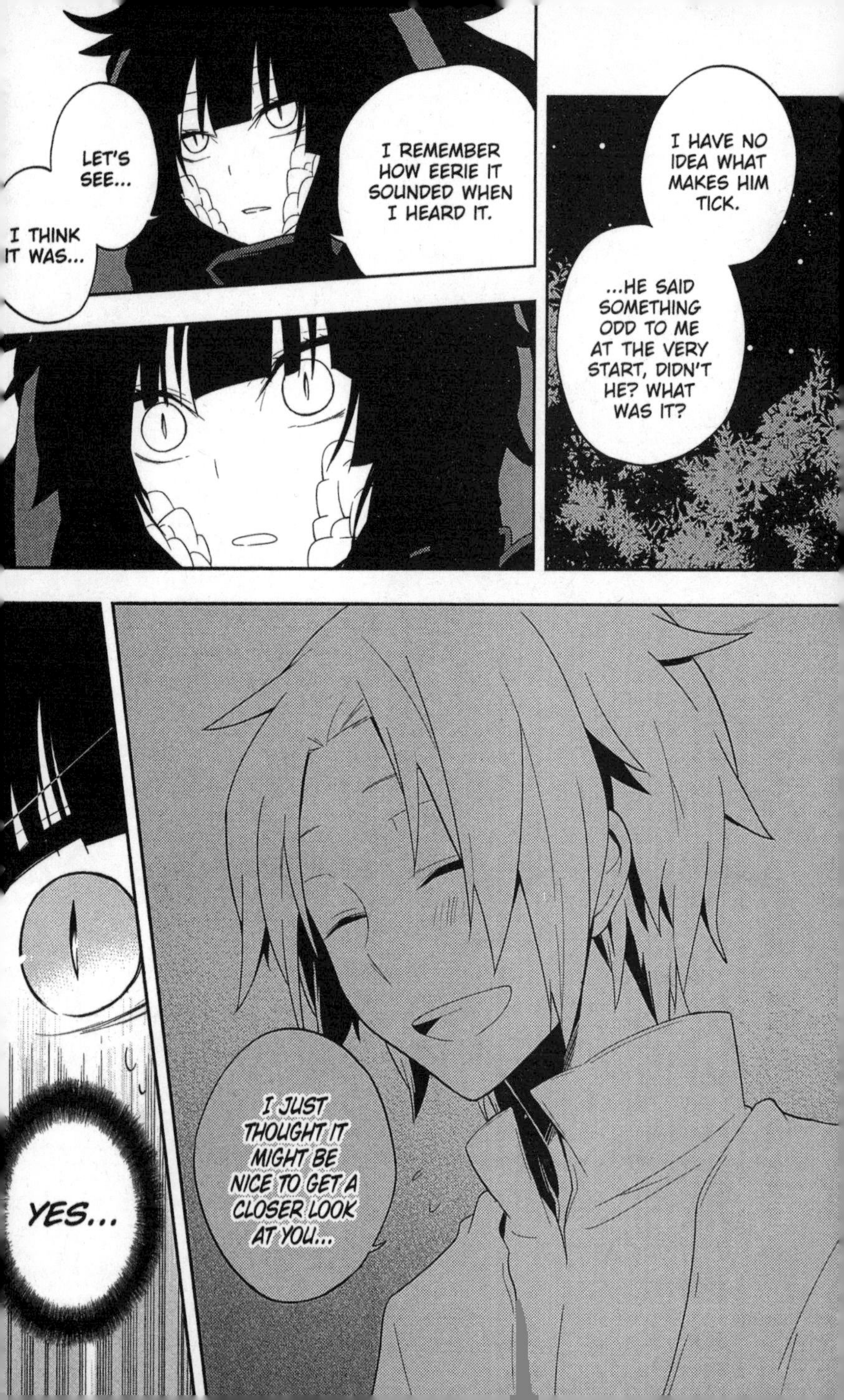
I HAVE NO IDEA WHAT MAKES HIM TICK.
...HE SAID SOMETHING ODD TO ME AT THE VERY START, DIDN'T HE? WHAT WAS IT?
I REMEMBER HOW EERIE IT SOUNDED WHEN I HEARD IT.
LET'S SEE...
I THINK IT WAS...
I JUST THOUGHT IT MIGHT BE NICE TO GET A CLOSER LOOK AT YOU...
YES...

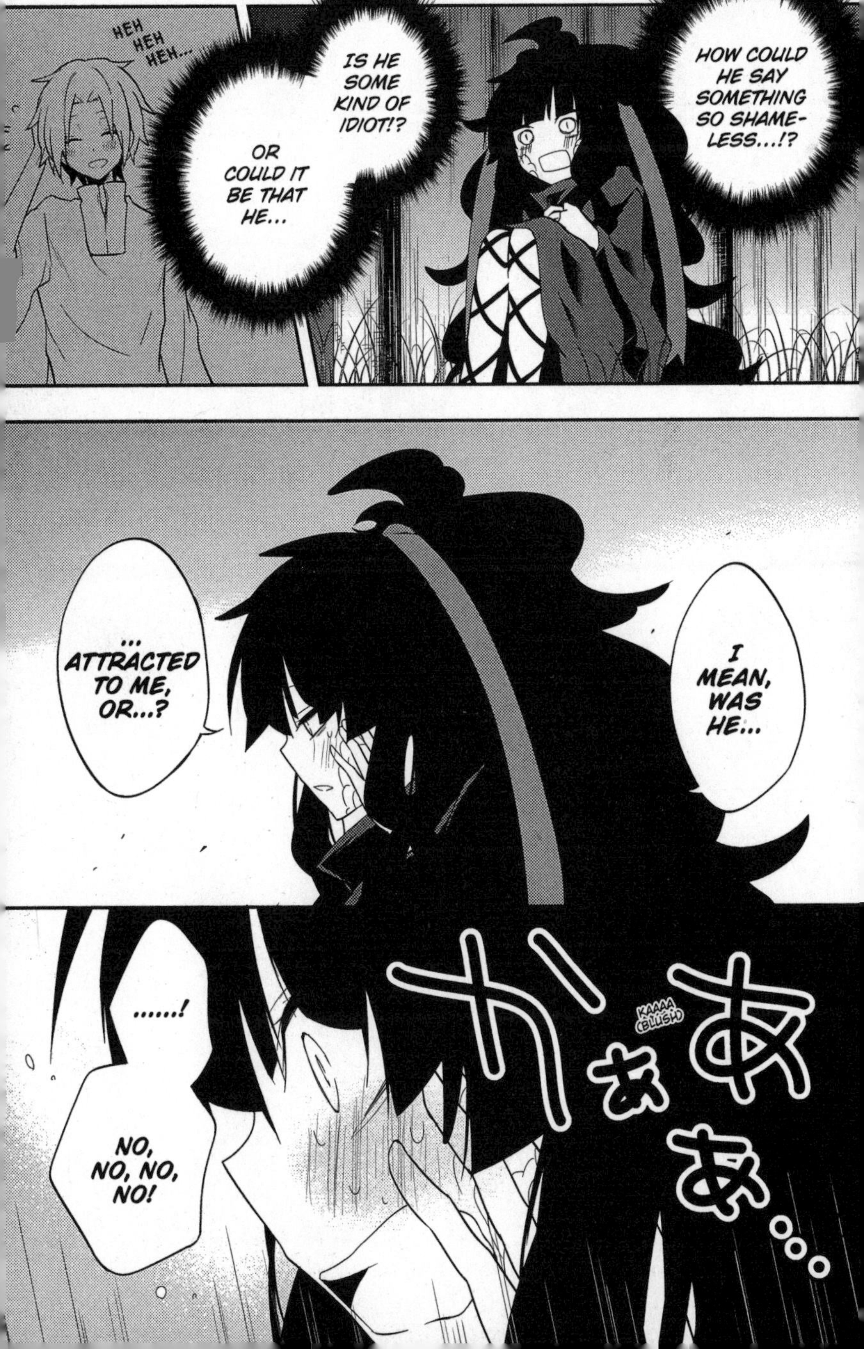

HOW COULD HE SAY SOMETHING SO SHAMELESS...!?
IS HE SOME KIND OF IDIOT!?
OR COULD IT BE THAT HE...
HEH HEH HEH...
I MEAN, WAS HE...
...ATTRACTED TO ME, OR...?
かぁぁ…
KAAAA (BLUSH)
......!
NO, NO, NO, NO!

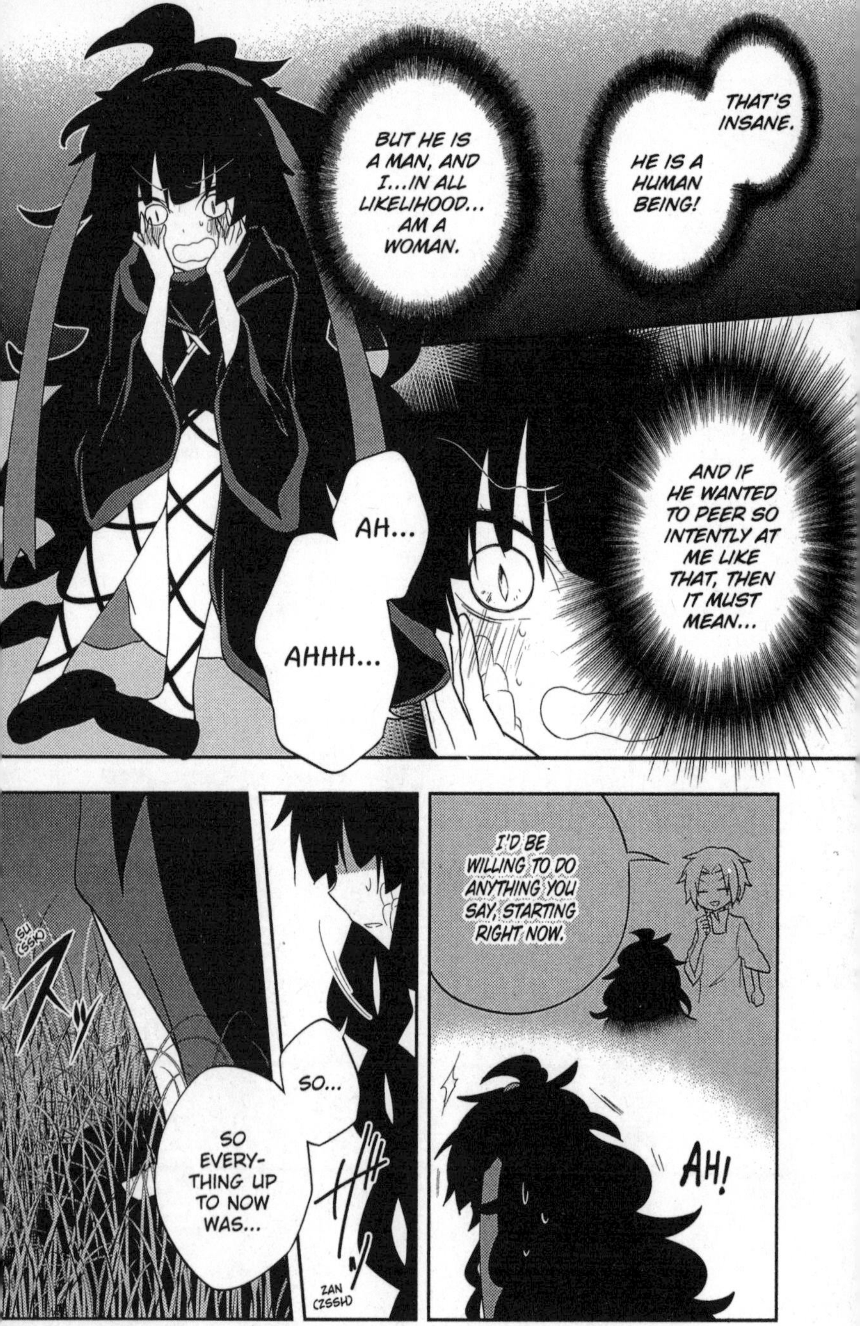
THAT'S INSANE.
HE IS A HUMAN BEING!
BUT HE IS A MAN, AND I...IN ALL LIKELIHOOD... AM A WOMAN.
AND IF HE WANTED TO PEER SO INTENTLY AT ME LIKE THAT, THEN IT MUST MEAN...
AH...
AHHH...
I'D BE WILLING TO DO ANYTHING YOU SAY, STARTING RIGHT NOW.
AH!
SO...
SO EVERYTHING UP TO NOW WAS...
ZAN (ZSSH)
SU (SSK)

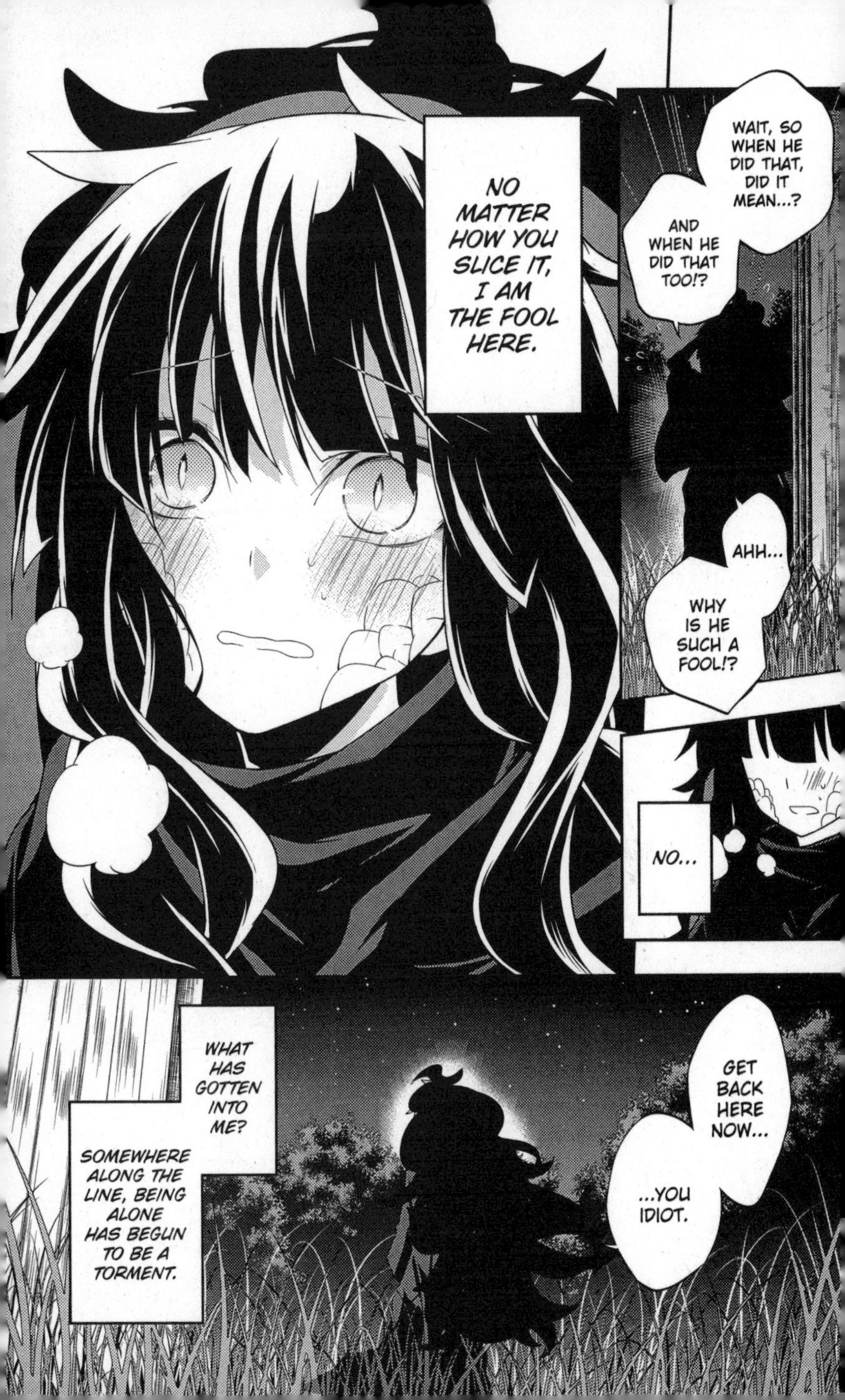
WAIT, SO WHEN HE DID THAT, DID IT MEAN...?
AND WHEN HE DID THAT TOO!?
AHH...
WHY IS HE SUCH A FOOL!?
NO...
NO MATTER HOW YOU SLICE IT, I AM THE FOOL HERE.
GET BACK HERE NOW...
...YOU IDIOT.
WHAT HAS GOTTEN INTO ME?
SOMEWHERE ALONG THE LINE, BEING ALONE HAS BEGUN TO BE A TORMENT.

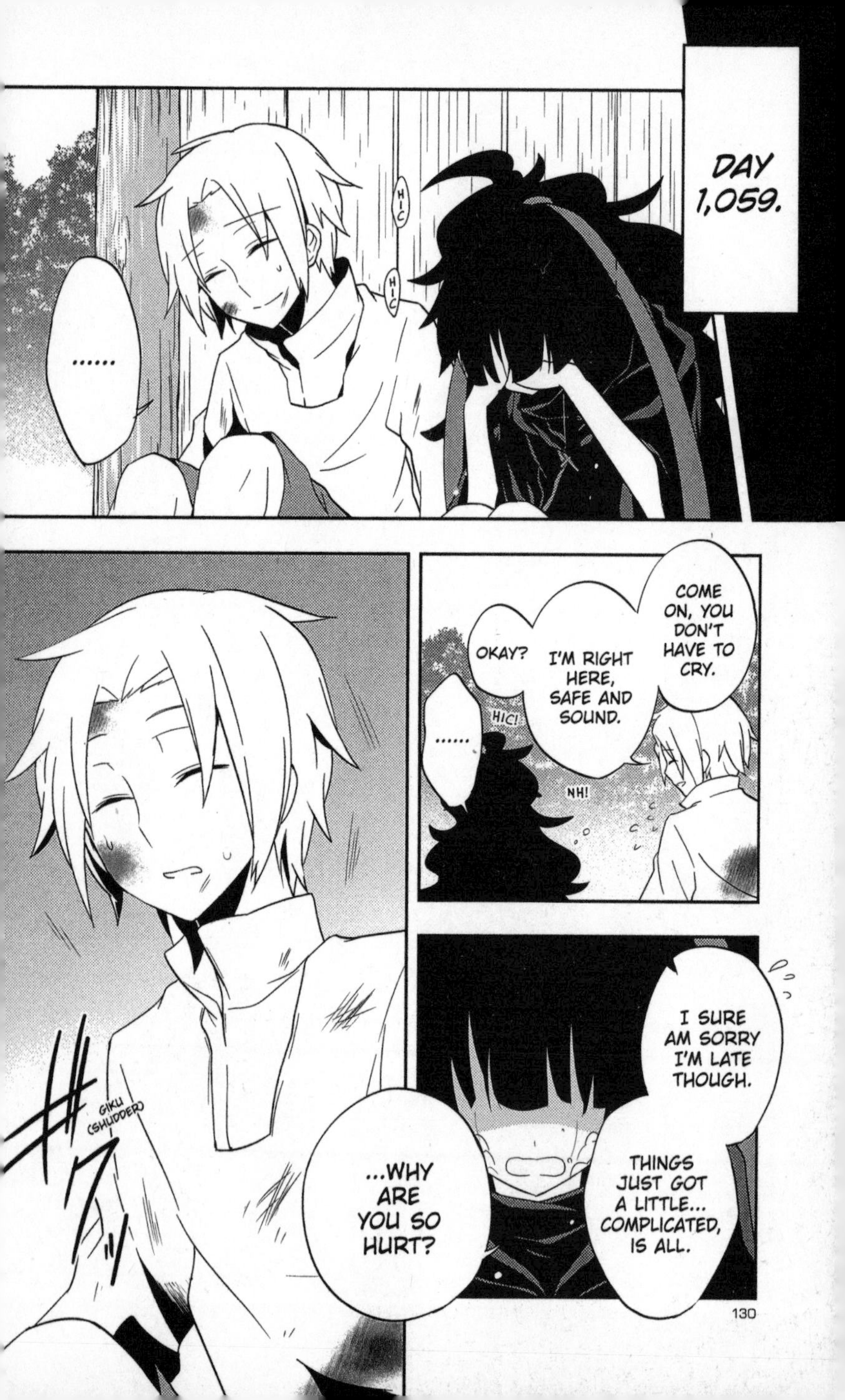
DAY 1,059.
HIC
HIC
......
COME ON, YOU DON'T HAVE TO CRY.
I'M RIGHT HERE, SAFE AND SOUND.
OKAY?
HIC!
NH!
......
I SURE AM SORRY I'M LATE THOUGH.
THINGS JUST GOT A LITTLE... COMPLICATED, IS ALL.
...WHY ARE YOU SO HURT?
GIKU (SHUDDER)

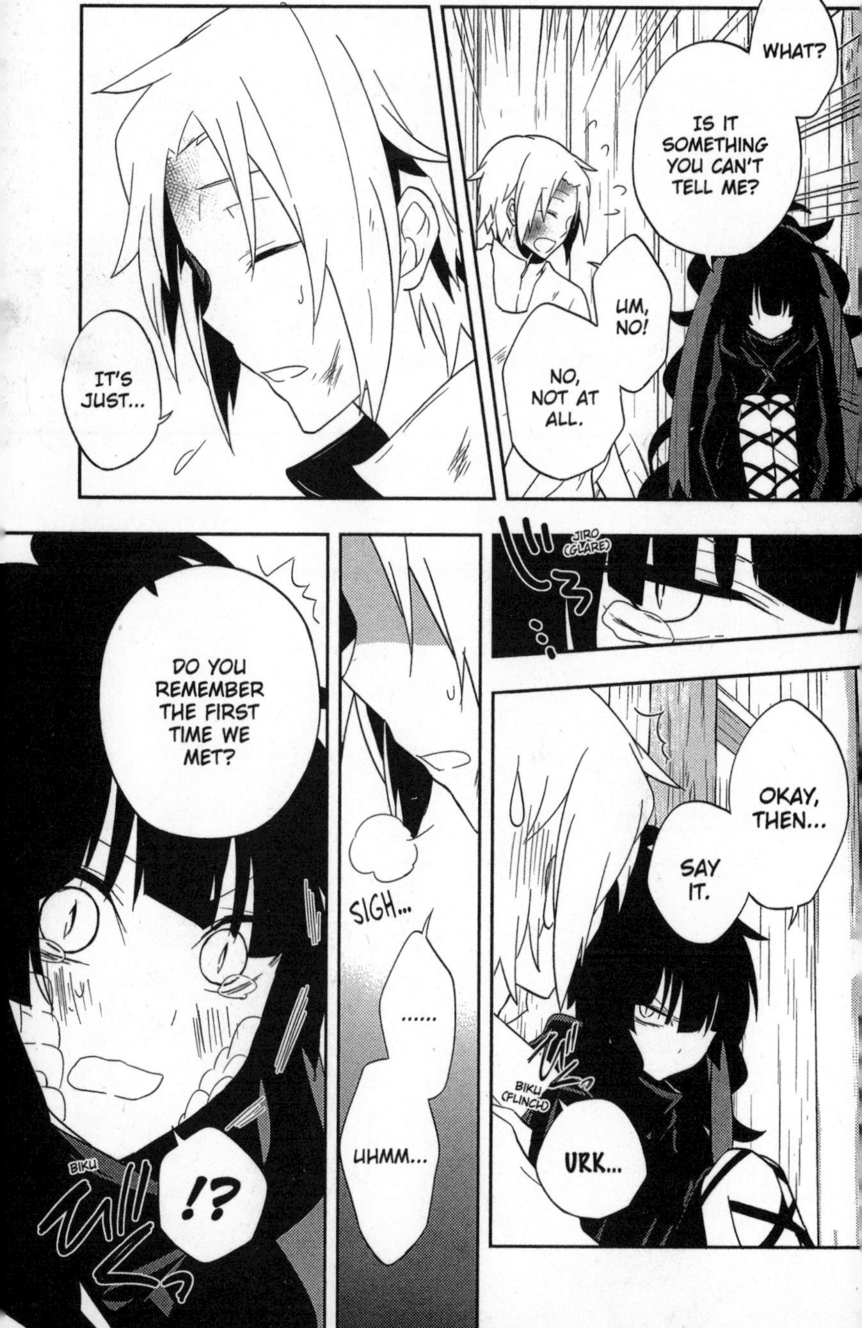
WHAT?
IS IT SOMETHING YOU CAN'T TELL ME?
UM, NO!
NO, NOT AT ALL.
IT'S JUST...
JIRO (GLARE)
...
OKAY, THEN...
SAY IT.
BIKU (FLINCH)
URK...
SIGH...
......
UHMM...
DO YOU REMEMBER THE FIRST TIME WE MET?
BIKU
!?

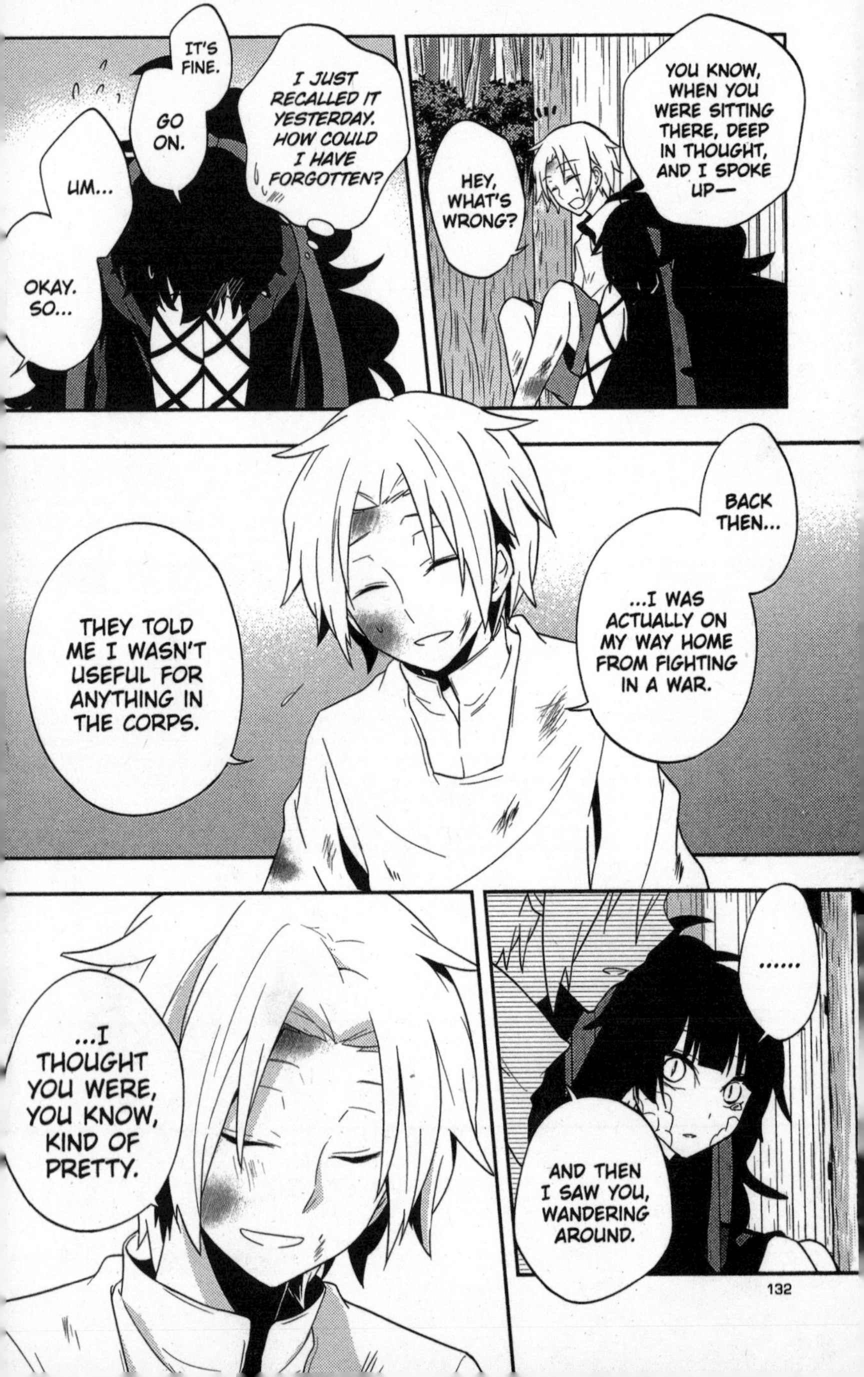
YOU KNOW, WHEN YOU WERE SITTING THERE, DEEP IN THOUGHT, AND I SPOKE UP—
HEY, WHAT'S WRONG?
I JUST RECALLED IT YESTERDAY. HOW COULD I HAVE FORGOTTEN?
IT'S FINE.
GO ON.
UM...
OKAY. SO...
BACK THEN...
...I WAS ACTUALLY ON MY WAY HOME FROM FIGHTING IN A WAR.
THEY TOLD ME I WASN'T USEFUL FOR ANYTHING IN THE CORPS.
......
AND THEN I SAW YOU, WANDERING AROUND.
...I THOUGHT YOU WERE, YOU KNOW, KIND OF PRETTY.

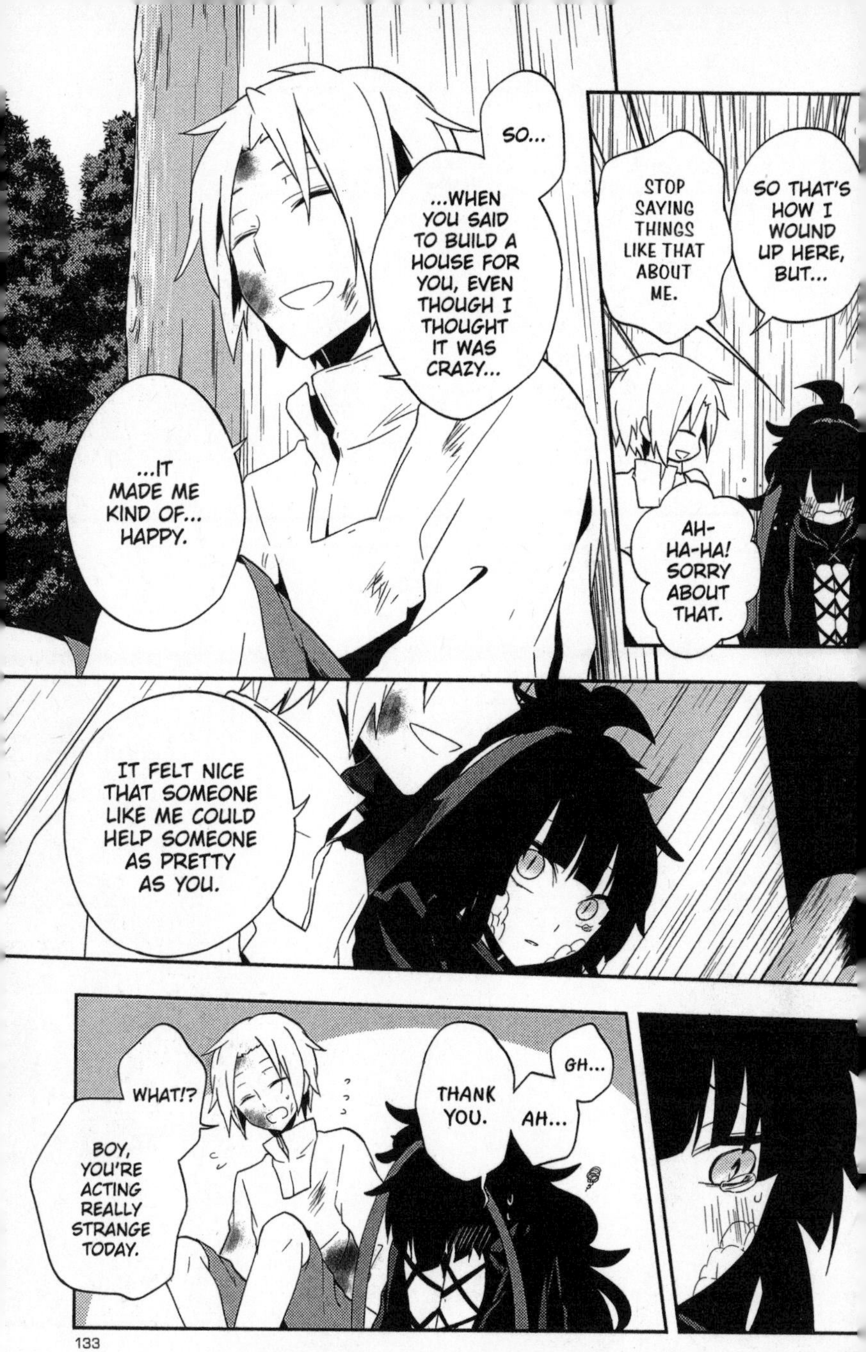
SO THAT'S HOW I WOUND UP HERE, BUT...
STOP SAYING THINGS LIKE THAT ABOUT ME.
AH-HA-HA! SORRY ABOUT THAT.
SO...
...WHEN YOU SAID TO BUILD A HOUSE FOR YOU, EVEN THOUGH I THOUGHT IT WAS CRAZY...
...IT MADE ME KIND OF... HAPPY.
IT FELT NICE THAT SOMEONE LIKE ME COULD HELP SOMEONE AS PRETTY AS YOU.
GH...
THANK YOU.
AH...
WHAT!?
BOY, YOU'RE ACTING REALLY STRANGE TODAY.

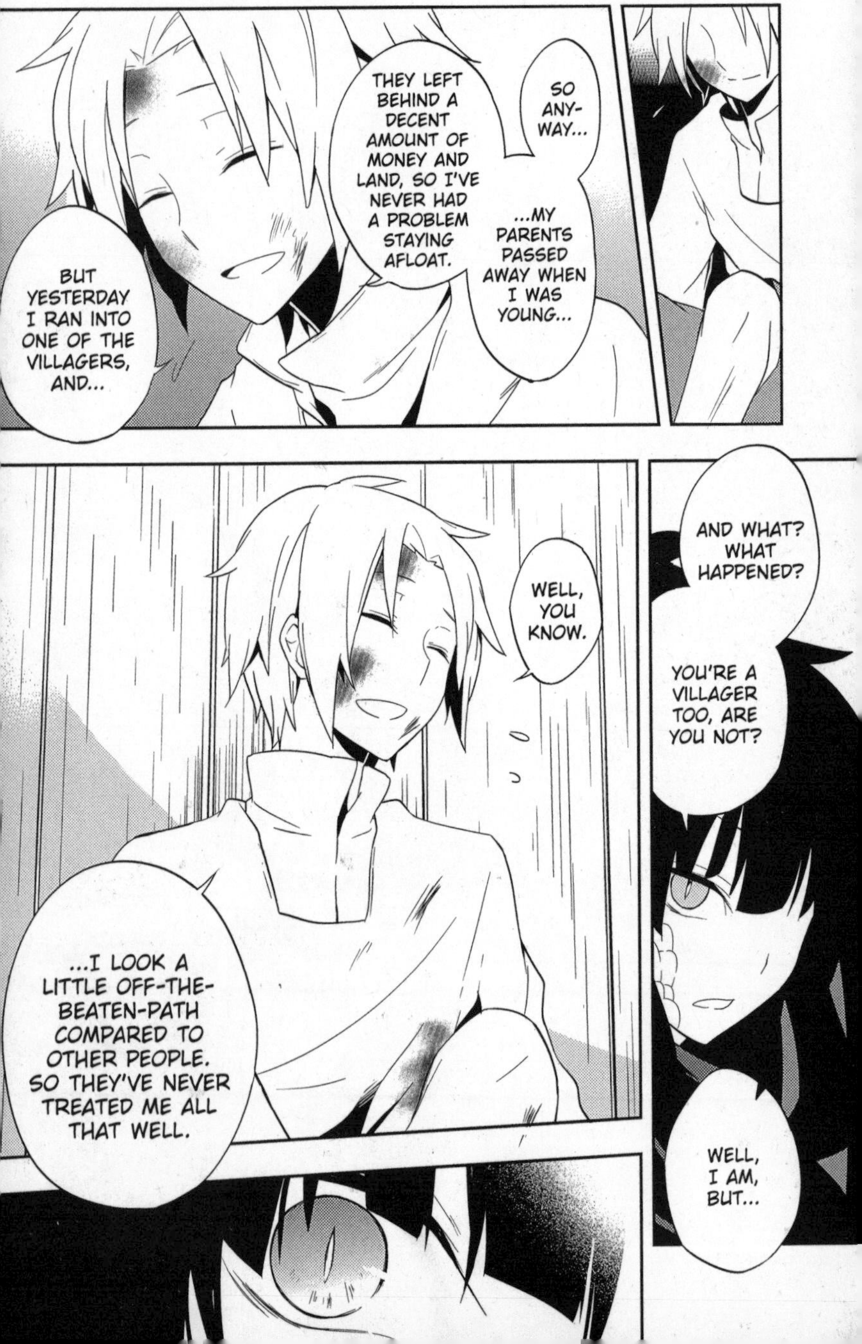
SO ANYWAY...
...MY PARENTS PASSED AWAY WHEN I WAS YOUNG...
THEY LEFT BEHIND A DECENT AMOUNT OF MONEY AND LAND, SO I'VE NEVER HAD A PROBLEM STAYING AFLOAT.
BUT YESTERDAY I RAN INTO ONE OF THE VILLAGERS, AND...
AND WHAT? WHAT HAPPENED?
YOU'RE A VILLAGER TOO, ARE YOU NOT?
WELL, I AM, BUT...
WELL, YOU KNOW.
...I LOOK A LITTLE OFF-THE-BEATEN-PATH COMPARED TO OTHER PEOPLE. SO THEY'VE NEVER TREATED ME ALL THAT WELL.

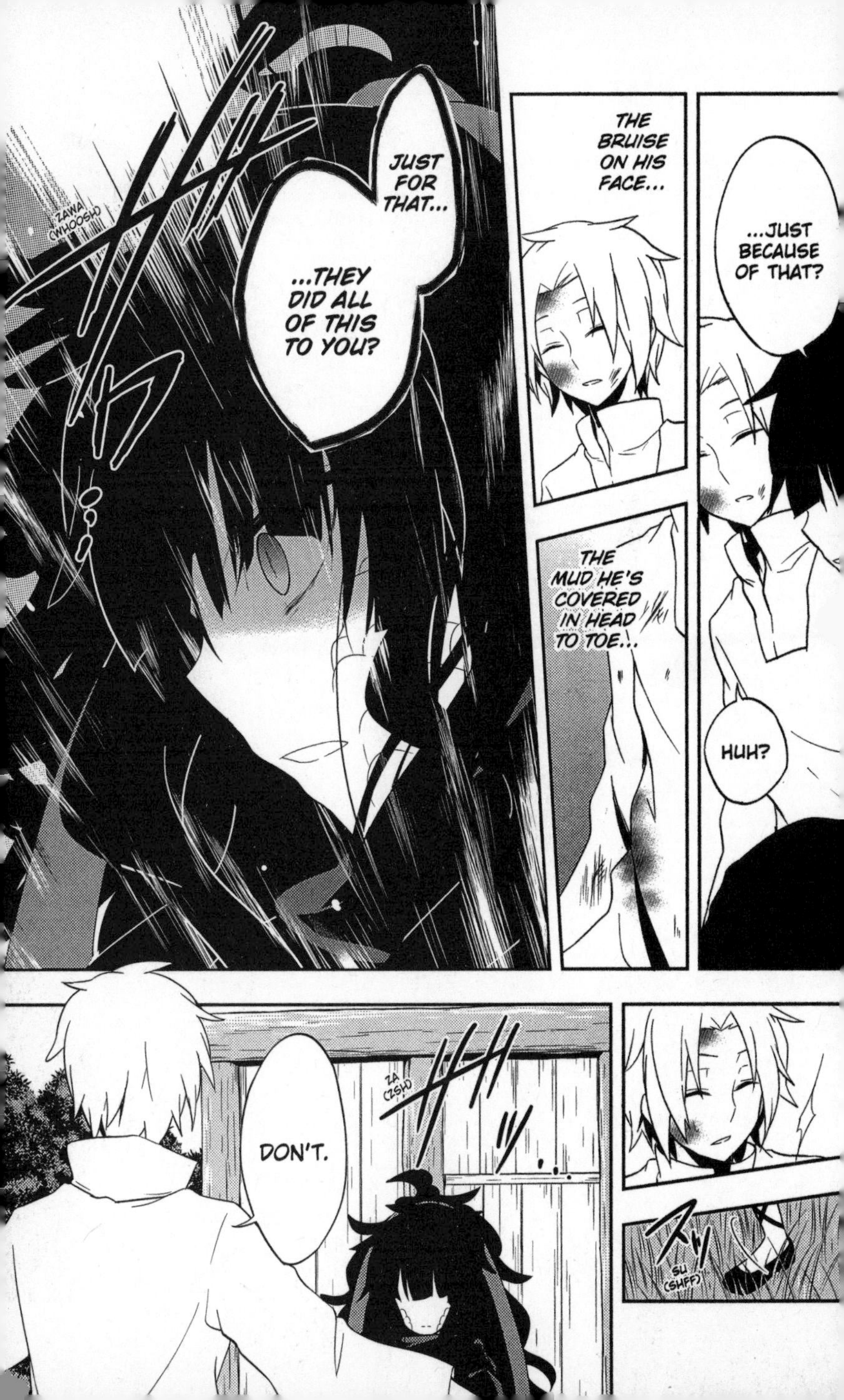

...JUST BECAUSE OF THAT?
HUH?
THE BRUISE ON HIS FACE...
THE MUD HE'S COVERED IN HEAD TO TOE...
JUST FOR THAT...
...THEY DID ALL OF THIS TO YOU?
ZAWA (WHOOSH)
SU (SHFF)
ZA (ZSH)
DON'T.

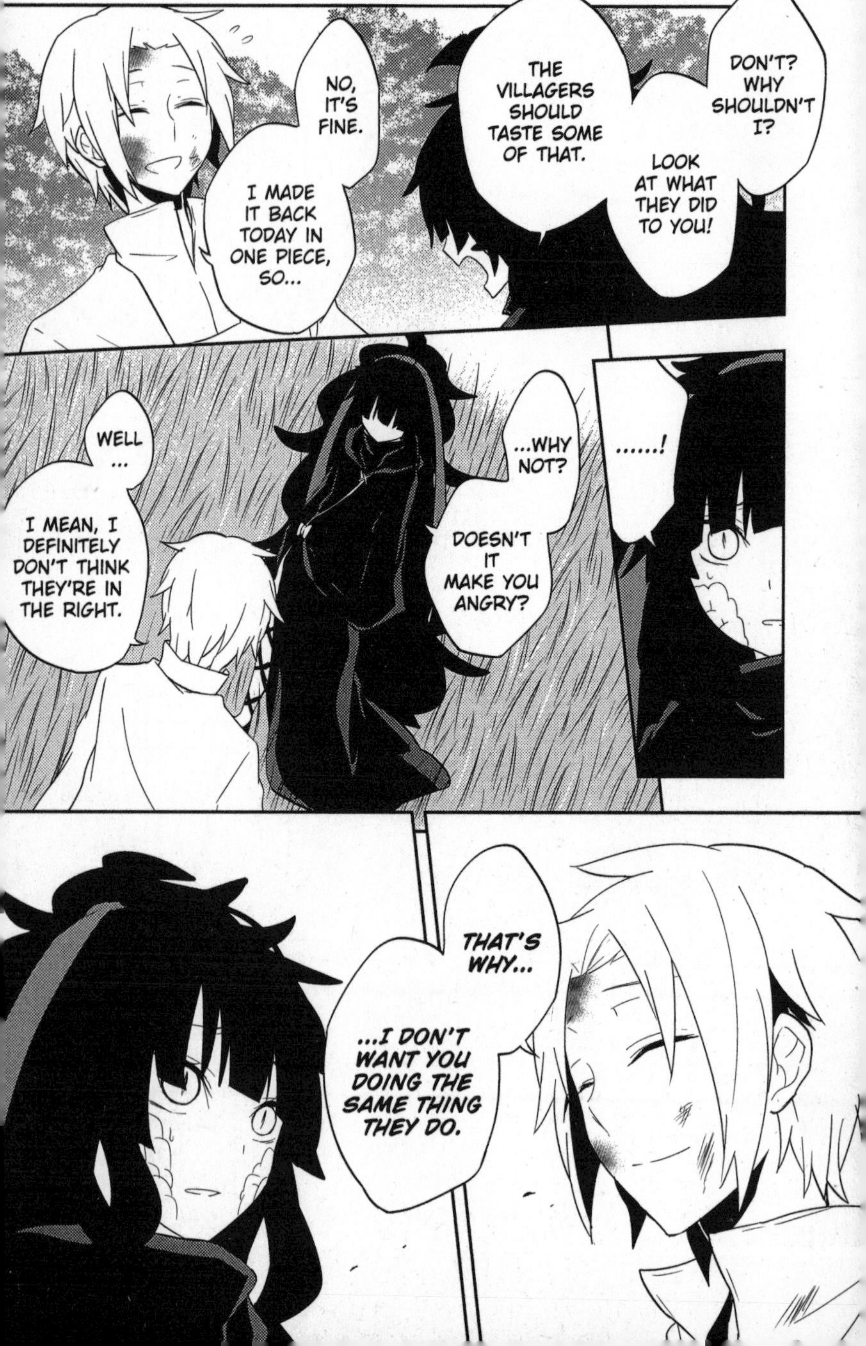
DON'T? WHY SHOULDN'T I?
LOOK AT WHAT THEY DID TO YOU!
THE VILLAGERS SHOULD TASTE SOME OF THAT.
NO, IT'S FINE.
I MADE IT BACK TODAY IN ONE PIECE, SO...
......!
...WHY NOT?
DOESN'T IT MAKE YOU ANGRY?
WELL ...
I MEAN, I DEFINITELY DON'T THINK THEY'RE IN THE RIGHT.
THAT'S WHY...
...I DON'T WANT YOU DOING THE SAME THING THEY DO.

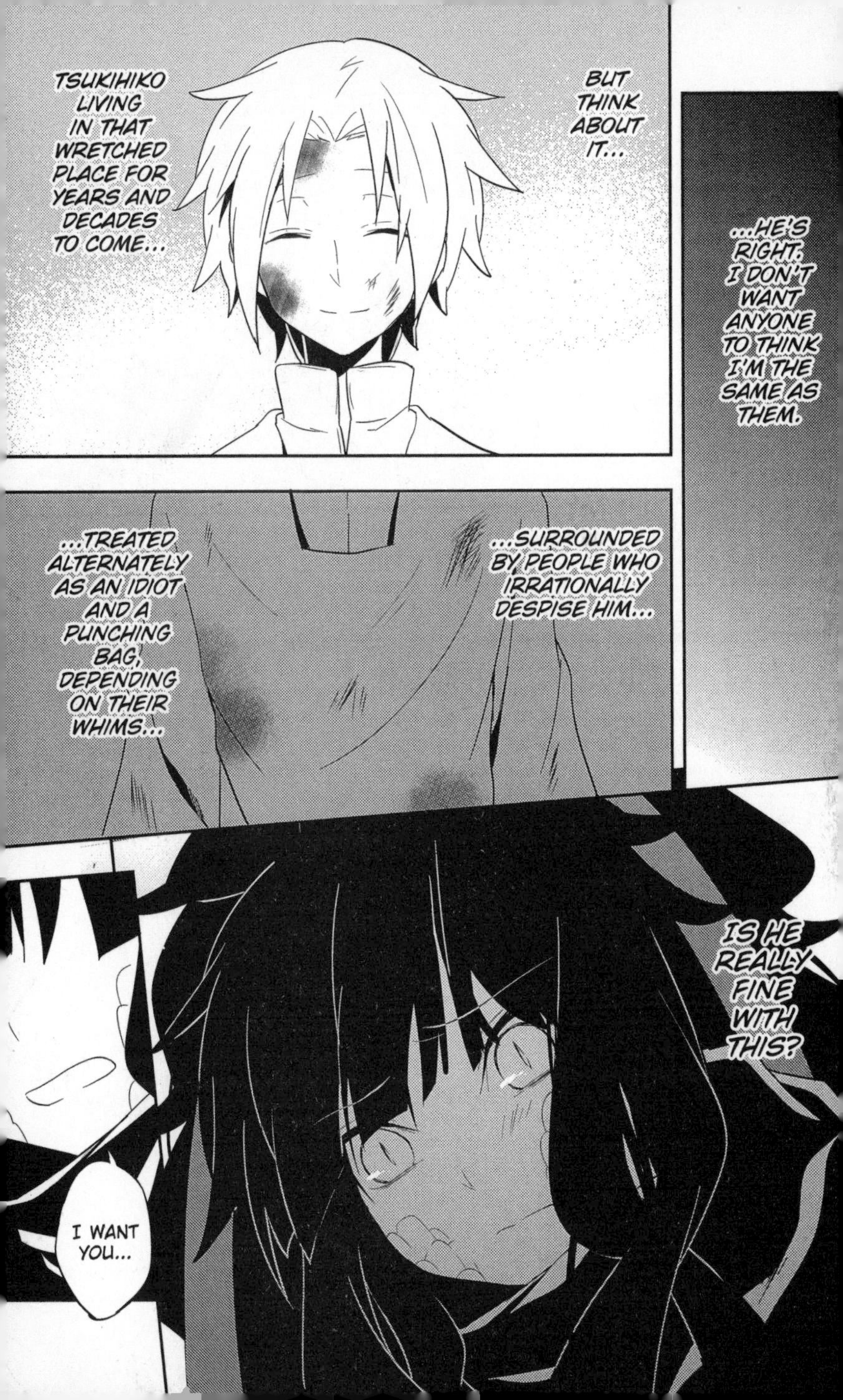
BUT THINK ABOUT IT...
TSUKIHIKO LIVING IN THAT WRETCHED PLACE FOR YEARS AND DECADES TO COME...
...SURROUNDED BY PEOPLE WHO IRRATIONALLY DESPISE HIM...
...TREATED ALTERNATELY AS AN IDIOT AND A PUNCHING BAG, DEPENDING ON THEIR WHIMS...
...HE'S RIGHT. I DON'T WANT ANYONE TO THINK I'M THE SAME AS THEM.
IS HE REALLY FINE WITH THIS?
I WANT YOU...

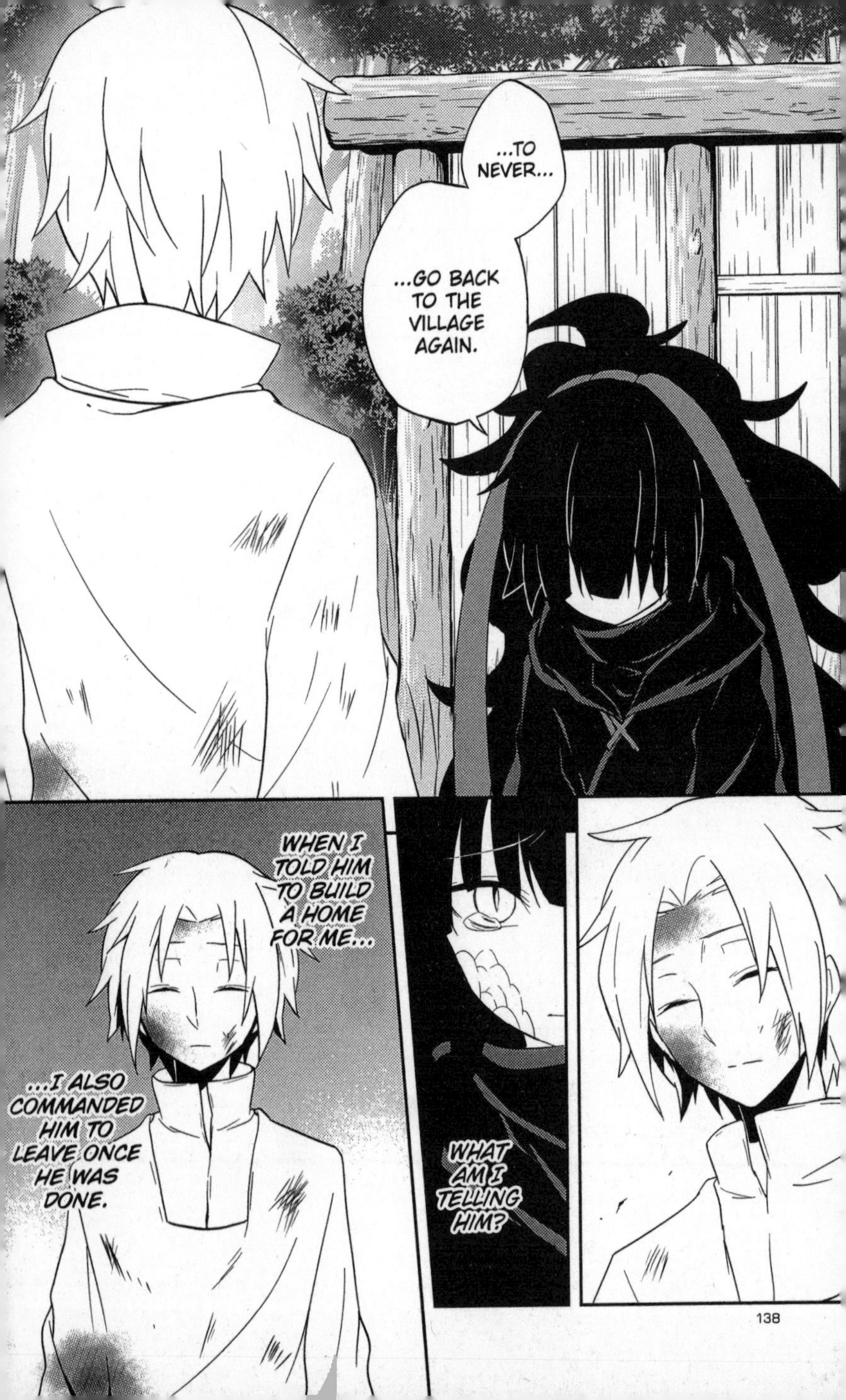
...TO NEVER...
...GO BACK TO THE VILLAGE AGAIN.
WHAT AM I TELLING HIM?
WHEN I TOLD HIM TO BUILD A HOME FOR ME...
...I ALSO COMMANDED HIM TO LEAVE ONCE HE WAS DONE.

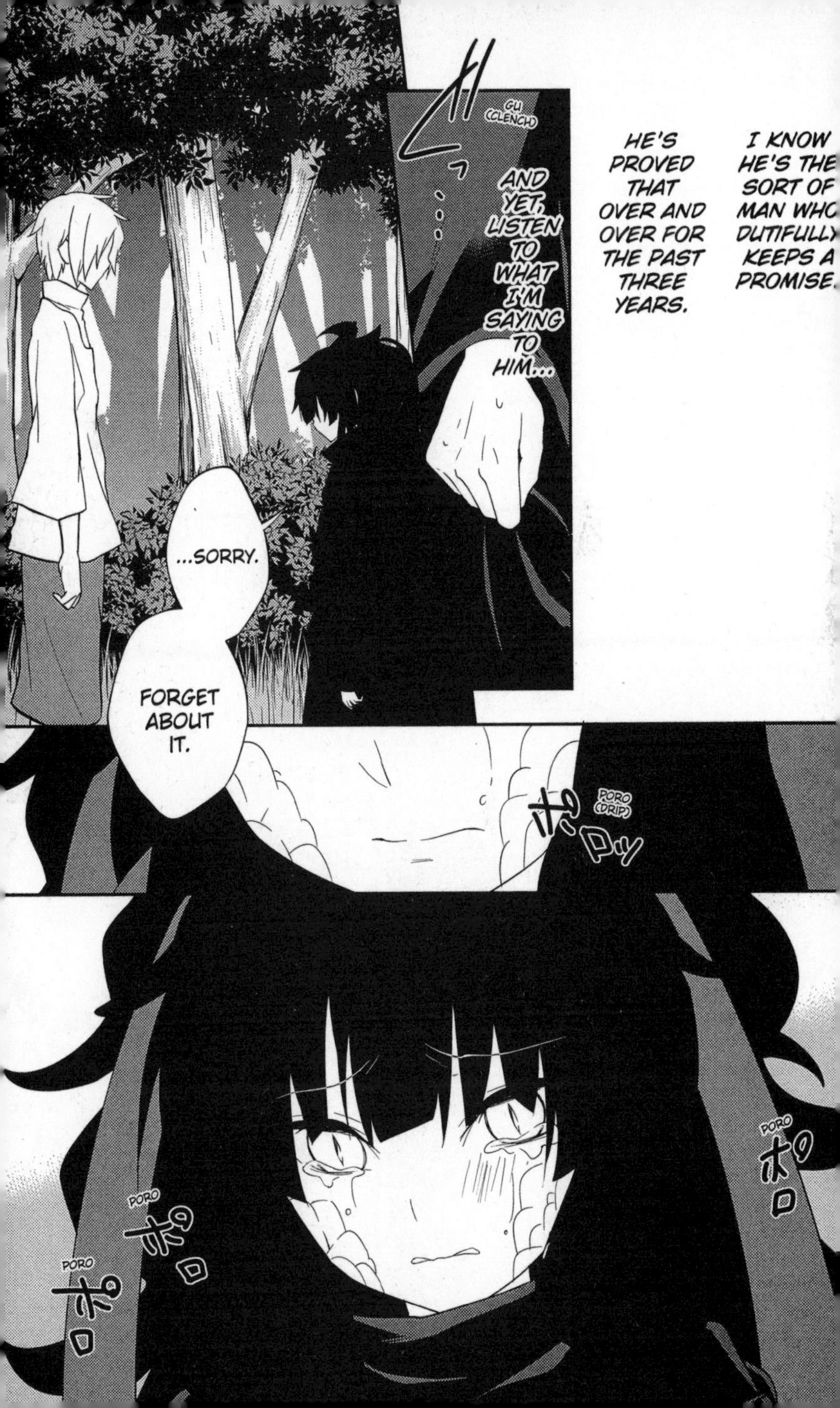
I KNOW HE'S THE SORT OF MAN WHO DUTIFULLY KEEPS A PROMISE.
HE'S PROVED THAT OVER AND OVER FOR THE PAST THREE YEARS.
GU (CLENCH)
AND YET, LISTEN TO WHAT I'M SAYING TO HIM...
...SORRY.
FORGET ABOUT IT.
PORO (DRIP)
PORO
PORO
PORO

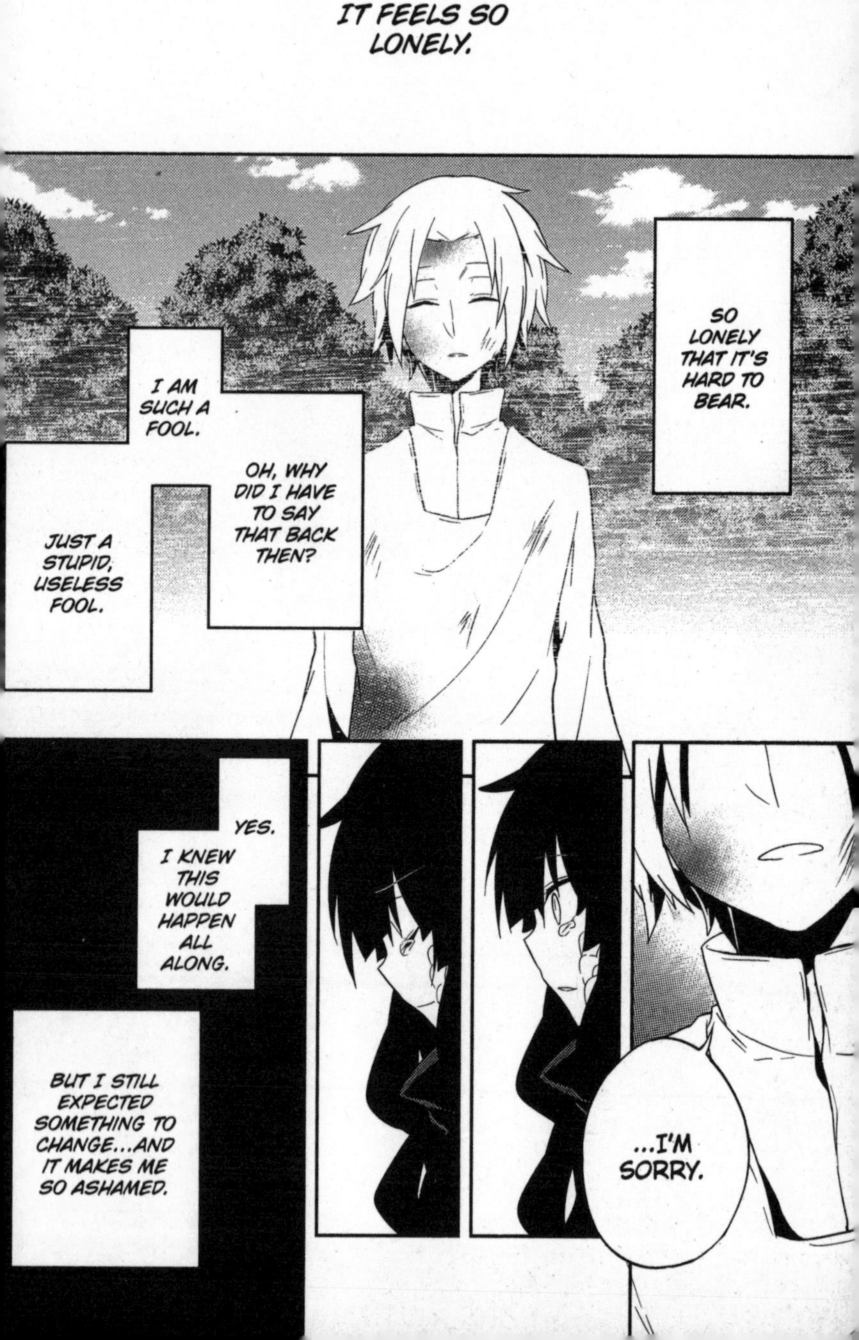
IT FEELS SO LONELY.
SO LONELY THAT IT'S HARD TO BEAR.
I AM SUCH A FOOL.
OH, WHY DID I HAVE TO SAY THAT BACK THEN?
JUST A STUPID, USELESS FOOL.
...I'M SORRY.
YES. I KNEW THIS WOULD HAPPEN ALL ALONG.
BUT I STILL EXPECTED SOMETHING TO CHANGE...AND IT MAKES ME SO ASHAMED.

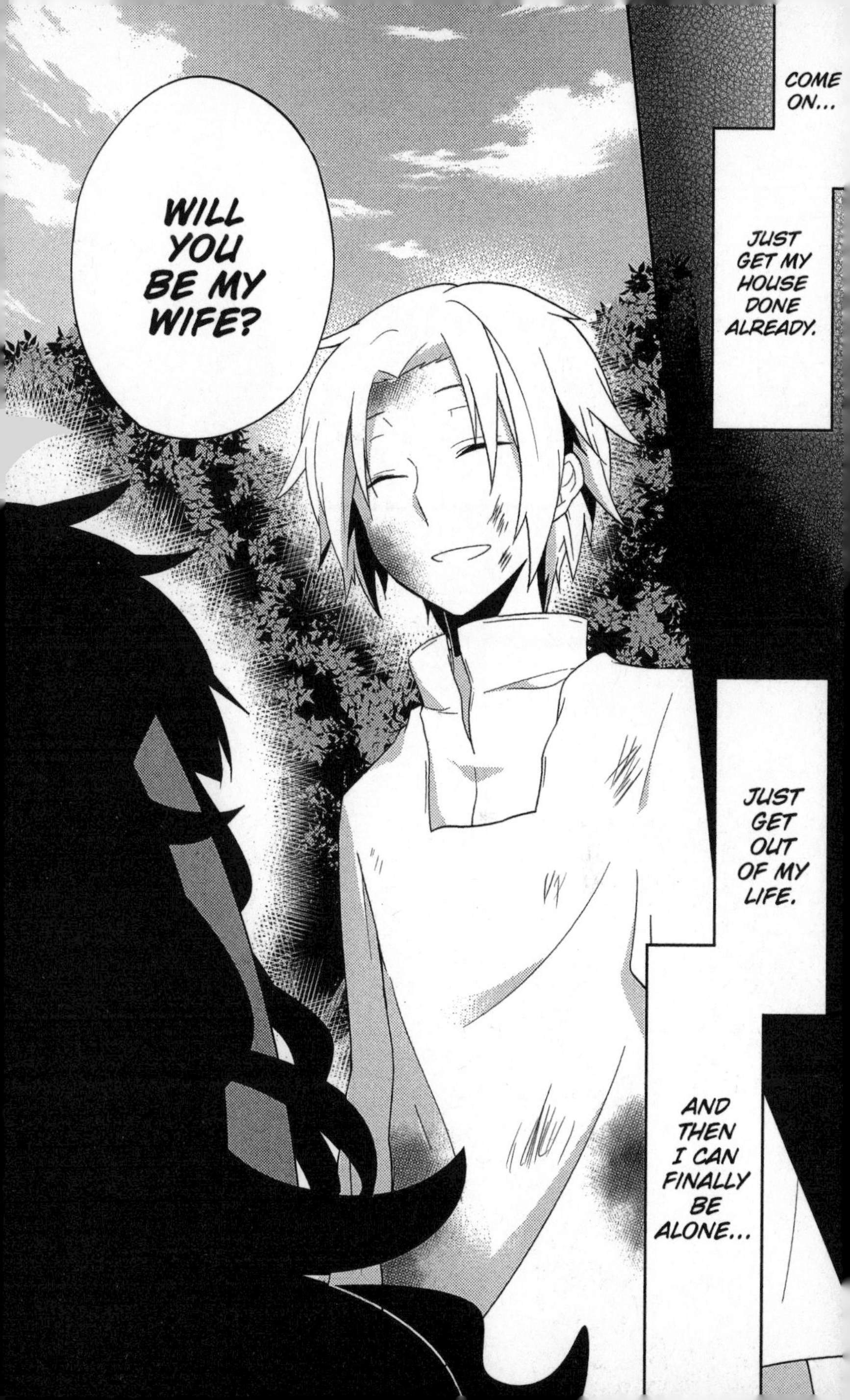
COME ON...
WILL YOU BE MY WIFE?
JUST GET MY HOUSE DONE ALREADY.
JUST GET OUT OF MY LIFE.
AND THEN I CAN FINALLY BE ALONE...

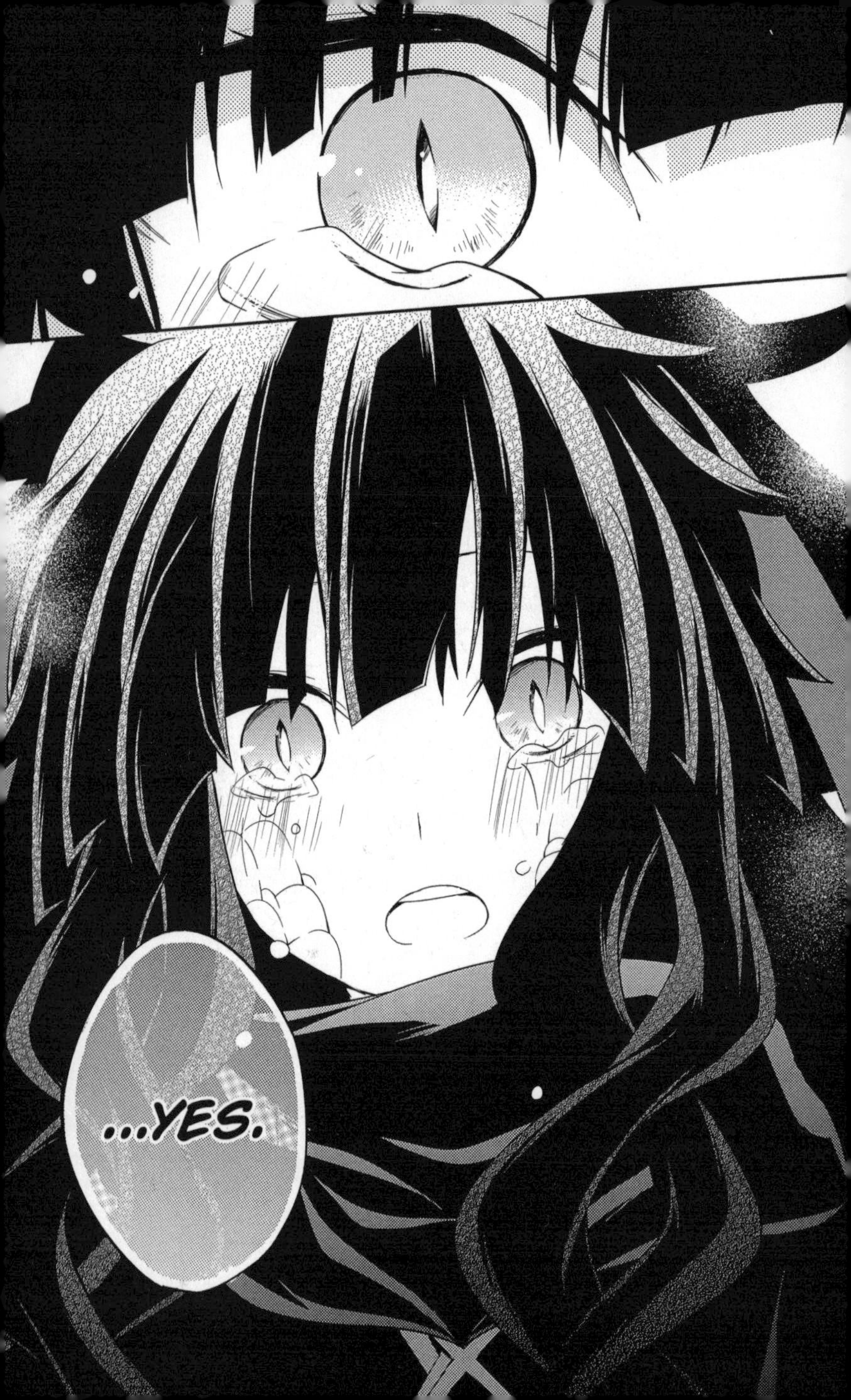
...YES.

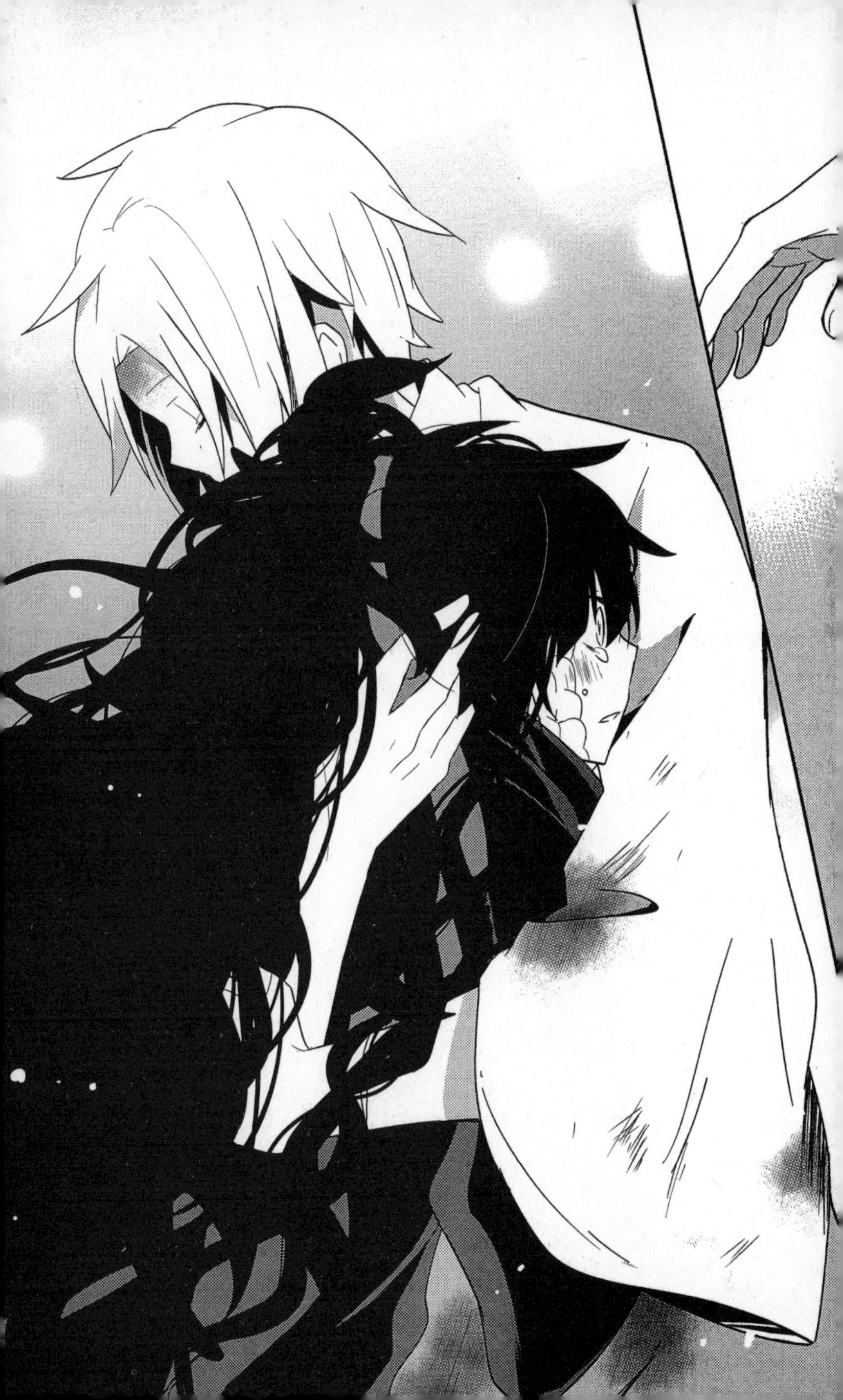

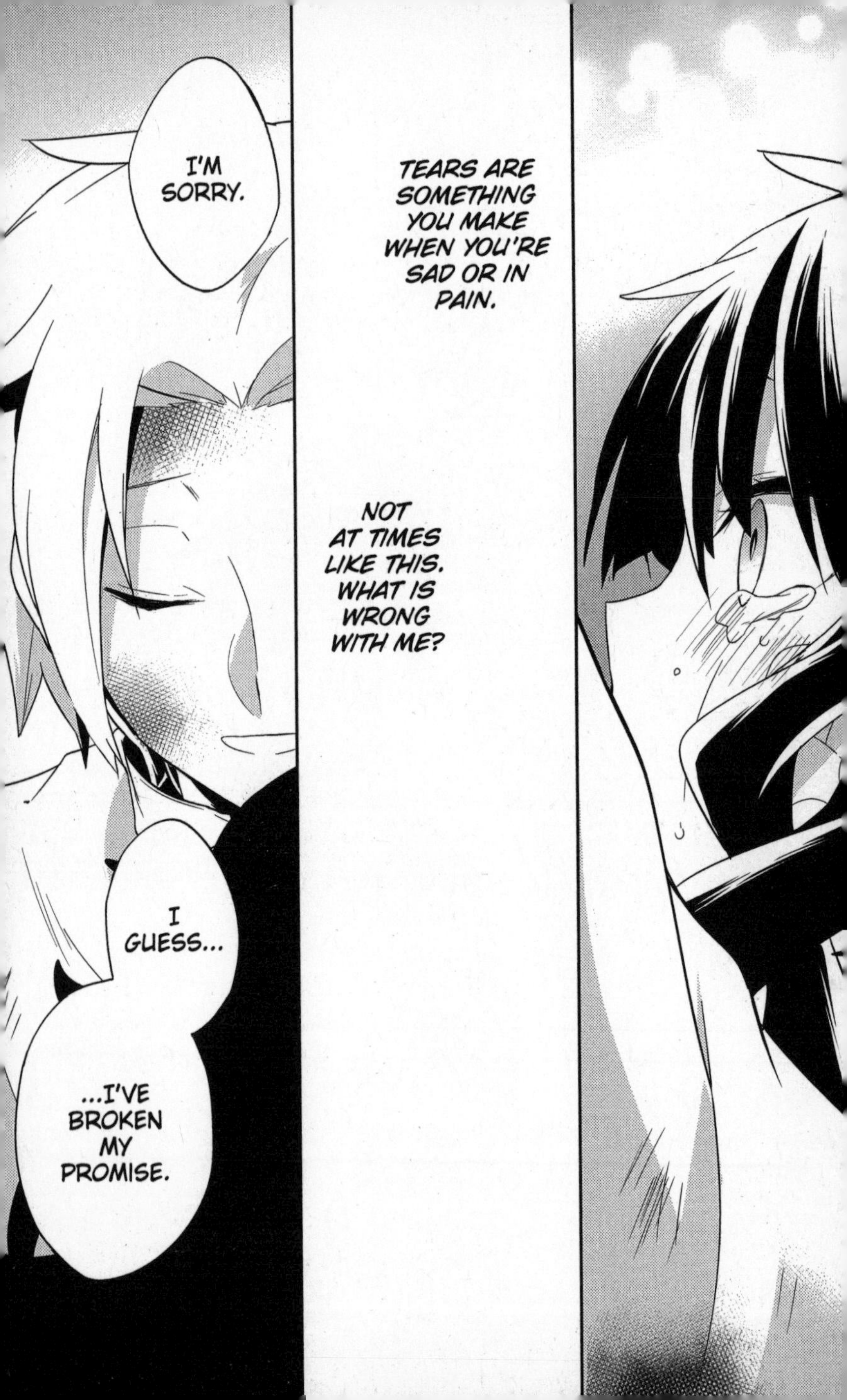
TEARS ARE SOMETHING YOU MAKE WHEN YOU'RE SAD OR IN PAIN.
NOT AT TIMES LIKE THIS. WHAT IS WRONG WITH ME?
I'M SORRY.
I GUESS...
...I'VE BROKEN MY PROMISE.

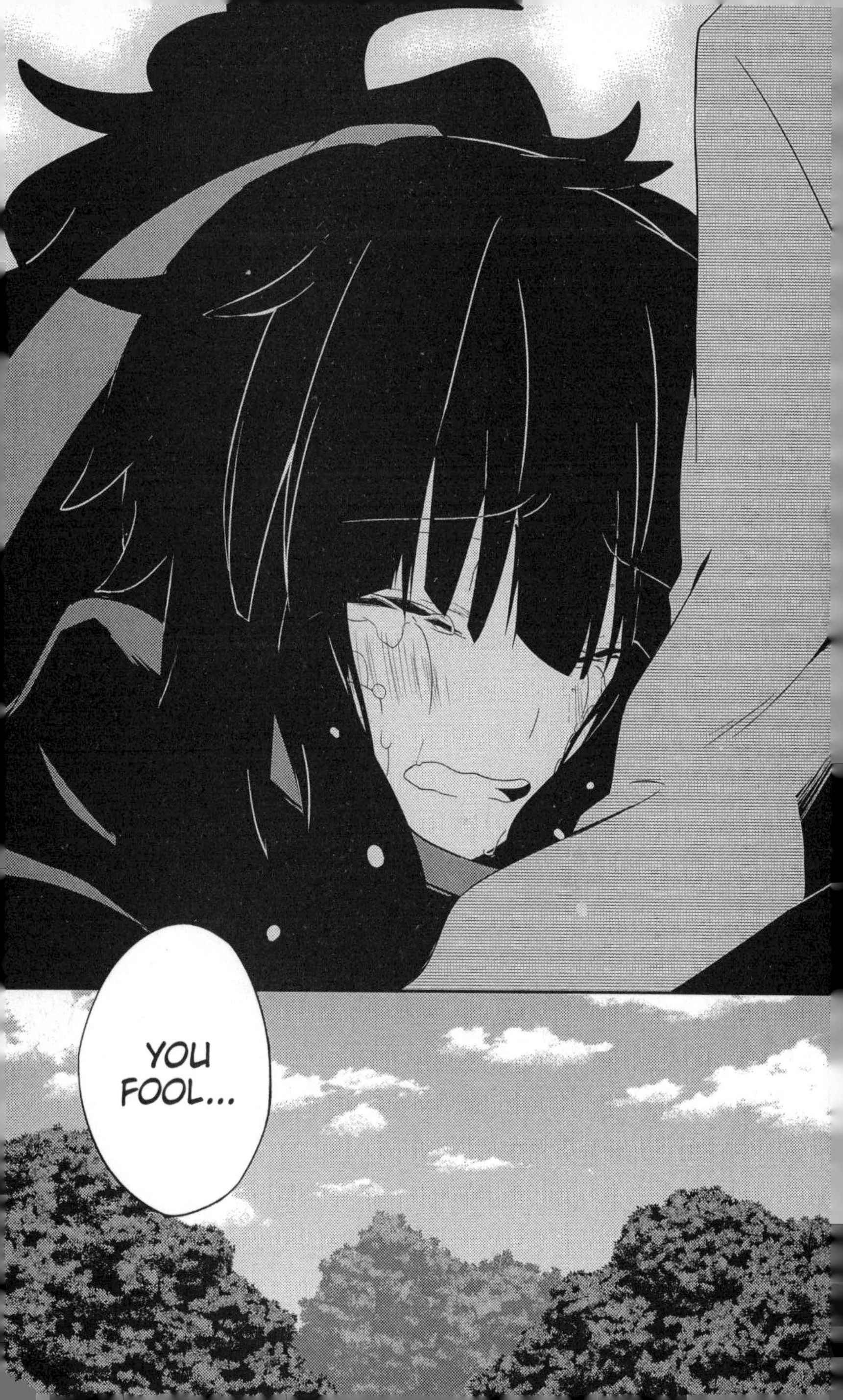
YOU FOOL...

KAGEROU
DAZE

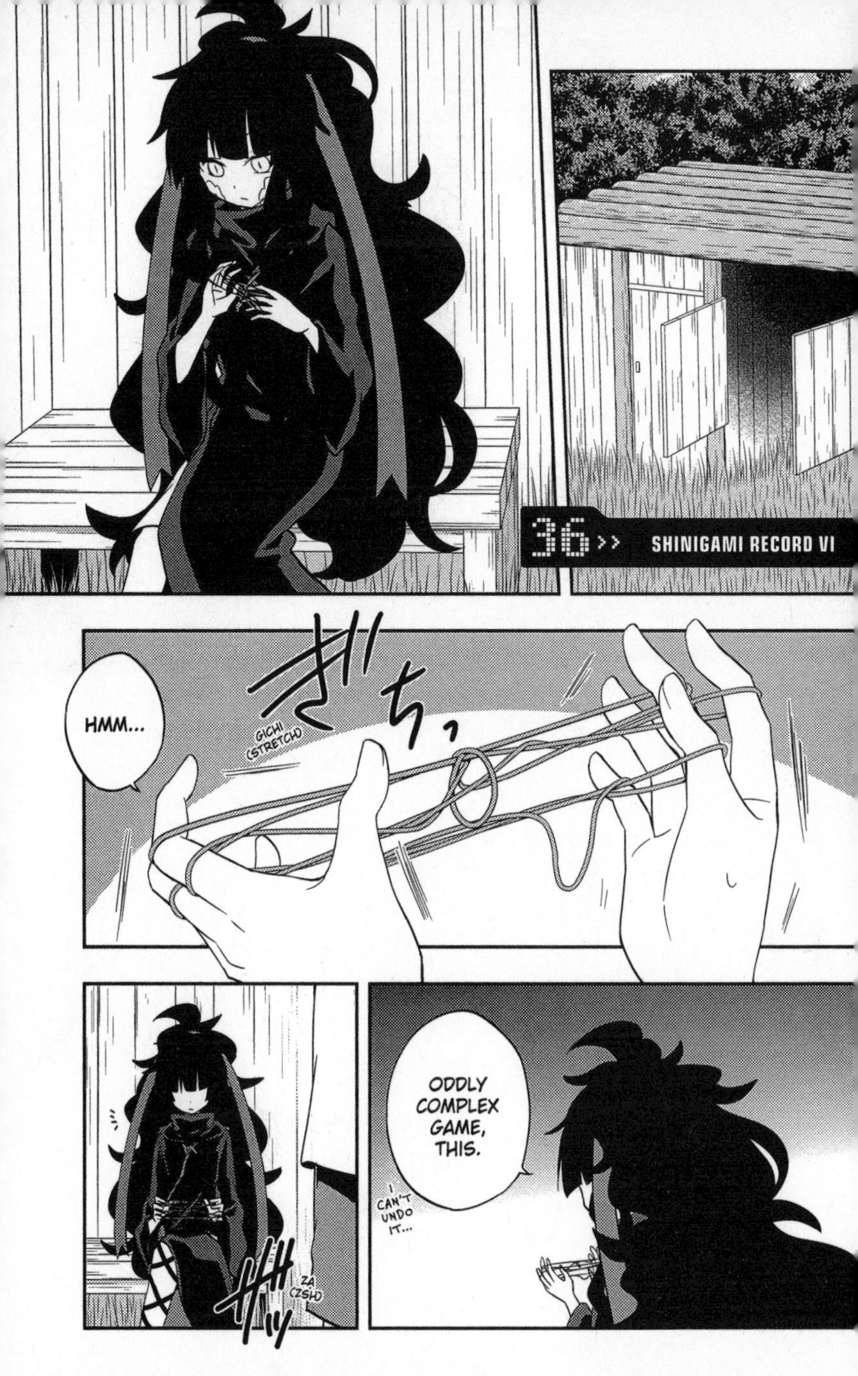
36 >> SHINIGAMI RECORD VI
HMM...
GICHI (STRETCH)
ODDLY COMPLEX GAME, THIS.
I CAN'T UNDO IT...
ZA (ZSH)

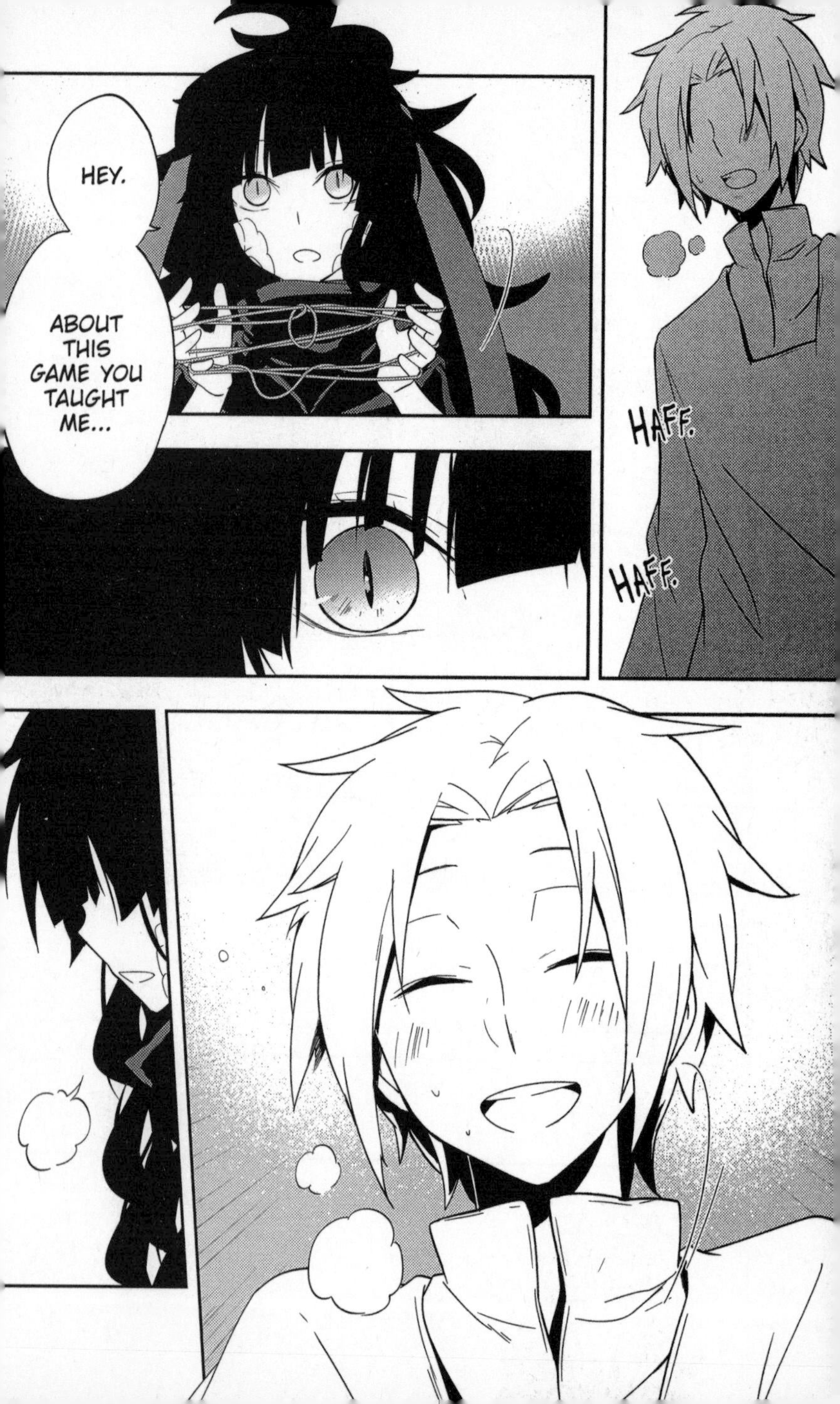
HAFF.
HAFF.
HEY.
ABOUT THIS GAME YOU TAUGHT ME...

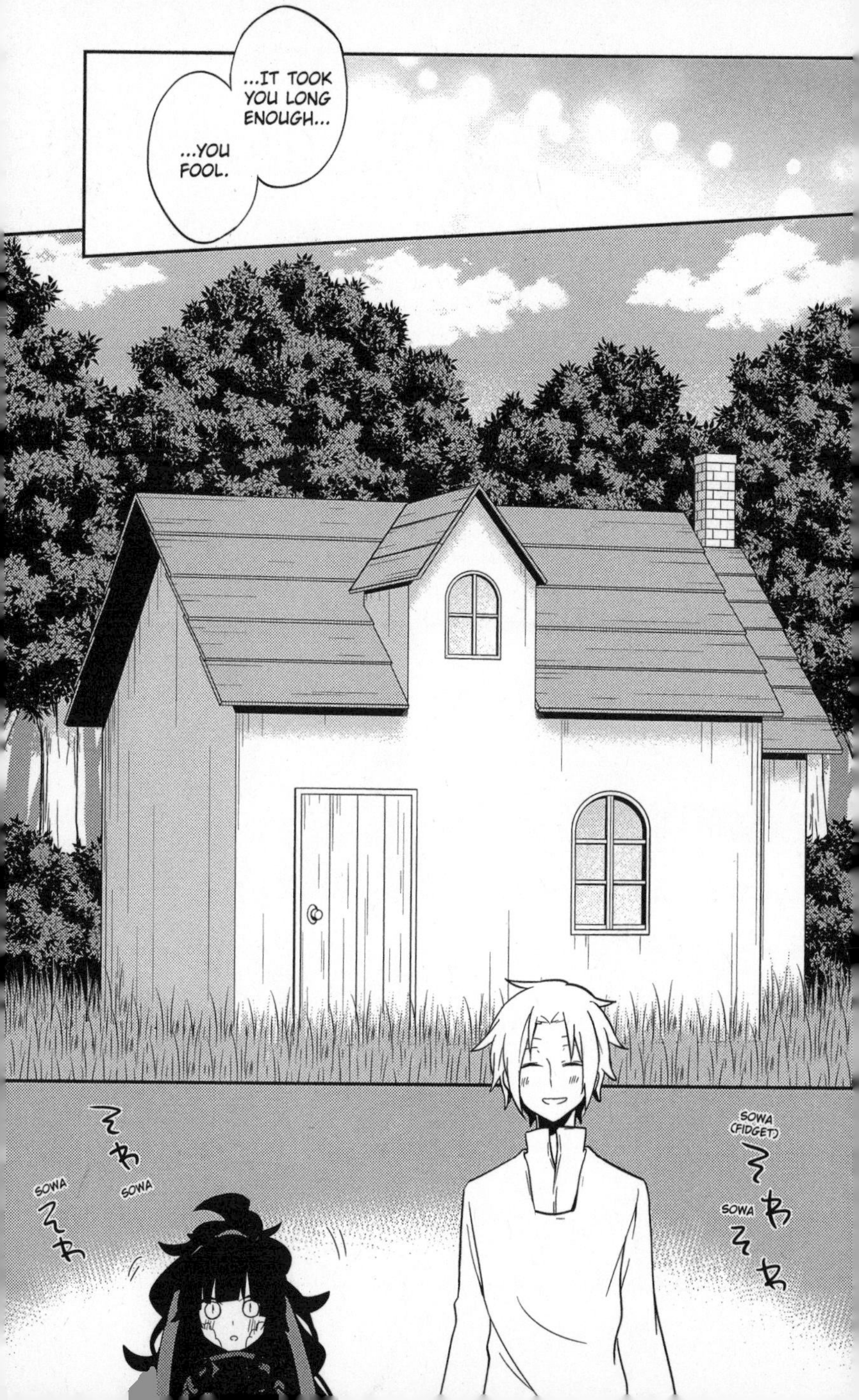
...IT TOOK YOU LONG ENOUGH...
...YOU FOOL.
SOWA (FIDGET)
SOWA
SOWA
SOWA

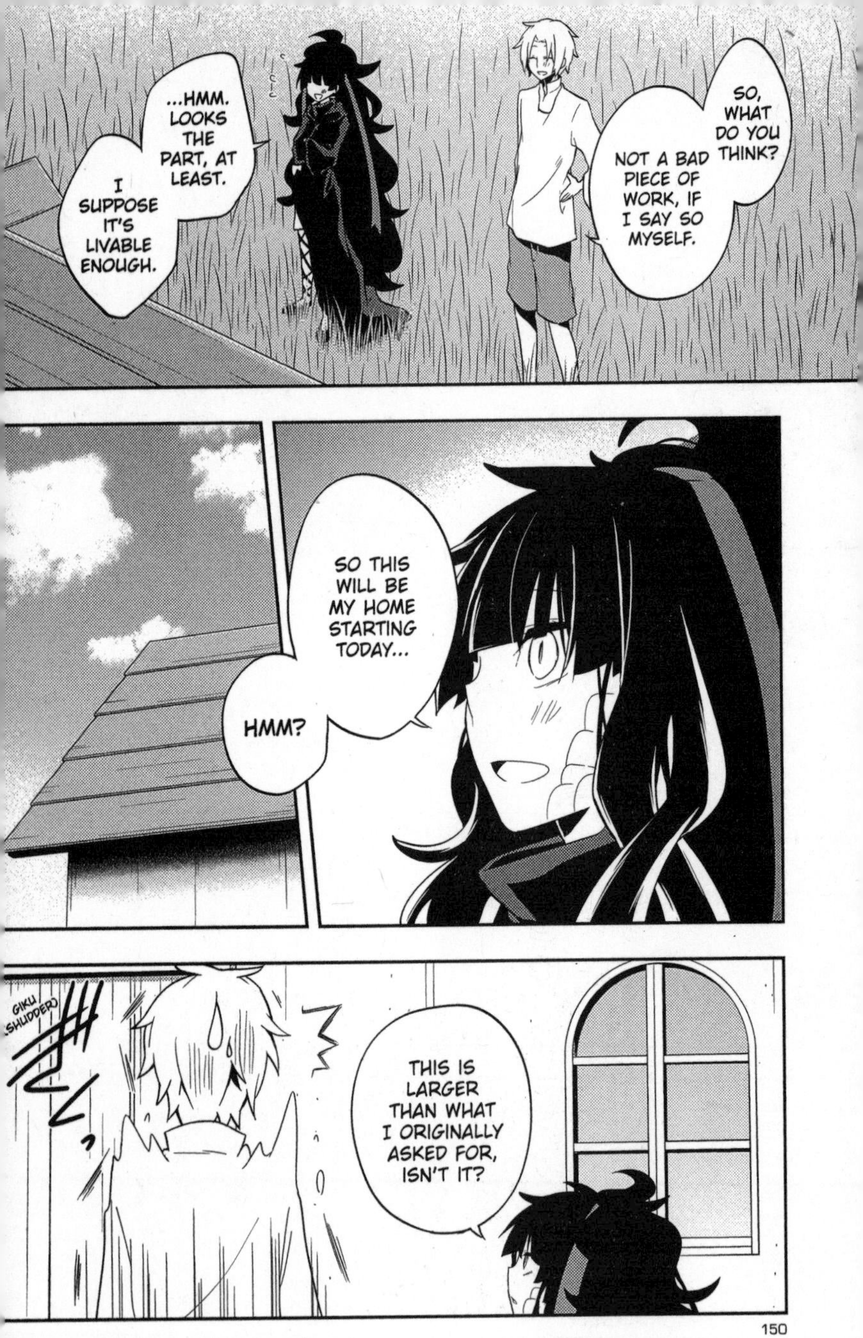
SO, WHAT DO YOU THINK?
NOT A BAD PIECE OF WORK, IF I SAY SO MYSELF.
...HMM. LOOKS THE PART, AT LEAST.
I SUPPOSE IT'S LIVABLE ENOUGH.
SO THIS WILL BE MY HOME STARTING TODAY...
HMM?
THIS IS LARGER THAN WHAT I ORIGINALLY ASKED FOR, ISN'T IT?
GIKU (SHUDDER)

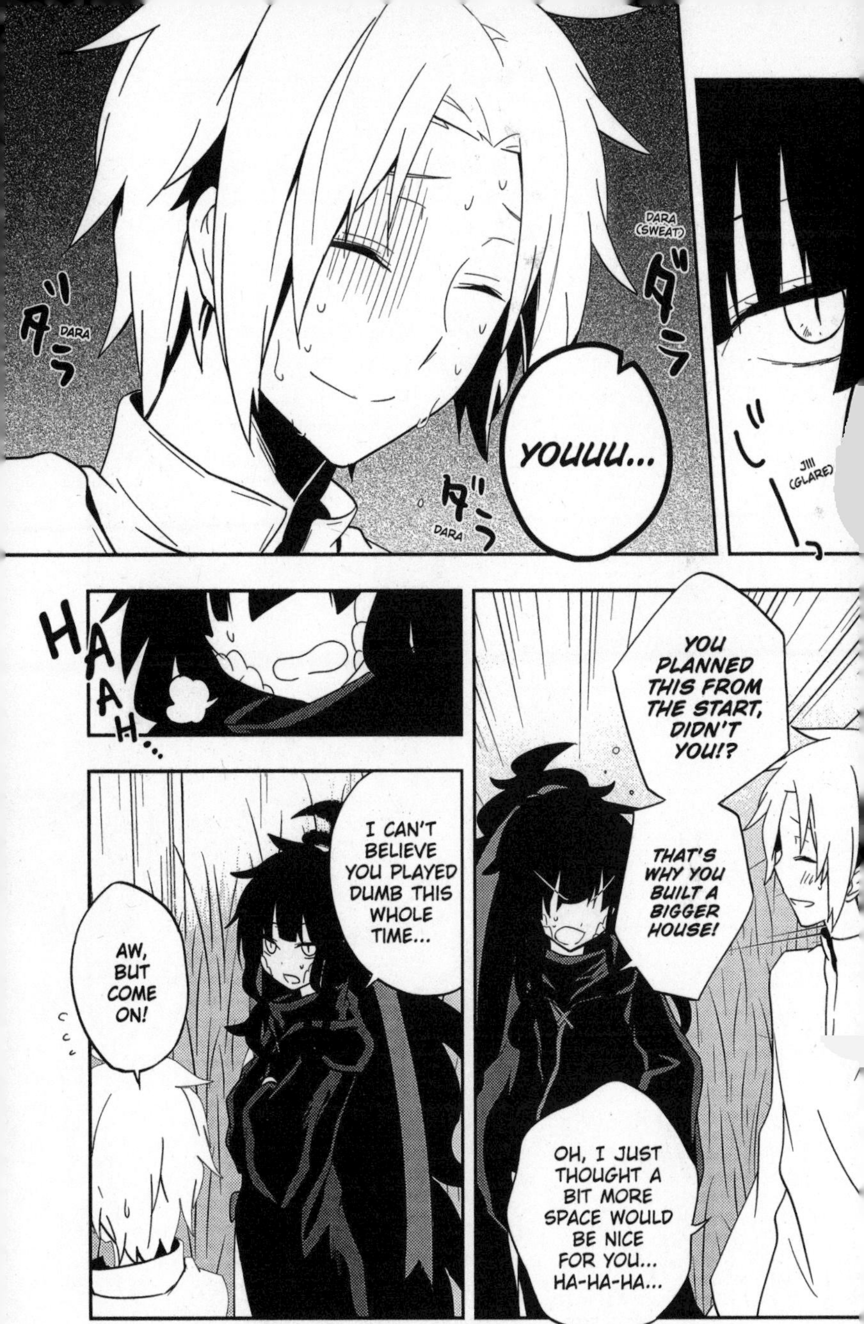
JIII (GLARE)
DARA (SWEAT)
YOUUU...
DARA
DARA
YOU PLANNED THIS FROM THE START, DIDN'T YOU!?
THAT'S WHY YOU BUILT A BIGGER HOUSE!
OH, I JUST THOUGHT A BIT MORE SPACE WOULD BE NICE FOR YOU... HA-HA-HA...
HAAAH...
I CAN'T BELIEVE YOU PLAYED DUMB THIS WHOLE TIME...
AW, BUT COME ON!

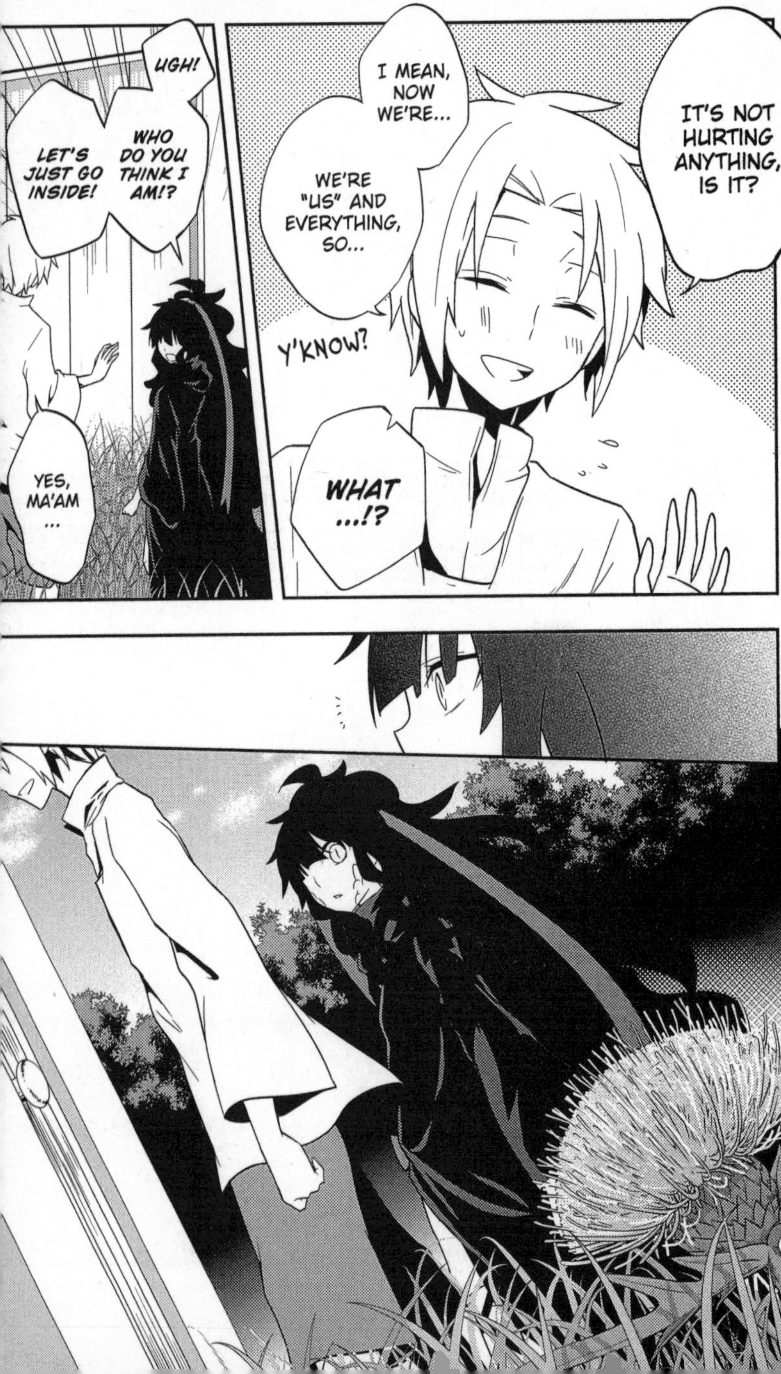
IT'S NOT HURTING ANYTHING, IS IT?
I MEAN, NOW WE'RE...
WE'RE "US" AND EVERYTHING, SO...
Y'KNOW?
WHAT ...!?
UGH!
WHO DO YOU THINK I AM!?
LET'S JUST GO INSIDE!
YES, MA'AM ...

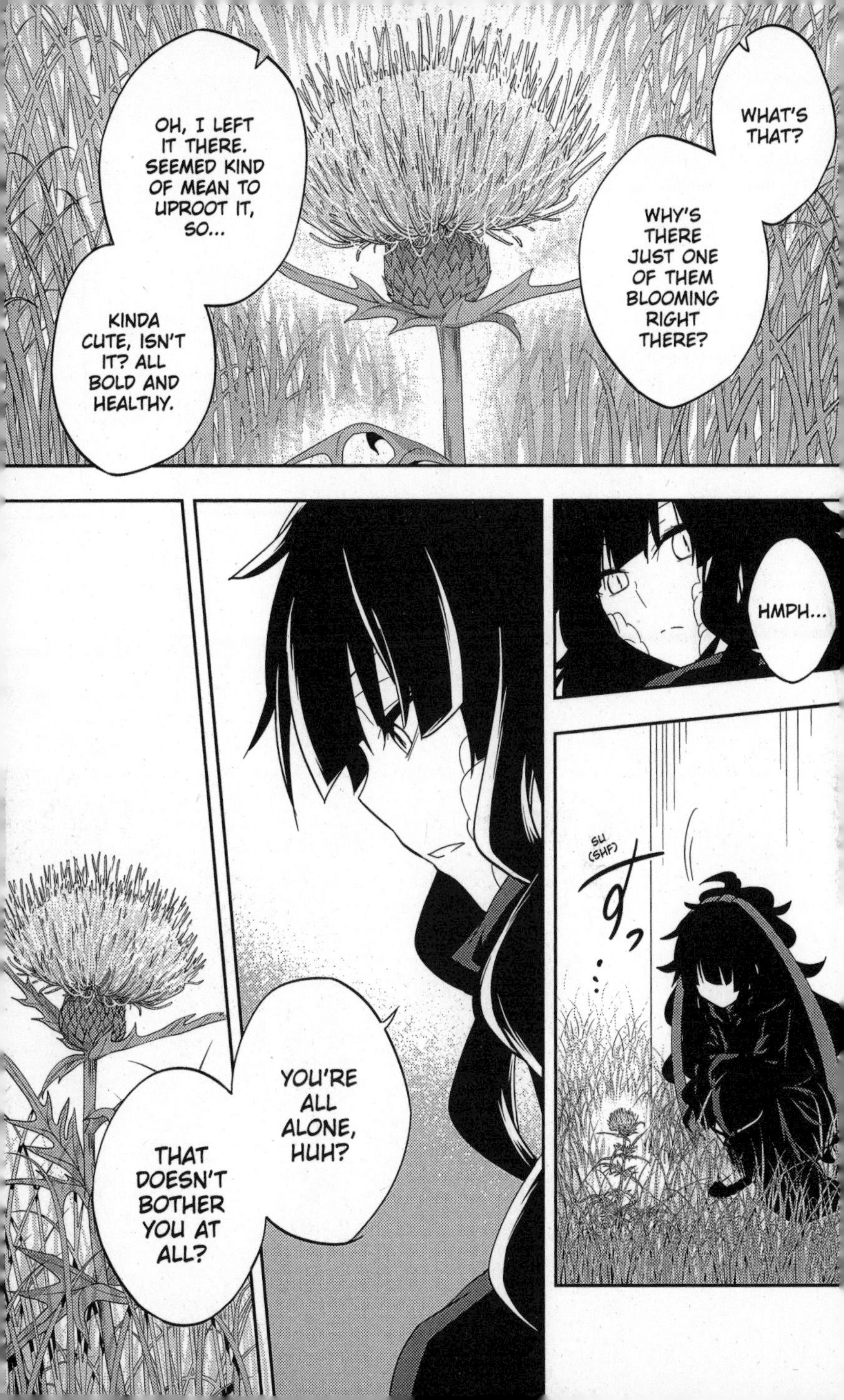
WHAT'S THAT?
WHY'S THERE JUST ONE OF THEM BLOOMING RIGHT THERE?
OH, I LEFT IT THERE. SEEMED KIND OF MEAN TO UPROOT IT, SO...
KINDA CUTE, ISN'T IT? ALL BOLD AND HEALTHY.
HMPH...
SU (SHF)
YOU'RE ALL ALONE, HUH?
THAT DOESN'T BOTHER YOU AT ALL?

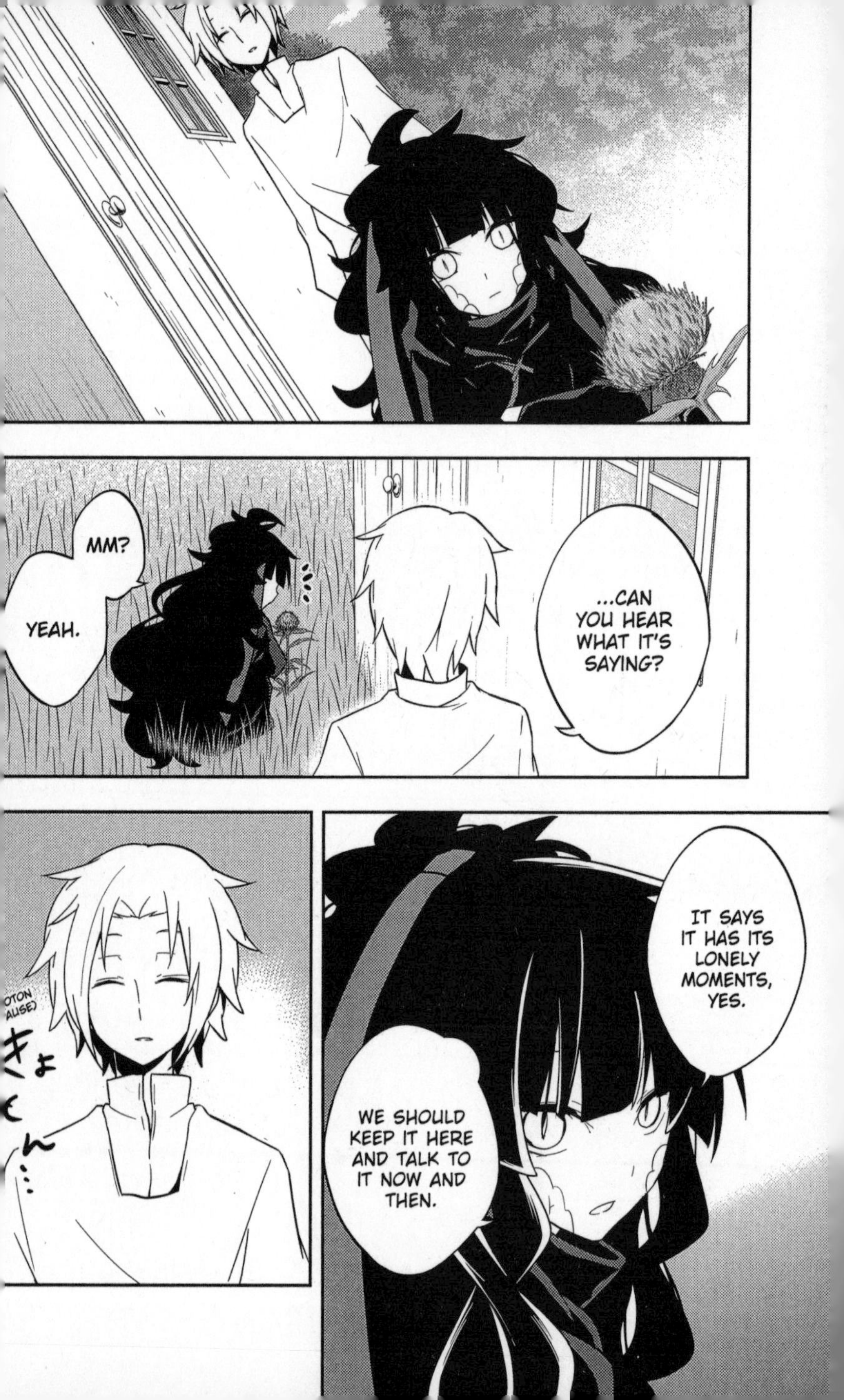
...CAN YOU HEAR WHAT IT'S SAYING?
MM? YEAH.
IT SAYS IT HAS ITS LONELY MOMENTS, YES.
WE SHOULD KEEP IT HERE AND TALK TO IT NOW AND THEN.
きょとん…

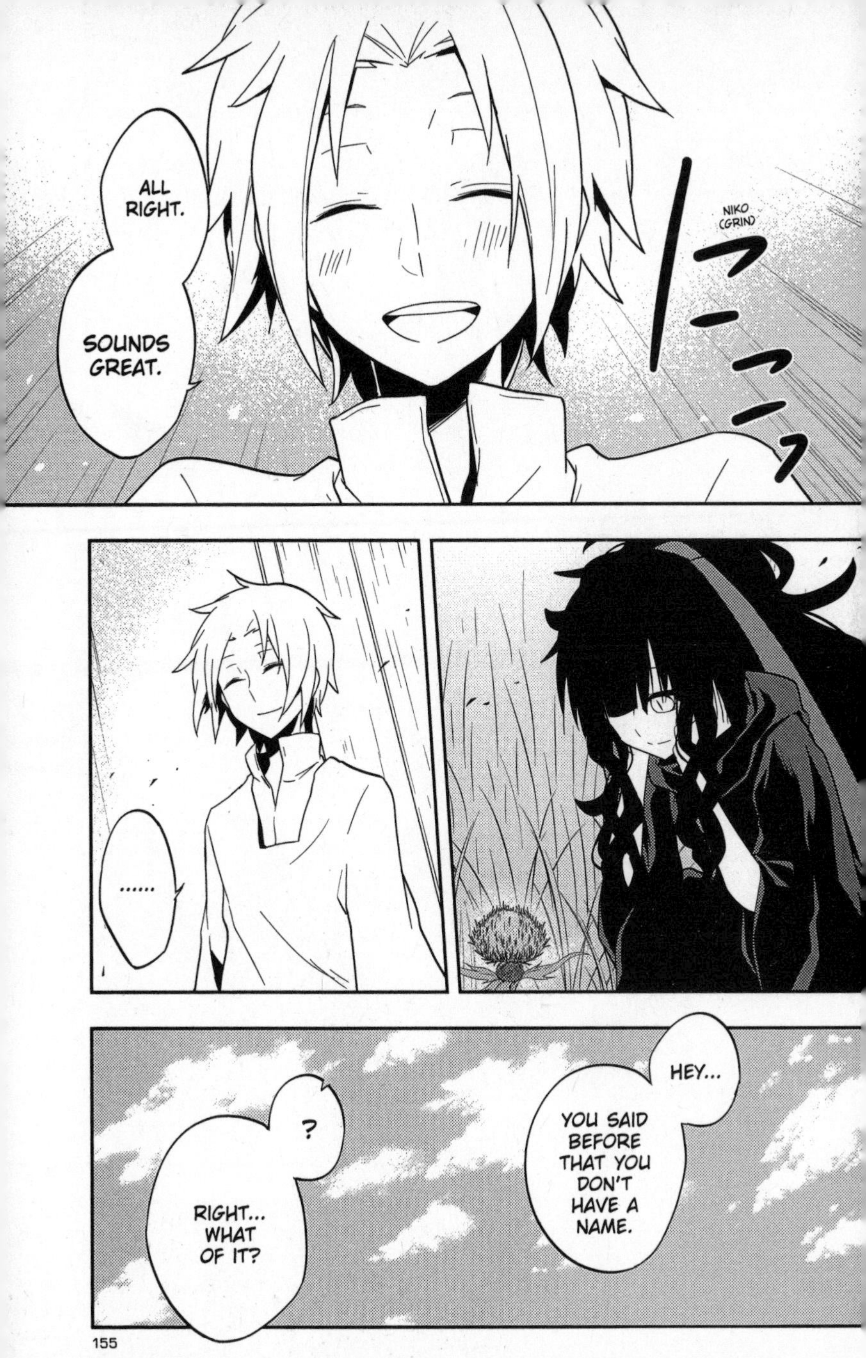
NIKO (GRIN)
ALL RIGHT.
SOUNDS GREAT.
......
HEY...
YOU SAID BEFORE THAT YOU DON'T HAVE A NAME.
?
RIGHT... WHAT OF IT?

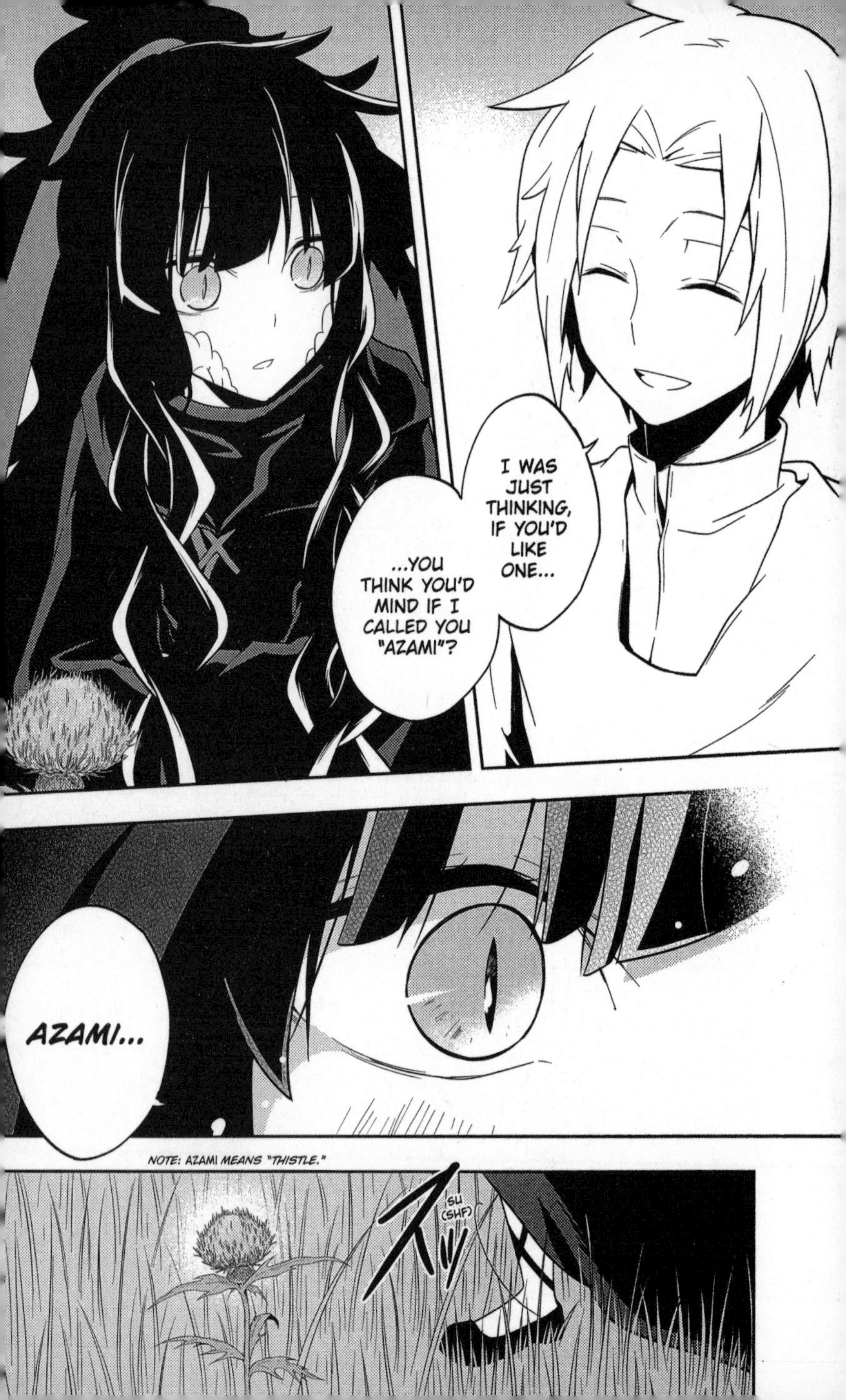
I WAS JUST THINKING, IF YOU'D LIKE ONE...
...YOU THINK YOU'D MIND IF I CALLED YOU "AZAMI"?
AZAMI...
NOTE: AZAMI MEANS "THISTLE."
SU (SHF)

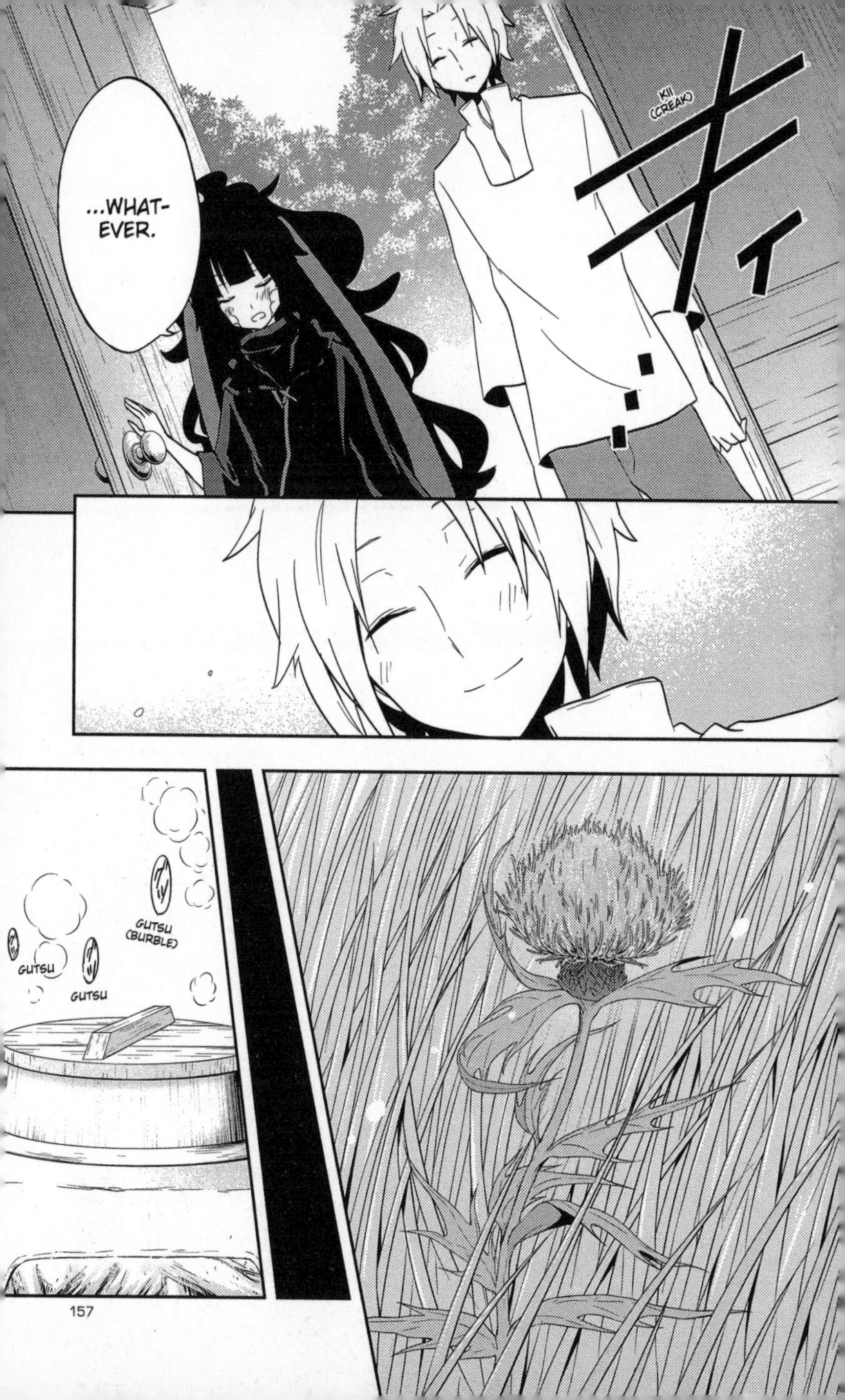
KII
(CREAK)
...WHAT-
EVER.
GUTSU
(BURBLE)
GUTSU
GUTSU

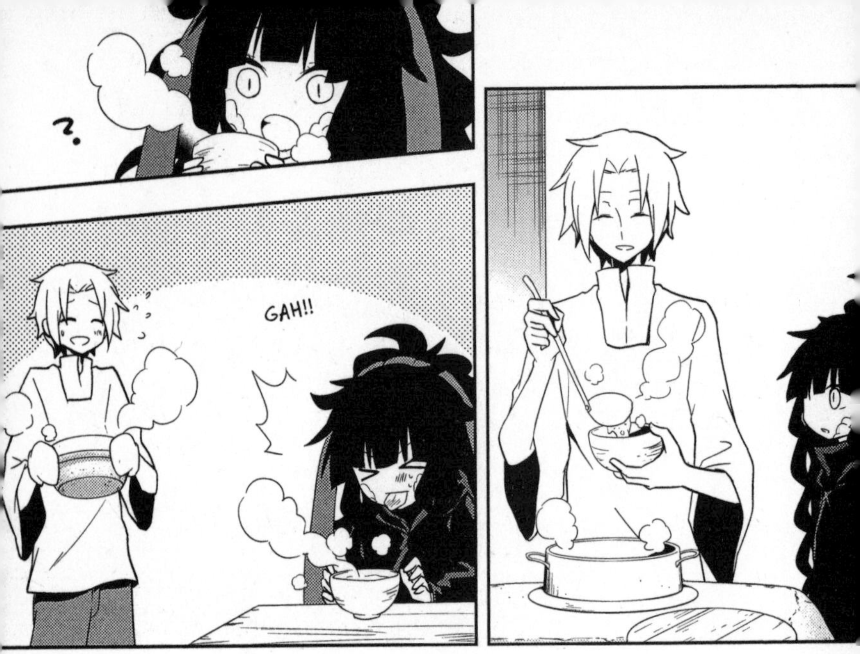
GAH!!

WHY DID ANYONE BOTHER CREATING THIS WORLD?

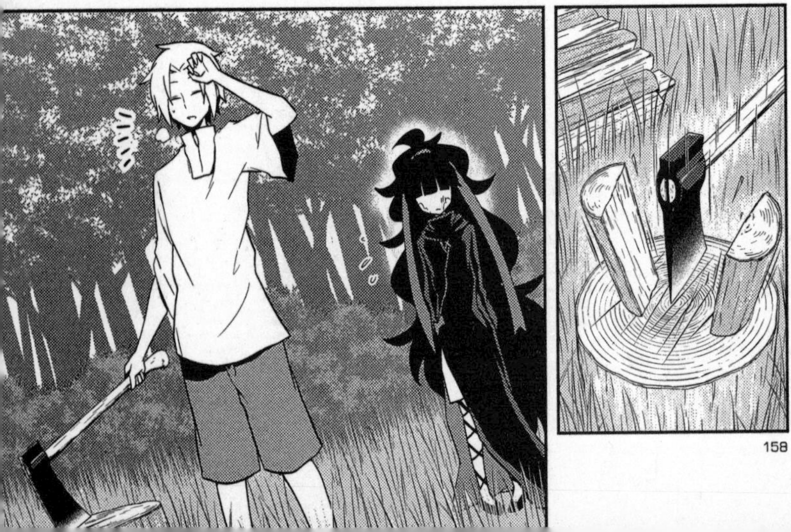

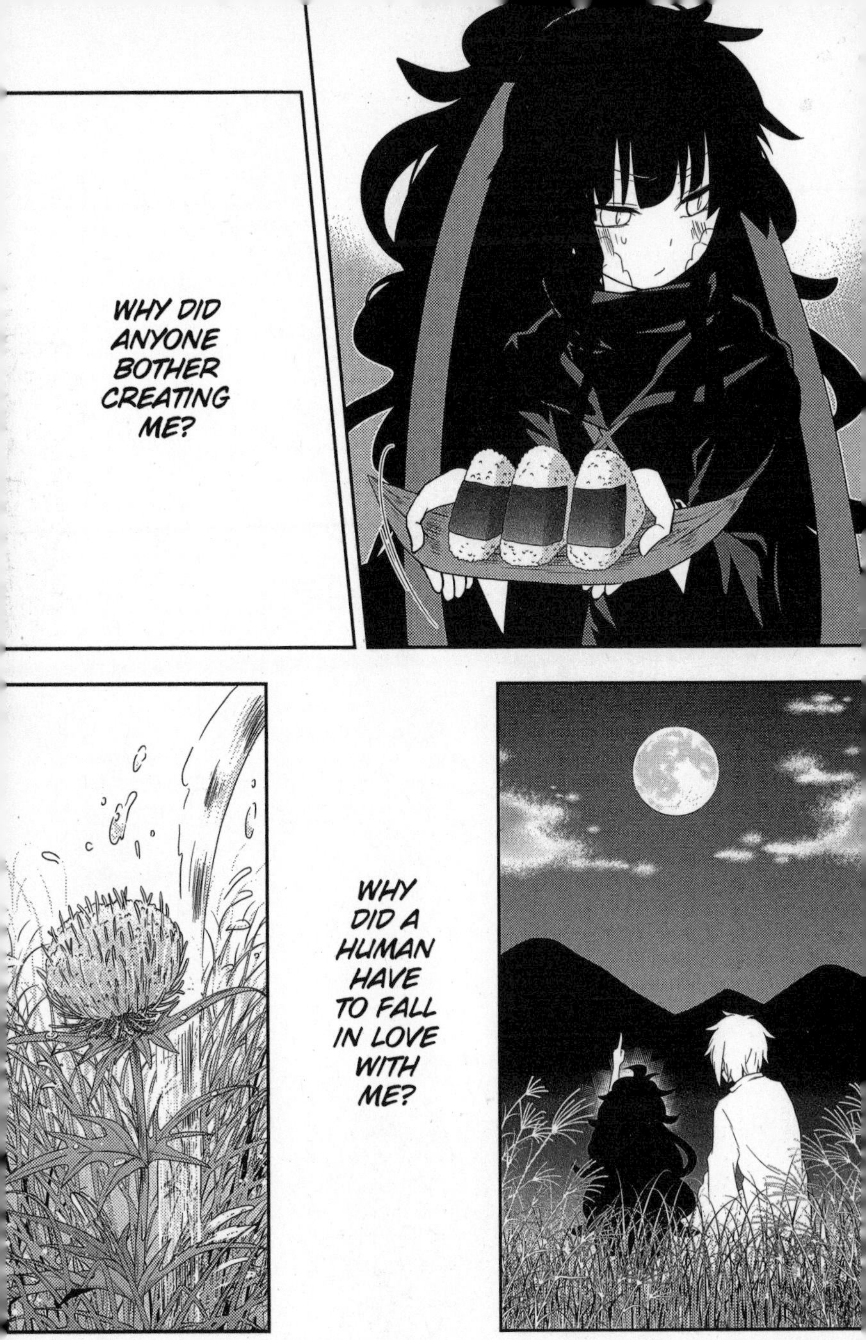
WHY DID ANYONE BOTHER CREATING ME?
WHY DID A HUMAN HAVE TO FALL IN LOVE WITH ME?

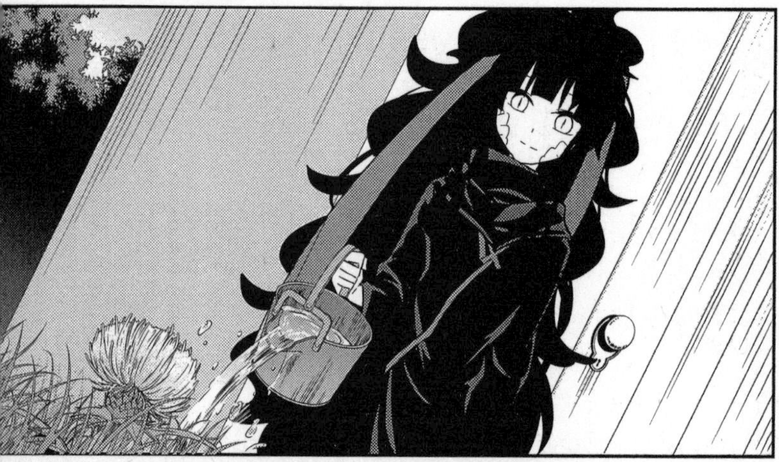

AND WHAT ARE THESE EMOTIONS THAT SEEM TO FILL MY HEART?

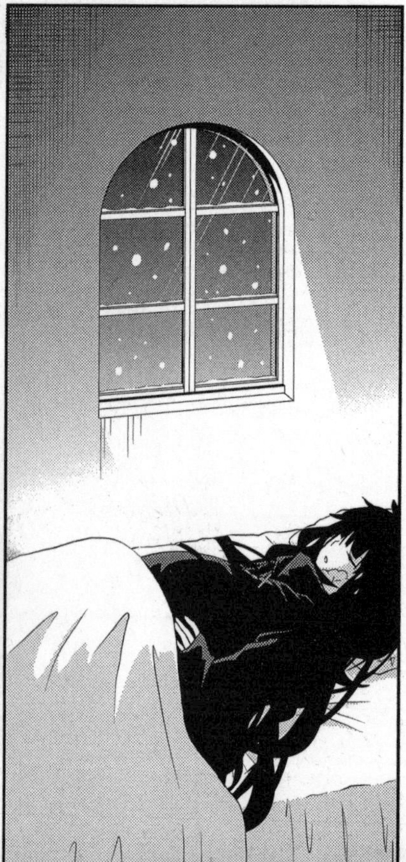

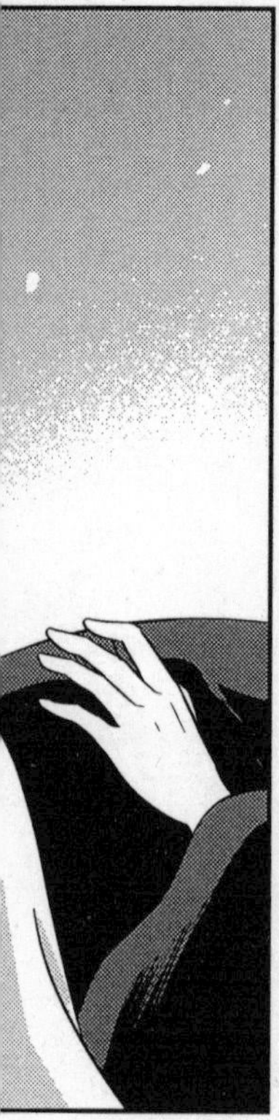

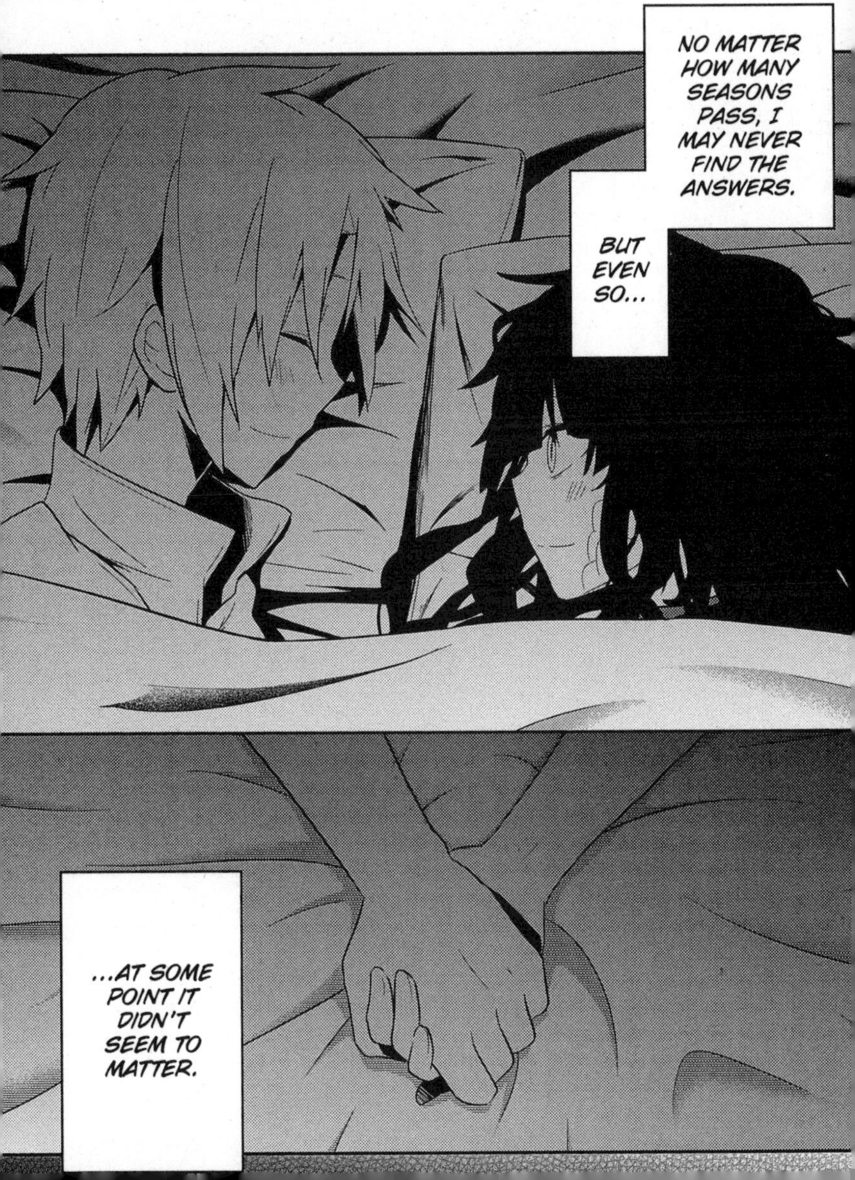
NO MATTER HOW MANY SEASONS PASS, I MAY NEVER FIND THE ANSWERS.
BUT EVEN SO...
...AT SOME POINT IT DIDN'T SEEM TO MATTER.

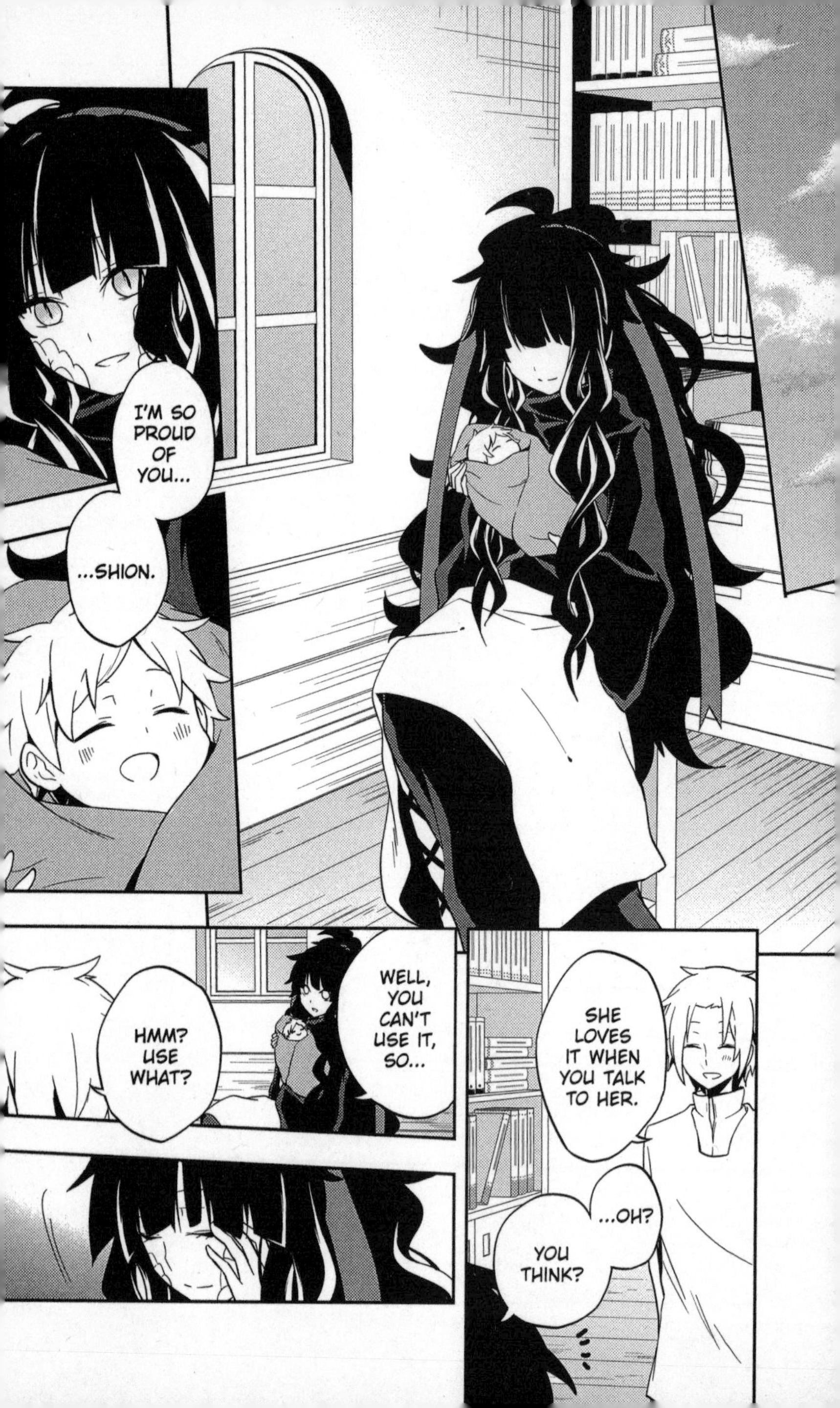
I'M SO PROUD OF YOU...
...SHION.
SHE LOVES IT WHEN YOU TALK TO HER.
...OH?
YOU THINK?
WELL, YOU CAN'T USE IT, SO...
HMM? USE WHAT?

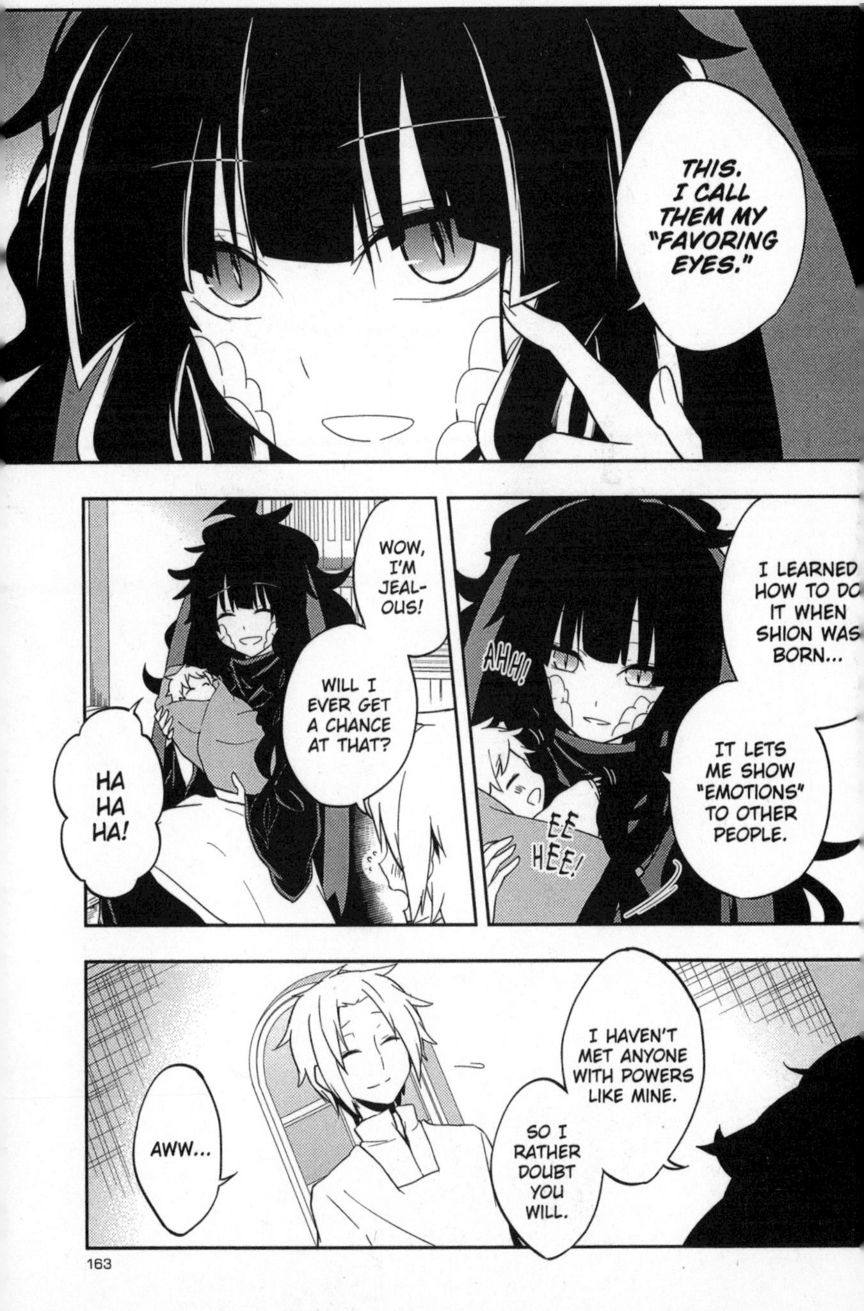
THIS. I CALL THEM MY "FAVORING EYES."
I LEARNED HOW TO DO IT WHEN SHION WAS BORN...
AHH!
IT LETS ME SHOW "EMOTIONS" TO OTHER PEOPLE.
EE HEE!
WOW, I'M JEAL-OUS!
WILL I EVER GET A CHANCE AT THAT?
HA HA HA!
I HAVEN'T MET ANYONE WITH POWERS LIKE MINE.
SO I RATHER DOUBT YOU WILL.
AWW...

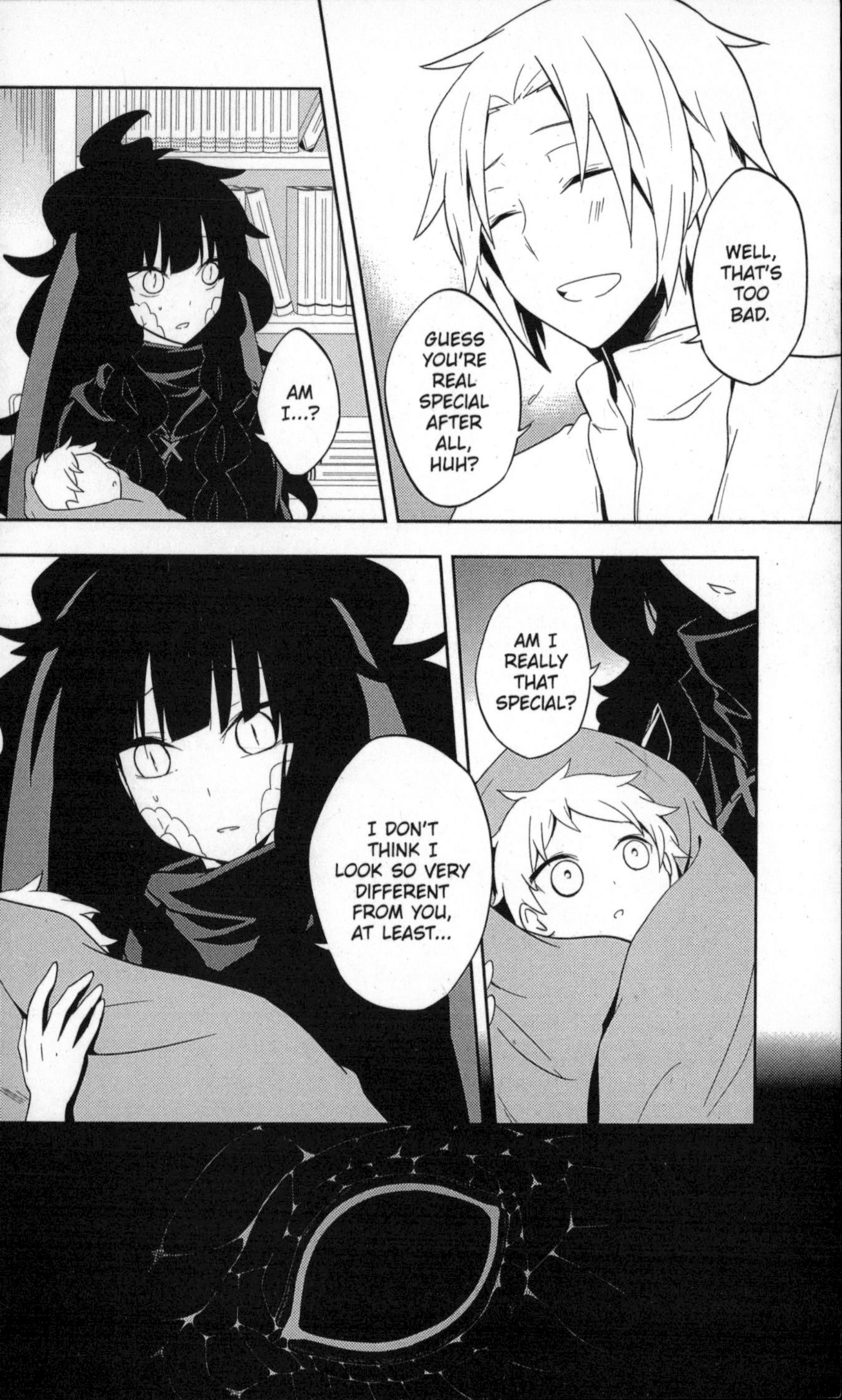
WELL, THAT'S TOO BAD.
GUESS YOU'RE REAL SPECIAL AFTER ALL, HUH?
AM I...?
AM I REALLY THAT SPECIAL?
I DON'T THINK I LOOK SO VERY DIFFERENT FROM YOU, AT LEAST...

..."TIME."

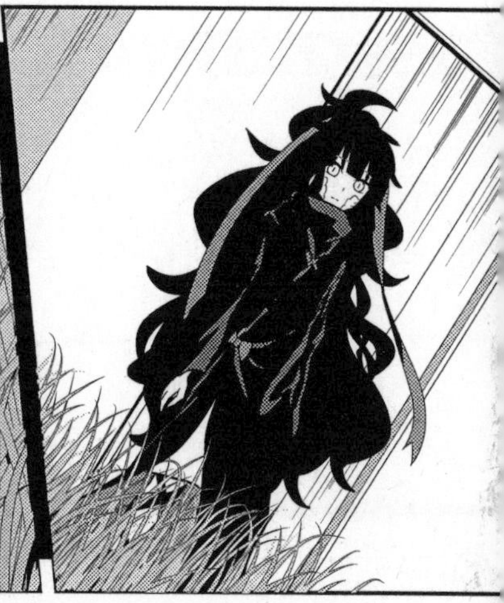

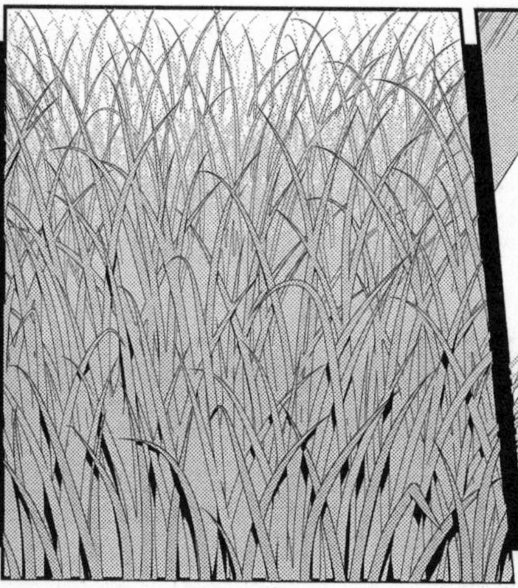

AGAINST THE EXISTENCE OF "TIME"
AND ITS POWER TO EAT AWAY
AT LIFE WITHOUT PREJUDICE,
ALL CREATURES ARE POWERLESS,
DOOMED TO FALL INTO THE GREAT VOID.

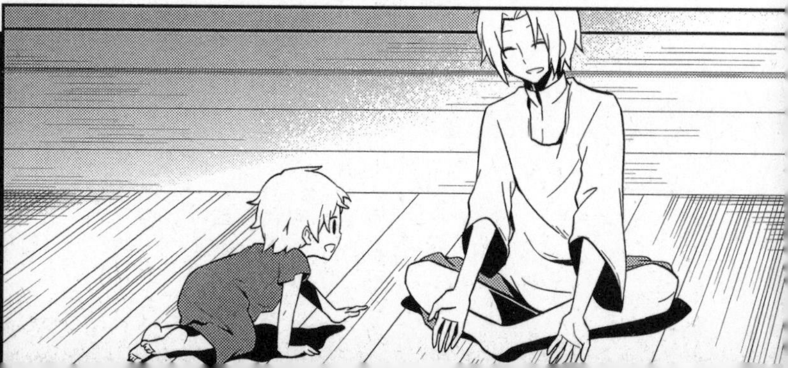

THE HUMAN RACE IS NO EXCEPTION. IN THEIR COUNTING SYSTEM, MOST HUMANS DIE ONCE THEY HAVE LIVED FOR EIGHTY YEARS OR SO.

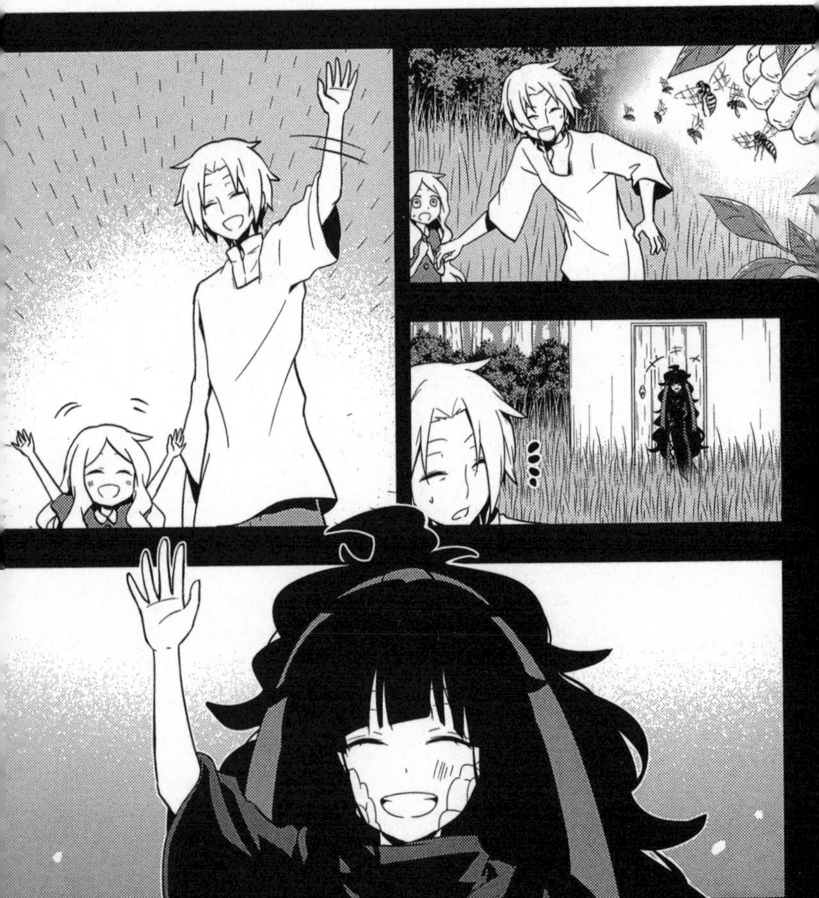

YES, ALL CREATURES EXCEPT ME FACE THE SAME FATE—DEATH—NO MATTER HOW MUCH THEY STRUGGLE.

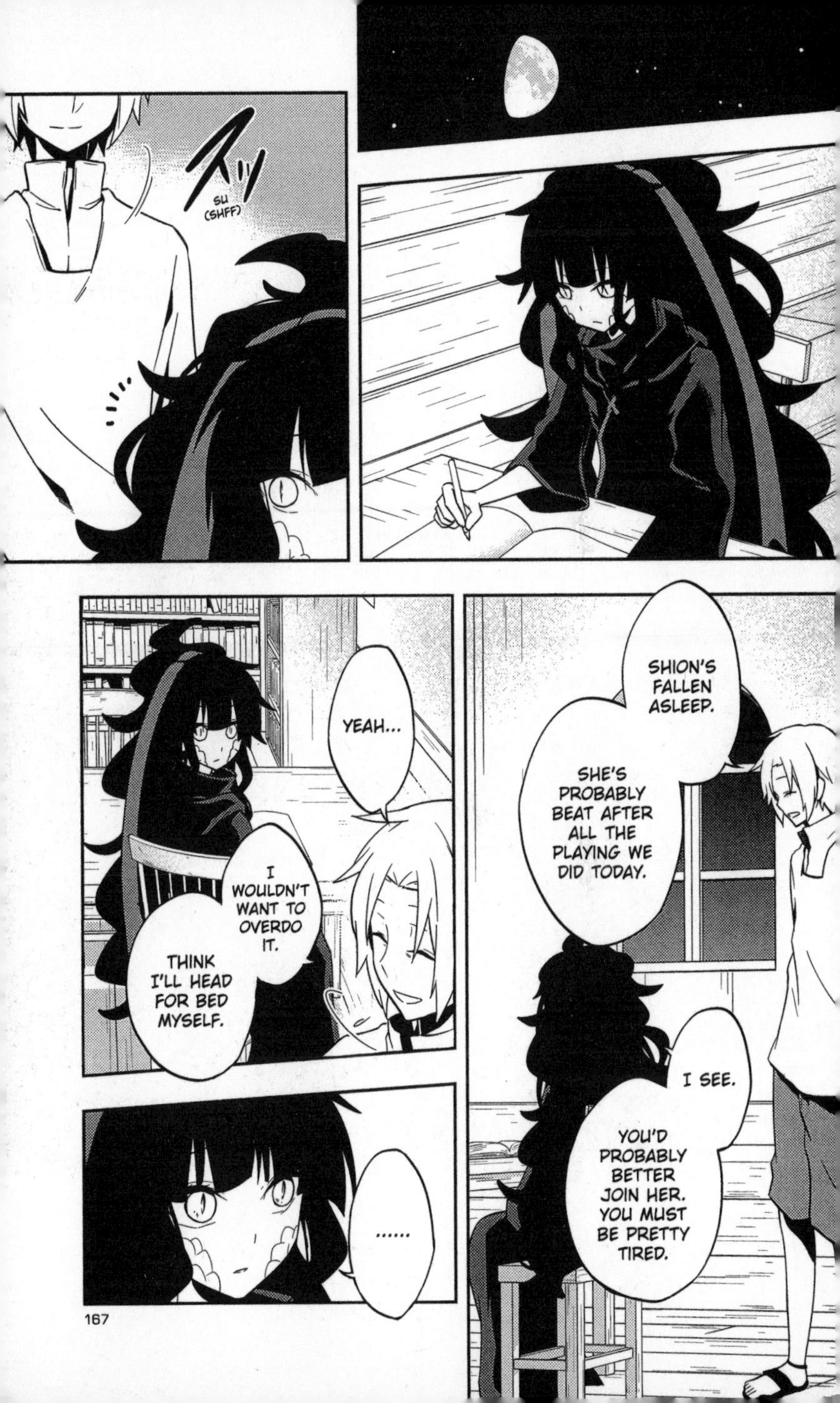
スッ
SU (SHFF)
SHION'S FALLEN ASLEEP.
SHE'S PROBABLY BEAT AFTER ALL THE PLAYING WE DID TODAY.
I SEE.
YOU'D PROBABLY BETTER JOIN HER. YOU MUST BE PRETTY TIRED.
YEAH...
I WOULDN'T WANT TO OVERDO IT.
THINK I'LL HEAD FOR BED MYSELF.
......

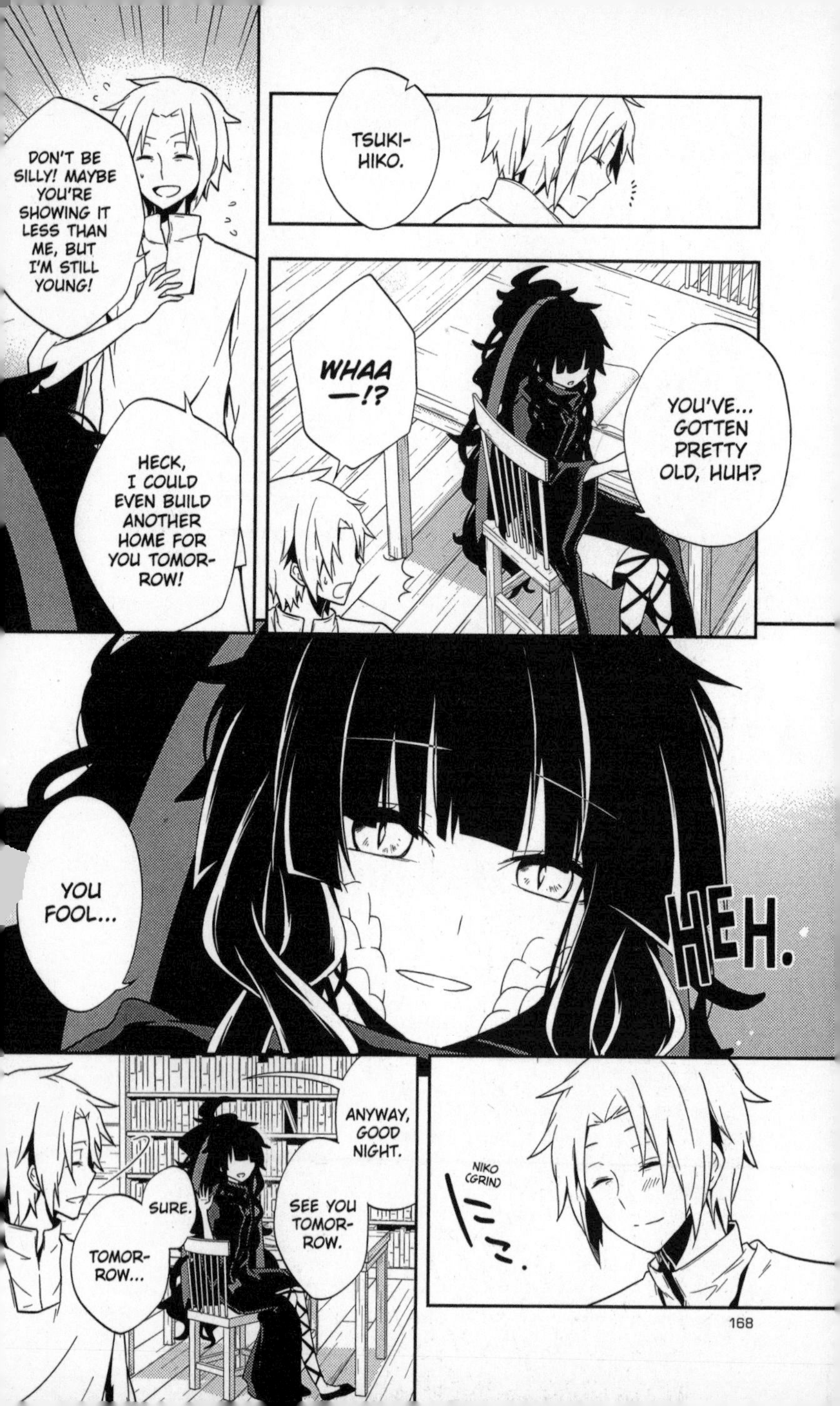
TSUKI-HIKO.
YOU'VE... GOTTEN PRETTY OLD, HUH?
WHAA—!?
DON'T BE SILLY! MAYBE YOU'RE SHOWING IT LESS THAN ME, BUT I'M STILL YOUNG!
HECK, I COULD EVEN BUILD ANOTHER HOME FOR YOU TOMOR-ROW!
HEH.
YOU FOOL...
NIKO (GRIN)
ANYWAY, GOOD NIGHT.
SEE YOU TOMOR-ROW.
SURE.
TOMOR-ROW...

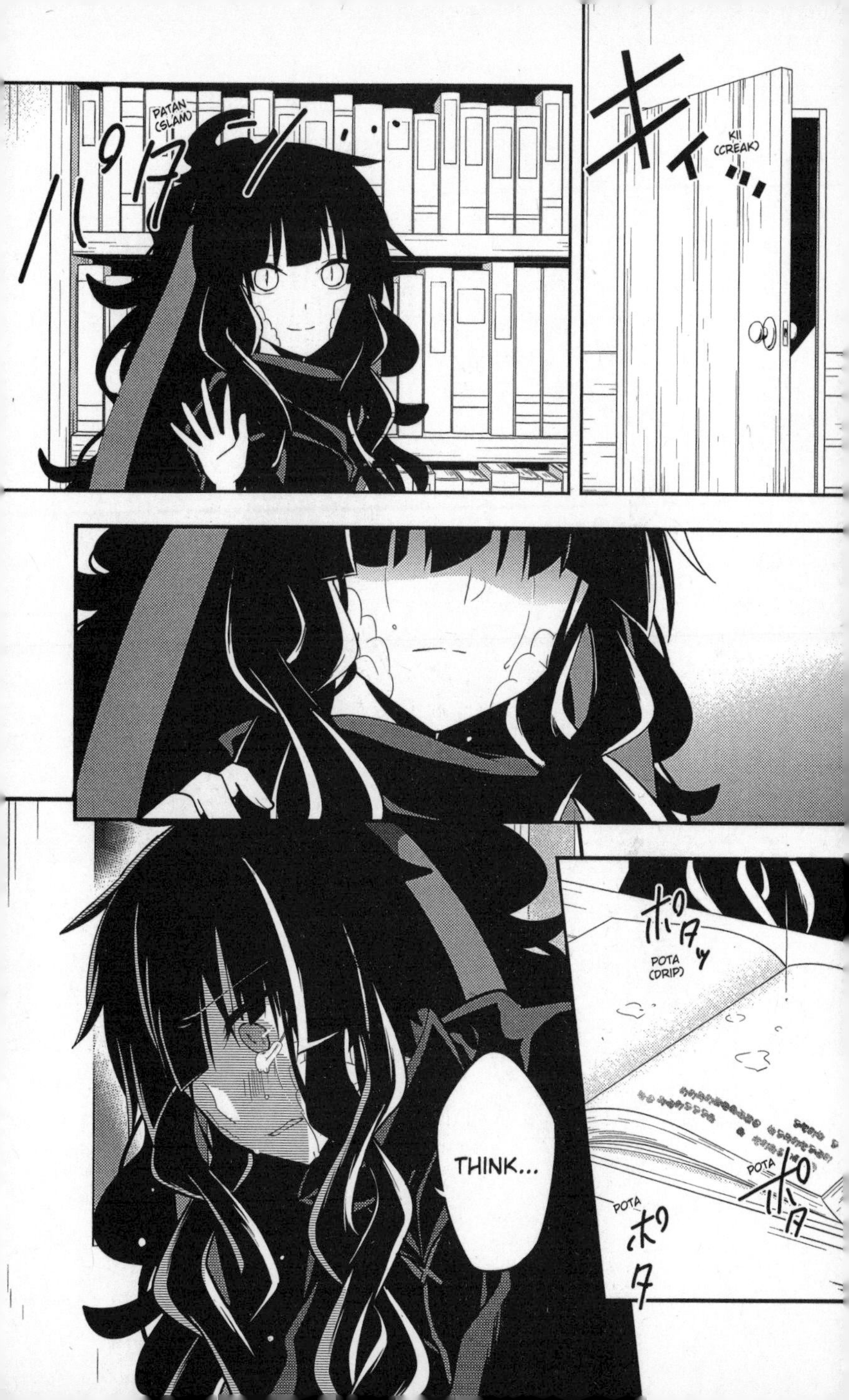
KII (CREAK)
PATAN (SLAM)
POTA (DRIP)
POTA
POTA
THINK...

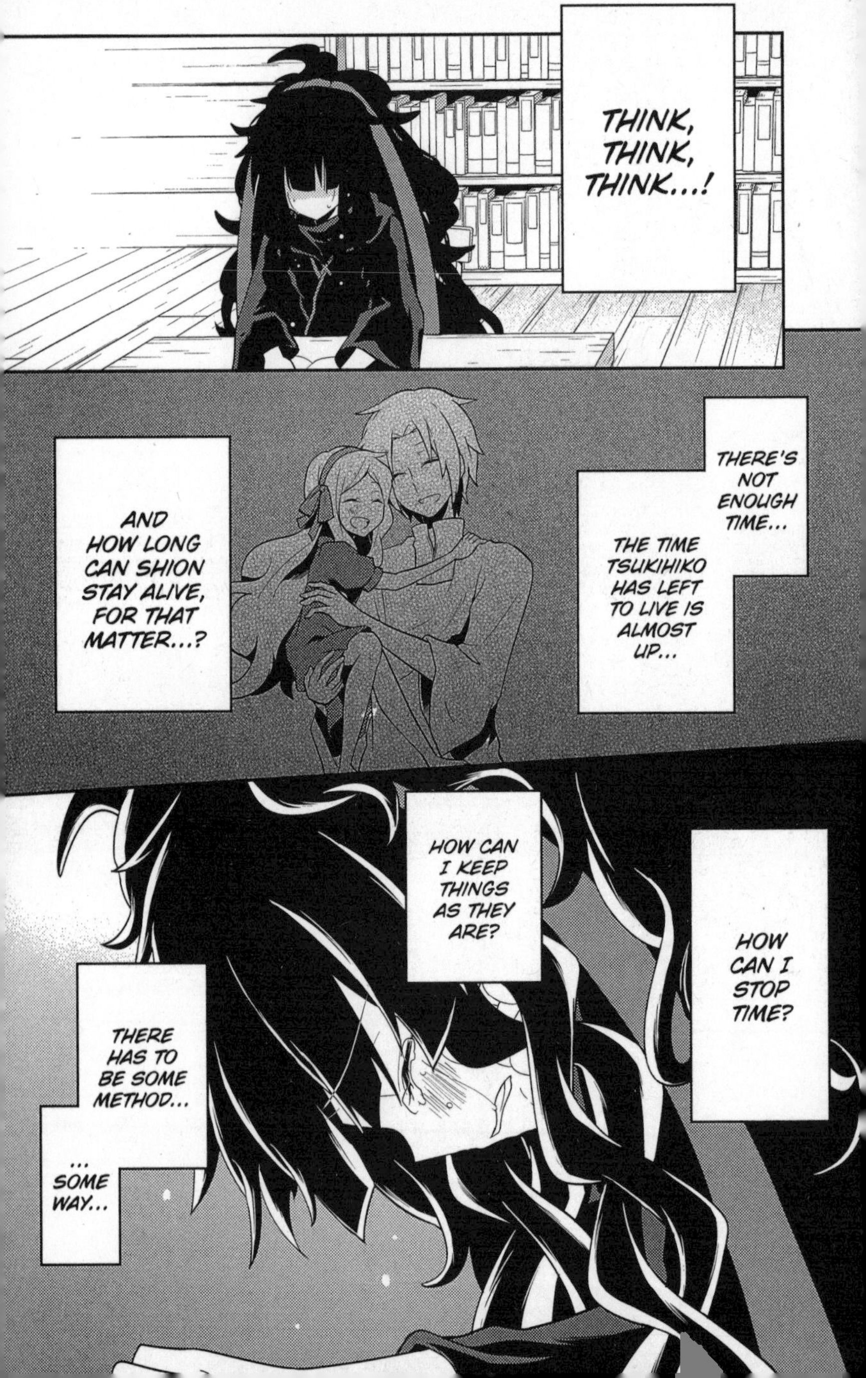
THINK, THINK, THINK...!
THERE'S NOT ENOUGH TIME...
THE TIME TSUKIHIKO HAS LEFT TO LIVE IS ALMOST UP...
AND HOW LONG CAN SHION STAY ALIVE, FOR THAT MATTER...?
HOW CAN I STOP TIME?
HOW CAN I KEEP THINGS AS THEY ARE?
THERE HAS TO BE SOME METHOD...
...SOME WAY...

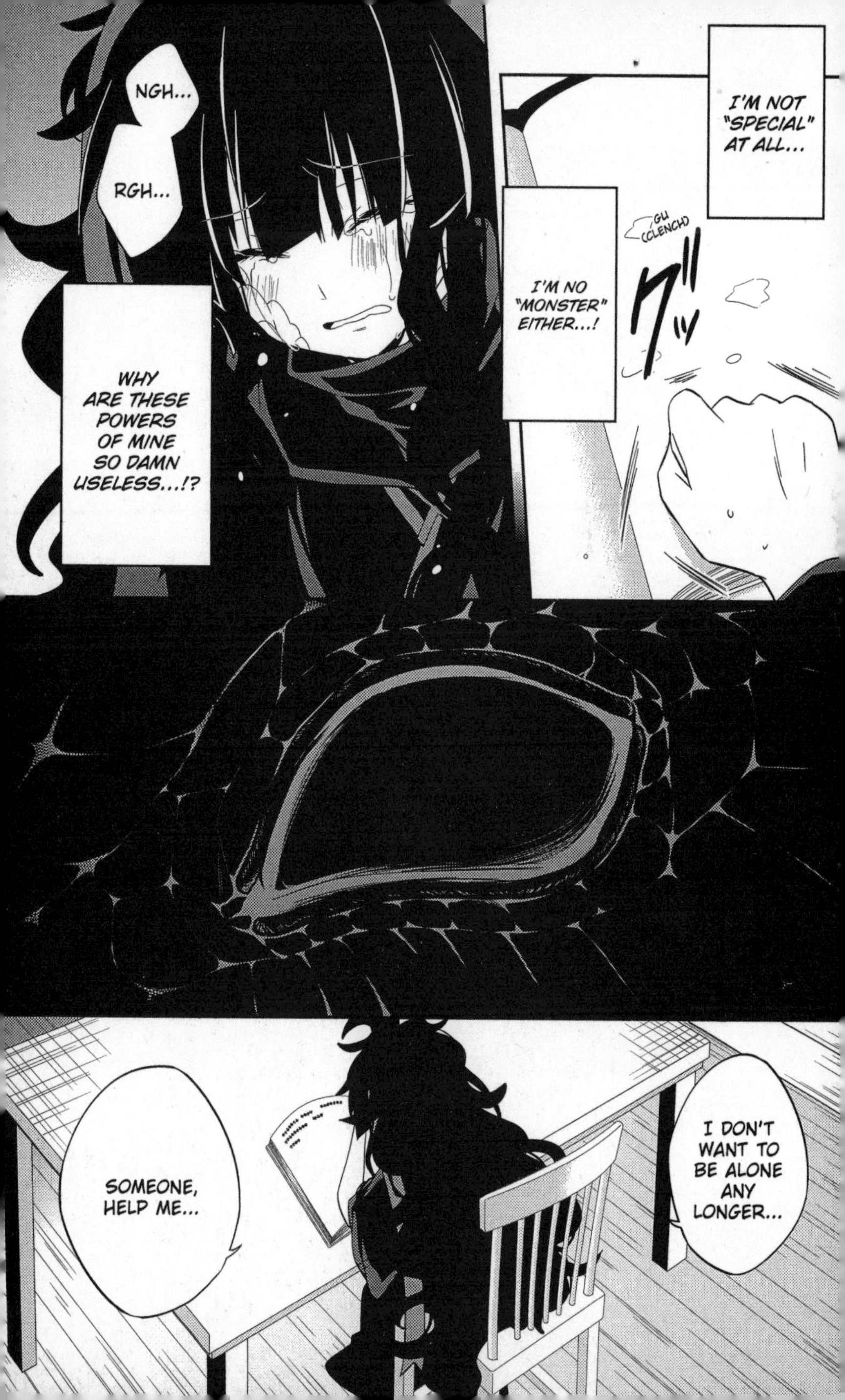
I'M NOT "SPECIAL" AT ALL...
I'M NO "MONSTER" EITHER...!
GU (CLENCH)
NGH...
RGH...
WHY ARE THESE POWERS OF MINE SO DAMN USELESS...!?
I DON'T WANT TO BE ALONE ANY LONGER...
SOMEONE, HELP ME...

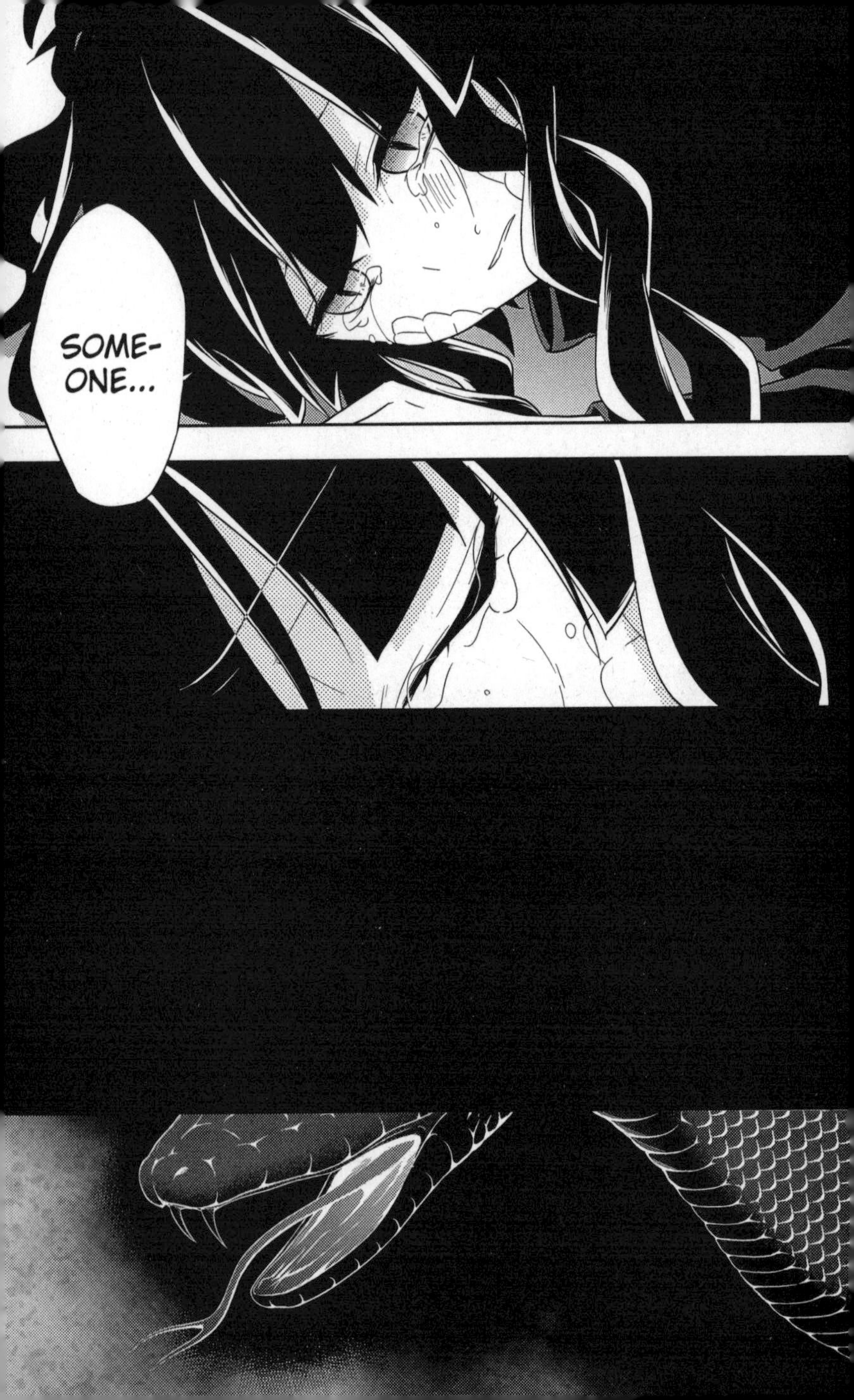
SOME-ONE...

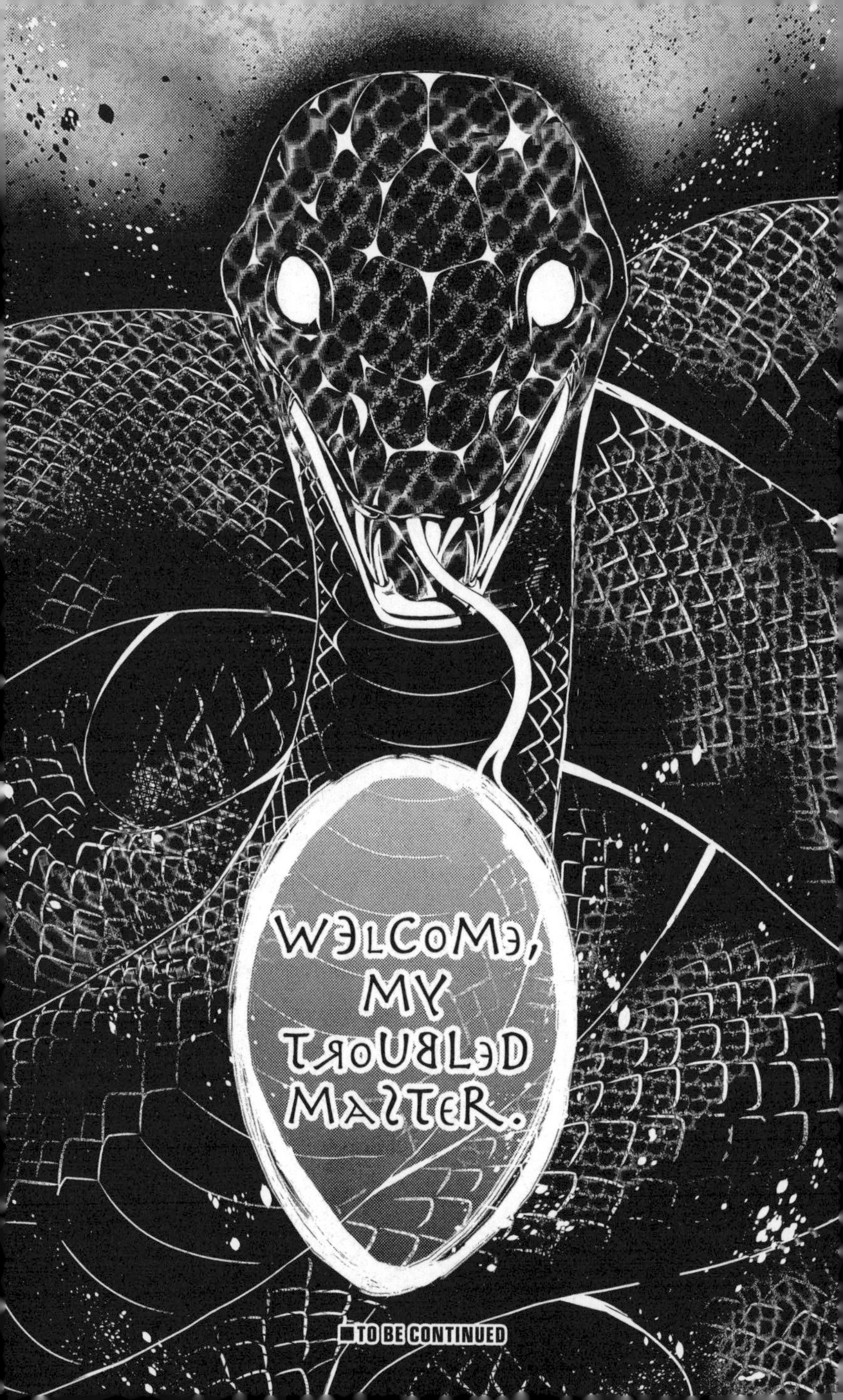
WELCOME, MY TROUBLED MASTER.
TO BE CONTINUED

IT'S HERE!

VOL.7!

Congratulations on getting Volume 7 out. Congrats, and thank you very much. Now the manga version's totally caught up to the novels. That's something I'm overjoyed to see, of course, but it also makes me feel a bit guilty. Therefore, I've made it my mission of sorts to make sure the original manga stories I'm creating are even more exciting than the novels, so hopefully that'll help earn me some forgiveness.

That aside, my handwriting's getting so messy that I'm honestly starting to get anxious. I feel like it's getting messier and messier with each passing volume. What an ordeal.

Here's to the next volume in the series!

You fool.

Jin

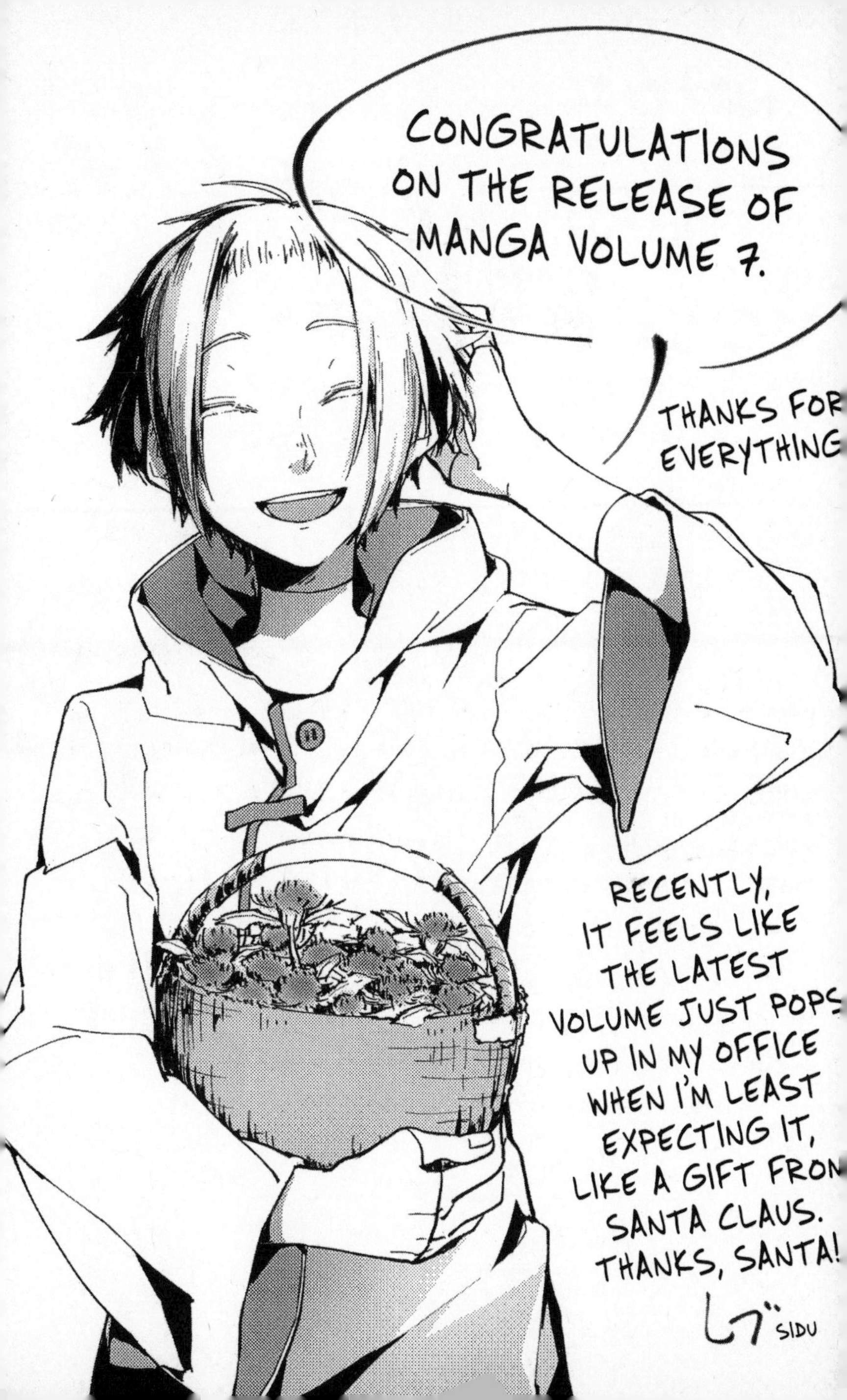
CONGRATULATIONS ON THE RELEASE OF MANGA VOLUME 7.
THANKS FOR EVERYTHING
RECENTLY, IT FEELS LIKE THE LATEST VOLUME JUST POPS UP IN MY OFFICE WHEN I'M LEAST EXPECTING IT, LIKE A GIFT FROM SANTA CLAUS. THANKS, SANTA!
しづ SIDU

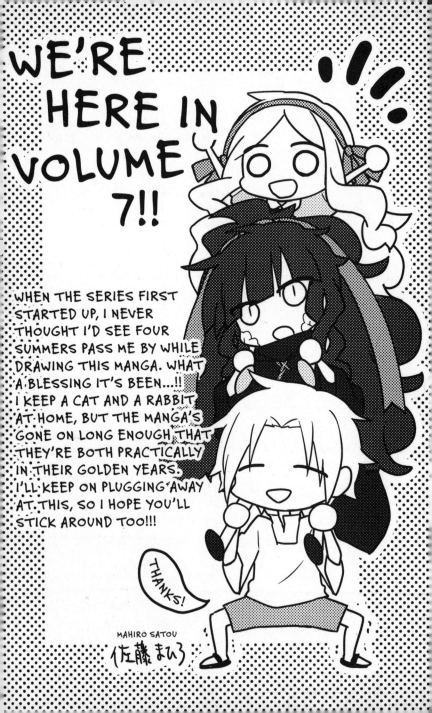

WE'RE HERE IN VOLUME 7!!

WHEN THE SERIES FIRST STARTED UP, I NEVER THOUGHT I'D SEE FOUR SUMMERS PASS ME BY WHILE DRAWING THIS MANGA. WHAT A BLESSING IT'S BEEN...!! I KEEP A CAT AND A RABBIT AT HOME, BUT THE MANGA'S GONE ON LONG ENOUGH THAT THEY'RE BOTH PRACTICALLY IN THEIR GOLDEN YEARS. I'LL KEEP ON PLUGGING AWAY AT THIS, SO I HOPE YOU'LL STICK AROUND TOO!!!

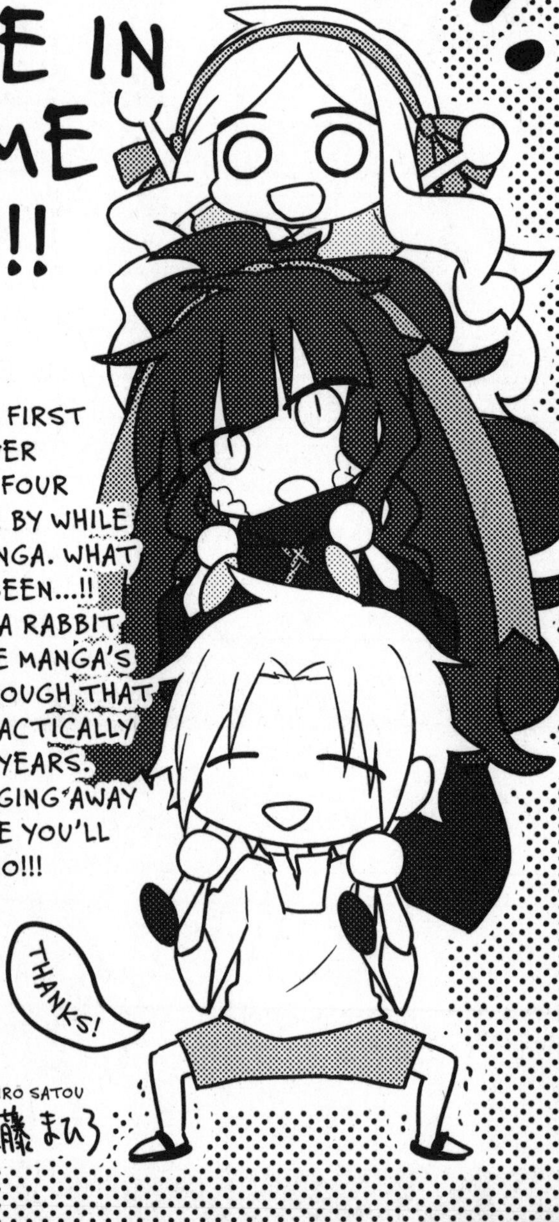
THANKS!

MAHIRO SATOU

佐藤まひろ

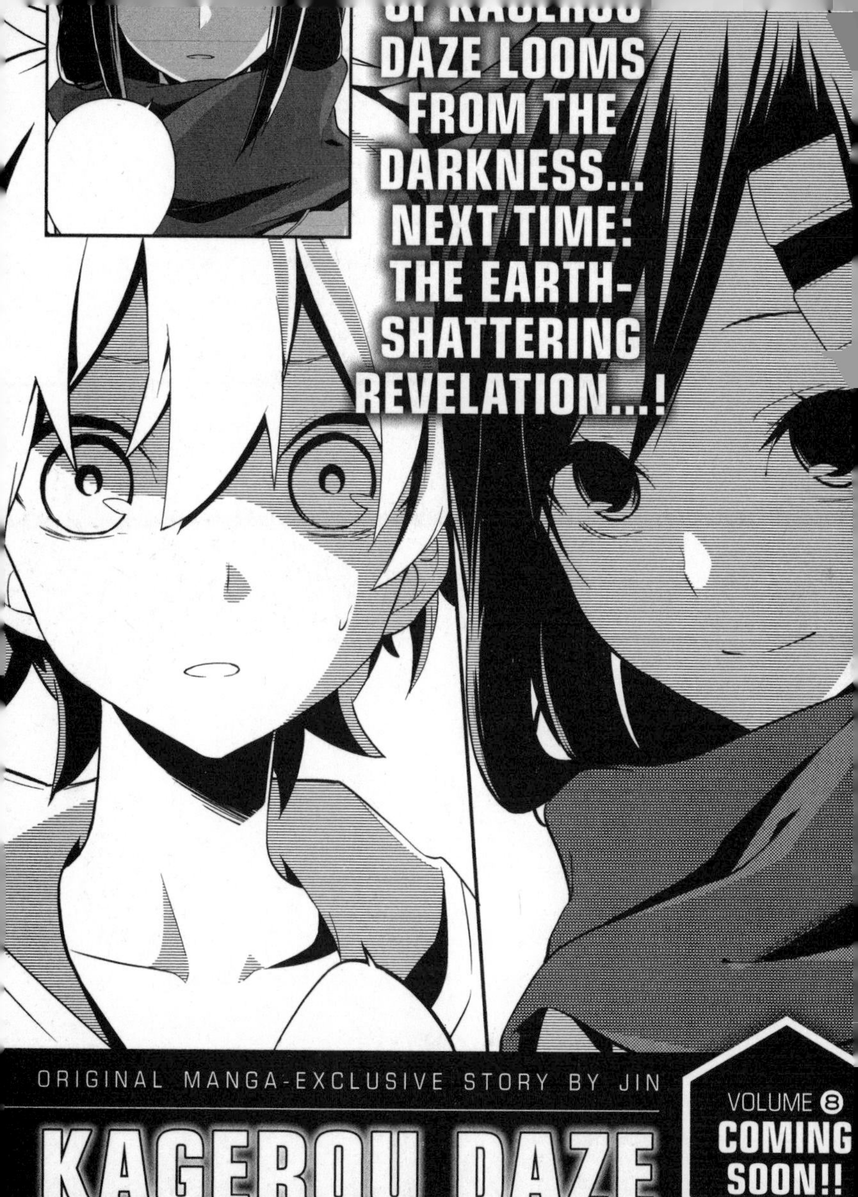
DAZE LOOMS
FROM THE
DARKNESS...
NEXT TIME:
THE EARTH-
SHATTERING
REVELATION...!
ORIGINAL MANGA-EXCLUSIVE STORY BY JIN
KAGEROU DAZE
VOLUME 8
COMING
SOON!!

KAGEROU DAZE 07

MAHIRO SATOU
Original Story: JIN
(SHIZEN NO TEKI-P)
Character Design: SIDU, WANNYANPUU-

Translation: Kevin Gifford • Lettering: Abigail Blackman

Kagerou Daze
© Mahiro Satou
© KAGEROU PROJECT / 1st PLACE
First published in Japan in 2015 by KADOKAWA CORPORATION.
English translation rights reserved by Yen Press, LLC under the license from KADOKAWA CORPORATION, Tokyo through TUTTLE-MORI AGENCY, Inc., Tokyo.

English translation © 2016 by Yen Press, LLC

Yen Press
1290 Avenue of the Americas
New York, NY 10104

Visit us at yenpress.com
facebook.com/yenpress
twitter.com/yenpress
yenpress.tumblr.com
instagram.com/yenpress

First Yen Press Edition: October 2016

Yen Press is an imprint of Yen Press, LLC.
The Yen Press name and logo are trademarks of Yen Press, LLC.

Library of Congress Control Number: 2016297061

ISBNs: 978-0-316-54535-8 (paperback)
978-0-316-43373-0 (ebook)

10 9 8 7 6 5 4 3 2 1

BVG

Printed in the United States of America